REGRET

REGRET
The Persistence of the Possible

Janet Landman

New York   Oxford   Oxford University Press   *1993*

Oxford University Press

Oxford   New York   Toronto
Delhi   Bombay   Calcutta   Madras   Karachi
Kuala Lumpur   Singapore   Hong Kong   Tokyo
Nairobi   Dar es Salaam   Cape Town
Melbourne   Auckland   Madrid

and associated companies in
Berlin   Ibadan

Copyright © 1993 by Oxford University Press, Inc.,

Published by Oxford University Press, Inc.,
200 Madison Avenue, New York, New York 10016

Oxford is a registered trademark of Oxford University Press

Library of Congress Cataloging-in-Publication Data
Landman, Janet.
Regret : the persistence of the possible / Janet Landman.
p. cm.   Includes bibliographical references and index.
ISBN 0-19-507178-6
1. Regret.   I. Title.
BF575.R33L36   1993   152.4—dc20   93-15209

1 3 5 7 9 8 6 4 2

Printed in the United States of America
on acid-free paper

For Stephen and Miriam

Acknowledgments

I've found that regret is something most people can relate to. As a result, most people have something interesting to say about it. My thanks to everyone who offered me your insights from your personal experience or your specialized knowledge.

A number of individuals contributed in important ways to my work on what I call the humanity of regret by referring me to relevant literary works. They include George Bornstein, Bert Hornback, Elizabeth Knoll, Nancy Kushigian, Harry Segal, David Winter, and Sabrina Zirkle. I am also grateful to an undergraduate student of mine, Paul Geddes, who phoned from Nashville, Tennessee, just to tell me about Charles Kuralt's chapter on regrets, and the unidentified graduate student in history who told me about Platonov's *The Foundation Pit* on the #5 Packard bus home from campus.

Many, many individuals have helped by talking with me about the nonliterary—philosophical, economic, and psychological—aspects of my work or by sharing relevant references from these disciplines. They include Elizabeth Anderson, Barnaby Barratt, Virginia Blankenship, Phyllis Blumenfeld, Donald Brown, David Buss, Al Cain, Nancy Cantor, Liz Cole, Paul Courant, Sue Cutler, Robyn Dawes, Colin Day, Randy Earnest, Bob Eggleston, Cleve Evans, Geoff Fong, Sidney Gendin, Tom Gilovich, Barbara Greenfield, Gerry Gurin, Pat Gurin, Doug Hofstadter (and the members of his Counterfactual Thought seminar), Theresa Hunt, Marita Inglehart, Daniel Kahneman, Miriam Landman, Randy Larsen, Jean Manis, Mel Manis, Hazel Markus, John Miyamoto, Warren Norman, Keith Oatley, Linda Perloff, David Schmidt, Carolin Showers, Keith Smith, Abigail Stewart, Joseph Veroff, Gary Wells, Bernard Williams, Ralph Williams, Frank Yates, and Bill Yeaton.

There is nothing quite like empirical research with intelligent colleagues to clarify fuzzy thinking. My thinking about regret has been considerably defuzzed through research collaborations with the following: Calvin Chin, Steve Fein, Jan Malley, Jean Manis, Mel Manis, Lucinda Orwoll, Abigail Stewart, Elizabeth Vandewater, and Camille Wortman. Thanks also to Lara Honos, Craig Nykiel, and David Pais for their bright and conscientious work as research assistants.

Another boost to my work came in the form of invitations for me to make presentations or otherwise participate in the following: the Social Environment and Health Research Seminar of the Institute of Social Research at the University of Michigan; the Personality Area Colloquium series of the University of Michigan's Department of Psychology; Doug Hofstadter's Counterfactual Thought seminar; and the 1989 Counterfactual Conference sponsored by Indiana University. The dialectic of intellectual action and reaction entailed in these experiences was invaluable.

My deepest gratitude goes to those who took the time to read and critically comment on versions of chapters at various stages of raggedness: Elizabeth Anderson, Hal Arkes, Robyn Dawes, Sidney Gendin, Stephen Landman, Christopher Peterson, Lance Sandelands, Jeri Sawall, Harry Segal, Sandra Vallie, Sidney Warshauski, and Frank Yates. Though none of you truly complied with my request for "ruthless" criticism, the critiques that you so generously gave me did significantly improve the end product. Thanks too for saving me from some real boners.

Many thanks to Hilarie Faberman, past Curator of Western Art at the University of Michigan Museum of Art, for taking the time to brainstorm with me possible book cover art. Also thanks to Deirdre Spencer, fellow CEW Scholar, and Head of the Fine Arts Library at the University of Michigan, for introducing me to DeChirico, and the ins and outs of the art library.

Joan Bossert, my editor at Oxford University Press, has given me more than I could ever repay. First, she gave me her belief in me and my ability to write this book. Later, she gave me what every author wants, perceptive and close readings. And most of all, she gave me the gift of prompting me for just a bit more, just a bit better.

This work benefited financially from a 1988 National Endowment for the Humanities Summer Fellowship. Research grants from the Department of Psychology of the University of Michigan funded library deliveries, computer searches, and payment of research subjects. I am very grateful to this department for providing me with so far over a decade's worth of intellectual stimulation, collegiality, and terrific students. To me this place has always been an intellectual banquet.

And thank you, Stephen and Miriam, for encouraging and supporting me and my work in a thousand ways, large and small. You know better than anyone how very important my work is to me. And you know that, even so, you are most important of all.

February 1993   J. L.
Ann Arbor, Michigan

Permission Acknowledgments

Many thanks to the following for permission to use copyrighted works:

Excerpt from "Fragment" by John Ashbery reprinted by permission of Georges Borschardt, Inc. Published in *The Double Dream of Spring.* Copyright © 1970 by John Ashbery.

Excerpt from "One Art" by Elizabeth Bishop. In *The Complete Poems 1927–1979* by Elizabeth Bishop. Renewal Copyright © 1979 by Elizabeth Bishop. Renewal copyright © 1980 by Alice Helen Methfessel.

Excerpts from *Great Expectations* by Charles Dickens published by The New American Library, Penguin USA.

Excerpt from "Remorse" by Emily Dickinson. From *The Poems of Emily Dickinson*, Thomas H. Johnson, Ed., Cambridge, Mass.: The Belknap Press of Harvard University Press. Copyright © 1951, 1955, 1979, 1983 by the President and Fellows of Harvard College. Reprinted by permission of the publishers and the Trustees of Amherst College.

Excerpts from *Notes from Underground* by Fyodor Dostoevsky, trans. by Mirra Ginsburg, Translation copyright © 1974 by Mirra Ginsburg. Reprinted by permission of Bantam Books, a division of Bantam Doubleday, Dell Publishing Group, Inc.

Excerpts from *Breathing Lessons* by Anne Tyler. Copyright © 1988 by Anne Tyler. Reprinted by permission of Alfred A. Knopf, Inc.; Penguin Books Canada Limited; and Chatto & Windus.

Excerpts from *Mrs. Dalloway* by Virginia Woolf. Copyright © 1925 by Harcourt Brace Jovanovich, Inc. and renewed in 1953 by Leonard Woolf. Reprinted by permission of Harcourt Brace Jovanovich, Inc., the Executors of the estate of Virginia Woolf, and The Hogarth Press.

Excerpt from the song "My Way" ("Comme D'Habitude"). Music by Jacques Revaux and Claude Francois. Original French lyrics by Gille Thibault. English lyrics by Paul Anka. Copyright © 1967 Societé des Nouvelles Editions Eddie Barclay and Jenne Musique for the World. Copyright © 1969 by Management Agency & Music Publishing, Inc. International copyright secured for the United States. All rights reserved. Used by permission.

Excerpt from the song "What I Did For Love" from *A Chorus Line*. Music by Marvin Hamlisch. Lyric by Edward Kleban. Copyright © 1975 by Marvin Hamlisch and Edward Kleban. All rights controlled by Wren Music Co., and American Compass Music Corp. All rights reserved. Used by permission.

Excerpt from the song "Nevertheless" by Bert Kalmar and Harry Ruby. Copyright © 1931 by Chappell & Co. (Renewed). Reprinted by permission of Chappell & Co.

Chapter 3 is a revision of a previously published article: J. Landman. (1987). Regret: A theoretical and conceptual analysis. *Journal for the Theory of Social Behaviour, 17*, 135–160. Revised and printed with permission of Basil Blackwell.

Contents

Prologue

The Science and Humanity of Regret

One morning, during the time I was writing this book, I spotted a posting relevant to regret taped on the wall of a medical office. It reads in part as follows:

> If I had my life to live over again, I'd try to make more mistakes next time. I would relax. I would limber up. I would be sillier than I have been this trip. I know of very few things I would take seriously. I would take more trips. I would climb more mountains, swim more rivers, and watch more sunsets. I would do more walking and looking. I would eat more ice cream and fewer beans. I would have more actual troubles and fewer imaginary ones.
>
> You see, I am one of those people who live prophylactically and sensibly and sanely hour after hour, day after day. Oh, I've had my moments and if I had it to do over again, I'd have more of them. In fact I'd try to have nothing else. Just moments, one after another, instead of living so many years ahead each day. I have been one of those people who never go anywhere without a thermometer, a hot water bottle, a gargle, a raincoat, aspirin, and a parachute. If I had it to do over again, I would go places, do things and travel lighter than I have . . . .

This was not the first time I had come across this piece (written by an author unknown to me). Many years earlier, on a bright crisp day in May I had sat under a tree, a copy of this piece of writing in my hand and the shock of recognition in my cortex, absolutely certain that I did not want to live the kind of life that would leave me with regrets like those. In a movie version of this incident, the strains of that impossibly sad song—"This Nearly Was Mine"— would no doubt have been swelling in the background. Call me corny, but there and then I launched a process of thinking and feeling that led to resolutions and eventually to choices that have, I think, mitigated for me the likelihood of suffering those particular regrets.

I relate this story in part to address a personal question I sometimes get—namely, where my interest in a subject so perversely negative as regret comes from. I think the story achieves another goal as well. Most important, it challenges the widely held view of regret as fundamentally negative, useless, even destructive. It challenges this view by suggesting what a dynamic, mobilizing, and rational experience regret can be—not only prospectively, as in this personal anecdote, but retrospectively as well. This is a theme that will be developed throughout this book.

Unlike related matters, such as depression, guilt, and shame, regret has only recently received scholarly attention. For me, regret's fascination stems in part from its prior neglect. That regret has largely escaped the attention of scholars before me means that it is a subject that offers space to move around in. This openness to new exploration, of course, comes at a price: exploration relatively unimpeded by the charting of others is also exploration relatively unassisted by the charting of others. All in all, like a mountain that is both *there* and heretofore *unclimbed*, regret holds for me an irresistible intellectual challenge—at once inviting and daunting. But on that day long ago, I had promised myself, among other things, to climb more mountains. So here I am.

If not a many-splendored thing, regret is a many-faceted thing. Bridging past and present, interior and exterior, actual and possible, the cognitive and the emotional, the individual and collective, regret calls for a wide-angle lens. From the very first, I found that I needed to reach out to disciplines other than my own, including some not noted for conversing sympathetically either with psychology or with one another—in particular economics, philosophy, and literature—but also anthropology, sociology, law, and medicine. This interdisciplinary approach proved not only necessary, but for me, welcome.

I like to be moved by what informs me. So I have immensely enjoyed turning to literature to find out what it has to say about regret. On the other hand, I have been able to indulge my taste for empirical analysis, not only through my own empirical investigations of regret, but also by becoming acquainted with an increasing number of fine empirical investigations of regret carried out by others. After having looked at regret from multiple perspectives, the act of writing this book has, finally, satisfied my appetite for synthesis.

Over the years I have more than once heard the arias of the humanities fall thuddingly upon the ears of science, and vice versa. Always I was left with a vague feeling that a handsome opportunity had been wasted—on both sides. Among its many satisfactions, the interdisciplinary approach has afforded me the pleasure of bringing together the analytic and the synthetic; nonfiction (the "facts") and fiction; propositional and narrative modes of thought;[1] the "ancient quarrel" between the philosophers and the poets;[2] what Yeats referred to, with the partiality of a romantic, as "logical straightness" versus "the crooked road of life";[3] and adding an invidious trio to the string of invidious duos, what Aldous Huxley called the "worlds of gray theory, green life and many-colored poetry."[4] I have found it challenging and rewarding to do my small part to resist the unfortunate processes of disciplinary balkanization through this interdisciplinary work.[5]

By a contradiction that is more apparent than real, the value of pluralistic inquiry stems from the commonalities, the differences, and even the incommensurability of the respective angles of refraction. An interdisciplinary approach offers descriptions, explanations, and hypotheses that are potentially fuller, more systematic, more precise, more particular, and more contextual—hence more valid—than either of the two cultures, working in isolation, offers. But it is always the differences that stand out. And science and the humanities do appear quite different from one another, especially in their methods and idiom.

First, the cultures of science and the humanities claim different *methods*. The scientific approaches, at their best, are virtuosos at taking implicit or inchoate ideas and transforming them into explicit (frequently systematic, sometimes formal, occasionally mathematical) theories. Both the psychological and the philosophical traditions boast venerable histories of the formal analysis of reason and emotion—which illumine the intellective/emotional phenomenon that is regret. Psychology also offers rich theory on unconscious motivation, which furthers the understanding of some of the more bewildering vicissitudes of regret. Philosophy, psychology, and economics all offer explicit perspectives on regret as a component of decision making. A foray into economic decision theory reveals, as well, a bit of a surprise: that ordinary people and decision theorists hold similar—that is, wary and dismissive—attitudes toward regret.

The study of regret is enriched too by the empirical procedures used by the culture of science. Psychology and economics in particular have taken this next step, transforming theory into specific hypotheses, and then testing them. Experimental studies permit control over certain variables—such as acts versus omissions, or near-misses versus misses-by-a-mile—that have been predicted to influence the intensity of regret. In experiments one can also hold constant important factors like outcome (e.g., so that everyone suffers the same loss of $1200), in order to tease out the independent influence of other factors. Survey studies let us examine the relationships between regret and personal factors over which experimenters have no control—for example, age, gender, and emotional concomitants. Survey studies also afford a look at how regret manifests itself outside the laboratory in the real and earnest domains of love and work. Finally, scientific methods have the related virtue of rendering hypotheses susceptible to disconfirmation—unlike the opinions expressed in tabloid television, graffiti, and at the dinner table. In other words, science offers to the study of regret its famed self-correcting mechanism for finding out when it is wrong.

Despite its considerable contributions, the scientific side of the great divide also has its limits. The experimental method is not the ideal method for garnering a richly fleshed-out picture of, say, the natural history of real people's regrets. I shudder to imagine the alarming experimental manipulations that would be necessary to investigate the kinds of regrets that people find most troubling—which tend *not* to revolve around monetary bets, to date the most common experimental stimuli. At the extreme, the living, breathing humanity of regret, like humor, can be obliterated by attempts to dissect it.

What about perhaps the most obvious method of studying regret—that is, talking with people about their own regrets? It would be lovely if one could study regret simply by talking with people about it in structured interviews or front-porch conversations. I've done a bit of that informally, and perhaps I'll give it a more systematic try yet. But unfortunately, this method too has its problems. Chiefly, many of us prove rather close-to-the-chest, inarticulate, or bewildered about something so personal, so emotional, and so distressing as regret.

For these reasons, there may actually be *no better* vantage point from which to investigate regret than in the depictions rendered by writers who by motivation and practice are extraordinary observers and portrayers of the human condition. Denis Donoghue explains:

> Literature would not be necessary, though it would still be desirable, if our ordinary meetings with people were not, on the whole, a muddle; or if most of our experience were not, as it is, concealed, deflected, sublimated, or otherwise opaque to one another. The normal conditions in which we meet one another are puerile. The advantage of literature is that it makes a more complete meeting possible.[6]

Lionel Trilling once characterized literature as "the human activity that takes the fullest and most precise account of variousness, possibility, complexity, and difficulty."[7] Unpacking this litany of praises one by one may help reveal what literature does that can contribute to our knowledge.

First, according to Trilling, literature offers a *full* account. In the past a number of social scientific theories have made the same claim—to impart full, comprehensive descriptions and explanations. Today those grand aspirations have been whittled down by specialization and by a modern distaste for overarching theory. Now we tend to be content to say more and more about less and less. That is not all bad, especially in light of the failures and excesses of certain grand theories; the Freudian theory of psychosexual stages, instinct theory and evolutionary theory as applied to human behavior, and (as I discuss later in this volume) economic decision theory are just a few that come to mind. In contrast, a good novel tends to offer a less imperialistic form of comprehensiveness. With respect to regret, Kazuo Ishiguro's *The Remains of the Day*, Henry James's *The Ambassadors*, and Virginia Woolf's *Mrs. Dalloway* are prime exemplars of the satisfying comprehensiveness of the treatment of regret to be found in literature—a claim that will be demonstrated throughout this volume.

Precision through literature? Precision is more often viewed as the monopoly of science, or literary criticism, or anything but literature itself. In contrast with systematic theory, literature is often disparaged as offering only those inferior anecdotal and impressionistic gifts sometimes referred to as "folk psychology"—about which, some sharp tongue once commented: " 'Ah yes, the province of such simple folk as Flaubert, Proust, and Henry James.' "[8] If it is precision we want, Trilling was of course right to direct us to literature. Especially with more evanescent and interior experiences such as perception, thought, and emotion, scientific description nearly always falls short. In contrast, literature contributes, as Diane Ackerman explains, a kind of precision of description beyond the reach of other approaches:

> we look to artists to feel for us, to suffer and rejoice, to describe the heights of their passionate response to life so that we can . . . get to know better what the full range of human experience really is.[9]

I cannot imagine anyone showing greater precision about the workings of the inner life in general and of regret in particular than authors like Henry James, Virginia Woolf, Fyodor Dostoevsky, and Kazuo Ishiguro. But you may judge this for yourself as you read the discussions of works of these and other authors in this volume.

The third value Trilling sees in literature is what he calls "variousness." The depictions of regret found in the novels, short stories, and poetry treated in this volume teem with variousness. They do so through the particulars—which are inevitably various. The variety extends far beyond what is regretted: lost youth, lost love, lost children, lost creativity, lost kingdom, lost innocence, and so on. Also various are the antecedents and occasions of regret, and the efforts to transform regret, all topics detailed later in this volume.

It strikes me that a major source of the "possibility, complexity, and difficulty" of regret is its contextuality. In Jerome Bruner's phrasing, science achieves its power through "context independence," and literature achieves its power through "context sensitivity."[10] The experiment's achievement of rigorously specifying causal conditions by rendering "everything else equal" comes at the price of isolating the individual from his or her personal history and social context. As something capable of changing over time (both within individuals and across historical periods), regret resists surrendering its secrets to approaches (not only the experimental method, but also formal theory, and mathematical models) that isolate the regretter from his or her temporal context.

Fortunately, we have literature, which (except for its more nonrepresentational forms) sets off to advantage the temporal and situational contexts of regret. "We look to artists to stop time for us," says Ackerman.[11] Dostoevsky stops time for us in *Notes from Underground* through his creation of a protagonist altogether obsessed with mistakes he made years before. Woolf stops time for us in *Mrs. Dalloway* through her celebrated method of taking the reader moment by moment through the thoughts of her regretful characters. In *Breathing Lessons* Tyler employs, like Woolf, a 24-hour time period, but Tyler does a bit more showing through the behavior of her characters than telling through their thoughts.

Even the most partisan must admit, on their sane days, that every method has its strengths and weaknesses. Plainly, therefore, you will learn different things about regret (or anything else) depending on where and how you look. Catholicity will get us further than parochialism.

The disciplinary cultures traditionally boast not only divergent methods but also *idiom.* Jacob Bronowski expresses (unfortunately in exclusionary language) one of the major differences in idiom: "whereas the scientist seeks to mean the same thing to everybody who listens to him, the artist is content to say something universal and yet mean different things to everybody who listens to him."[12] One way that scientific discourse seeks to mean the same thing to everybody is through verbal redundancy. One way that literary discourse seeks to mean different things to everybody is through its use of rich, evocative, even "reckless" language.[13] Literature (and more broadly, the humanities) also differs from science in its preference for the style of discourse called (in another context) "thick description."[14] In thick description "small, but very densely textured facts"[15] are transformed into "piled-up structures of inference and implication."[16] In contrast, scientific discourse prefers thin description, in which inference is closely tied to a relatively circumscribed, straightforwardly outlined set of empirical observations.

Narrative exposition is an aspect of language frequently viewed as clearly and definitively literary. Here too the disciplinary differences have been exaggerated. Science's reliance on narrative is being increasingly noticed. Misia Landau, for example, brilliantly details the narrative nature of human evolutionary theory.[17] An experience like regret is often more fully portrayed through stories than through the usual scientific idioms. Margaret Atwood expresses the thought well: "the way in which we understand ourselves is less through theory than through story."[18]

Metaphor is another aspect of language often considered peculiarly literary. Science has frequently looked upon metaphor with a suspicious eye, dismissing it as a cheap mode of thought, yet fearing its rhetorical power. There is some validity to this view. A vivid, colorful metaphor can ride roughshod over pallid scientific evidence and rational argumentation. Consider, for example, the persuasive power (especially among those sympathetically predisposed) of metaphors like "The U.S. is the Great Satan," "Saddam Hussein is a modern Hitler," and labeling a contested confirmation hearing a "high-tech lynching."

Of course, metaphor is not limited to literary and political contexts. Science also regularly consorts with metaphor. "The skeleton of a theory is a string of causal statements, although . . . the heart of any theory is a metaphor or image," says David Kenny in a volume detailing sophisticated methods of statistical analysis.[19] In psychology, theories to describe and explain the mind have for the past few decades relied heavily on the computer metaphor and its batch of related metaphors, such as *encoding, input, output, storage, capacity,* and *retrieval.*

A central reason that metaphor is so often enlisted by both science and the humanities is its epistemological value. For metaphor is neither the harmless coquette nor the all-powerful seductress she is sometimes made out to be; rather, the responsibly chosen metaphor is a perfectly legitimate mode of knowing and understanding.[20] As Jean Cocteau expressed it, art is "science in the flesh." Literature, expressly through metaphor, has a way of putting flesh on matters such as the experience of regret.

Regret has been imaged as a waste of hard currency (explicitly and unsympathetically in a novel by Anne Tyler, implicitly and sympathetically in formal decision theory); a "baffling geography" (Baldwin); a perilous slope (Lampedusa); soul-tearing teeth, a self-gnawing mouse, and a self-biting snake (Baudelaire, Dostoevsky, and Hemingway, respectively); an arrow in the heart (Woolf); footfalls echoing in the memory, disturbing the dust on a bowl of roses (Eliot); the forward/backward rush of a sacredly contrary brook (Frost).[21] As I discuss in later chapters, each of these, and other, images reveals particular elements of the nature and experience of regret (and conceals others).

For the most part, science and literature demand somewhat different sorts of *processes* of the knower. Science mostly works on the mind (though at its best, it works on the imagination as well). It instructs the reader in the ways of nature, in the present case "human nature,"[22] or (as I prefer) the human condition. Literature, although it also works on the mind, works equally through imagination and the heart. Literature instructs not only through its meaning but through the psychological processes it requires of its readers. Proust was correct in asserting through his protagonist Marcel that "the most important truths about human psychology cannot be communicated or grasped by intellectual activity alone:

powerful emotions have an irreducibly important cognitive role to play."[23] As literary theorist Wayne Booth suggests, "Don Quixote might have been rescued by reading *Don Quixote* and Emma Bovary's best hope would have been to read *Madame Bovary*."[24]

But the literary process goes further than mirroring. Like all forms of art, literature "does not reproduce what we see. It makes us see," said Paul Klee. The thinking and feeling we do in response to literature can "make us see" any number of truths about the nature of human phenomena that otherwise might have escaped our notice. Brecht saw art as a hammer. A hammer can make us see by shaping reality: as in the hammer used by the sculptor to reveal the shape "hidden inside" the block of marble; or, alternatively, as in the hammer used to hit someone over the head. In this vein, Kafka offered another violent image for what goes on when we read, comparing good literature with an ax—useful for breaking up the frozen sea within. This metaphor captures particularly well, I think, the harrowing experience that regret can be. When we refer to something as art, we are in part honoring a certain honesty about the human condition that is sometimes called verisimilitude. It seems to me that the brutally honest observations about the human condition to be found in art somehow possess a greater potential to transform the reader than the more dispassionate observations produced by science.

Literature also allows vicarious role-playing, in which readers can work safely on distressing aspects of life, among which is regret:

> Art is rehearsal for those real situations in which it is vital for our survival to endure cognitive tension, to refuse the comforts of validation by affective congruence when such validation is inappropriate because too vital interests are at stake; art is the reinforcement of the capacity to endure disorientation so that a real and significant problem may emerge.[25]

As I argue later in this volume, one of those situations in which it may be vital to endure tension and disorientation to allow a significant problem (and thus a solution) to emerge is precisely the situation in which regret is at issue.

Finally, literature can work by virtue of encouraging a dialectical process in its readers. I know: it's a dreadful word, "dialectical," weighted down with pretentious-sounding tone and surplus meanings, evoking images of armchair radicals and all-too-real gulags. I regret this, but I haven't found a better word to express the process of going forward toward enlightenment by going backward, by forever questioning what is. I believe the tolerant reader will find its usage in this book surprisingly helpful.

Of course, in and of itself, neither literature nor science can save us; we must do that ourselves. Through processes that engage both our minds and our hearts, literature and science together can serve the interests of scholarly and personal illumination.

In investigating widely differing, even incompatible, approaches to regret, I found the makings of that most elusive of all gifts—a synthesis. As Italo Calvino suggested in another context, literature offers such a synthesis:

> Since science has begun to distrust general explanations and solutions that are not sectorial and specialized, the grand challenge for literature is to be capable of weaving together the various branches of knowledge, the various "codes," into a manifold and multifaceted vision of the world.[26]

As will become evident throughout this volume, the literary genres of comedy, romance, tragedy, and irony serve the function of "weaving together the various branches of knowledge" into a single but "manifold and multifaceted vision" of regret.

In sum, the interdisciplinary approach, at least my variant of it, seeks neither to deny differences between and among disciplinary cultures nor to exaggerate them. The cultures are not identical. They have somewhat different objectives, methods, languages. They have different merits and different limitations. Yet there is considerable common ground uniting them. All in all, I believe that regret in particular can only benefit from a marriage of art and science, with its talent for illuminating such a complex experience of "felt thought."

Looking back on what animated my pluralistic approach to regret, I can say that I have not been disappointed. Through exploring the worlds of gray theory, green life, and many-colored poetry—or the way of "logical straightness" and the "crooked road of life," I have been able at least partially to satisfy my goals in the following ways: (1) by questioning certain assumptions specific to each approach, thereby lowering some of the barriers separating them; (2) by providing a summary of the thinking and the empirical findings concerning regret produced by each discipline; (3) by specifying certain theoretical, conceptual, and empirical foundations upon which future inquiry might be constructed; and (4) by suggesting an integrative understanding of regret in the light of differing intellectual traditions. The approach taken here has, I believe, helped contribute as well to the understanding for its own sake of a most significant human experience.

This is, then, a somewhat unconventional book. It makes use of varied kinds of materials—including lexicographical constructions, mathematical models, psychological theory, philosophical analysis, empirical results, autobiographical accounts, humor, fiction, and poetry. The volume is part theoretical and conceptual analysis. It is part report of my own empirical research, part review of others' research. It is partly about specific regrets and partly about the general conditions that evoke and follow from regret. It is part speculative essay, part poetics of regret.

What is more, different chapters rely on different quotients of contributions from science and humanities. The differences between literary and scientific discourse discussed earlier make for virtually unavoidable shifts of diction across chapters, depending on how heavily each relies on scientific, as opposed to literary, sources. My own appreciation for the integrity of literary language makes for a strong sense of the limitations of paraphrase of literary passages. I have intentionally indulged in quoting rather more lavishly than is usual, trusting that the quoted writers will be honored and most readers delighted.

These more or less unusual features of this book follow from my decision to eschew the more obvious structural strategy that would have constructed separate, walled-off disciplinary enclaves like: The Psychology of Regret, The Philosophy of Regret, The Economics of Regret, Regret in Literature. Instead, I have persuaded the disciplines to come together in the same room where I then asked them to talk with each other about the kinds of concerns many of us have about regret. I hope readers will find, as I have, the conversation more enlightening than the monologues would have been.

Finally, some readers may be put off by the fact that I present no formal theory of my own of regret. This reflects my assessment that formal theory-building would at this point require premature closure, and my own growing preference for a particularistic, rather than a totalizing, approach. Through its construction as well as its content, then, this volume says that regret itself is neither a static experience nor a seamless whole, but at least in its fullest human form, is a more or less open-ended, back-and-forth, dynamically cumulative—yes, a dialectical—experience. Now that you've been forewarned, I hope that the inevitable bumps, twists, and turns will not so much put off as challenge you. Overall, I do think that the gain in variety of the view outweighs the loss in smoothness of the ride.

Overview

Too often, we rush to sidestep or conquer regret. I want to see what we can learn from lingering with it first. In Chapter 1, I detail the destructive and constructive consequences of regret, arguing particularly for regret's often-underrated benefits. Thereby I introduce one of the main themes of this book, the value and the authority of regret.

Chapter 2 examines the meaning of regret as concept, as well as its differences from the related concepts of disappointment, sadness, undoing, remorse, and guilt.

In Chapter 3 I lay the groundwork for locating regret in worldviews drawn from the literary genres of the romance, comedy, tragedy, and irony. Each of these stances toward regret is defined and explained through illustrative metaphor and novels: Dickens's *Great Expectations*, Henry James's *The Ambassadors*, Dostoevsky's *Notes from Underground*, and Woolf's *Mrs. Dalloway*, respectively. Through the rest of the volume I return again and again to these (and other) literary works, asking what they offer to the comprehensive understanding of regret.

Chapter 4 takes up the issue of what sorts of things people most often regret.

The most technical chapter is Chapter 5. There I look at the major philosophical, psychological, and economic decision models in which regret figures. I find, among other things, that the inclusion of regret as a valued player in decision models remedies a number of their otherwise serious shortcomings. I hope the nonaficionado will hang on (or skim) through this necessarily equation-studded chapter.

Chapter 6 focuses on the personal antecedents of regret and Chapter 7 on the situational antecedents of regret, as well as its everyday occasions. Of all the chapters, Chapters 6 and 7 are most informed by empirical research.

In Chapter 8 I explore through literature and psychological theory a variety of possible paths toward the transformation of regret. The question of transformation culminates in Chapter 9 with a dialectical model of the transformation of regret and the related transformation of the self. Finally, applying a dialectical approach to the interdisciplinary knowledge presented in previous chapters, I advance an integrative position on the contrary wisdom of regret.

REGRET

1

The Uses of Regret

In 1985 I set about buying a car. I wanted to make a decision I wouldn't regret. Knowing something about decision theory, I asked myself what I valued most in a car (my "subjective utilities," in the jargon of economic decision theory) and the likelihood of getting what I wanted (the "subjective expected probabilities"). The two most important qualities to me were cost and reliability. As for cost, I decided to buy a used car, to avoid paying the high interest of a loan on a new car. My vivid images of a car that spent more time in my mechanic's garage than mine, or of me stranded with a broken-down car and helped out by an ax-murderer (the subjective probabilities don't always jibe with the objective ones), told me to buy a car less than three years old. I knew about the illogic of failing to make use of statistical information, so I went right to *Consumer Reports* to look up the repair information on 1982 and 1983 cars. It didn't take me long to identify a couple of makes for which the expected probabilities of reliability were very high. So when an ad for a two-year-old Toyota Corolla appeared in the paper, I immediately went over to see it. Everything seemed in order during the test drive, and it was Sunday, when my mechanic wasn't available, and of course the owner had another buyer very keen on this car, so I bought it.

Two weeks later—to make a long story short—I learned that my new used car had to have the transmission rebuilt, to the tune of almost $600. At that moment I felt a good strong pang of regret over my decision.

Just what is regret? The short answer is that regret is a more or less painful judgment and state of feeling sorry for misfortunes, limitations, losses, shortcomings, transgressions, or mistakes. It can be experienced in anticipation of a decision or retrospectively, after a decision. The long answer is that—depending on which philosopher, psychologist, statistician, or economist is doing the defining—regret is (among other things) an emotion,[1] not an emotion,[2,3] a result of comparing reality with what might have been,[4,5] a cold calculation of payoffs,[6] a tepid judgment,[7] or a hot self-protective defense mechanism[8].

Then, too, depending in part on how it is defined, regret evokes strong feelings pro and con. An acquaintance of mine tells me that regret is wrong—in fact, a sin—because all things come together for the good to those who believe. Others view regret specifically as a moral emotion capable of awakening the kind of sense of responsibility for wrongs that results in the remediation of those wrongs.[9] In classic decision theory, whenever we carefully make the best choice possible at the time, regret for a bad outcome is an irrational self-indulgence.[10] But some modern economists dispute this, arguing that it is eminently rational to include regret in decision making, since it is one of the inescapable consequences of our decisions.[11] Finally, as the playwright Eugene Ionesco wrote in his memoirs, his regret at growing old afforded him an oddly consoling sense of temporal integrity: "The only thing I have left is my regret at being someone else. It is this regret that makes me continue to be myself . . . ."[12] So there are at least two sides to this story, a side that rejects regret as wrong, irrational, and dysfunctional versus a side that prizes regret as essential to rational decision making and to moral and personal integrity.

Our attitudes about regret are complicated. Regret repels us, and it fascinates us. I would bet that Ford Motor Company has been interviewed at least as often about the Edsel, its mistake, as about the Mustang, its success. And though we might hesitate out of delicacy to query our grandparents about their regrets, my burgeoning file on the regrets of public figures like Woody Allen, Paul Newman, Sammy Davis, Jr., Tallulah Bankhead, B. B. King, Lee Atwater, and William Burroughs attests to the avid public interest in the topic.

What is it about regret that makes it a modern siren song? In part regret shares the fascination of the coin toss, the lottery, and the horror genre. Journalists pander to our endless fascination with randomness and its role in causing intense regret. At seemingly every air crash, for example, they flock to the scene, nosing out the story of the passenger who at the very last minute switched onto (or off of) the doomed flight. Perhaps reading accident and disaster stories lets us safely work out how it feels to happen to be in the wrong place at the wrong time. Regret, like horror books and films, may remain perennially fascinating because it allows us to play with forbidden terrors, thereby to master them. Which brings us back to the other side of our fascination with regret—repudiation. Our powerful and conflicting feelings suggest that in this time and place regret, like sex in the Victorian era, may be something of a cultural taboo, something not spoken of in polite company.

Destructive Functions of Regret

If we as a society were asked to compose a portrait of regret, I imagine her (inevitably, I'm afraid, it would be a female) as a stringy-haired, boneless woman sunk in the dead arms of the past. We would paint her half-sitting, half-lying in the shadows of a musty room empty of everything but cobwebs and ghosts—forever staring with glazed eyes out a window, forever straining to hear ancient footfalls, which, were they to appear, would be muffled by the drone of her mutterings about what might have been.

I believe that the rejection of regret implicit in this portrait is part of a larger cultural framework that repudiates *emotion* and is convinced that emotion is irrational. The bias in favor of reason and opposed to emotion is at least as old as ancient Greek civilization. In *The Republic* the human soul is said to consist of three principles: (1) the rational element, which Plato called *reason*; (2) the passionate element, meaning the emotions, such as anger and love; and (3) the appetitive or concupiscent element, controlling our desires for food, fame, money, or other gain. Plato argued that "reason ought to rule."[13] The Platonic metaphors for these psychic elements reveal the same judgment: reason is the "shepherd" and the passionate and appetitive elements the "dogs."[14] For Aristotle, the soul is divided into two parts, rational and irrational, and the irrational part into two subparts, the vegetative (concerned with bodily nutrition) and the appetitive or concupiscent (concerned with other desires and pleasure). Like Plato, Aristotle asserted that the irrational principle should be "amenable and obedient" to the rational principle.[15]

Centuries later, in the hands of Freud, these elements became ego and id. The Freudian metaphor of horse (the irrational id) and rider (the rational ego) again presumed a state of conflict between reason and unreason, and retained the idea that reason should always master unreason. Modern psychology, too, emphasizes the intellective over the emotional. Cognitive psychologists, for instance, discourage the overuse of vivid, concrete, imaginable, immediate, and emotional information and encourage the use of unemotional statistical or base-rate information in problem solving, inference, and decision making.[16] Psychotherapies that focus on cognition proliferate, while those few focused on emotion per se shortly become the objects of derision. Even the view of emotion arising from psychological research remains so far decidedly cognitive—giving short shrift to what is emotional about emotion.

In an ethos so skeptical of emotion, the wisdom of the adage "No use crying over spilled milk" seems almost beyond question. The very titles of both of the other books that I am aware of that are substantially devoted to regret convey a clearly disparaging attitude toward regret: *Woulda, Coulda, Shoulda: Overcoming Regrets, Mistakes, and Missed Opportunities* (A. Freeman and R. DeWolf, 1989, HarperPerennial)[17] and *Overcoming Regret: Lessons from the Road Not Taken* (C. Klein and R. Gotti, 1992, Bantam).[18] Both titles promise to tell us how to "overcome" regret—as if it were a mortal enemy or a fatal disease. A writer for *The Michigan Daily,* the University of Michigan student newspaper, once categorically declared regret "God's greatest curse to humankind."[19] Rhetorical hyperbole aside, many of us ruefully nod.

We are not the only culture whose distrust of emotion offers fertile ground upon which to breed a basic distrust for regret. However, I suspect there are a number of quintessentially American sources of our discomfort with regret, in particular its seeming failures of future-oriented pragmatism, can-do exteriority, and optimism.

The only *past* we much like is the sentimental past of nostalgia, a cozy place furnished with golden oldies, retro watches, and vintage vehicles. Otherwise, we keep our distance. For to reflect on the real, unsentimentalized past is to open oneself up to regret, feeling sorry about past mistakes, misfortunes, and missed opportunities. In shunning the past, we shun regret.

"History is bunk," declared Henry Ford. Although the statement has been widely misunderstood (apparently Ford was criticizing the dry-as-dust mode of *teaching* history),[20] I suspect that many

Americans agree with the (misunderstood) sentiment. Former President Bush, for one. When Mr. Bush was asked after his 1988 election whether he had any second thoughts about the negative campaigning, his reply was a dismissive "That's history."[21] Our dislike of the past is betrayed by other cultural clichés as well—"That was then; this is now" and "You can't turn back the clock," for instance.

The results of a 1984 survey of readers of *Psychology Today* gives sustenance to the intuition that many of us avoid the past. The survey asked respondents whether they considered themselves oriented primarily toward the past, the present, or the future. Only 1 percent of the nearly 12,000 respondents described themselves as oriented toward the past.[22] One might legitimately question these results on the grounds of the unrepresentativeness of the sample; but given the strength of the cultural pull away from the past, I suspect that the results aren't too far off the mark.

Repudiation of the past is an axiomatic criterion of rational decision making, according to the long reigning theory of economic choice. Standard decision theory commands us, among other things, to base our decisions only on our best guesses of future consequences. From this perspective, it is therefore imperative to ignore "sunk cost"—which is what you have already paid into an enterprise in the past.[23,24]

A classic example of the sunk-cost problem is the case of the money-eating car. Imagine a variant on my opening example. You bought a new car, which in its first three years has clocked more time in the shop than on the road. Now it has just been diagnosed as needing a costly ring job. Some people (not adherents of standard decision theory) engage in this line of thinking: "I should get rid of this lemon now and not put another cent into it. But I could have gotten rid of it before and didn't. Now I've sunk too much money into this thing to get rid of it, so I'll have the expensive ring job done."

According to standard decision theory, this kind of thinking— sometimes referred to as "knee-deep-in-the-Big-Muddy" thinking,[25] because of the sense of being hopelessly mired in a swamp— is irrational. It is irrational because it factors in the past. Psychological decision theorist Robyn Dawes explains: "Rational decisions are based on an assessment of future possibilities and probabilities. The past is relevant only insofar as it provides information about possible and probable futures."[26] Even more to the point, as Ronald deSousa explains, because "the past is held in common between all possible futures, past investment could not possibly be relevant to the present decision."[27]

Past-bashing has a long beard. It is at least as old as the political theory and mathematics of the Enlightenment. Ideologically, the Enlightenment was much occupied with attacking blind faith in and blind obedience to the past, as represented by custom, tradition, and religious dogma. The past was even mathematically discredited—by probability theory—which challenged, among other things, the "gambler's fallacy," that nearly irresistible belief that if, say, a fair coin has turned up heads on ten previous tosses, there is a higher than 50 percent chance of its turning up tails on the eleventh toss. As probability theory points out, even after a string of heads, the best guess of the future probability of the coin's turning up tails is still 50 percent, because the future outcome is entirely independent of past outcomes. "Coins have no memories," quips Robyn Dawes.[28]

The economic analysis clearly has merit when it comes to coins, cars—and extravagant space-based weapons programs. It is arguable, however, whether it applies across the board. For decisions whether to leave or remain with a particular job or partner, for instance, it is not clear that we should always discount personal history. In general, the economists' dismissal of the past may have limited applicability to decisions regarding how to conduct oneself as a human being in relationship to others. Since Einstein, we can no longer view time as an inferior, incidental adjunct to reality. Time is at the very heart of reality.[29]

What was formerly a justifiable and salutary political, social, and mathematical critique has now calcified into yet another form of dogma. Yet many of us recite the catechism. History is bunk. And regret is bunk. Or worse—as Lillian Hellman observed: "We are a people who do not want to keep much of the past in our heads. It is considered unhealthy in America to remember mistakes, neurotic to think about them, psychotic to dwell upon them."

But wait. What about Santayana's famous "Those who cannot remember the past are condemned to repeat it"? We do not, I think, reject wholesale Santayana's defense of looking backward. Even standard decision theory accommodates part of Santayana's idea: the theory acknowledges the rationality of taking account of the past—to the extent that it provides information about future consequences.[30] If there is something *pragmatic* to be gained in regretting a mistake, then we may, however reluctantly, give it a go. Otherwise, regret seems a failure of American pragmatism. To the

extent that a mistake seems unamenable to corrective action, we
disavow regret as useless. We can't help but agree with Harry Tru-
man when he said: "Never, never waste a minute on regret. It's a
waste of time."[31] Or with Katherine Mansfield when she wrote:
"Regret is an appalling waste of energy; you can't build on it; it's
only good for wallowing in."[32] (At this juncture I want to assure
any readers who might be starting to wonder about my patriotism
that other governmental systems will be getting an equivalent share
of criticism later in this chapter.)

A related, though less obvious, reason for the cultural allergy
to regret is an ideal of (a myth of) unconflicted rationality. If conflicting values and demands are resolvable by the astute application of cost-benefit analysis, then regret is simply uncalled for. If
the national budget cannot support both Stealth bombers and student loans, then the rational would-be student cheerfully goes off
to the hamburger stand or the barracks rather than to college. If
one's health insurance provider judges hospitalization to be unnecessarily costly, then the rational patient picks up her pallet and
limps quietly home to mend. In contrast, regret sometimes entails
an admission that the available choices are inadequate or incommensurable; that taking one road in that yellow wood means aban-
doning another heartbreakingly lovely road; that the most cogent
calculation of costs and benefits fails to touch human wish, need,
or desire.

We find deeply implausible Elizabeth Bishop's sadly ironic assertion: "It's evident the art of losing's not too hard to master."[33]
Which touches on one of America's worst fears—the dread of being
a loser. (Victims, maybe. Survivors, yes. Losers, no). We deny regret
in part to deny that we are now or have ever been losers. In the
reigning economic models of decision, human beings are "calculating machines" who decide their preferences based on the calculation of utilities and probabilities. And regret is viewed as a violation of the rationality of that decision model. But losers, with their
sticky regrets, not only fail to fit the calculating-machine model,
but often (in the words of Murray Kempton) "don't count in the calculations" performed at the societal level.[34] We know this and we
quake.[35]

The typically American quality of *can-do exteriority* provides
another basis for our quarrel with regret. Regret arouses our discomfort with interiority and passivity. A person with regrets is putatively passively thinking things over and feeling bad. But the
American way is to be up and *doing*. Perhaps in part because it is

so difficult for us to believe that acts of consciousness can also be great acts, we (many of us) scorn "navel gazing" and speak mockingly of "wallowing" in regret.

I once noticed on a rack of books in a doughnut shop a book that on its cover urged: "Set yourself free from the paralysis of analysis."[36] From a similarly anti-intellectual perspective, regret tends to be viewed as harmful because paralyzing. There seems to be an irresistible assumption that regret is *in principle* incompatible with action. Think of Lot's wife, turned to a pillar of salt, and thus immobilized, because she looked back.

Excessive regret *can* provoke excessive hesitation.[37] It may even supplant action. As writer Nora Ephron put it in her essay "Revision and Life," "you can spend so much time thinking about how to switch things around that the main event has passed you by."[38] This seems to have been the downfall of Geoffrey Fermin, the protagonist of Malcolm Lowry's novel *Under the Volcano*. Unlike his half-brother Hugh, who lived by the philosophy that regret for unchangeable things is futile, Geoffrey clung to his regrets and thereby failed to act upon opportunities to reverse his descent into an alcoholic hell.[39] The helplessness of some forms of regret appalls cando, pragmatic-minded Americans. Insofar as regret is focused on things we can do nothing about, we find it a frighteningly passive experience.

Existential discomfort with the limits of personal control may explain some of our denial of regret. Just as we in scientifically savvy late-twentieth-century America reject fate and destiny as explanatory concepts, we emphatically avoid thinking about those misfortunes that seem unforeseeable, unpredictable, or uncontrollable. When events throw in our face the fact of our helplessness before chance—say, a child was at the last minute switched onto that plane that crashed—we squirm out from under the knowledge. In an effort to retain a (however beleaguered) sense of being masters of our fate, we suppress as irrational our response of unqualified regret.

Paradoxically, the opposite is also true. It is not only when regrettable occurrences lie outside our control, but also when they lie clearly within our control, that regret chafes. At times, regret entails an admission of personal deficiency (what philosopher Amelie Rorty has called "character regret") or poor judgment (what Rorty calls "agent regret," regret for having contributed to a state of affairs that one judges harmful or undesirable).[40] No one enjoys admitting that his or her judgment, let alone character, is poor. You can imagine how our used-car owner must have felt when she found out that a cursory check of the transmission fluid would have firmly disabused her of the desire to purchase that particular car. On top of her regret for the monetary cost of this mistake, she suffered the self-recrimination of knowing she had made the decision less than brilliantly. Who needs it?

Finally, in a militantly *optimistic* society founded on deeply progressivist assumptions, regret (along with similarly "negative" emotions such as guilt, remorse, and sadness) seems a destructive lapse of optimism. By now a solid body of psychological research has convincingly demonstrated that those who accurately ac-knowledge personal shortcomings, unpleasant realities, and lack of personal control tend to show a host of unpleasant emotions, par-ticularly depression.[41] There is also empirical evidence directly supporting the intuition that *regret* possesses unpleasant emo-tional concomitants, including depression, neuroticism, and gen-eral psychological distress.[42] Regret *can be* a mood-dampener—at least in the short run.

But we find it hard to think of regret as "merely" depressing. We tend to think of it more like we think of crack cocaine, as ruinous because inexorably done to excess. Following philosopher Gabrielle Taylor's analysis of pride,[43] there are at least three ways in which regret might prove destructive through sheer excess: an excessive amount of time might be spent in regret; the intensity of the emotion might be excessive; and excessive importance might be assigned to the regretted matter.

In *Brothers and Keepers*, John Edgar Wideman expresses the torment of excessive regret:

> We come too far to turn back now. Too far, too long, too much at stake. We got a sniff of the big time and if we didn't take our shot wouldn't be nobody to blame but ourselves. And that's heavy. You might live another day, you might live another hundred years but long as you live you have to carry that idea round in your head. You had your shot but you didn't take it. You punked out. Now how a person spozed to live with something like that grinning in his face every day? You hear old people crying the blues about how they could have been this or done that if they only had the chance. How you gon pass that by? Better to die than have to look at yourself every day and say, Yeah. I blew. Yeah, I let it get away.[44]

If jeremiads about the shot you did not take and the chance you let get away grin in your face *every day*, they have become excessive.

In this case, what folk singer Tom Paxton said about nostalgia applies equally well to regret: "It's all right to look back—as long as you don't stare."[45]

Wideman's passage also describes regret that is excessive in its *intensity*—"*Better to die* than have to look at yourself every day and say, Yeah. I blew. Yeah, I let it get away." But is regret generally experienced this intensely?

To find out, I asked a sample of almost 150 college students: "How painful do you generally find the experience of regret?" I asked them to rate the degree of painfulness on a scale of 1 (not at all painful) to 5 (extremely painful). On the average, this sample rated their experience of regret as a temperate "somewhat painful" (the average was 3.1 on the 5–point scale). Only one percent of the students rated their usual experience of regret as "extremely painful."[46] That one percent, though not representative of most people, may be representative of those who resonate to Wideman's "better to die . . ." sentiment.

In Ibsen's play *The Wild Duck,* a young man, Gregers Werle, has wreaked havoc in the life of a couple by informing Hjalmar that his wife Gina was seduced before their marriage by her employer (who happened to be Gregers Werle's father). Seeing Hjalmar's catastrophic reaction, Gina asks him: "Do you regret the fourteen - fifteen years we have lived together?"

Hjalmar: "Tell me. Haven't you—every hour, every day—regretted the web of deceit you've spun around me like a spider? Answer me! Haven't you really been going about in an agony of regret and remorse?"

Gina: "Oh, my dear Hjalmar, I've had so much to do, looking after the house and all the everyday jobs . . . "

Hjalmar: "So you never gave a thought to your past life?"

Gina: "No. God knows, I'd nearly forgotten all that old business."

Hjalmar: "Ah, this blunt, insensitive placidity! There is something shocking about it, to my mind. Just think! Not a single regret!"[47]

In this exchange, the sympathies of most modern audiences lie, I think, with Gina. Hjalmar seems to be granting entirely too much *importance* to something that Gina (the individual, after all, to whom the event actually occurred) considers unimportant, especially in comparison with their years of marriage.

Of course, whether a particular regret is being assigned excessive weight is even harder to judge than whether the regret is excessively intense or preoccupying. It is simply not possible to rank objectively the importance of all possible regrets. Importance depends to a large extent on deeply personal and subjective matters such as one's values and needs, and what one cares about.[48] In *The Wild Duck*, something that Hjalmar considers all-important Gina has dismissed. One person may consider it highly important to, in Wideman's words, have failed to take his or her shot at the big time, however that is defined. Someone else may consider this particular sort of regret rather trivial. Still, we need not drown in an ocean of relativism here; certain matters do lend themselves to consensus—for example, that regret over neglecting a friend who then commits suicide *should* receive greater weight than regret over having eaten the all-pork hot dog instead of the tofu dog. In any case, like the elderly deposed Prince in Lampedusa's novel *The Leopard*, we tend to consider regret a "perilous slope," a treacherous emotion bound to drag us down to the Slough of Despond.

For all these reasons—regret's sometime admission of randomness, of incommensurable conflicts, and of personal deficiency or blame; its failure of future-oriented optimism, pragmatism, exteriority, and action—regret is almost un-American. Our feelings about regret may be grounded in our American worldview, which in the language of literary genres is essentially comic (as opposed to romantic, ironic, or tragic)—in its Horatio-Alger progressivist assumptions and its preference for action as the solution to life's problems. Furthermore, it is *true* that regret can prove useless and harmful, not only on the counts just detailed, but also insofar as it is phony or misplaced.

Probably the most common case of *nongenuine regret*, that occurring in RSVPs ("I regret that I cannot attend . . . "), may often amount to nothing more than a fairly innocuous mode of social etiquette. Other sorts of phony regret, however, can prove more insidious.

A number of philosophers of emotion, including Robert Solomon, view remorse and regret as closely related emotions. Therefore, when Solomon criticizes remorse as "an extremely self-indulgent emotion, more concerned with its esteem in its own eyes than with the victims of its folly,"[49] we can assume that he intends the accusation to apply as well to regret. Likewise, because guilt and regret are emotional cousins, surely some of the hazards of guilt acidly articulated by Lillian Hellman also apply to regret: "I am suspicious of [it] in myself and in other people: it is usually a way of not thinking, or of announcing one's own fine sensibilities the better to be rid of them fast."[50] In 1991 Los Angeles Police Chief Daryl Gates gave the appearance of expressing regret the better to deny it when he said after the beating by his officers of motorist Rodney King: "We regret what took place. I hope he gets his life straightened out. Perhaps this will be the vehicle to move him down the road to a good life instead of the life he's been involved in for such a long time."[51]

Some of the suspicion with which we regard regret comes from getting a nasty whiff of the kind of self-serving and socially debilitating uses detailed by Solomon and Hellman. Regret primarily concerned with bolstering one's esteem in one's own eyes or the eyes of others is simply phony. Phony regret, what Forster refers to in *A Passage to India* as "the canny substitute," is perhaps the most obviously bad form that it can take.

Regret may be wrong in yet another way. It may be misplaced—that is, based on a bad, immoral, or self-alien value.[52] A student who regrets *not* cheating on an exam or *not* "improving" a written assignment with some shrewd plagiarism is showing misplaced regret. Yet, many regrets resist definitive judgment as to whether or not they are misplaced. Person X regrets a divorce from a partner whom Person Y perceives as an utterly destructive force in Person X's life. There is probably no metric that can definitively declare Person X's regret misplaced. However, some matters do admit of consensual judgments of misplaced regret. Morally serious agents will agree that the individual is showing misplaced regret who regrets *not* having cheated on an exam, plagiarized, or joined his compatriots in a successful bank robbery.

Even if a particular experience of regret is genuine and not misplaced, still it could prove self-serving. Some people may express regret for the sole purpose of eliciting sympathy from others. Alternatively, forever rehashing regret may serve the "sick" purpose of perpetual self-punishment. Some individuals may, as Freeman and DeWolf put it, have "been taught—and deeply believe—that if you err, especially if you err seriously, then you should and must suffer forever."[53] The protagonist of Dostoevsky's *Notes from Underground* has been interpreted as representing a fictional illustration of masochistic regret, as evidenced by passages such as the following:

I would feel a certain hidden, morbid, nasty little pleasure in the acute awareness that I had once again committed something vile that day . . . and I would gnaw and gnaw at myself . . . until the bitterness would finally begin to turn into a kind of shameful, damnable sweetness and, in the end—into a definite, positive pleasure! Yes, a pleasure! I stand by that. . . .[54]

Emily Dickinson's assessment of remorse—that it is "the Adequate of Hell"[55]—applies also to excessive forms of regret: to experience continuous, unending regret could fulfill the need for eternal suffering reasonably well, at least here on earth.

For others, obsessive regret, though painful, may serve the purpose of relieving existential anxiety that they find even more painful. Such persons may "prefer" constantly replaying their regrets to acknowledging lack of omniscience or omnipotence. One can imagine a parent whose child is killed on her walk home from school by a hit-and-run driver constantly torturing himself with regrets about not having collected his child from school that day. Still, this parent may actually find obsessive regret less distressing than facing his utter helplessness to have saved his child from an essentially random event. Perhaps this is what is meant by writer Jonathan Baumbach's phrase "the dim solace of regret."[56]

Hellman is right that in this time and place regret is viewed as at minimum unhealthy, or worse, neurotic (self-destructively painful), and even irrational. Moreover, regret *is* sometimes a force for no good. Obsessively recycling, replaying, and rehashing mistakes, losses, and misfortunes *can* be an exercise in lamentation or immobility. But it is another thing entirely to claim that simply because regret is unpleasant and fruitless (at least in an immediately pragmatic sense) it is therefore irrational.

Rather than rush to sidestep or conquer regret, let us see what we can learn from lingering with it first. Regret need not necessarily be a futile waste of time, a failure of rationality, or a "perilous slope" down to depression. Regret can also constitute a path leading onward and upward. Regret is better viewed as a form of practical reason appropriately informed by emotion. Like anything human, it can go wrong. It all depends on what you do with it.

Constructive Functions

Yes, regret is sometimes "wrong" in the senses just discussed. Still, these are arguably less grievous sins than the sins of the other extreme—the complete absence of regret characteristic of overly well-defended optimists, fatalists, rationalizers, and sociopaths.

But regret need not fall at either of these extremes. Regret properly handled serves a number of beneficial purposes. Because human beings are capable of *development,* regret need not be a static experience like staring or wallowing or inertia. Regret soundly practiced will be a dynamic, changing *process.*

Following sociologist Fred Davis's analysis of nostalgia,[57] I conceive of the dynamics of regret as a chain of events roughly comparable to sensation, perception, and cognition. First-order, or "primary," regret is the immediate, unreflected experience: as in that almost sensory pang I felt when my mechanic showed me the black, metal-flaked transmission fluid from my new used car. If first-order regret is like sensation, second-order or "reflexive," regret is like perception, the process of consciously registering the meaning of that primary experience—for example, consciously acknowledging regret to oneself: "Yikes. I think I made a big mistake." Third-order, or "analyzed," regret entails further psychological processing of the reflected-upon experience—say, questioning whether one *ought* to reflect on it, as opposed to suppressing it, or engaging in "emotion management," problem-solving, or action to undo, re-do, or repair the regretted matter, as in: "I'm really sorry I bought that car without having a mechanic look it over. Now I'll have the transmission rebuilt, and learn a good lesson from this mistake for the future." It is particularly at the higher-order levels that the constructive effects of regret are realized and where Proust's phrase "the ephemeral efficacy of sorrow"[58] applies as well to regret. This claim rests on a view of regret as a temporally dynamic experience, on a nonliteral view of the past, and on respect for the rationality of emotion.

Regret and the Continuity of the Past and the Present

Pragmatist that she was, Lady Macbeth lectured her husband for his guilty meditations following their multiple murders: "What's done is done." There is, of course, literal truth to the idea of past-as-done-deed. There *is* a sense in which the past is unchangeable and irremediable. Sartre did have whooping cough when he was five years old.[59] The *Challenger* did explode in 1986. I did buy a car in need of a major repair. These things cannot be undone.

However, there is another sense in which what's done is not done, the past is neither unchangeable nor irremediable—and anything but dead. As Sartre asserted, the personal meaning of the brute facts of the past is changeable. While it is an implacable fact that Sartre had whooping cough as a child, that the *Challenger* exploded, and that I bought a car that needed a costly repair, the personal significance of those facts has the potential to shift.[60]

Faulkner crisply asserted this nonliteral side of the truth when he wrote that "The past isn't dead. It's not even past."[61] The following excerpt from a poem by John Ashbery expresses with more plenitude the enduring power of the past:

> Out of this intolerant swarm of freedom as it
> Is called in your press, the future, an open
> Structure, is rising even now, to be invaded by the
> present
> As the past stands to one side, dark and theoretical
> Yet most important of all. . . .[62]

William James expressed both sides of this truth when, in the same breath in which he averred that the past can never "in strict scientific literalness" be undone, he also implied that the past lives on in the present: "Every smallest state of virtue or of vice leaves its never so little scar."[63]

Freud is perhaps the foremost thinker for whom the past is (in Ashbery's words) not only "dark and theoretical" and (in Faulkner's words) not only not dead, but (as for Ashbery) "most important of all." A foundation stone of the Freudian theory of the psyche is the idea that "in mental life nothing which has once been formed can perish."[64] This statement originally referred primarily to the instincts, understood by Freud as innate, hardwired psychic and somatic impulses of an erotic or aggressive nature. However, it applies more broadly to anything in mental life—thoughts, feelings, wishes, memories, images, and so on. According to psychoanalytic theory, mental processes are never eradicated; they can be muffled by defensive maneuvers or channeled into socially approved forms of expression. But defensive maneuvers never destroy the original processes. On the contrary, according to Freud:

> the instinct-presentation develops in a more unchecked and luxuriant fashion if it is withdrawn by repression from conscious influence. It ramifies like a fungus, so to speak, in the dark and takes on extreme forms of expression.[65]

It follows that whatever truth there is to our assumption that regret is inevitably done to excess may actually arise from our attempts to repress it. In the dark it grows like a fungus and takes on extreme forms. At the very least, psychoanalysis as a theory of the human condition tells us that the past ramifies in the present. Psychically, the truth is: that was then, *this* is then. At the same time, as a method of treatment, psychoanalysis tells us that we have the power to reformulate the meaning of our past to at least some degree.

The past is not dead, it is not even past. Perhaps the past, like time, is most important of all. As a consequence, it is vitally important to direct our powers of reflection onto the past and to attempt to discern its enduring influence. Insofar as new understanding reveals ways of undoing, redoing, or repairing past missteps, regret becomes no more irrevocable or irremediable than the past.

Regret and the Rationality of Emotion

Despite the strong presumptions to the contrary, I believe that emotion in general and regret in particular are not necessarily irrational. Indeed, emotions have enormous epistemological, moral, and utilitarian value. Not to make the assertion that reason ought to be ruled by emotion, I argue that reason is necessary but not sufficient to responsible human conduct. Reason and emotion typically play interdependent roles in human conduct. Furthermore, they should.

Although emotion has mostly been considered disruptive of rationality, as Stuart Hampshire put it, human beings "are only half rational."[66] Emotion is an undeniable part of what it is to be human. To aspire to be something we are not—whether disembodied angels, "ideally rational agents," or calculating machines—is futile and counterproductive. We are therefore not warranted in demanding as a condition of rationality the suppression of emotion. In fact, we might well question the judgment of individuals capable of living life unemotionally.

Due to the strength of the prevailing wisdom, it is not necessary to belabor cases in which emotion threatens rationality. Instead, let us consider an example in which the *suppression* of emotion threatens rationality. Consider a thoroughly "rational man," Rudolph Hoess.[67] As commandant of Auschwitz for three years, Hoess supervised the murders of 2.9 million individuals. Even while awaiting execution for his crimes, Hoess defended these killings as just and rational.

Oh, he had his reservations: he regretted those acts in which he or his subordinates had experienced or displayed emotion as they carried out the "Final Solution." By Hoess's lights, all emotion, whether beneficent or malevolent, was to be suppressed. Thus Hoess excoriated both those Nazis who had sadistically enjoyed brutalizing their victims, and also those who had been unable to control their "good nature and kind heart."[68] Here is Hoess describing his own difficulty in properly "stifl[ing] all softer emotions" at the door of the gas chamber:

> On one occasion two small children were so absorbed in some game that they quite refused to let their mother tear them away from it. Even the Jews in the "special attachment" were reluctant to pick the children up. The imploring look in the eyes of the mother, who certainly knew what was happening, is something I shall never forget. The people in the gas chamber were becoming restive and I had to act. Everyone was looking at me; I nodded to the junior non-commissioned officer on duty and he picked up the screaming, struggling children in his arms and carried them into the gas chamber accompanied by their mother, who was weeping in the most heart-rending fashion. My pain was so great that I longed to vanish from the scene; yet *I might not show the slightest trace of emotion.*[69]

As Robyn Dawes points out, this chilling self-description of a rational man casts doubt on the assumption that, if only reason were to master emotion, rational decisions and acts would follow. One wishes that Hoess, hyperrational, hypoemotional, and thereby monstrously inhuman, had factored his emotional reaction to the weeping mother and screaming children into his decision-making process—and had permitted that emotion to influence what he construed as the dictates of reason.

Emotion, like ideation, is informative. It tells us what we care about, or what we should care about.[70] It can make us think twice in order to avoid doing something we will later regret, or should later regret. A valid theory of rationality ought not only to accept with resignation the role of emotion but to insist on it—by virtue of its epistemological and moral value.

Emotion has pragmatic, utilitarian value as well. By the early 1990s, most scholars studying emotion had come to appreciate the possible evolutionary usefulness of emotion in serving our survival as well as other important functions.[71] Stuart Hampshire argues that the passions—"when these are circumscribed as the reflective passions"—ought to be the "equal partner" of reason.[72] Even Plato acknowledged the dangers associated with a tyranny of rationality:

"when *either* of the two [i.e., reason and the passions] prevails, it fails in attaining its own pleasure."[73] In a recent book entitled *Passions Within Reason: The Strategic Role of the Emotions*,[74] Robert H. Frank has argued the less obvious side of Plato's assertion—that when reason prevails entirely over passion, "it fails in attaining its own pleasure."

Frank's thesis takes as its starting point the body of empirical research that has established the paradoxical truth that "in many situations the conscious pursuit of self-interest is incompatible with its attainment."[75] But Frank advances an even bolder claim: that "passions often serve our interests very well indeed."[76] This is so, according to Frank, not because of hidden, intangible, subjective, or distal gains (like personal satisfaction in knowing one has behaved well, or survival of the genes of one's kin)—but because passion-driven behavior "often confers material benefits on the very individuals who practice it."[77]

Frank provides a fascinating example grounded in a narrow, but widely held, variant of classic decision theory, one in which self-interest in general and one's own time and money in particular reign supreme. The example goes like this. Smith is thinking about stealing Miller's $200 leather briefcase. If Smith steals it, Miller has a decision to make: whether or not to press charges. To do so will involve a possible gain—justice: Smith's spending 60 days in jail. Pressing charges will also entail considerable losses for Miller—time and aggravation spent in court, and $300 in lost earnings—that is, $100 more than the value of the briefcase.

How rational then would it be for Smith to steal the briefcase? According to Frank, Smith's decision will likely depend on his knowledge of whether or not Miller is a "pure rationalist"—that is, an adherent of this common variant of standard decision theory. As Frank explains, "If Smith knows that [Miller] is a purely rational, self-interested person, he is free to steal the briefcase with impunity."[78] However, if Miller is not a pure rationalist, but someone willing to lose time and money to see justice done, and if Smith knows this, then Smith knows it would not be in his best interest to steal the briefcase. Because Miller is known not to be ruled by rational self-interest alone, Miller benefits materially—by avoiding the theft of his briefcase. The same principle applies not only in the case where someone values justice over time and money, but also in other forms of conduct sometimes judged irrational under orthodox decision theory—such as self-destructive vengeance, behaving with honesty even when one could get away with dishonesty, and altruism. In these cases and others, emotion can enhance the material consequences of the emotional individual.

I want to be very clear here. My defense of emotion should not be taken as an anti-intellectual romanticizing of emotion. Clearly, the exercise of uninhibited, unreflected emotion can make for faulty decisions and acts. We've known that at least since Plato. But the suppression of emotion, and its dissociation from reflective thought, can make for equally faulty decisions and acts. Like cognition, emotion is not nefarious but neutral, and potentially a force for rationality and human decency. The reason-versus-emotion dichotomy is a false dichotomy. Judgment is never free of emotion; nor is emotion ever free of judgment. Ideally, reason and sentiment ought to collaborate in the exercise of rationality.

In the light of these views of regret as a temporally dynamic process, of the past as living on in the present, and of emotion as a normal, not irrational, element of humanity, what then are the constructive purposes of regret? The benefits may be utilitarian or ethical in nature; they may occur before or after a decision or event; and they may accrue to the individual or society.

Regret's Benefits for the Individual

PRAGMATIC FUNCTIONS OF REGRET

By pragmatic or utilitarian regret, I mean regret for undesired consequences (or for failing to achieve desired consequences) that are neutral with respect to human decency or morality.[79] Regret possesses a number of benefits of a utilitarian or pragmatic sort—including remunerative, instructional, correctional, and motivational benefits.

Material Reward. As Robert Frank has pointed out, individuals are at times materially rewarded for being the kind of persons who act out of sentiments like regret.[80] For example, those with a reputation as individuals who do not suppress regret may be more likely than those without such a reputation to be occupationally rewarded for their presumed thoughtfulness prior to making decisions and their presumed ability to learn from past decisions that proved mistaken.

Forewarning. From a pragmatic point of view, when I was buying that used car, I would have been smart to have vividly imagined ahead of time my possible regret, and to have used my anticipated regret to motivate me to have the car checked out by a mechanic. Before making a decision of any consequence, it is not morbid but a very good idea to think through exactly how one might come to regret the decision. Anticipatory regret can enhance decision making by putting the decision brakes on long enough to identify and appraise each of the relevant alternative courses of action.[81] To blunt the pain of regret may be to forgo potentially valuable information.

Instruction. Eventually, whether or not you've troubled to weigh each possible alternative, you have to come to a decision. (Even someone paralyzed by indecision has through inaction decided not to decide.) Retrospective regret, although arguably more torment-ing than anticipatory regret, can prove just as useful. Like pain, regret provides valuable information, telling us that something is wrong. Regret has epistemological value.

Remembrance of things past, which almost inevitably brings with it some measure of regret, has the potential to serve the func-tion of shining an instructional light on the future. Of course, the process of looking backward commands no inherent power to pro-mote this understanding. Life in general and life's missteps in par-ticular are not *inevitably* understood at all, forward or backward. Still, our best hope for understanding life and its missteps is to study the past.

How is it that regret-driven reflection might improve upon the past in the future? Perhaps surprisingly, recent research finds a number of cognitive benefits to accompany the negative emotions. First of all, there is the body of research on "depressive realism," the fact that, relative to nondepressed people, (nonclinically) de-pressed individuals often show greater accuracy of judgment.[82] Sec-ond, compared with people in elated moods, people in (nonclini-cally) depressed moods have been found to show more attentive, more careful, more analytic processing of information.[83] For ex-ample, depressed subjects have been observed to be influenced only by strong but not by weak persuasive arguments, while elated sub-jects were equally influenced by strong and weak arguments.[84] By extension, it may be that regret stimulates high-quality thinking. Because it signals that all is not well, it may produce more watch-fulness.

Another way that regret might make for a better future is through the application of what is called counterfactual thought—thinking about possible but unactualized states. Imagining how things might have been different has the potential to free one from the thrall of the past to entertain a new future. To use the fine phrase of Daniel Kahneman and Dale Miller (researchers of counterfactual thought): this higher-order processing of regret might be referred to as the "power of backward thinking."[85] As Sartre points out in an acute, though less-than-colorful, assertion: "freedom is interiorized as the internal negation of the given."[86] In its own role as an internal negation of the given, regret stimulates thoughts and feelings that form a bridge between a regretted past and a better, freer future.

To return to the unfortunate car purchase: these lines of research suggest that I was better off consciously regretting the mistake than suppressing it. In fact, facing my regret over that purchase did push me to clarify exactly where I had gone wrong. "Negating this given" did lead me to analyze carefully what I might have done differently—that is, not only consult *Consumer Reports* but *also* a good mechanic before buying the car. The regretter has a better chance than the non-regretter to avoid making the same mistake in the future.[87] To blunt the pain of regret is to forgo valuable information.

Mobilization. Not only does emotion have epistemological value; it has motivational value. In fact the words *emotion* and *motivation* share the same root, the Latin *movere*, to move.[88] Regret too has motivational value. Regret does not *in principle* paralyze. It has just as much potential to mobilize thought and action. Once again, like pain, regret may not only tell us that something is wrong, but it can also move us to do something about it.

Those working from a clinical perspective have long stressed the importance of acknowledging and integrating negative feelings and personal experiences—to the end of unfixating those who were fixated, and unparalyzing those who were paralyzed. Regret is one of those painful feelings that can be used in the service of greater mental health and personal integrity.

Researchers studying political empowerment have pointed to the critical role of acknowledging distress over an undesirable status quo—in order to develop the will to take action.[89] Hanging onto illusions about a bad situation can prevent us from developing the will to take action. Psychologist Faye Crosby has uncovered a common tendency of individuals to acknowledge that there is discrimination against their social group, while simultaneously denying suffering any "personal disadvantage" whatsoever; this may account for much quietism among objectively disadvantaged groups. Conversely, there is research evidence that thinking counterfactually can serve to prepare one to improve the future.[90] Taken together, these lines of thought suggest that acknowledging regret for personal suffering and societal discrimination has the potential to stimulate the will to take action.

How might regret prove mobilizing? For one thing, regretful thought can function as experimental action. Again, I was better off consciously regretting my car-buying mistake than suppressing it. In fact, facing my regret over that purchase did mobilize me to have a mechanic do a thorough check before I bought my second used Corolla some years later, after the one with the rebuilt transmission eventually died.[91]

So what about all that research that has found that facing a negative reality acts as a depressant—for example, social psychologist Shelley Taylor's[92] research with cancer patients? No doubt it is right, particularly in circumstances in which that negative reality is difficult or impossible to change. In such circumstances, regretful realism might prove demoralizing and immobilizing. It is equally important to recognize, though, that optimistically putting the best face on things can *also* drain motivation to change things that can and should be changed. To blunt the pain of regret is to blunt the will to take action to correct what has gone wrong.

Regret then need not be *only* a doleful experience. Regret may be at the same time a sorrow and an opportunity. Political theorist Antonio Gramsci's terse description of the proper stance toward social change—"pessimism of the intellect, optimism of the will"— applies as well to the experience of regret.

ETHICAL FUNCTIONS OF REGRET

Regret has been defined as one of the "moral sentiments," along with guilt, remorse, and shame.[93] Just as the process of reflecting on and feeling sorry about mistakes and misfortunes constitutes the first step toward pragmatic improvement, the process of reflecting on and feeling sorry for moral failures, one's own or those of one's society, constitutes the first step toward reconstruction and integrity. Regret thus serves intrinsically, as well as instrumentally, beneficial purposes.

In the novel *Under the Volcano* Malcolm Lowry wrote that "conscience had been given to man to regret [the past] *only* in so far as that might change the future" (emphasis added). I take issue with Lowry's "only." Regret has uses other than the pragmatic. The nonutilitarian—indeed, counterutilitarian—nature of certain regrets is here expressed with eloquent irony by Benjamin DeMott:

> If we pause too long in contemplation of a former self, studying some lesson or other, we run the risk of forgetting how to take our present selves for granted. And down that road there's a risk of starting to treat life as a mystery instead of the way smart people treat it—as a set of done and undone errands.[94]

Selfhood, personal development, or character is one aspect of life better taken as a mystery than as a set of done and undone errands. Part of the mystery of selfhood lies in its lack of inevitability; it is a task, not a given. Despite the popularity of metaphors like "finding oneself," I believe it is not useful to construe self-development as a process of uncovering one's inner self—as if the self were the secret heart at the center of an artichoke. I prefer to think of personal development as a historical, dialectical process in which (to paraphrase Kierkegaard), one lives forward and understands backward.[95] Or as I once overheard an unknown graduate student say, the self is a verb. Robert Frost expressed the historical and dialectical nature of selfhood—and how regret is implicated in it—through the striking metaphor of a "West-Running Brook":

> The universal cataract of death
> That spends to nothingness—and unresisted,
> Save by some strange resistance in itself,
> Not just a swerving but a throwing back,
> As if regret were in it and were sacred.
> It has this throwing backward on itself
> So that the fall of most of it is always
> Raising a little, sending up a little . . .
> It is this backward motion toward the source,
> Against the stream, that most we see ourselves in . . .
> It is most us.[96]

Frost's metaphor invokes a complex vision. If human life is like a brook, it is essentially linear rather than cyclic in nature, and thus tragically limited rather than happily unlimited. Yet there is in a human life also "this backward motion toward the source, against the stream"—again, not a cycle, but a dialectic, a back-and-forth. In fact, says Frost, this backward motion is "most us." The past is that hovering fact that renders regret, through the activity of understanding backward, "most us," and therefore hallowed.

Perhaps it was this sense of the sacredness of regret that Ionesco was referring to in the following passage:

> I can't quite explain to myself how I could allow myself to reach the age of 30, 35, 36. I don't understand how I could have failed to try to prevent this catastrophe. . . . A reverse metamorphosis: I became a caterpillar. Whatever became of the person I was, the person I must still be, the frail child, the brand-new being? . . . Where have I disappeared to? . . . The only thing I have left is my regret at being someone else. *It is this regret that makes me continue to be myself,* or the child that I was, that I am.[97]

Here Ionesco expresses nostalgia for his lost childhood and regret for the reverse metamorphosis of aging. The bittersweet experience of regret links Ionesco's present caterpillar-self with his prior butterfly-self. Regret thus affords him a sense of continuity with his past, a sense of personal integrity which may itself have ethical (as well as pragmatic) benefits.

But just as some of what is "most us" (Frost) is far worse than caterpillar-like, some forms of regret, perhaps especially character regret, taste not bittersweet, but simply bitter. The culpable inaction of the protagonist of Camus's *The Fall,* faced with the woman committing suicide; the smoldering shame and cruelty of Dostoevsky's Underground Man; the accusatory resentment and wasted talent of the writer/protagonist of Hemingway's "The Snows of Kilimanjaro"; the years of evading his work responsibilities of the protagonist of Kurosawa's film *Ikiru*—these and other aspects of the self resemble Hemingway's image of regret as a self-biting snake more than Ionesco's caterpillar-self. Yet even when regret puts us in touch with "worse selves," it contributes significantly to a comprehensive sense of integrity that comes of sustaining one's link with who one was, while also sustaining one's link with one's present better self. Regardless of how bad are the regretted matters, genuine regret signifies that you have standards of excellence, decency, morality, or ethics you still care about—a good thing in itself. In addition, remaining in connection with your better values through regret can further the purpose of moving you to behave differently if a similar situation should present itself in the future.

How critically important for selfhood it is to remember who we once were is clarified by examining its negation. In an essay titled "The Self and Memory in *1984*," psychologist Joseph Adelson analyzes how in George Orwell's *1984* the destruction of the self was accomplished through eradicating the personal past. "Winston Smith's argument [against the Party's attempt to destroy his selfhood] is Cartesian: 'I remember, therefore I exist.' "[98]

But memory is only part of integrity. Feeling and judgment are other parts. The capacity to recognize and to "own" one's thoughts and feelings, even if they are unpleasant, also furthers personal integrity. Although "smart people" (as DeMott put it) may find it counterproductive to own their regret, it is a condition of personal integrity to do so. In the following passage from *The God That Failed*, Richard Wright shows such integrity. Although Wright eventually came to regret his membership in the Communist party, which he left in 1936, nevertheless, he did not wholly disavow the impulse that had originally led him to Communism:

> I remembered the stories I had written, the stories in which I had assigned a role of honor and glory to the Communist Party, and I was glad that they were down in black and white, were finished. For I knew in my heart that I should never be able to write that way again, should never be able to feel with that simple sharpness about life, should never again express such passionate hope, should never again make so total a commitment of faith.[99]

In this passage Wright shows another facet of the multidimensional matter that is regret. At one level, he judges his party membership to have been a mistake. At another level, he looks back with approval on the passionate idealism of the younger self who had made that mistake.

In *The Sound and the Fury* the narrator's father declares that a "man is the sum of his misfortunes." This is going too far in a morose direction, but it is half true. Wright demonstrates in the above passage the wisdom of recognizing that he is the sum of his clever decisions as well as his mistakes, his fortunes as well as his misfortunes. To the extent that individuals are not alienated from their past—better *or* worse—but are at one with it, they are strengthened. I believe this is what Shakespeare meant when he had Albany in *King Lear* say: "Where I could not be honest, I never yet was valiant." Like other moral sentiments, regret is not particularly pleasant. But it is essential to a full humanity, as philosopher John Rawls wrote:

> the moral feelings are admittedly unpleasant, in some extended sense of unpleasant, but there is no way for us to avoid a liability to them without disfiguring ourselves.[100]

Like other moral sentiments then, regret functions as "a guardian of our goodness."[101]

In a related vein, regret confronted can lead to the healthy recognition that we are who we are partly by virtue of who we are *not*. One's limitations and missed boats define one's character as much as one's positive acts. Philosopher José Ortega y Gasset understood this:

> Everything that we are in a positive sense is by virtue of some limitation. And this being limited, this being crippled, is what is called destiny, life. That which is missing in life, that which oppresses us, forms the fabric of life and maintains us within it.[102]

Even if one never made a mistake and never lost something wonderful, one is inevitably limited. Human beings cannot simultaneously take both roads in that yellow wood. Or as Anne Morrow Lindbergh wrote, fashioning a different metaphor: "One cannot collect all the beautiful shells on the beach." Those who recognize themselves as historically constituted beings will inevitably experience some regret—for a past that was unlovely, for a self that was stillborn, or never conceived, for some of the beautiful shells that had to be left behind on the shore. Much as it takes a lot of work to keep a beach ball submerged in a lake, attempting forcibly to submerge regret drains the individual of energy for other things. The route to a vigorous sense of integrity—and more important, to an actual state of integrity—lies partly in fully experiencing regret.

Finally, I wish to return to an idea I raised earlier: the link between regret and action. I have acknowledged the potential destructiveness of regret that substitutes for action. Here I wish to qualify that condemnation. As moral philosopher Michael Stocker points out, not *all* judgment worth having is judgment worth applying directly to action.[103] More specifically, philosopher Gabrielle Taylor argues that regret that does not lead to action is not always worthless or harmful: "No action need follow from regret, or even need be expected to follow."[104] Hume's answer with respect to grief applies also to certain regrets: "To the claim 'Your sorrow is fruitless,' Hume replied, 'Very true, and for that very reason I am sorry.'"[105] Someone who regrets having neglected a distressed friend who then committed suicide is experiencing regret that is fruitless, in the sense that there is no action that can be taken that will bring back the friend. Yet it is not fruitless, in the sense that it serves the function of connecting the regretful individual with values that are part of what make him or her humane.

Insofar as one does not—despite the personal pain it brings—repudiate the value of being attentive to and patient with those in distress, one is undoubtedly a better person. It is better to have (right) values, even at the cost of the pain of regret, than to be devoid of them. It is a "peculiarly utilitarian or pragmatic crassness which asks only where the action is and gets its answer by looking only at the bottom line," writes Michael Stocker.[106]

Social Benefits of Regret

In the utopian world of *Erewhon*, the 1872 novel by Samuel Butler, someone whose spouse dies, who comes down with an illness, or who suffers a financial loss is in trouble with the law. In Erewhon, losses, misfortune, and mistakes are criminal offenses. As a consequence, people refuse to talk or even think about such things.[107] Andrei Platonov, whose work of the 1920s to the 1950s was suppressed by his government, the USSR, wrote in *The Foundation Pit* about a "fictional" state in which regret is a political crime, and in which the state mandates "the duty of joy."[108] Citizens of this state are exhorted to compete to display the most patriotic—that is, the sunniest—moods. To keep at bay regret for the old system, the government purposely keeps workers' bodies and minds so occupied with physical labor and radio propaganda that they have no time for an interior life, with its potential to engender the politically subversive state of regret. In their taboos on regret, Butler's and Platonov's fictional societies are not too different from the society—mine—that Hellman described, where it is "considered unhealthy . . . to remember mistakes, neurotic to think about them, psychotic to dwell upon them."

The view of emotion as a purely internal state, a purely private matter, is itself a cultural construction. In fact, as anthropologists tell us, non-Western cultures more often construe emotion as referring to social interaction than to internal states.[109] Regret, like virtually all emotion, has social origins, social implications, and social norms that regulate its expression. Accordingly, the constructive functions of regret apply not only at the individual level but also at the social level. (I believe that the individual/social and personal/public distinctions forever need to be challenged; but for organizing purposes they remain a useful fiction.) Among the social benefits of regret are those I have described for individuals: the pragmatic and ethical benefits of utilitarian reward, instruction, correction, motivation, and integrity, among others.

First, societies capable of regret may find themselves the beneficiaries of better material payoffs than those incapable of regret. During the Persian Gulf War of 1991, Iraqi missiles repeatedly attacked Israel's cities. At first it was assumed that Israel would immediately and massively retaliate, although it was feared that retaliation would drastically escalate and transform the war from one in which an Arab-Western coalition fought united against Iraq to one in which the Arab (Saudi Arabian, Egyptian, Syrian) sectors of the coalition would join Iraq to attack Israel. To the world's surprise, Israel refrained from retaliation, a decision apparently based in part on anticipation of later regret. In turn, Israel gained considerable worldwide sympathy and goodwill, which was expected after the war to result in increased cooperation with and aid from the West. More generally, regret may serve not only the material welfare of the individual,[110] but also the survival of the species—especially insofar as it reduces aggression.

Just as acknowledging problems represents the first step to individual betterment, so is it the first step to ameliorative social action. The writer Ronald Cassill imagined the biblical Noah acting on this insight: "I'd like to find and join a chorus of people who say this stuff is rain and it's going to keep coming, so let's build an ark."[111] Far from a paralyzing force, anticipatory regret ("we'll regret it if we don't build an ark") has the power to mobilize collective action and make for smarter social decisions.

Retrospective regret can also make for better decisions following societal mistakes or for problem-directed action to correct regrettable social circumstances. In an analysis of the genre of autobiography and its relationship to historical and cultural attitudes toward the individual, J. N. Morris proposes a fascinating explanation of why something so interior as reflective self-consciousness might impel action to change the world:

> [T]he great progress made during this century and the last toward more equitable social arrangements and institutions has been achieved partly as a result of the accession to consciousness of literally millions of humble persons of a sense of their worth and dignity as individuals. . . . Almost paradoxically, the high value that men came to put on private experiences, freeing them from impotent, accepting anonymity, encouraged them to combine with others to force the social recognition of their new conceptions of themselves on the public world. Self-consciousness is, that is to say, a subversive force.[112]

Morris's insight does appear paradoxical in a culture that dichotomizes the individual and the social, rather than viewing them as interdependent and interembedded. But his is a deep truth about the human condition: it is conceivable that the richer and stronger one's inner life, the richer and stronger one's engagement with the outer world. Just as self-reflection can be a subversive force, so can reflection on the collective status quo. Regret, too, can be a subversive force.

Clear-eyed scrutiny of the past, and of the status quo, that residuum of the past, is a *sine qua non* for social change. For this reason it is not surprising how frequently authors familiar with totalitarian suppression take as their theme the strategic deployment of denial of the past and denial of regret as modes of social control. Platonov's *The Foundation Pit* and Butler's *Erewhon* have many comrades. In *1984* Orwell condemned party institutions in the totalitarian Oceania (such as the Ministry of Truth, the memory hole, and doublethink) for falsifying the past. In *The Book of Laughter and Forgetting*, one of Milan Kundera's characters highlights the connection between suppression of the past and the maintenance of totalitarian forms of government: "The first step in liquidating a people . . . is to erase its memory."[113]

In disconnecting individuals from their past, the process of denying and rewriting the past effectively depersonalizes, disorients, and isolates those individuals. In *1984* Orwell captures the sense of personal disorientation and social isolation in a chilling simile:

> cut off from contact with the outer world, and with the past, the citizen of Oceania is like a man in interstellar space, who has no way of knowing which direction is up and which is down.[114]

Disconnecting people from their collective past effectively precludes the possibility of collective protest, in part because it truncates their standards of comparison. Someone with "no way of knowing which direction is up and which is down" has all she can do to try to attain and maintain a measure of perceptual equilibrium. Floating and tumbling in an ever-changing "interstellar space," she will likely be more preoccupied with achieving stability than with imagining still other, still better, possible worlds. Again, in this way, denial of the past serves as a means of social control. In contrast, individuals able to sustain their connection with the past are in a better position to imagine alternative worlds and to take action to free themselves from an oppressive present. Imagination is a rebel.

Denial of the past as a mode of social control is not limited to fiction or to totalitarian states. In a study of women homemakers who chose to undertake demanding careers in the mid-1970s, psy-

chologists George Rosenwald and Jacqueline Wiersma[115] noticed
that at the initial interview these women almost uniformly told a
story of a radical break with, a clean sweep of, even the death of,
the old self. Their "initial self-descriptions signal[led] a wish to dismiss and even excise the prior life from remembrance."[116] In subsequent interviews, these women eventually recognized the falsi-
fication of the past entailed in their initial stories. In fact, their
past selves had never died. Instead, the women's career changes
actually reflected fundamental continuities in themselves—and
fundamental discontinuities in their social situations. The researchers noted how the women's initial "disparagement of
history"[117] served the purposes of social control: "the memory of
origins seems much too coldly regarded in many circles—as though
the memory, rather than the origins themselves, were a shackle on
the oppressed."[118] In describing her life change in terms of complete and utter rebirth, the woman "curses her past, not the sexual-
occupational role system."[119] In so doing, she leaves herself vulnerable to further exploitation by that role system. In Scheler's
words, "The eternal fugitive from the past sinks deeper and deeper
into the dead arms of that very past."[120] In contrast, the process of
reflecting on and "owning" a regretted past possesses socially relevant educative and liberating functions.

Still, the disparagement of regret proceeds on the societal level
as well as the individual level. In the 1980s we in America heard
early and often about the "prophets of doom and gloom" who were
supposedly causing a national "malaise" that was undermining the
hope of the populace. Christopher Lasch, however, articulates well
the fallacy in this sort of claim:

> a denial of the past, superficially progressive and optimistic, proves on
> closer analysis to embody the despair of a society that cannot face the
> future.[121]

Decent Americans regret the fact that in 1988 a U.S. Navy captain
was, through a dreadful accident, responsible for killing 290 civilians while patrolling the Persian Gulf. Decent Americans regret
the fact that in 1991 several hundred Iraqi civilians were killed in
the U.S.-led destruction of a Baghdad bomb shelter. Decent Americans regret these incidents as intensely as we regret the high proportion of American and other deaths in the Gulf War that occurred by "friendly fire." Facing these and other collective regrets,
rather than expending valuable energy forcibly suppressing them,
stands to enhance a country's integrity, thus strengthening it for

future action based on a firm foundation rather than on shifting desert sands.

ETHICAL FUNCTIONS OF REGRET AT THE SOCIAL LEVEL

A number of great thinkers have highlighted the *moral* benefits for society of regret, and its emotional cousins such as guilt, shame, and remorse. In *The Theory of Moral Sentiments*, Adam Smith described remorse as the safeguard of society.[122] Spinoza argued that, although moral emotions like regret are not pleasant, such emotions are "productive of more profit than disadvantage," precisely because of this social function. Because human beings will inevitably sin, "it is better that they should sin in this way. For if men . . . were ashamed of nothing, . . . *by what bonds could they be united or constrained?*"[123] Nietzsche[124] and Freud[125] advanced a similar idea, arguing that the moral feeling of guilt is the most effective protector of civilization, whose disintegration is ever threatened by the erotic and aggressive drives of its members (albeit at some considerable cost to the individual).

In this vein, Mrs. Moore in Forster's *A Passage to India* was thoroughly disgusted with her son Ronny when he advised her that "he was not in India to behave pleasantly." She understood that "one touch of regret—not the canny substitute but the true regret from the heart—would have made him a different man, and the British empire a different institution."[126] Regret is a guardian of goodness for societies as well as individuals.

Conclusions

Earlier in this chapter, regret was personified as a paralyzed woman sunk in the dead arms of the past. By now, another picture has, I hope, emerged. In this new portrait regret is a person of will and integrity standing firm on a base of her own personal past, standing hand-in-hand with others, strong enough to resist being sucked into the tempting but deadly Memory Hole. She may meet life with an ironic expectation of ambiguity, ambivalence, limits, mistakes, and good and bad luck; yet she is not emotionally disengaged. She may be a semi-romantic, in that she engages in a heroic struggle against personal and social evils; yet she renounces the romantic demand for absolute answers to the human predicament. This figure of regret is someone whose free and active inner life and engagement with others fortify her in facing forward and outward with courage.

Finally, I want to make it clear that to reclaim the authority of regret is not to recommend a hair-shirt approach to life. It is merely to acknowledge reality: misfortunes, losses, and mistakes are an inevitable part of life. So is death. Perhaps it all boils down to death: for if we weren't mortal, we could always re-do the unhappy things in some future. In the face of these realities, regret is inevitable, rational, and a moral imperative.

In an essay concerning the memorial to the Holocaust erected in Washington, D.C., in 1983, writer Lance Morrow eloquently summarized a number of the pragmatic and moral costs and benefits of regret, among which are some discussed in this book—for example, education, relief, and finally redemption:

> Life likes to forget a little. The living, if they are sane, want memory and death and obsession to observe certain house rules. . . . [But] a memorial can relieve the poor mind of the responsibility of obsessive remembering. . . . it is a form of tutoring in the truth. . . . Only the faculty of moral memory can begin to redeem the worst deeds. . . . Memory is eventually a moralist, and memory educates the beast.[127]

Though there is no redemption in the mere act of acknowledging regret, there is no redemption without it.

Just as the medieval emotion of accidie (gloom and fear over losing God's grace due to one's spiritual laziness) has disappeared over time,[128] I sometimes wonder whether we aren't sliding toward a regret-free world. In a humorous story, Garrison Keillor once referred to the present as "a regretless time" in which:

> your own best friend might spill a glass of red wine on your new white sofa and immediately *explain* it—no spontaneous shame and embarrassment, just "Oh, I've always had poor motor skills," or "You distracted me with your comment about Bolivia." People walked in and stole your shoes, they trashed your lawn and bullied your children and blasted the neighborhood with powerful tape machines at 4:00 A.M. . . . and if you confronted them about these actions they told you about a particularly upsetting life-experience they'd gone through recently, such as condemnation, that caused them to do it.[129]

But seriously. It is conceivable that each time regret is dismissed as useless or irrational, the capacity for genuine regret may be weakened, until at last it atrophies. A regret-free world, lacking the potential benefits of regret I have discussed here, would no doubt prove a barbarous place to live.

2

What We Talk About When We Talk About Regret

The word *regret* has refashioned itself over time. An all-but-archaic use of the term emphasized losing someone or something dear, as in Shelley's "that fair lady whom I regret." Though this usage flowers in nineteenth-century novels by Jane Austen and others, I have never heard the term used in this way in contemporary colloquial speech. The former meaning of *regret* has been largely taken over by nouns like *nostalgia*[1] and verbs like *miss* or *long for.* Shelley's "that fair lady whom I *regret*" would today read "that fine woman whom I *miss.*" The romantic, bittersweet connotation of *regret* seems to have drifted to an unromantic, simply bitter, emphasis on gaining something unpleasant. The modern sense of *regret* hauls a heavier load of pathology—an emotional tone and a stance that desires distance from the past. The semantic drift of the word *regret* supports the idea developed in the previous chapter that part of our modern quarrel with regret concerns our quarrel with the past.

The central question of this chapter is what it is we are talking about when we talk about regret.[2] To explore this question, I make use of a medley of sources: theory, empirical research, the lexicon, and common parlance. My aim is first to specify the defining features of regret and then to distinguish regret from similar concepts—namely, disappointment, sadness, undoing, remorse, and guilt. My listing of conceptual sources should alert the reader to my strategy, which is to avoid an exercise of defining the concept in arid isolation from the experience. My hope, then, is to go beyond mere "word games" or "semantics."

In Chapter 1, regret was briefly defined as a more or less painful judgment and state of feeling sorry for misfortunes, limitations, losses, shortcomings, transgressions, or mistakes. Webster's Unabridged Third New International Dictionary (my lexicographical source from now on) tells us that the word *regret* is of Scandinavian origin, kin to the Old Norse word *grata,* to weep. This information paints a picture of a broad concept, incorporating both cognitive aspects (remembering, imagining, and having misgivings, for example) and emotional aspects (sorrow, grief, or pain).

The present analysis argues for the following extended definition. Regret is a more or less painful cognitive and emotional state of feeling sorry for misfortunes, limitations, losses, transgressions, shortcomings, or mistakes. It is an experience of felt-reason or reasoned-emotion. The regretted matters may be sins of commission as well as sins of omission; they may range from the voluntary to the uncontrollable and accidental; they may be actually executed deeds or entirely mental ones committed by oneself or by another person or group; they may be moral or legal transgressions or morally and legally neutral; and the regretted matters may have occurred in the past, present, or future.

What Is Regret?

Regret as an Intellective Matter

"I regret buying this lemon of a car"—this statement expresses the intellective, cognitive, or judicial sense of regret. Even if the remark were embellished with expletives and exclamations, the experience has rather less to do with sorrow, grief, or psychic pain (emotion) and more to do with cognitive processes of judgment and evaluation.

Some philosophers and psychologists take the extreme view that regret (and all emotion) is *primarily* a matter of critical judgment and only secondarily or not at all a matter of feelings. The proposition "I never feel the slightest pang of regret for what I did," according to philosopher E. Bedford, is *not,* despite its claim, describing a feeling. Instead, it is stating a purely cognitive evaluation, that is, "the justification of a choice."[3] As Stuart Hampshire explains, the question "'Do you regret that decision?' [e.g., to buy that car] is a question that requires me to *think,* and to think practically, about the decision, and not merely to inspect my feelings."[4]

Although I take issue with efforts to reduce emotion to cognition, regret does entail a significant degree of cognitive appraisal. Especially relative to other emotions such as anger or fear, regret does seem more cognitively elaborated. And relative to related emotions such as remorse and guilt, regret may often (though not always) be experienced more as a matter of "cool" cognitive assessment than of "warm" emotional reactivity.

Regret is associated with counterfactual thought, or imagining states contrary to fact: especially what might have been. The process of beginning with the actual (the "facts") and imagining the possible ("counterfactuals") is a type of induction, in that it proceeds from a set of particular givens to a broader set of possibles.[5] The importance of counterfactual thinking was first highlighted in the philosophical approach called "possible worlds," or ways the world might be or might have been.[6] As illustrated by philosopher Saul Kripke, when two dice are tossed, only one out of a possible 36 "possible worlds" is actualized—a 5 and 6, for instance. The ability to imagine or mentally construct the remaining 35 possible states of being is one form of counterfactual thought.[7] Whenever we wonder what would have happened had we taken one job rather than another, or what we would do if we won the lottery, we are engaging in counterfactual thought.

Modern legal theory also recognizes the practical importance of counterfactual thought, in some instances replacing causal rationales with counterfactual ones. For example, under the old New York fire rules, based on the principle of proximate cause, a person was held responsible only for the first building damaged by a fire negligently set, not for any other buildings that caught fire. But a more modern principle of legal responsibility is the *"sine qua non"* principle—that is, the "but for" principle, which asks "whether the harm *would have happened* without the act."[8] Reasoning counterfactually, "but for" the first fire, the other buildings would not have been damaged. Therefore, the negligent person is held legally responsible for all the buildings damaged.

We may think counterfactually through a "simulation heuristic"—a mental process of inventing alternatives to actual life outcomes and events in an effort to deal with past and present realities, to predict future events, to assess causation, and so forth.[9] According to psychological researchers Daniel Kahneman and Amos Tversky, who authored these ideas, in the process of "running mental simulations" (e.g., imagining life if you had taken that other job, if that first fire had not started, or if you had won the lottery), the "counterfactual emotion" of regret makes itself felt.[10] One implication of this view is that the intensity of regret will depend in part on how easily one can imagine alternatives to an unpleasant reality. The more readily counterfactuals come to mind, the greater the regret. For example, regret tends to burn hotter for missing a plane by 5 minutes than by 20 minutes, presumably because it is easier to imagine the counterfactual state of not having missed the plane in the former than in the latter instance.[11]

Economic decision theory contributes another thoroughly cognitive perspective on regret. In a number of these theories, regret is added to the traditional utility functions long thought to describe rational decisions.[12] These models typically define regret as the difference in payoff between a chosen and an unchosen action.[13] According to regret theories, the expected utility of choice X (the alternative chosen) is a mathematical function of the expected utility of X minus the amount of regret for not-X (the better alternative not chosen). These mathematical formulations represent the coolest of all cognitive formulations of regret—about which much more in Chapter 5.

Economist Robert Sugden focuses on the type of regret involving being sorry for one's *mistakes*. In Sugden's two-part definition regret entails not only a "painful sensation of recognizing that 'what is' compares unfavorably with 'what might have been,' "[14] but also "self-recrimination or repentance or self-blame"—"the state of mind you have when you come to believe that a previous decision involved an error of judgement, that it was wrong at the time you made it."[15] Thus, the individual who is sorry for having bought the lemon of a car without having first checked *Consumer Reports* (where that model's dismal repair record would have raised red flags) will experience greater regret than someone who bought a car that turned out to be a lemon despite an impeccable record in *Consumer Reports*. Self-recrimination represents a twofold exemplification of the exercise of critical judgment and counterfactual thought—first, when one compares the actual outcome with the outcome that might have been, and second, when one compares one's decision processes with those that might have been.

It seems to me that personal responsibility and thus self-recrimination ought not be viewed as a *defining* feature of regret. In fact, Freud's view, as we will see in Chapter 8, would surely be that regret with intense self-recrimination deserves to be called "neurotic" regret, not "normal" regret. However, whenever our regret includes a sense of personal responsibility and self-recrimination, we will likely feel worse than when these elements are absent.

The cognitive revolution in social science has begun to change the previously prevailing view of emotion as first and foremost a biological experience. The 1980s saw the cognitive aspects of emotional experience emphasized by many investigators of emotion (including Ellsworth and Smith; Frijda; Kemper; Lazarus; Oatley; Ortony, Clore, and Collins; D. Russell and McAuley; J. A. Russell; and Weiner).[16] Although I am more interested in emotion as a dynamic process than in its abstracted structure, Ira Roseman's structural approach is of particular relevance to me because of his inclusion of regret in the set of emotions examined. Roseman argues that different emotions are aroused by distinguishable combinations of cognitive dimensions, such as (pardon the jargon) perceived locus of agency (e.g., self, other, circumstances), motivational state of the actor (appetitive, aversive), situational state (motive-consistent, motive-inconsistent), probability of outcome (certain, uncertain), and perceived personal power (strong, weak).[17] In a series of vignette experiments and self-report studies, Roseman and his colleagues systematically varied these five dimensions in different stories and asked subjects to rate the nature and intensity of certain emotions—among them, regret—experienced by themselves or by the protagonists of the stories.[18] As predicted, which emotion people named depended on the specific pattern of these cognitive dimensions. In Roseman's findings, regret was characterized by a particular pattern in which the self or a circumstance was agent; the motivational or situational state consisted of the presence of something undesirable or the absence of something desirable; and a negative outcome had occurred with or without certainty and with or without perceived personal power.[19]

Like the economic regret models, Leon Festinger's cognitive dissonance theory locates regret in the context of decision making.[20] In a typical experiment, subjects are first asked to rank their preferences for two or more options among a group of like things (e.g., phonograph records, hair styles, or job placements). In such a situation, the mere process of making a choice arouses dissonance, or physiologically measurable tension.[21] Most people dissolve this state of tension by changing their attitude—in this example, by denigrating the option not chosen, idealizing the option chosen, or both.

However, not everyone manifests the typical pattern of altering their attitudes to correspond to the dissonance-arousing choice elicited in the initial phase of an experiment. Instead, some subjects—as many as 62 percent in one study—evidence regret for their dissonance-arousing behavior.[22] When given the chance, these people reverse their initial preferences, undoing their earlier decision.[23] Of course, regret is a bête noir for the theory of cognitive dissonance, inasmuch as it represents the opposite of dissonance reduction. Regret represents a *failure* to rationalize or justify one's prior behavior or decision through cognitive maneuvers that may be conscious or unconscious.

So how did Festinger explain regret? It depends when you asked him. At first he explained regret as a defensive operation designed to avoid dissonance by "psychologically revoking the decision."[24] Later, perhaps as the academic zeitgeist turned increasingly away from psychodynamics, Festinger de-emphasized the defensive and emphasized the merely cognitive interpretation of regret. On this later view, regret results simply from attentional processes, specifically from an increase in the salience of dissonant thoughts immediately after acting or making a decision.[25] Upon choosing one of two alternatives, one's attention may be temporarily focused on the undesirable aspects of the chosen alternative and the desirable aspects of the rejected alternative: "But then again, Elvis's instrumentals are so primitive and the Beatles's so interesting." Neo-Festinger hypothesized that it was simply this attentional pattern that explained regret—never mind those unnecessarily complicated defensive strategies postulated by paleo-Festinger. However, as will be seen later, this purely cognitive account of dissonance, and thus of regret, has not received empirical support.

An implication of the cognitive dissonance branch of psychological decision theory is that insofar as choice is inescapable and insofar as conflict between choices, claims, or even ways of life is inevitable,[26] regret is also an inevitable, natural, normal human experience. Because it is not possible to have it all, and because we know it, regret is inevitable. A similar implication of the cognitive, inductive, and counterfactual models is that regret may be viewed as a normal, inevitable, and direct consequence of *rationality*—that is, "a direct consequence of the capacity to recognize and to name differences . . . and the capacity to conceive multiple alternatives."[27] In the face of less-than-satisfying realities, it is normal to acknowledge that the world is less satisfactory than it might have been and to imagine how it might have been better—hence regret.

These perspectives suggest the following conclusions: (1) Regret, as perhaps all adult emotional activity, has a significant cognitive component. (2) Regret is intimately associated with higher-order cognitive processes such as critical judgment, induction, counterfactual thought, and decision making. (3) But regret is not reducible to cognition. In brief, it is necessary but not sufficient to define regret as a cognitive phenomenon.

Regret as an Emotional Matter

To modify a cartoon by Jerry Van Amerongen ("The Neighborhood"), consider a faculty member who loses his "struggle with subtlety"[28] during a faculty meeting and calls the dean "dummy butt." One can imagine this individual later expressing an exquisitely emotional sense of regret: "I keenly regret calling the dean 'dummy butt'." More serious examples of emotionally freighted regret include being sorry for an unwise marriage, for hasty words hurled at a loved one, or for neglecting a distressed friend who then commits suicide.

Though we generally know it when we experience it, emotion is another of those things we are hard-pressed to define. In fact, I have attended more than one presentation in which distinguished scholars of emotion refused to define it. Paul Kleinginna and Anne Kleinginna, in an attempt to clarify the issue, reviewed over 90 definitions of emotion found in the psychological literature. Their composite working definition follows:

> Emotion is a complex set of interactions among subjective and objective factors, mediated by neural/hormonal systems, which can (a) give rise to affective experiences such as feelings of arousal, pleasure/displeasure; (b) generate cognitive processes such as emotionally relevant perceptual effects, appraisals, labeling processes; (c) activate wide-spread physiological adjustments to the arousing conditions; and (d) lead to behavior that is often, but not always, expressive, goal-directed, and adaptive.[29]

This chapter focuses mostly on the first and second criteria identified by Kleinginna and Kleinginna, the emotional and cognitive dimensions of regret. Chapter 8 focuses on the expressive and goal-directed aspects of regret.

Although regret may not be the first emotion to come to mind when one thinks of the activation of physiological reactions, this too is an essential dimension of certain experiences of regret. Virginia Woolf portrayed some of these in the novel *Mrs. Dalloway*, for example, in the following conversation Clarissa Dalloway is having with Peter Walsh, a suitor she rejected years ago, though with some regret:

> Do you remember the lake? she said, in an abrupt voice, under the pressure of an emotion which caught her heart, made the muscles of her throat stiff, and contracted her lips in a spasm as she said "lake."[30]

Later their regretful reminiscence brings both Clarissa and Peter to the physiological reaction of tears. Yes, regret too includes the bodily reactions that are a necessary element of emotional experience.

As stated in this definition, emotion always has an appraisal component. But emotion is not reducible to cognition. In contrast to certain resolutely cognitive perspectives discussed earlier, my view is closer to that of Sartre, who reminds us that emotion is not simply "a reasoned calculation."[31] Regret likewise cannot be reduced to an unemotional calculation or any other type of cognition. Why not? In addition to the physiological involvement just mentioned, it is the intertwined feelings of distress that mark these particular appraisals as something more than intellective judgments.

All theories of emotion posit a hedonic, or pleasurable, dimension as a defining feature of emotion. Emotion always has to do with pleasurable or unpleasurable feelings. Taking the lead from philosopher Patricia Greenspan,[32] let us imagine that you and a close friend are both in the running for a particular job—say, vice-president of your organization. You both want it very much. Your friend gets the job and you don't. In such a circumstance, many people would experience mixed feelings, or a state of ambivalence, meaning that you simultaneously rejoice in his win and regret it. Some scholars would deny that this is a case of contrary emotions but is really a case of contrary judgments: "His winning is a good thing. His winning is a bad thing." Now imagine that, being a reasonable person, you try to get hold of yourself in this difficult situation by changing how you think about it. After a few days, you eventually come to a state in which you truly think, based on your assessment of the weight of the logical arguments on both sides, that "on the whole" his winning is a good thing. You have now resolved your state of holding contrary beliefs. Still, for many of us, the set of contradictory feelings would persist. What is left over—the lump in the throat, the subvocal groan, the lift of the heart—is the *emotion.* These leftover feelings of both pleasure and regret (or whatever the particular mix of contrary emotions) show that emotion is not reducible to judgment, not even evaluative judgments.

Rooted as it is in tears, the very origin of the word *regret* gives away its emotional nature. Regret is *by definition* an emotion, as evidenced in its lexicographical allusions to sorrow, grief, pain, disappointment, dissatisfaction, longing, remorse, and "comparable *emotion.*" Philosopher Amelie Rorty assumes the emotional side of regret when she writes that regret is "characteristically felt as a particular sort of painful feeling, a pang, a stab, waves of stabs . . . ."[33] Recall, too, Kahneman and Tversky's referring to regret as a "counterfactual emotion."[34] Finally, the fact that a number of investigators of emotion have included regret in their analyses provides *a priori* support.[35] In a taxonomic study of the vocabulary of emotions, for example, *regret* was categorized by raters in a set of terms denoting the negative emotion of sadness; *regret's* most closely related terms were: *guilty, remorseful, apologetic, repentant,* and *sorry.*[36]

Empirical evidence and subjective experience support the hedonic and hence emotional nature of regret. When researchers asked subjects to rate the unpleasantness of a number of terms, they found that regret was rated as significantly *unpleasant,*[37] which corroborates the common wisdom. What rational person, after all, would make this kind of dinner-table announcement: "Gee, Dear, I had such a lovely day; for some reason I felt tremendously regretful all day!"?

Emotion is also a matter of something we care about. Many researchers of emotion have pointed out the defining role of personal concerns and goals in emotion. According to Nico Frijda, writing in his book *The Emotions,* emotion is "awareness of situations as relevant, urgent, and meaningful" with respect to oneself.[38] Among a list of "laws of emotion," Frijda includes this one: "Emotions arise in response to events that are important to the individual's goals, motives, or concerns."[39,40] The greater the concern, the more intense the emotion. The fact that regret of necessity entails something we *care* about represents another important reason for regret's irreducibility to a "reasoned calculation." Regret is always about something we "take personally"—often something we ourselves have done or been, but at least something we care about.

Another reason that regret often feels more like an emotion than like a simple cognitive judgment is the fact that regret often entails a judgment about oneself—one's doing (agent regret) or one's being (character or status regret).[41] Unlike other intellective activities (e.g., discrimination learning, concept formation, memory for nonsense syllables), regret is more likely to entail acts of self-representation, self-reflection, and self-appraisal. And as William James points out, one's sense of self is based primarily on "warm," feeling-based self-representations rather than on "cold intellectual self-estimation."[42] Like James, proponents of the object-relations school within clinical psychology and psychiatry define the self as "consisting of multiple self-representations and their related *affect* [i.e., emotional] dispositions."[43]

The notion of *possible selves*, analogous to the earlier-discussed idea of possible worlds, adds to the understanding of regret as necessarily emotional to the extent that it is personal. Psychological researchers Hazel Markus and Paula Nurius define possible selves as cognitive and affective representations of the self in some currently unactualized state.[44] Possible selves represent wished-for or rejected aspects of the self. Hence imagining possible selves has the potential to evoke emotions such as regret. In the language of possible selves, one might construct (consciously or not) mental images of oneself as, say, bewildered teenager or lottery winner, leading to thoughts like: "I regret my past self of bewildered teenager" or "I regret that my currently actualized self is not that of major lottery winner."

If common sense as well as theorists such as James, Markus, and others are right that the self-concept necessarily involves feelings, then self-pertinent regret is unlikely to amount merely to cool cognitive appraisal or dispassionate comparison of actual versus possible utilities. Indeed, Markus and Nurius found that people who felt the worst in the present were those who also reported the greatest number of negative (regrettable) past selves.[45] Even more directly pertinent are the recent experimental research findings that regret is greater when the self (as opposed to someone else or simply circumstances) is the agent of the act.[46]

This examination of the nature of emotion in general and of regret in particular leads to the following conclusions: (1) Emotion cannot be reduced to cognition. (2) Despite its relatively high degree of cognitive involvement, regret is nevertheless an emotion, due in part to its component of psychic pain. (3) Regret is emotional because it always implicates the self to some degree—if not the self as agent or character, then the self as caring about the regretted matter. Taken together with the previous examination of the cognitive aspects of regret, these lines of thought support the conclusion that it is necessary but not sufficient to define regret as an emotional phenomenon.

Regret as Reasoned Emotion and Felt Thought

Notwithstanding the separation of thought and emotion just enacted for analytic purposes, I believe that this distinction is often overdrawn. T. S. Eliot, for instance, appeared to overdraw the dissociation between reason and emotion in his essay "Tradition and the Individual Talent."[47] There he made his case for impersonality, which does not mean unemotionality, but personal emotion so transmuted by art that it takes on universal resonance. This was to be accomplished, thought Eliot, by a "fusion" of thought and emotion. And in a later essay "The Metaphysical Poets," Eliot makes this point with more conviction, stating: "in the seventeenth century a *dissociation of sensibility* set in, from which we have never recovered."[48] For Eliot, the best art is characterized by the "unification of sensibility"—by which he meant the unification of "states of mind and feeling."[49] I agree—and not only when it comes to art. More generally, human beings ought to aspire to the unification of thought and emotion. Our emotion, moods, concerns, interest, motivation, energy, desire should not be understood as sloppy "deflections" from some so-called more "normal" state free of emotion, moods, concerns, interest, motivation, energy, and desire.[50] Paraphrasing Robert Zajonc,[51] personal and emotional judgment is better understood *not* as a special case of the general case of impersonal and nonemotional judgment. Personal, emotional judgment *is*, and ought to be, the general case.

The present analysis argues then that regret is conceptually, logically, and experientially a matter of thought and feeling as interdependent and co-constitutive. Indeed, to regret entails a whole host of psychic processes, including thinking, imagining, feeling, comparing, evaluating, doubting, denying, refusing, or affirming (e.g., a good lost or a standard unattained).

Theory and research in the area of cognitive dissonance give further sustenance to the idea that regret is a matter of reason and emotion working in concert. According to Festinger,[52] immediately following a choice between alternatives, we experience dissonance—in this case, in the form of post-decision regret—which serves the function of defending against internal conflict by "psychologically revoking the decision." As previously noted, Festinger eventually sought to downplay this earlier psychodynamic explanation and to explain dissonance—and regret—in purely cognitive terms, as a consequence of a temporary heightening in salience of the desirable features of a rejected alternative and/or the undesirable features of a chosen alternative.[53] However, the purely cognitive account has not been supported by data. In fact, subjects who are experimentally compelled to attend to dissonant elements of their decisions evidence not more *regret*, as predicted by the cognitive account, but more defensive justification.[54] Thus, in a review of the cognitive dissonance literature, Robert Wicklund and Jack Brehm reject a purely cognitive understanding of dissonance phenomena in favor of the original motivational explanation—precisely because of the existence of regret: "If dissonance reduction were simply a matter of noting relevant cognitions and proceeding to a reasoned conclusion, there would never be any reason to suspect the appearance of regret."[55]

A final argument for the dual operation of thought and emotion in regret depends on making a distinction between decision process and decision outcome. Coaches often make this distinction when they say things like "The loss may not show it, but we played great"—or less often, "You can't tell it from the win, but our playing was lousy." Sugden referred implicitly to this distinction in his two-part definition of regret as entailing both a desire for a better outcome and self-recrimination for the erroneous way in which one made the decision.[56] Regret, however, does not require both these conditions, but can reasonably follow from either one alone. As philosopher Bernard Williams points out, even when people deliberate well, if things turn out badly (e.g., investing a minor dependent's money in real estate that seems safe and promising but that loses money), they can feel justified about how they made the decision at the very same time that they regret the outcome.[57] Conversely, if people deliberate badly and things turn out well (taking the dependent's money to Las Vegas and winning), they may regret their decision processes at the very same time that they rejoice (or breathe a sigh of relief) over the outcome. In these cases, the regret over the outcome seems to carry more feeling (pain and sadness over thwarted desire) in contrast to the regret over the process, which seems more a matter of judgment—unless the judgment applies preeminently to the *self*, in which case, the judgment of self-recrimination ("how stupid I was") seems unavoidably emotional as well.

Both rational and empirical analyses, then, support the conclusion that regret is not merely cognitive, nor merely emotional, but a matter of thought and emotion as co-constitutive aspects of a whole: that is, felt reason and reasoned emotion.

How Does Regret Differ from Similar Concepts?

As the dictionary reminds us, regret holds membership in a family of related concepts, among which are disappointment, sadness, undoing, remorse, and guilt. Exactly how does regret overlap with and differ from each of these?

Regret versus Disappointment

At least one of the definitions of *regret* directly links it with disappointment: "sorrow caused by circumstances beyond one's control or power to repair: grief or pain tinged with disappointment . . . ." *Disappointment* is defined as "the act or an instance of the failure of expectation or hope: frustration."

But the two are not synonymous. Disappointment and regret have been contrasted in economic decision theory, with separate predictions for each.[58] There disappointment is defined as the difference between actual versus expected outcomes, and regret as the difference between the outcomes of a chosen versus an unchosen option. The two entities are not mutually exclusive, but an essential difference is disappointment's, and not regret's, dependence on expectations (estimated probabilities) of various outcomes. Within this rather technical framework, it is more precise to say that I am disappointed with than that I regret an unexpected negative outcome. The child is *disappointed* when the Tooth Fairy forgets his third lost tooth. The child's parents *regret* the lapse.

Regret versus Sadness

Sadness is defined as: (1) sorrowfulness, unhappiness, gloominess; (2) a general term usually without implications regarding cause or intensity of unhappy feeling. Synonyms are: *depression, melancholy, dejection, gloom, blues.*

As previously mentioned, regret's connection with sadness appears in both the lexicon and empirical research. Recall the Scandinavian origin of *regret* in the word for weeping, and one of the definitions of the verb form: to remember with sorrow or grief; to mourn the loss or death of. Recall, too, the empirically derived tax-

onomy of the semantics of emotion which located regret in a group
of negative emotions characterized primarily by *sadness*.[59]

How then does regret differ from mere sadness? Researchers
recently found that, within the sadness grouping, regret appeared
in the category that implied personal agency or responsibility.[60] But
this is at variance with what I shall argue about regret. My inclination is to reject personal responsibility as a *defining* characteristic of regret, while acknowledging that it may validly distinguish
certain states of regret from prototypical states of sadness. Whereas
regret more adequately describes the phenomenal state of the
aforementioned trustee who gambled away the child's inheritance,
sadness (and perhaps anger) for the loss more adequately describes
the (grown) child's mental state. This example illustrates a subtle
distinction between sadness and regret. Although they overlap,[61]
sadness (and nostalgia[62]) more often concerns the loss of desirable
entities or states, while regret as often concerns the gaining of undesirable entities or states. More clearly, *sadness* lacks *regret*'s
connotation of having made a mistake.

Regret and sadness are neither semantically synonymous nor
experientially identical. Sadness need not entail regret. When a child
leaves home for college, a parent may be sad (or nostalgic) without
regretting the event. Striking employees may be saddened by their
loss of income, yet not regret the act of striking.

Regret versus Undoing

Webster's *Third Unabridged International Dictionary* defines *undoing* this way: "to make of no effect or as if not done; to make
null; to bring to naught; to cancel." Just as regret and counterfactual thought may co-occur, so may regret and undoing—which in
its purely mental form is itself a form of counterfactual thought.
Regret is frequently, though not always, associated with efforts to
imaginatively cancel or nullify losses or errors. The same individual who expresses regret for having bought a lemon of a car might
well attempt to "make [that purchase] null," "to bring [it] to naught,"
"to cancel" it—if not in fact, then at least in imagination. The
same goes for the individual who is sorry for having "lost his struggle with subtlety" during a heated faculty meeting. The individual
who regrets having neglected a depressed friend who later committed suicide unfortunately lacks the ability to cancel his or her neglect in actuality. However, this fact would not prevent many of
us from canceling the neglect over and over in tortured imagina-

tion. In fact, as Hume pointed out, the fact that undoing is not possible makes us all the more sorry.

Within the psychoanalytic perspective, undoing is a defense mechanism "whereby the subject makes an attempt to cause past thoughts, words, gestures or actions not to have occurred."[63] Also according to Freud, undoing represents and embodies a state of ambivalence or conflict between two opposing impulses of equivalent strength, "invariably" love and hate.[64] By the same token, Freudian undoing often, but not always, entails an individual's doing or thinking the polar opposite of an earlier act or thought.

Freud observed the operation of undoing as a defense typical of individuals with obsessive and compulsive disorders.[65] In "Notes Upon a Case of Obsessional Neurosis," Freud reported vivid examples of undoing in his patient who has come to be known as the "Rat Man."[66] In one instance, on the day in which his woman friend was to leave for holiday, the Rat Man was irresistibly compelled to move a stone to the side of the road lest his friend's carriage be overturned by it later. After a few minutes, deciding that this behavior was absurd, he was irresistibly compelled to return and replace the stone to its original spot in the road.

The Freudian concept of undoing encompasses not only overt deeds but also a variety of internal acts, such as "wishes, temptations, impulses, reflections, doubts, commands, or prohibitions."[67] Following Freud, Otto Fenichel delineates a similarly broad conception of undoing: "something positive is done which, actually or magically, is the opposite of something which, again actually or in imagination, was done before."[68] (This formulation also retains the Freudian construal of doing and undoing as entailing polar opposites.)

Lady Macbeth's famous handwashing is an example of something's being done to attempt to "magically" expunge something that was actually done. The Rat Man's behavior is more complex. In one sense it illustrates the case in which someone does something *in actuality* to cancel something that was actually done— that is, moving and re-moving the stone.[69] But in another sense, both the initial act of moving the stone out of the road and the subsequent act of undoing that act represent "magical" acts; both are significant only in their status as physical instantiations of symbolic personal meanings.

Even in Festinger's less deeply psychoanalytic formulation,[70] regret is associated with undoing in both its overt and mental forms. In fact, Festinger's measure of regret is but an inference based on the subject's act of undoing (i.e., reversing the original decision). Moreover, early Festinger explained regret as a defensive operation that served to "psychologically" revoke—or undo only in imagination—the conflictual decision.[71]

Finally, mental undoing of a distinctly nonpsychoanalytic order has been investigated recently in the context of research on the simulation heuristic and counterfactual thought, introduced earlier. The idea is that people may assess causation and probabilities, imagine possible past events, and predict future events by mentally undoing actual states and imagining states contrary to fact. In a later chapter I shall discuss empirical investigations of mental undoing which support, among other things, the idea that a regrettable life event or outcome unleashes the process of mental undoing in an effort to manage one's regret.

What then is the relationship between undoing and regret? It seems to me most likely that undoing and regret are concomitants of one another, emerging together in the context of reflecting on a particular scenario. The family and friends of a victim of a fatal auto accident certainly regret his taking the unfortunate route or leaving at the unfortunate time—at the same time that they imagine undoing these antecedent events.[72]

Alternatively, undoing might precede the conscious awareness of regret. Someone may not recognize that he or she is regretful and may even deny regret, yet be troubled with obsessive if-onlys that "generate a characteristic feeling, which then itself generates further thoughts, scenarios of what one has done, instant replays of this angle and that, how it could have gone differently. These thoughts then cause more rueful feelings. . . ."[73] At some point in such a sequence of mental undoing, the individual might become aware of feeling regretful.

Finally, the emotion of regret (not necessarily consciously experienced) may precede thoughts and acts of undoing, the sequence suggested by Zajonc.[74,75] To me, however, the more interesting and tractable questions focus not on questions of temporal priority but on consequences.

Overt undoing, when that is possible, has the potential to reduce or cancel regret. If I am able, by making use of my state's "lemon law," to undo my purchase of a defective car, then I have diminished or eradicated my regret. But chances are that I won't engage in the overt undoing unless I first engage in some mental undoing. Thus mental undoing may serve as a goad to future behavior—thinking backward in time in order to plan for a future in which regret is minimized.

But regret *need* not entail undoing. According to Amelie Rorty, "it is not a condition of regret that the agent would undo the action if he could."[76] Philosopher Gabrielle Taylor illustrates this point:

> when feeling regret she need not think that she would undo the action if she could. She may regret an action (sacking an employee) which overall she still considers necessary and beneficial. . . . It is possible also to regret an action but accept it [i.e., not wish to undo it] under the same description: she regrets sacking the employee because the girl was so easily crushed, but she had to be sacked, nevertheless, because she was so inefficient.[77]

That regret need not entail undoing was poignantly expressed by Jesse Mahojah, at 77 one of six remaining full-blooded members (all over 70) of the Kaw tribe. In an interview by William Least Heat-Moon, Jesse Mahojah regrets the passing of his tribe, its language, and its culture: "In fifty years there won't be much Kaw Indian left—there won't be much blood at all. The decision's made, and we all helped make it: I married a white woman."[78] However, when Heat-Moon asks him "whether he would do anything differently if he could go back to the year he graduated from high school," Mahojah asks "Like what?" Heat-Moon asks him point blank whether he might marry a Kaw woman. Jesse Mahojah replies: "You're asking me to forsake some fifty years of love."[79] Then he falls silent.

No doubt regret frequently accompanies undoing. However, regret (in contrast with remorse and guilt, as I will now argue) does not require that the person would undo the antecedent event (if that were possible).

Regret versus Remorse

Remorse is defined as "gnawing distress arising from a sense of guilt for past wrongs (as injuries done to others)." Synonyms are *self-reproach* and *penitence*. Recall that in the lexicon *regret* is explicitly linked with *remorse*: "grief or pain tinged with . . . remorse or comparable emotions." Hence remorse is by definition a close relative of regret. Empirically, too, regret and remorse have been linked. In a taxonomic study of the vocabulary of emotions, researchers recently found that raters listed *remorse* as one of the terms most closely related to *regret*.[80] Both regret and remorse can be painful or distressing emotions concerning a past personal transgression.

However, regret and remorse differ on a number of dimensions, including personal agency, responsibility, and control. It will be recalled that the lexicographical definition of regret included matters beyond one's control. Four centuries ago, Montaigne, too, thought that "repentance [defined above as synonymous with remorse] does not properly affect things that are not in our power; regret, indeed, does."[81] In a similar vein, Solomon defines remorse as the response to a state of affairs for which one is to blame, whereas regret is the response to "circumstances beyond my control."[82] I agree with Montaigne and Solomon on remorse, but not on regret, which I argue involves *both* circumstances over which one has control and those over which one has no control. In an analysis with which I wholly concur, philosopher Irving Thalberg argues that personal responsibility is a defining feature of remorse but only a characteristic feature of regret.[83] I may regret events over which I have no control, such as the passing of summer,[84] or the secret acts of a member of the National Security Council; but one feels remorse only over one's own voluntary acts. Recently, this assertion received empirical support; regret was found to apply to *both* conditions of agency: self and circumstances.[85] There are events for which *no one* is responsible that are, nonetheless, regrettable by me—as long as they are things I care about. At the same time, it may well be that regret over matters in which the self played an active role will prove more intense than other matters.[86]

Thalberg identifies other ways in which remorse and regret differ.[87] First, one might regret the acts of another person but one feels remorse only with respect to one's own acts. Second, one might regret doing something morally innocuous or even virtuous, but one feels remorse only for acts that one considers morally wrong.[88] An example is the commonplace situation in which you are unable to attend a social event to which you are invited; in this morally neutral circumstance it is ordinarily appropriate to feel and to express regret rather than remorse. Having to inform a mother of her son's death exemplifies a morally upright act that may evoke regret, but not remorse.[89] Third, remorse and regret differ in that one might appropriately regret one's future actions (having to notify the mother tomorrow of the death of her son), but remorse applies only to past acts.

Remorse also necessitates mental undoing, whereas regret does not. Similarly, an intention not to commit the same offense in the future is a defining feature of genuine remorse but not of regret. As Montaigne observed, one might regret that one is so constituted that one "can do no better" in the future.[90] In addition, one might regret that it will be necessary to do something in the future that one might prefer not to do (again, inform a mother of her son's death); but remorse necessitates a firm resolve not to commit the same act again.

Other distinctions between remorse and regret can be clarified by examining the differences between remorse and guilt. As Freud explained, remorse applies to overt acts, while guilt applies not only to overt conduct but also to the "perception of an evil *impulse*."[91] The Freudian construal of remorse conforms to the lexicographical use of the term, which necessitates an actual offense. Thalberg presents a vivid illustration of the difference: "We can feel guilty about *intending* to take a double portion of strawberries, but nobody ever feels remorse for his unexecuted designs."[92] This is not to say, of course, that remorse does not apply to sins of omission, or failures to act—for example, failing to have responded helpfully to a depressed friend who later commits suicide. Inaction or acts of omission are proper objects of remorse—and of regret.

Just as guilt follows not only from overt deeds but from covert ones, one may regret not only overt acts but also one's inner acts—for example, thoughts, attitudes, wishes, or impulses. For example, people may regret their social prejudices even when they have not acted on them; however, in such instances, there will be no remorse because there was no overt act. Of course, just as one is legally and morally *more* culpable for acts than for unexecuted intentions, it follows that the intensity of one's regret for overt acts is likely to exceed that of one's regret for unexecuted acts.

In sum, remorse applies with respect to one's own past, voluntary, overt, and morally wrong acts (or failures to act). Regret applies to all of these circumstances but also to others—for example, one's own unexecuted intentions, thoughts, wishes, impulses; one's own future, involuntary, and morally innocuous or virtuous acts; and circumstances and the acts of others that share the forgoing characteristics. In general, remorse entails a measure of personal responsibility for wrongs that is not a necessary feature of regret. Of regret and remorse, "regret is by far the broader notion."[93]

Regret versus Guilt

Definitions of *guilt* include the following: delinquency or failure in respect to one's duty; an offense; responsibility for an offense; fault; state of deserving punishment; the fact of having committed a breach of conduct; and the state of consciousness of one who has committed an offense. Guilt is thus both a state of being and a state of mind; and it applies to both moral and legal transgressions.

Guilt is often defined in terms of regret, with guilt said to entail "regret over the 'bad thing' that was done."[94] And with respect to how distressing they are, regret and guilt are more similar than not, an intuition that has empirical support. When researchers had subjects rate a number of emotion terms, among which were *regretful* and *guilty*, on the dimension of pleasure, regret and guilt were judged to be significantly and equally unpleasurable.[95]

What then are the "appropriate" objects of regret versus guilt? First, recall that guilt concerns both overt acts and purely mental acts while remorse is limited to overt acts. Like guilt, *regret* concerns both overt deeds and unexecuted or entirely psychic acts, as illustrated by the example of regret for one's unexpressed social prejudices.

Second, it is appropriate to speak of regret and guilt with reference both to acts and to failures to act, which again are not identical with purely mental acts. For example, someone may regret (and feel guilty for) having robbed a bank. Someone else may regret (but not feel guilty for) his decision *not* to join his friends in a bank robbery that successfully netted a million dollars for each participant.[96]

Agency is a third dimension on which regret subsumes guilt. It is appropriate to speak of regret both with reference to one's own free and voluntary acts (or omissions) and also with reference to acts over which one had no personal control. In contrast, guilt is limited to events over which one had some measure of personal responsibility or control.[97] Thus, someone might regret the secret and unconstitutional acts of members of one's government, but not feel guilty, because these acts lay outside the aegis of his or her knowledge or personal control.

Contrary to this distinction, though, is the idea of collective guilt, guilt as a response not only to one's own offenses but also the offenses of others with whom one has a relationship of some import. This controversial notion has been advanced as a form of

co-responsibility incurred, for example, by certain national and religious organizations for the Holocaust,[98] or more broadly as the
co-responsibility of all members of a group for the acts of some of
its members. A compelling argument made by Hannah Arendt
against the idea of collective guilt is that it justifies the evil-doer.
If everyone is guilty, no one is.[99]

More defensible (due to the less stringent entailment of personal control in regret than guilt) is the notion of collective regret,
whereby the members of a group experience misgivings, dissatisfaction, or distress of mind over the acts of other members of their
group. For example, the people of a colonizing or aggressing nation
might experience collective regret over their nation's acts. The notion of collective regret makes sense also insofar as the self is implicated by virtue of the regretted matter's being something you
care about.

To consider issues of responsibility for offenses is to enter the
domains of legality and morality. And herein lies a fourth way in
which regret subsumes guilt. As denoted in the lexicon, guilt concerns legal and moral matters.[100] The moral nature of guilt has
received empirical support.[101] One study, for example, had respondents rate their own experiences of guilt on a number of theory-
based dimensions, among which was moral nature of the offense.
These subjects did link guilt with moral failings.[102] In sum, guilt
is limited to circumstances entailing an offense against a legal or
moral precept—or entailing something the agent considers to constitute a legal or moral transgression.[103]

Some scholars argue that regret differs from guilt with respect
to the moral nature of the offense. Roseman views regret and guilt
as "opposite" in precisely this feature: "The difference between
Regret and Guilt is like the difference between making a mistake
and committing a sin or crime."[104] Solomon also describes guilt as
entailing "extreme" blame and regret as entailing no blame because it concerns circumstances beyond one's control.[105]

Despite the *prima facie* plausibility of this distinction, I believe it is at variance with psychological experience, in which one
can and does regret not only one's mistakes but also one's sins and
crimes. Indeed, the categories are not so easy to distinguish. Was
Macbeth guilty but not regretful about the murder of Duncan and
the others? Would a morally developed driver of a train that deliv-
ered people to their deaths in Auschwitz experience guilt but not
regret? I don't think so. In both cases it seems sensible to describe

the experience as at once guilty and regretful. In general, it seems impossible to imagine experiencing guilt without regret, but quite possible to imagine experiencing regret without guilt.

Thus regret is once again the broader concept. Regret is not limited to instances in which there is legal, moral, or psychological culpability but includes instances of legally, morally, and subjectively innocuous acts. Furthermore, regret is not limited to one's own free and voluntary acts and failures to act, but also includes certain acts and omissions of others with whom one shares group membership. But regret also applies to matters over which one has no control.[106]

Conclusions

This conceptual and theoretical analysis of regret and related concepts suggests that regret is a superordinate concept that subsumes certain defining features of disappointment, sadness, remorse, and guilt, but that regret can also be distinguished from these. In addition, regret is phenomenally associated with undoing. The fact that there is some overlap between and among these concepts and experiences conforms to the results of research that find that emotions tend to occur in clusters, especially positive and negative clusters, rather than in isolation.[107] If negative emotions (e.g., anger, depression, and anxiety) typically occur together (or are so reported)[108] and if the emotions of shame and guilt often occur together (or are so reported),[109] then it should come as little surprise that regret, disappointment, sadness, remorse, and guilt might co-occur.

Finally, this analysis highlights the complex nature of regret as experience. Regret bridges the interior and the exterior; the cognitive and emotional; the actual and the possible; the past, present, and future. Perhaps it is not surprising that such a complex matter can be experienced from within a number of different frameworks.

3

Worldviews of Regret: A Literary Framework

How we experience regret has, I believe, much to do with personal and cultural values that are deep and fundamental, though often tacit and unexamined. Just as the text of life cannot be reduced to a single universally agreed-upon text, but supports multiple possible meanings, interpretations, or constructions, regret cannot be reduced to a single unitary concept or phenomenon but requires a many-dimensioned analytic framework. In this chapter I begin an exploration of regret within the framework of the literary categories of romance, comedy, tragedy, and irony—as illustrated in Dickens's *Great Expectations*, James's *The Ambassadors*, Dostoevsky's *Notes from Underground*, and Woolf's *Mrs. Dalloway*, respectively. In addition, I examine a more modern exemplar of regret in a mixed mode (romantic and ironic) as found in *Breathing Lessons* by Anne Tyler.[1,2] Finally, I take a look at literary metaphors for regret emerging from within each of these worldviews. I shall be returning to these novels and their corresponding modes of regret in later chapters, combing through them for whatever they can contribute to an understanding of the substance, antecedents, occasions, sequelae, and transformation of regret.[3]

Four Worldviews of Regret

The concepts of romance, comedy, tragedy, and irony rarely show up in psychological, philosophical, or economic analysis. Nevertheless, their roots in the humanities are entirely congruent with the kind of phenomenon that regret is—a subjective, personal experience dependent on a subjective and personal interpretation of reality. Precisely because of the subjective nature of regret, these worldviews (modes, attitudes, stances, mentalities, constructions) come especially well equipped to illuminate regret in its complexity.

Much of my framework is based on the work of four scholars: Northrop Frye, George Steiner, Roy Schafer, and Dan McAdams. In his classic *Anatomy of Criticism,* Frye was the first to classify literary plots into the four archetypal categories of comedy, romance, tragedy, and irony.[4] My framework is also informed by Steiner's analysis of tragedy, which contributes clear distinctions between the tragic and ironic modes and which fleshes out the understanding of the romantic mode.[5] I have relied as well on Schafer's examination of how psychoanalysis reflects aspects of the comic, romantic, tragic, and ironic "visions of reality"[6]—that is, "ways of looking at experience and imposing meaning on it."[7] Along with Schafer, I caution the reader that "there are no terse definitions of these terms on which philosophers and critics generally agree."[8] McAdams has contributed to my framework certain organizing categories within each of the stances—particularly those of "central problem" and "general sentiment."[9]

I do not think of this framework as a typology. It is more modest than that. Rather than types (clearly distinct, discontinuous, empirically derived categories),[10] I think of the mentalities as heuristic conceptual configurations that to a certain degree overlap. I believe that the present framework proves useful both as a "communications convenience"[11] and as a viewing device capable of revealing deep coherence existing in surface incoherence. Once they have been delineated in some detail, it should be feasible, in principle, for the interested scholar to test to what extent these stances represent empirically distinctive patterns of psychological organization.[12]

The Romantic Worldview

In the romantic stance, life is viewed primarily as a quest involving individual struggle and ultimate heroic triumph, characterized by the following features:

- View Of Time

  Ahistorical, atemporal because based on the hope of sudden, discontinuous leaps forward.

- Central Attitudes

  1. Striving against obstacles.
  2. Belief in the existence of certainties, absolutes, and clear divisions between right and wrong, good and evil, hero and villain, etc.
  3. Belief in the possibility of justice, reform, progress, perfectibility, happy endings, reconciliations, redemption, and heroic rebirth following struggle.

- Central Problem

  How to journey onward and upward so as to emerge victorious.[13]

- Nature of Obstacles

  External, situational forces—not internal, or personal failings; and controllable forces.

- Preferred Solution

  Action.
  Emotion.
  Fantasy (involving individualistic, heroic, triumphal quest).

- Outcome

  Triumph.

The romantic disposition toward regret arises out of the conviction that, although misfortune, mistakes, shortcomings, failings, and transgressions are inevitable aspects of the heroic quest that is life, they are obstacles that will in the end be overcome by struggle. Moreover, the individual will be a better person—a hero— for having struggled against and triumphed over adversity.

The Comic Worldview

The comic stance toward life in general, and regret in particular, is an essentially optimistic one characterized by the following features:

- View of Time

  Time as cyclic, in the sense that it is assumed that spring follows winter and the past is refurbishable.

- Central Attitude
  Belief in the possibility of justice, reform, progress, perfectibility, happy endings, reconciliations, redemption, and rebirth.
- Central Problem
  "How to find happiness and stability in life . . . by minimizing interference from environmental obstacles and constraints."[14]
- Nature of Obstacles
  Controllable, external forces.
- Preferred Solutions
  Exercise of reason.
  Action.
- Outcome
  Happy resolution.

The comic stance toward regret is one in which misfortune, mistakes, shortcomings, failings, and transgressions come out all right in the end. Therefore, regret is a brief interruption on the way to resolution, rather as travelers have to stop periodically for gas on the way to their vacation destinations. To add another metaphor, regret in the comic mode is just a blip on the essentially sensible screen of life.

The comic and romantic mentalities share these features: (1) belief in progressive, melioristic development; (2) ascription of conflict and misery to external and controllable forces; and (3) an emphasis on reasoned action as a primary solution to conflict and unhappiness.

The comic and romantic stances differ from one another in these four ways. (1) Both are based on a progressivist assumption; but in the comic view progress is expected to be fairly smooth in its evolution, and in the romantic view progress takes place in discontinuous leaps. (2) Whereas in the comic stance good and evil are aligned on a continuum, the romantic view is that good and evil are drastically different. (3) The romantic stance entails an emphasis on certainty not characteristic of the comic stance. (4) The romantic stance prizes the articulation of heroic emotion and fantasy as precursors of the overt action it (along with the comic stance) endorses.

The Tragic Worldview

In the tragic vision life is viewed as a process of decline and deterioration culminating in death. Yet in this view decline and death are *not* perceived as a good night into which one ought to go gentle. Rather, these facts call for wailing and gnashing of teeth, defiantly shaking one's fist at the gods, and in the words of Dylan Thomas, "raging against the dying of the light." The tragic stance entails the following features:

- View of Time
  1. Time as linear: "time is seen to be continuous and irreversible; choices once made are made forever; a second chance cannot be the same as the first; life is progression toward death without rebirth."[15]
  2. or, time as entailing cyclic-but-futile phases of advance and decline.
- Central Attitudes
  1. "Responsiveness to the great dilemmas, paradoxes, ambiguities, and uncertainties pervading human action and subjective experience."[16]
  2. "A sense of the inescapable dangers, terrors, mysteries, and absurdities" of life.[17]
  3. An awareness of the "loss of opportunities entailed by every choice and by growth in any direction; . . . [and] the reversal of fortune."[18]
  4. Belief in the existence of certainties, absolutes, and clear divisions between right and wrong, good and evil, hero and villain, etc.
  5. a. Lack of belief in the possibility of justice, reform, progress, perfectibility, happy endings, reconciliations, redemption, and rebirth.
     b. Refusal to accept these circumstances.
- Central Problem
  "How to avoid or minimize the danger and absurdities of life which threaten to overwhelm even the greatest human beings."[19]
- Nature of Obstacles
  1. Internal failings, splits, ambivalences, polarities.
  2. Uncontrollable forces that "lie outside the governance of reason or justice," and "which can neither be fully understood nor overcome by rational prudence."[20]

- Preferred Solution
  Articulated emotion.
  Reflective thought, with the goal of good reality testing, or seeing "the truth," no matter how dark.
- Outcome
  Irreparable disaster or catastrophe.

The tragic stance shares three features with the romantic stance: (1) a dualistic, absolutistic assessment of right and wrong, good and evil, hero and villain; (2) the expectation that there will be obstacles in one's path; and (3) an emphasis on the articulation of emotion in response to life's obstacles.

The tragic mentality differs from the romantic in that the tragic mentality: (1) views obstacles as primarily internal and uncontrollable (as in the tragic flaw of ancient and modern heroes), rather than external and controllable; (2) emphasizes the articulation of reason rather than fantasy as a preferred mode of meeting life's obstacles; (3) eschews belief in perfection and resolution; but (4) refuses to accept this limitation. From within the tragic perspective, regrets are as irremediable as they are unforeseeable, inevitable, and catastrophic.

The Ironic Worldview

Where the tragic vision is heavy and dark, the ironic stance is at once light and dark. From the ironic perspective, it is an undeniable fact that life presses on nearly everyone a mix of good and ill. But acceptance, rather than defiance, is the prescribed response to this fact.

- View of Time
  1. Time as linear: "time is seen to be continuous and irreversible; choices once made are made forever; a second chance cannot be the same as the first; life is progression toward death without rebirth"[21]
  2. or, time as entailing cyclic-but-futile phases of advance and decline.
- Central Attitudes
  1. "Responsiveness to the great dilemmas, paradoxes, ambiguities, and uncertainties pervading human action and subjective experience."[22]

2. "A sense of the inescapable dangers, terrors, mysteries, and absurdities" of life.[23]
3. An awareness of the "loss of opportunities entailed by every choice and by growth in any direction; . . . [and] the reversal of fortune."[24]
4. Belief that there are no certainties, absolutes, clear divisions between good and bad, right and wrong, hero and villain, etc.
5. Belief in, and detached acceptance of, the impossibility of perfection or resolution.

- Central Problem

  "How to solve some of the mysteries of life, to gain some perspective on the chaos, ambiguities, and contradictions of human living."[25]

- Nature of Obstacles

  1. Internal failings, splits, ambivalences, and polarities.
  2. Uncontrollable forces that "lie outside the governance of reason or justice," and "which can neither be fully understood nor overcome by rational prudence."[26]

- Preferred Solutions

  Reflective thought, with the goal of good reality testing, or seeing "the truth."

  Detached acceptance.

- Outcome

  Mixed blessings, compromises, trade-offs.

The ironic vision is identical to the tragic vision in these features: (1) viewing time as linear and thus irreversible; (2) viewing obstacles as primarily due to internal and uncontrollable forces; (3) valuing good reality-testing: "We see—and value seeing—that which we are most powerfully disinclined to see"[27]—that is, loss, injustice, decline, destruction, death.

But the ironic differs from the tragic stance in that the ironic stance: (1) eschews absolutistic and dualistic views of right and wrong, good and evil, hero and villain; (2) prescribes detached acceptance of the impossibility of perfect resolution of conflict; (3) implies neither unequivocally happy endings (as in the comic and the romantic visions) nor unmitigated catastrophes (as in the tragic vision), but mixed blessings, compromises, and trade-offs. From within the ironic perspective, regret is an inevitable but not cata-

Four Modes of Experiencing Regret

	Romantic	Comic	Tragic	Ironic
View of Time	Ahistorical, atemporal: sudden, discontinuous leaps.	Cyclic: second chances.	Linear, irreversible.	Linear, or futilely cyclic.
Central Attitudes	1. Belief in striving against obstacles. 2. Belief in certainties and absolutes. 3. Belief in progress, perfectibility, and heroic rebirth following struggle.	Belief in progress, perfectibility.	1. Expectation of dangers, dilemmas, loss. 2. Refusal to accept these facts. 3. Belief in certainty and absolutes.	1. Expectation of dilemma, ambiguity, uncertainty, loss. 2. Detached acceptance of these facts.
Central Problem	How to venture heroically.	How to maximize happiness and minimize pain.	How to avoid the worst fates.	How to gain some perspective.
Nature of Obstacles	External, controllable.	External, controllable.	Internal, uncontrollable.	Internal, uncontrollable.
Preferred Solutions	1. Action. 2. Emotion. 3. Fantasy	1. Exercise of reason. 2. Action.	1. Seeing the truth. 2. Feeling the truth.	1. Seeing the truth. 2. Accepting the truth.
Outcome	Triumph.	Happy resolution.	Irreparable loss.	Compromises, trade-offs, mixed blessings.

strophic human experience occasioned by the facts that every human gain necessarily entails loss and every human virtue vice.

These mentalities—the romantic, comic, tragic, and ironic—represent four different analytic frameworks with which we perceive, organize, and interpret the raw material of life's regrets. It is worth repeating here some of the most important similarities and differences among them; these are also revealed in graphic form in the table on page 64. The romantic and comic modes share the progressivist assumption, the ascription of life's obstacles primarily to external and controllable forces, and an orientation to action. The tragic and ironic modes both reject the progressivist assumption, they both ascribe life's obstacles primarily to internal and uncontrollable forces, and they share a respect for seeing the truth of reality. The romantic and tragic modes share a belief in certainty and absolutes.

A Literary Portrayal of Regret in the Romantic Mode

In *Great Expectations* Dickens tells the story of the fall from grace and the rising again of Pip, an impoverished boy whose misfortune it is to have his great wish—to be a "gentleman"—granted. In the first third of the book, Pip lives near the marshes with his only living relative, his older sister, and her blacksmith husband, Joe Gargery. Following the deaths of their parents, Pip's sister has, none too gently, raised him. Throughout Pip's dismal childhood, Joe, Pip's only ally, tries to protect Pip from Pip's sister's anger and abuse. One day Pip encounters in the marshes an escaped convict who threatens Pip's life unless he returns with food and a file. Pip does so, but later the convict is caught.

Someone else who plays a crucial role in Pip's life is Miss Havisham, a wealthy, bitter old woman for whom time stopped the day she was abandoned by an unscrupulous fiancé. She asks to have young Pip visit her once a week. At Miss Havisham's, Pip falls in love with Estella, whom Miss Havisham has raised as an adopted daughter for the purpose of wreaking vicarious revenge on men. Under the influence of Miss Havisham, Pip becomes embarrassed by his unrefined background, and he determines that he must become a "gentleman." Suddenly his wish is granted, when he is told that a secret benefactor wishes to finance his leaving for London at age twenty-one to be educated as a gentleman.

In the middle third of the book, Pip throws off the yoke of his past and squanders his fortune in London. Having assumed all along that Miss Havisham is his benefactor, Pip finally learns, to his mortification, that the benefactor is actually the convict, Abel Magwitch (alias Provis), he had helped long ago.

The last third of the book details Pip's handling of this news, including his initial reluctance to have anything to do with Provis, his later decision to assist Provis to escape from an assassin, and his determination to stand by Provis after his recapture and trial. Eventually, he is reconciled with Joe and his past, and ends on friendly terms with Estella, who, like Pip, has been ennobled by suffering.

Pip's Regrets

Estella's scornful reaction to meeting the young Pip[28] awakens his first regret, the beginning of his loss of innocence. For the first time, he is ashamed of his social status, feeling that his clothing, his hands, and his speech are "coarse." In reaction, he resolves to shuck off his commonness along with the rest of his past, and to make of himself a "gentleman." He also embarks on the road to getting an education by having a young woman friend, Biddy, teach him to read and write. But soon he feels that he has learned everything she has to teach him and that he has outgrown her.

However, Pip is not entirely of one mind on this subject. He vacillates between regret for and idealization of his past:

> I would decide conclusively that my disaffection to dear old Joe and the forge, was gone, and that I was growing up in a fair way to be partners with Joe and to keep company with Biddy—when all in a moment some confounding remembrance of the Havisham days would fall upon me, like a destructive missile, and scatter my wits again.[29]

Some time after his change of fortune, Pip comes to regret having abandoned Joe and Biddy and the simple goodness of life with them:

> When I woke up in the night . . . I used to think, with a weariness in my spirits, that I should have been happier and better if I had never seen Miss Havisham's face, and had risen to manhood content to be partners with Joe in the honest old forge.[30]

More regrets follow from Pip's discovery that it is Provis, the criminal, who is his benefactor, rather than the ostensibly more respectable Miss Havisham. He feels that this fact does not redound to his glory: "I have found out who my patron is. It is not a fortunate discovery, and is not likely ever to enrich me in reputation, station, fortune, anything,"[31] Pip complains to Miss Havisham. In the end, however, he is sorry for his earlier ill-treatment of Provis and comes to his aid in his hour of need.

The Romantic View of Regret in Great Expectations

If anyone is known for a romantic attitude, it is Dickens. In *Great Expectations* regret spurs the characters on to suffering and struggle leading to reform, reconciliation, and redemption. Like other romantic forms, this work takes seriously the possibility of discontinuous leaps forward, most especially Pip's sudden gift of "great expectations" from a secret benefactor. The work is shot full of absolutes, particularly in its cast of characters, many of whom are portrayed at any particular point in time as either absolutely good (Joe and Biddy) or evil (Compeyson, Provis's adversary). "Good" characters progress toward the better. Pip himself, after wrong turns and suffering, reforms his own character so that in the end he becomes a miracle of filial devotion to Provis, magnanimously forgives Miss Havisham the harm she has done him through Estella, and reconciles with Joe, Biddy, and a reformed Estella. Rather than merely indulging in the heroic fantasy characteristic of some romances, Pip throws himself into deeds that amount to a triumphal quest. There is also the romantic's ascription of conflict and misery to external, situational forces, particularly with respect to Provis, the good-hearted convict who, it is implied, but for his unfortunate background might not have been a felon at all. Finally, the romantic dismissal of reason and science appears in Dickens's famed penchant for coincidence: "coincidence was his [Dickens's] favorite contraption, the ultimate, irrational rescue, a slap in the face of science."[32] In its plot (if not in every nuance of each character), *Great Expectations* presents a thoroughly romantic stance toward regret.

Romantic Metaphors for Regret

Romantic metaphors for regret may be as rare in fiction as a regretless adult in real life. The closest thing to a simile for regret in this novel of Dickens is the romantic reference to "some confounding remembrance of the Havisham days," which would fall on Pip "like a destructive missile." Heroically, Pip survived these dramatically formidable assaults.

The only other arguably romantic metaphor of regret I have

unearthed appeared in a piece of nonfiction. In a review of Elia Kazan's novel *The Arrangement*, James Baldwin wrote of regret as a "momentous gap" and a "baffling geography":

> When more time stretches behind than stretches before one, some assessments, however reluctantly and incompletely, begin to be made. Between what one wishes to become and what one *has* become there is a momentous gap, which will now never be closed. And this gap seems to operate as one's final margin, one's last opportunity, for creation. . . . Some of us are compelled, around the middle of our lives, to make a study of this baffling geography . . . .[33]

Baffling geography—a puzzling picture of the earth. What does this metaphor reveal about regret? That this gap is both "momentous" and offers a "last opportunity for creation" represents a quintessentially romantic vision. If only the individual were to struggle mightily, it is by implication still possible, if not to close the yawning void, at least to seize the opportunity to *create*—something. But what? Baldwin's metaphor suggests to me an image of regret as an enormous canyon over which a bridge is about to be constructed—perhaps a magnificent bridge[34] at last linking what one has become with what one wished to become. In Baldwin's passage there is at least a sense of hope for a last-minute transformation (if not such a grand metaphorical Bridge of Sighs) that is quite romantic.

A Literary Portrayal of Regret in the Comic Mode

In *The Ambassadors* Henry James paints a complex, but ultimately sanguine portrait of regret. The protagonist, Lambert Strether, is a 55-year-old editor of a minor literary magazine in Woollett, Massachusetts. Since the death of his wife and 10-year-old son years earlier, he has lived alone in Woollett. He has just been dispatched to Paris by his widowed patron, Mrs. Newsome, to try to convince her 28-year-old son, Chad, to return to Woollett from Paris. If Chad returns, he will receive a handsome inheritance, and ownership of his father's business. If he does not return, he will forfeit them. Mrs. Newsome wants Strether to talk Chad into leaving Europe and marrying Mamie Pocock, the younger sister of her daughter Sarah's husband, Jim. If Strether succeeds in his mission, it is understood that he will receive the undying gratitude of Mrs. Newsome in the form of a financially gratifying marriage.

In Europe, Strether eventually discovers that Chad has an alli-

ance with an older woman (38 years of age), Mme Marie de Vionnet, who is separated from her husband. Instead of bringing Chad
Woollett's censure, Strether finds himself surrendering to what he
sees as the civilized charm of Chad and Madame de Vionnet, and
the unconventional beauty of their life together. When Mrs. Newsome finds that Strether is going to be no help to her, she dis-
patches Sarah (with Jim and Mamie) to Europe to make one last
effort to persuade Chad to return to America. Sarah primly steels
herself against Chad's life and friends. In the end, Chad chooses to
remain in Paris with Madame de Vionnet, although it is left ambiguous how much longer he will remain true to her. During his
three-month sojourn in Europe, Strether has failed in his ambassadorial function but has succeeded in saving his own soul.

It is unusual to have an author's statement as to the meaning
of a literary work. But, according to James himself, the theme of
this book is regret and the transformation of regret. His explanation requires a lengthy quote:

> The remarks to which he [Strether] thus gives utterance contain the
> essence of *The Ambassadors* . . . : "Live all you can; it's a mistake
> not to. It doesn't so much matter what you do in particular so long as
> you have your life. If you haven't had that what *have* you had? I'm
> too old— too old at any rate for what I see. What one loses one loses;
> make no mistake about that. Still, we have the illusion of freedom;
> therefore, don't, like me today, be without the memory of that illu-
> sion. I was either, at the right time, too stupid or too intelligent to
> have it, and now I'm a case of reaction against the mistake. Do what
> you like so long as you don't make it. For it *was* a mistake. Live,
> live!"
>
> Such is the gist of Strether's appeal to the impressed youth, whom
> he likes and whom he desires to befriend; the word "mistake" occurs
> several times, it will be seen, in the course of his remarks—which
> gives the measure of the signal warning he feels attached to his case.
> He has accordingly missed too much, though perhaps after all consti-
> tutionally qualified for a better part, and he wakes up to it in condi-
> tions that spring of a terrible question. *Would* there yet perhaps be
> time for reparation?—reparation, that is, for the injury done his char-
> acter; for the affront, he is quite to say, so stupidly put upon it and in
> which he has even himself had so clumsy a hand? The answer to which
> is that of my action, not to say the precious moral of everything, is
> just my demonstration of this process of vision.[35]

According to James himself, then, what Strether regrets is not
having "lived" his life. But what exactly does this mean? First,

Strether suffers regret related to his life's work: he regrets "his long grind and his want of odd moments, his want moreover of money, of opportunity, of positive dignity."[36] He recognizes that, because of his failure to have forged much of an identity or to have produced anything of value himself, having his name on the cover of the *Review* carries inordinate importance to him:

> It's exactly the thing that I'm reduced to doing for myself. It seems to rescue a little, you see, from the wreck of hopes and ambitions, the refuse heap of disappointments and failures, my one presentable little scrap of an identity.[37]
>
> He was Lambert Strether because he was on the cover, whereas it should have been, for anything like glory, that he was on the cover because he was Lambert Strether.[38]

As these passages show, Strether is perfectly aware that his paltry pride in seeing his name in print does not begin to assuage his regret. He continues to suffer precisely because the source of his regret lies deeper than his knowledge of having failed to achieve occupational and financial success:

> this acceptance of fate was all he had at fifty-five to show. He judged the quantity as small because it *was* small, and all the more egregiously so since it couldn't, as he saw the case, so much as thinkably have been larger. He had not had the gift of making the most of what he tried, and if he had tried and tried again—no one but himself knew how often—it appeared to have been that he might demonstrate what else, in default of that, *could* be made. Old ghosts of experiments came back to him, old drudgeries and delusions and disgusts, old recoveries with their relapses, old fevers with their chills, broken moments of good faith, others of still better doubt; adventures, for the most part, of the sort qualified as lessons.[39]

What Strether is here exhibiting is what Amelie Rorty terms "character regret"—regret for what he *is*.[40] Indeed, James himself described Strether as experiencing regret "for the injury done his character"—by his own self-constraint. More specifically, Strether regrets the limitations of sensation, of generous imagination, and of accomplishment characteristic of him as he had lived life in Woollett.

Strether represents a sophisticated version of the speaker of the long quote with which I opened this book: someone who lives "prophylactically and sensibly and sanely hour after hour, day after day. . . . [who] never goes anywhere without a thermometer, a hot water bottle, a gargle, a raincoat, aspirin, and a parachute." And like this first speaker, Strether regrets having lived this life of excessive sobriety.

The Comic View of Regret in The Ambassadors

The Ambassadors manifests a predominantly comic construction of regret—most of all by taking seriously the possibility of redoing the mistakes of the past. The plot trajectory follows Strether's largely successful journey of redoing, which is further detailed in Chapter 8. This novel suggests what Schafer calls a cyclic view of time in which the past can be repaired and "redone, if not undone"[41]. Strether repairs his past in at least three interrelated ways: by expanding his perceptions and sympathies, by living vicariously through beloved others, and by living more fully himself than before. When he is dispatched to Europe, Strether gets a second chance. In refusing to carry out Mrs. Newsome's ambassadorial wishes, to persuade Chad to give up his "scandalous" alliance and go back to America, Strether experiences something like a rebirth: "I'm making up late for what I didn't have early."

Alongside the second-chance element is another comic (as well as ironic) aspect of this novel: the allergy to absolutes and certainties. This shows itself in Strether's reminiscences about his past, which are typically painted in variegated hues rather than black and white: "broken moments of good faith, others of still better *doubt*," for example. But the most momentous discovery of shades of gray for Strether centers on the gradual but drastic change in his initial understanding of the nature of Chad's alliance with Madame de Vionnet. When Strether happens upon the couple on their outing in the boat, he is confronted with a fact that he had never really allowed himself to acknowledge—the erotic implications of the couple's connection. Instead, he had earlier understood someone's characterization of the connection as a "virtuous attachment" in Woollett's sense of a platonic relationship, rather than in the more worldly sense in which it was intended. At the sight of the couple "caught" in their otherwise discreetly private affair, Strether's black-and-white view is considerably complicated.

In James's novel the comic dominates, but, like all good fiction, there are elements of the other modes as well. Most notable is James's own non-comic comment on this work in the Preface: "What one loses one loses; make no mistake about that." However, in the novel itself this sentiment is absent or rather deeply buried. Similarly, James does not manifest the comic (and roman-

tic] ascription of Strether's failures to external circumstances. Instead, he has Strether demonstrate the ironic and tragic mentality
of freely admitting to himself his own contribution to his regrettably cautious life: "he had not had the gift of making the most of
what he tried."

The element that best illustrates Strether's non-comic limita-
tions is his final failure to maintain or deepen his seemingly prom-
ising relationship with his guide, Maria Gostrey. Strether seems at
the end just as clueless as he was at the beginning of his stay in
Europe about how to achieve and sustain intimacy with another.
In fact, for the life of me I can never believe James's description of
Strether as a man who at one time had a wife and child; for me
Strether remains the very soul of bachelorhood—before and after
Europe. But when Strether explains to Maria that he must leave
her "to be right. . . . [so as not] to have got anything for myself,"
he may be showing that he is not quite so liberated as one might
wish. Even if the reader is not meant to accept this sanctimonious
explanation at face value but rather as a subtly tactful exit on
Strether's part, Strether is still lacking the gift of making the most
of what he tries. The aborted relationship illustrates the non-comic
assessment of the fault as lying not entirely in external circumstances (e.g., the moralistic parochialism of Woollett, Massachusetts) but in one's character. Strether's inability to pursue his connection with Maria Gostrey sadly illustrates James's non-comic
claim in the preface that "what one loses one loses."

A third non-comic aspect is the romantic battle going on inside
Strether not only between the absolutes of platonic versus nonvir-
tuous relationships but also between the two near-absolutes—good
old Europe and bad new America. There is very little gray in
Strether's worshipful attitude toward all things European, including the "European" characters, particularly Chad and, even more,
Madame de Vionnet, who tend to approach romantic perfection in
Strether's eyes. Of Chad, Strether exclaims: "He's excellent." Of
Madame de Vionnet he gushes: "She's perfect." And "You *are* as
wonderful as everybody says!" professes Strether to Madame de
Vionnet. Interestingly, Strether's romantic illusions on this point
furnish the basis of the central comedy—in the traditional sense of
the term—that is, his almost humorous blindness to the true nature of Chad's alliance with Madame de Vionnet.[42]

Notwithstanding these non-comic elements, however, the novel's mentality remains primarily comic. Strether's "failure" at discharging his ambassadorial duties in conformity with Mrs. New-

some's wishes represents the great success of his life. Although Strether's rebirth is partial, rebirth it is.

James's Metaphors for Regret

James's metaphors for regret range from the noncommittal "old ghosts" to the more malign "old fevers with their chills" to the even more tragic "wreck of hopes and ambitions" and "refuse heap of disappointments and failures." What do these metaphors reveal about regret?

Most strikingly, despite Strether's ultimate success in resolving his regrets, none of James's images is unreservedly optimistic. One is after all *haunted* by "old ghosts" (about which more later). Fevers and chills are nasty conditions from which one hopes to escape into health. Even more malign are wrecks and refuse heaps, for which the best that can be hoped is that they might nourish, rather than befoul, the soil in which they decompose.

Other Comic Metaphors for Regret

Comic literary metaphors for regret, like romantic ones, appear rare to nonexistent. Even in *The Ambassadors*, a long work that portrays regret in a relatively optimistic mode, the metaphors for regret do not fit the comic mode. As yet, I have not found in literature a single metaphor for regret that I would characterize as clearly comic. The closest things to comic metaphors for regret I've come upon are these (to be discussed in greater detail in later chapters, especially Chapters 5 and 9): (a) as-yet-unbalanced but ultimately balanceable financial accounts, an image that implicitly underlies a number of the theoretical and economic models of regret in psychology and economics; and (b) a malfunctioning information-processing machine, an image common in modern cognitive psychology.

Interestingly enough, though, the very act of literary creation and revision serves not uncommonly as a comic metaphor for life and its regrets. Nora Ephron writes in this vein about the process of literary revision. She describes the development of her interest in writing fiction in her thirties:

> whole new areas of possible revision opened before me. What should I have done instead? What could I have done? What if I hadn't done it the way I did? What if I had a chance to do it over? What if I had a

chance to do it over as a different person? These were the sorts of questions that kept me awake and led me into fiction, which at the very least (the level at which I practice it) is a chance to rework the events of your life so that you give the illusion of being the intelligence at the center of it, simultaneously managing to slip in all the lines that occurred to you later. Fiction, I suppose, is the ultimate shot at revision.[43]

Ephron's implication is that being painfully aware of what in your life you would like to be able to revise can bring a certain kind of hope—as long as you have not arrived at the final draft.

This idea relates to the theme of *The Ambassadors* in that the process of revising one's fictional creation is analogous to the novel's theme of the reform and rebirth of one's life. The process of revising one's life is an essentially optimistic activity congruent with the comic perspective. The corollary is: as long as there's regret, there's hope.

A Literary Portrayal of Regret in the Tragic Mode

It is possible to enter the text of Dostoevsky's *Notes from Underground* in such a way as to highlight regret. This is not to claim that regret is the *only* or even the *primary* theme of this rich, complex book. Though a regret-centered analysis may lack the capacity to illuminate every corner of the mystery of the Underground Man (or, for that matter, the characters of other works examined here), it has potential value for those of us who wish to understand regret.

The nameless narrator of *Notes from Underground* is a painfully ruminative, alienated, socially isolated, 40-year-old former civil servant, a brutally honest individual, a tormented soul. In his own words the narrator is an "antihero,"[44] a defiantly self-immolating, nonconforming recluse who typically elicits more revulsion than admiration in others (including readers). With this complex character, Dostoevsky keeps the reader constantly off balance.

This narrator tells an imaginary audience about two crucial events from his past. Both illustrate, among other things, excruciating shame and character regret.[45]

At the age of 24, the narrator badgers an acquaintance, Simonov, into inviting him to join a party for Zverkov, an old schoolmate. Despite the facts that the narrator expresses nothing but contempt for Zverkov and the expense exceeds his financial wherewithal, the narrator attends the party. He goes, primed to take offense. And sure enough, feeling that he has been insulted, he alien- ates all present by insulting them—or doing his best to insult them (though Zverkov crushes him by letting him know he is incapable of insulting them, since he is too insignificant). Even though the others are clearly disgusted with him, he then insists on joining them in their visit to a house of prostitution. There he encounters Liza, a young prostitute with whom he has sex. Afterward, stricken with a mix of compassion and contempt, he attempts to persuade her to abandon her demeaning life. He succeeds in breaking through her defensive armor and reduces her to tears. Impulsively, he in- vites a reciprocal intimacy with Liza by giving her his home ad- dress.

He attempts to undo the Zverkov fiasco by writing a jauntily rationalizing letter of apology to Simonov. But his regret with re- spect to Liza proves more complicated and recalcitrant. "As the evening advanced and the dusk gathered, my emotions, and with them my thoughts, kept changing and growing ever more confused. Something would not die down within me, in the depths of my heart and my conscience; it refused to die down and scalded me with anguish."[46] He doesn't know what it is, but he feels "as if some crime were weighing on my heart."[47] He imagines rescuing Liza from her plight and sharing with her a happy married life. Then again he mocks himself for these fantasies and rues his over- ture to Liza, judging it to have been sincere and even noble, and at the same time exaggerated and Machiavellian. Most of all, he re- grets having invited Liza into his life by having given her his ad- dress. On the one hand, he is terrified that she will actually come to his home and find that, far from being a heroic savior, he is an impoverished nothing. He veers wildly between thoughts that he is not good enough for her and has unconscionably manipulated her—and desires to drive her away if she comes to him—because of his shame at what she will then "have on him."

In the novel's second central event, Liza does visit his flat, where she finds him in squalid surroundings in the midst of a humiliating conflict with his servant, whereupon he bursts into tears and launches into a speech again meant to crush her. She sees through the cruel words to his pain, and embraces him. He sobs in her arms. Then, recoiling from his feelings for her, he forces himself on her sexually as a "means of revenge, of inflicting new humiliation upon her."[48] As the ultimate affront, he presses money into her hand as she leaves.

Immediately after he has driven Liza from his home, he discov-

ers that she has refused the money and he acutely regrets his behavior. He runs out in an unsuccessful effort to find her. He has
destroyed whatever chance he may have had for happiness.

Dostoevsky's Metaphors for Regret

In this work, Dostoevsky's metaphors for regret coincide with his
metaphors for consciousness, the wellspring of regret: regret is a
poison, a disease, and a mouse gnawing at itself.

First, regret is a poison, a "poison of unfulfilled desires turned
inward."[49] The Underground Man's unfulfilled desires for respect
and love and dignity poison his soul.

Second, recall that in *The Ambassadors* Henry James too (albeit more vividly than Dostoevsky) equates regret with disease—
"old fevers with their chills." In *Notes from Underground* consciousness and regret are also portrayed as dis-ease, in the sense of
a disturbance of well-being or psychic tranquility.

Third, in Dostoevsky's most extended, most vivid, and most
original metaphor, he likens regret to a mouse biting at itself: "he
honestly feels himself, with all his heightened consciousness, to be
a mouse, not a man . . . an acutely conscious mouse, but a mouse
all the same."[50] "I would gnaw and gnaw at myself."[51] He is a
mouse who in the end will "slip back ignominiously into its hole
with a smile of feigned contempt in which it doesn't itself believe."[52] The underground is his claustrophobic mouse hole located below the earth where the real life takes place.

What do these metaphors reveal? First, they reveal a fusion of
cognitive (consciousness, excessive consciousness) and emotional
(dis-ease; "a poison of unfulfilled desires turned inward") aspects
in regret. Furthermore, the narrator allies himself with desire over
reason—particularly in a long polemic against the Socratic
assumption[53] that human beings do "vile things"[54] only so far as
they do not recognize their own true interests. Instead, the narrator
insists, people do vile things with their eyes wide open, simply to
assert the validity of desire over the claims of rationality:

> You see, gentlemen, reason is unquestionably a fine thing, but reason
> is no more than reason, and it gives fulfillment only to man's reason-
> ing capacity, while desires are a manifestation of the whole of life—I
> mean the whole of human life, both with its reason and with all its
> itches and scratches.[55]

The metaphor of the self-gnawing mouse reveals a type of regret that arises from the working of a divided psyche. Yes, Dostoevsky's man/mouse smiles contemptuously at the world above
ground, but the smile is "feigned"; moreover, this man/mouse knows
full well that his contempt is feigned—and for that reason he gnaws
at *himself.*

Finally, these images of poison, disease, and self-gnawing mouse
all reveal the painful, noxious, shattering experience that regret can
be. Yet, despite the element of pain revealed by these metaphors,
Dostoevsky also has his protagonist express "pleasure" in regret for
the vile things he has done:

> I reached a point where . . . I would feel a certain hidden, morbid,
> nasty little pleasure in the acute awareness that I had once again com-
> mitted something vile that day, that what had been done could no
> longer be undone; and I would gnaw and gnaw at myself . . . until
> the bitterness would finally begin to turn into a kind of shameful,
> damnable sweetness and, in the end—into a definite, positive plea-
> sure! Yes, a pleasure, a pleasure! I stand by that.[56]

In what sense are we to understand this man's claim to take
pleasure in his regrets? This is what the narrator has to say by way
of explanation:

> This pleasure comes precisely from the sharpest awareness of your
> own degradation; from the knowledge that you have gone to the ut-
> most limit; that it is despicable, yet cannot be otherwise; that you no
> longer have any way out, that you will never become a different man,
> that even if there were still time and faith enough to change yourself,
> you probably would not even wish to change; and if you wished, you
> would do nothing about it anyway, because, in fact, there is perhaps
> nothing to change to.[57]

Dostoevsky's answer has four elements. First, we are told, the
pleasure comes "from the sharpest awareness of your own degra-
dation." Taking pleasure in the consciousness of one's own degra-
dation is the desperate act of a masochist. As such, it is a fatally
tragic character flaw.

The second source of pleasure in regret comes "from the
knowledge that you have gone to the utmost limit." There will be
no halfway measures for this uncompromising individual, but only
absolutes and extremes.

Third, the narrator says that the pleasure in regret comes from
facing the facts that one's state "is despicable, yet cannot be oth-

erwise; that you no longer have any way out, that you will never become a different man, that even if there were still time and faith enough to change yourself, you probably would not even wish to change." Of all the narrator's explanations of how anyone can possibly take pleasure in regret, this is perhaps the most understandable. It is, in a sense, comforting to think that it is too late to change; then one need only lie back and accept one's fate rather than continue the struggle. Of course, Dostoevsky's scaldingly self-critical character does not stop with the easy comforts. He has to add the damning accusation that, even if it were not too late, one can take pleasure in knowing that one would not want to change. The protagonist expresses the same incommensurable conclusions when he asserts that "you are somehow to blame even for the stone wall, although, again, it is entirely obvious that you are not to blame at all."[58]

Finally, the narrator claims that there is pleasure in considering that "there is perhaps nothing to change to," an ambiguous statement suggesting a sense of complete and utter hopelessness alongside a sense of defiant, nihilistic self-complacency. Knowing what we know about this character, we do well to accept both sentiments as self-contradictory convictions stemming from a thoroughly divided psyche.

Even if Dostoevsky intended these thoughts as a satire and parody of the scientific determinism of the day, as critic Joseph Frank[59] suggests, they also succeed in articulating what I believe is a not-uncommon inner struggle between fatalism and its denial, and between self-recrimination and its denial, a struggle central to the modern experience of regret.

The Tragic View of Regret in Notes from Underground

The Underground Man is a man with the tragic preference for "truth" over social and emotional equilibrium. The working of a tragic vision can also be seen in his refusal to accept any overlap between good and bad, hero and villain, and his correlative refusal to accept the impossibility of attaining the absolute perfection of his ideals. On the contrary, this character consistently maintains an absolutistic, uncompromising stance. With his tragic linear sense of time, he is convinced that it is too late to change. Most of all, there is tragedy in his insistence that regret must be irremediable: "how preferable it is to . . . refuse to reconcile yourself to a single one of those impossibilities and walls."[60]

Notes from Underground provides not a breath of an optimistic construction on the part of the dour narrator. But, again, as in all fine literature, more than one worldview is sustained in this book. Along with the tragedy, the Underground Man manifests a strongly romantic perspective.

First, he habitually indulges in regressive fantasies of glory: "I was tormented by remorse, and I would try to drive it away . . . But I had a way out, which reconciled everything: escape into 'the lofty and the beautiful'—in my dreams, of course. I was a terrible dreamer."[61] Moreover, these fantasies typically hinge on a sudden, discontinuous leap out of the mayhem of the past—an impulsive, decisive duel with Zverkov; a precipitous, but happy marriage with Liza—an element characteristic of the romantic vision.[62]

In his exaltation of the claims of desire over those of reason he again shows himself to be a model of romanticism. "You see, gentlemen, reason is unquestionably a fine thing, but reason is no more than reason, and it gives fulfillment only to man's reasoning capacity, while desires are a manifestation of the whole of life." At heart he is a romantic, demanding of life a metaphorical palace[63] and not just a chicken coop for shelter.

This character thinks in absolutes, another highly romantic element: he is in his own estimate at one moment a villain and at the next moment a hero. A final romantic characteristic of the protagonist is his sometime conviction that all his problems are external in origin: "it is entirely obvious that you [i.e., himself] are not to blame at all."[64,65]

The Underground Man at times reaches for an ironically detached view of himself in which he doesn't take himself too seriously, particularly in his choice of the humble mouse metaphor. But in the end his effort after detachment fails: as in his admission that the mouse wears a "smile of feigned contempt *in which it doesn't itself believe."* Ultimately, *Notes from Underground* portrays a thoroughly tragic experience of regret.

Other Tragic Metaphors for Regret

Dostoevsky's tragic images of regret as a disease, a poison, and a mouse gnawing at itself are only three among a host of tragic metaphors for regret in literature. In Virginia Woolf's *Mrs. Dalloway* we will discover another tragic metaphor for regret—an arrow lodged in one's heart. As we have already seen, even in James's comic novel, *The Ambassadors,* the metaphors for regret were tragic: the

refuse heap of disappointments and failures, the wreck of hopes
and ambitions, old ghosts.

The ghost metaphor turns out to be one of the most common
of all metaphors for regret. Along with James, both Sherwood Anderson in *Winesburg, Ohio* and Maxine Kumin in a poem "History
Lesson" write about regret in terms of ghosts. In the play *Dear
Brutus,* James Barrie has a child ask her father to define "might-
have-beens." He defines them as "ghosts"[66] and "shades . . . made
of sad folk's thoughts."[67] In a similar vein, Scheler declares: "The
eternal fugitive from the past sinks deeper and deeper into the *dead
arms* of that very past."

Why have so many writers equated regrets with ghosts? I suspect that it is explained by the elements of unreality and of a
haunting past in both. First, regret is about comparing reality with
possibility. It makes little difference to the human heart or head
that possibility is not real. Second, the ghost metaphor discloses
the way in which the past has the power to haunt us in the present. To some (especially proponents of economic decision theory),
these very elements are what make regret irrational, as senseless
as believing in ghosts. But to me, these elements are part of what
makes regret fascinatingly human. When we regret, we bring together in the psyche the actual and the possible, the past and the
present.

Curiously, immediately after finishing *The Ambassadors*,
wherein the protagonist's life blossoms after previous stunting, James
wrote the short story "A Beast in the Jungle," in which the protagonist tragically misses the opportunity of his life and too late becomes aware of the loss. In this story, the title metaphor, the
crouching beast in the jungle, is a metaphor for regret, for becoming aware—too late—of what might have been, and for being de-
voured by that awareness. In "The Beast in the Jungle," what might
have been was the opportunity for John Marcher to have loved and
been loved by May Bartram—parallel to the Underground Man's
squandered opportunity with Liza, and Strether's with Maria Gostrey.

Brutish zoological images do seem to lend themselves to expressing tragic regret. In Hemingway's "The Snows of Kilimanjaro"
Harry, the protagonist, is dying of a gangrenous leg on Kilimanjaro.
He is consumed with regret concerning all the years he wasted his
literary talent through disuse. He regrets the literature he will now
never write, "things that he had saved to write until he knew enough
to write them well."[68] He regrets his marriage, particularly his de-

pendence on his wife's money; he quarrels with her, and is sorry for doing so. Reminiscent of Dostoevsky's self-gnawing mouse, Hemingway compares self-recriminatory regret to a snake biting itself: "Now if this was how it ended, and he knew it was, he must not turn like some snake biting itself because its back was broken."[69] In the poem "The Irreparable," too, Baudelaire writes that the "might-have been with tooth accursed/Gnaws at the piteous soul of man."[70] All these metaphors reveal how certain experiences of regret feel like something is eating at you. They disclose the pain and the pathology of the self-recriminatory characteristic of regret, particularly as it is experienced in the tragic mode.

Regret in the tragic sense—irremediable regret—is also commonly construed as something that, like the fire of hell, burns. For Emily Dickinson, remorse (a close cousin of regret) is "the Adequate of Hell." In *Notes from Underground*, the narrator describes his regrets as "scalding"; in his memoir *Present Past, Past Present*, Ionesco refers to "burning regrets"; and in *Heart of Darkness* Conrad describes regret as "unextinguishable."

Dickinson and Dostoevsky also share the disease metaphor: for Dickinson, "Remorse . . . is cureless—the Disease/Not even God— can heal."[71] Again like Dostoevsky, Dickinson points to the element of excessive consciousness: "Remorse—is Memory—awake." So does James in "The Beast in the Jungle," where he delineates the horror of waking—that is, the horror of becoming aware of exactly how much one has foregone. In *Krapp's Last Tape* Beckett's protagonist had at age 39 memorialized the great regret of his life by recording its description on audiotape. Now in his old age, Krapp replays this tape in which he describes his having broken off with his love, Bianca. He wonders: "Could I have been happy with her, up there on the Baltic, and the pines, and the dunes. [Pause]. Could I? [Pause]. And she?"[72] and "Perhaps my best years are gone. When there was a chance of happiness."[73] Then he makes a last tape in which he repudiates his youthful self as "a stupid bastard." Through the trope of replaying old audiotapes, Beckett concretizes Dickinson's notion of "memory awake."

Regret is sometimes compared to cultural entities, such as music and theatre. In *Out of Africa* Isak Dinesen describes tragedy in general as "the key—the minor key—to existence."[74] John Edgar Wideman relates regret to singing the blues: "You hear old people crying the blues about how they could have been this or done that if they only had the chance."[75] F. Scott Fitzgerald said that for Americans there are no second acts, a theatrical metaphor for regret that concisely expresses the irremediable nature of regret as viewed from within the tragic perspective.

Finally, regret lends itself to geographical metaphor. There are Baldwin's "momentous gap" and "baffling geography" discussed in the section on romantic metaphors for regret. In *The Leopard* Lampedusa images regret as a "perilous slope."[76] A regretful tone pervades Jonathan Galassi's poem entitled "Still Life": "somewhere you're always twenty-four," and "one of us says what we didn't say,/feels what we didn't feel." There are strong images of a little lake with a brilliant, mirror-like surface but murkiness under the surface: "We could have cracked/its [the lake's] mirror with a rock,/ a branch that might have lifted/something muddy to the surface."[77] Here regret is represented in the rock and the branch, which might have been used, but weren't, to break that glassy surface to expose to the surface (to consciousness) "something muddy" that unfortunately, perhaps even tragically, remained unexamined.[78] And in the novel to be considered next, Virginia Woolf's *Mrs. Dalloway,* regret is similarly compared to looking into the glassy depths.

A Literary Portrayal of Regret in the Ironic Mode

Of the literary works discussed in detail here, Virginia Woolf's *Mrs. Dalloway* yields perhaps the most abundant treasure concerning regret. The plot of this novel takes place soon after World War I on a single June day in the life of the protagonist Clarissa Dalloway, a middle-aged woman recovering from heart problems. The story revolves around Clarissa Dalloway's preparations for a party she is giving that evening. The central event is a surprise visit after a lapse of five years by Peter Walsh, a former suitor whom thirty years ago she had rejected in favor of Richard Dalloway. Peter has returned from India for a visit prior to his hoped-for wedding with Daisy (who is unfortunately a married woman with two children). Peter Walsh and Clarissa Dalloway share emotional reminiscences about their past friendship and obliquely her rejection of him. The narrative concludes with the party, which Clarissa Dalloway considers a great social success. However, it is not a success for Peter, who suffers through it with mixed feelings of tenderness and estrangement toward Clarissa Dalloway, who appears to be purposely keeping him at arm's length. Throughout the day, the bells of Big Ben regularly toll the half hour, with the incantatory phrase "the leaden circles dissolved in the air" regularly marking the passage of the "irrevocable" hours.

The novel, though not dour, simmers with regret. Clarissa Dalloway ambivalently regrets that she gave up Peter Walsh and married Richard Dalloway; Peter Walsh clearly regrets this. There are numerous subplots entailing regret as well; but for the present purpose it is sufficient to focus on the regrets of Clarissa Dalloway and Peter Walsh.

Clarissa Dalloway's Regrets

Periodically Clarissa Dalloway suffers pangs of regret for having given up Peter Walsh. This feeling comes to light early in the day, as she anticipates Peter's imminent visit:

> For they might be parted for hundreds of years, she and Peter; she never wrote a letter and his were dry sticks; but suddenly it would come over her, If he were with me now what would he say?—some days, some sights bringing him back to her calmly, without the old bitterness; which perhaps was the reward of having cared for people; they came back in the middle of St. James's Park on a fine morning— indeed they did.[79]

One question confronting the reader is whether Clarissa Dalloway's regrets are objectively warranted, or whether she is simply a malcontent. Sally, an old friend of Clarissa and Peter, gives credence to the "validity" of Clarissa's feelings; in those youthful days Sally had begged Peter to:

> carry off Clarissa, to save her from the Hughs and the Dalloways and all the other "perfect gentlemen" who would "stifle her soul" (she wrote reams of poetry in those days), make a mere hostess of her, encourage her worldliness.[80]

So, if Sally can be believed, Clarissa Dalloway does have reason to regret her marriage, although Clarissa herself never frames her regrets in precisely these terms—never focuses sharply on the costs she has incurred by having married Richard, but instead focuses only on the losses she has incurred by not having married Peter.

As is typical of regret as portrayed in this novel, Clarissa's regret is thoroughly ambivalent. On the one hand, she yearns for the sense of engaged stimulation she experiences when she is with Peter Walsh, an unconventional, talkative, emotional man; on the other hand, she finds his opinionated emotionality tiresome after a time. On the one hand, she desires the tranquility and conventionality of life with Richard Dalloway, who adores and pampers her;

on the other hand, his constitutional inability to touch her at an emotional level leaves her desolate.

Clarissa's rueful state of mind seems to recruit even more regret, until she finds herself regretting even her physical appearance and age:

> Oh if she could have had her life over again! she thought, stepping on to the pavement, could have looked even differently!
>
> She would have been, in the first place, dark like Lady Bexborough, with a skin of crumpled leather and beautiful eyes. She would have been, like Lady Bexborough, slow and stately; rather large; interested in politics like a man; with a country house; very dignified, very sincere. Instead of which she had a narrow pea-stick figure; a ridiculous little face, beaked like a bird's. That she held herself well was true; and had nice hands and feet; and dressed well, considering that she spent little. But often now this body she wore . . . this body, with all its capacities, seemed nothing—nothing at all. She had the oddest sense of being herself invisible; unseen; unknown; there being no more marrying, no more having of children now, but only this astonishing and rather solemn progress with the rest of them, up Bond Street, this being Mrs. Dalloway; not even Clarissa any more; this being Mrs. Richard Dalloway.[81]

This passage shows a progression in Clarissa Dalloway starting from reflection on less distressing regrets for her pea-stick figure and ridiculous little face, and moving on to more deeply distressing, though related, regrets—her sense of being invisible, derivative, and inconsequential and her conviction that the life remaining to her is intolerably narrow and predictable.

Later that morning, when Peter pays her his surprise visit, Clarissa's regret flares into more acute suffering for having given him up. As they converse, Peter—always quick to laugh and quick to cry—breaks into tears, she draws him to her and kisses him, then holds his hand, and feels "extraordinarily at her ease with him and lighthearted," when:

> all in a clap it came over her, If I had married him, this gaiety would have been mine all day!
>
> It was all over for her. The sheet was stretched and the bed narrow.
>
> . . . He has left me; I am alone for ever, she thought, folding her hands upon her knee.
>
> Peter Walsh had got up and crossed to the window and stood with his back to her, flicking a bandanna handkerchief from side to side.

Masterly and dry and desolate he looked, his thin shoulder-blades lifting his coat slightly; blowing his nose violently. Take me with you, Clarissa thought impulsively, as if he were starting directly upon some great voyage.[82]

In contrast to Clarissa's unspoken romantic impulse, Peter responds to Clarissa quite demonstratively:

"Tell me," he said, seizing her by the shoulders. "Are you happy, Clarissa? Does Richard—"
The door opened.
"Here is my Elizabeth," said Clarissa, emotionally, histrionically perhaps.[83]

Peter Walsh's Regrets

Even after all the years, Peter Walsh's regret over Clarissa's rejection of him has the unambivalent sting of a fresh wound. He and Clarissa have been reminiscing about the past when he thinks:

it almost broke my heart too, he thought; and was overcome with his own grief, which rose like a moon looked at from a terrace, ghastly beautiful with light from the sunken day. I was more unhappy than I've ever been since, he thought. And as if in truth he were sitting there on the terrace he edged a little towards Clarissa; put his hand out; raised it; let it fall. There above them it hung, that moon.[84]

Sometimes she too wants to keep reminiscing:

Do you remember the lake? she said, in an abrupt voice, under the pressure of an emotion which caught her heart, made the muscles of her throat stiff, and contracted her lips in a spasm as she said "lake".
. . .[85]
She looked at Peter Walsh; her look, passing through all that time and that emotion, reached him doubtfully; settled on him tearfully; and rose and fluttered away, as a bird touches a branch and rises and flutters away. Quite simply she wiped her eyes.
"Yes," said Peter. "Yes, yes, yes," he said, as if she drew up to the surface something which positively hurt him as it rose. Stop! Stop! he wanted to cry. For he was not old; his life was not over; not by any means. He was only just past fifty.[86]

At this point Peter takes out his old pocketknife and clenches it in his fist—for him a sign of emotion displaced. He finds remembering staggeringly painful. Clarissa mourns the anticipated emptiness of the years remaining to her; Peter quarrels with the same expectation.

The Ironic Stance Toward Regret in Mrs. Dalloway

Beginning with the choice of metaphors, *Mrs. Dalloway* represents a rich example of an ironic experience of regret. None of Woolf's images (except for the arrow lodged in the heart) is on a sufficiently grand scale to warrant the designation of romantic or tragic. Neither are they ameliorative, or comic. Instead, their modesty of scale and ambiguity of emotional connotation places them in the ironic mode. Permeating this book is the ironic vision of life as an ambiguous matter in which loss of opportunity is "entailed by every choice."[87]

Second, there is never a sense in which time is viewed as a cyclical phenomenon; instead, time is viewed linearly, very much as a "progression toward death without rebirth."[88] This is particularly the case with Clarissa, who seems most clear-sighted and accepting—perhaps even morbidly welcoming—of this fact. But it is also the case with Peter, whose fruitless quarrels against middle age testify to his conviction of the irreversibility of age.

Moreover, in *Mrs. Dalloway* there are few or no certainties, absolutes, clear divisions between good and bad, heroes and villains. The two major characters, Clarissa Dalloway and Peter Walsh, come across as attractive individuals who nevertheless have their faults. Their choices too are portrayed as mixed in motive and in outcome. We also see the ironic ascription of conflict and misery to internal failings, splits, ambivalences, and polarities—particularly in the case of Clarissa Dalloway, who is torn by her needs for unquestioning approval, support, and tranquility (offered by Richard) versus her needs for challenge, excitement, and emotional engagement (offered by Peter) versus her need for a comfortable intimacy that seems most fulfilled in her friendships with other women. Furthermore, there is never a suggestion that one might overcome these inner divisions simply through the exercise of reason. A final characteristic of an ironic vision—that of ironic detachment—plays itself out in the character of Clarissa, but not in that of Peter, who in this respect is a far more emotionally involved, and thus romantic, character. Indeed, this very characteristic of Peter's is one of the things that she finds most devastatingly attractive, particularly in contrast to her own—and her husband's—more arid detachment.

Woolf's Metaphors for Regret

Virginia Woolf has Clarissa Dalloway compare regret to "an arrow sticking in her heart"[89] and to "a clap," as of thunder.[90] Metaphors articulated by Peter Walsh include "a sleeper jolting against him in a railway carriage,"[91] "time flapping on the mast,"[92] looking into the "glassy depths,"[93] and "grief, which rose like a moon looked at from a terrace, ghastly beautiful with light from the sunken day."[94] What do these metaphors reveal about the nature of regret?

The first two metaphors, those spoken by Clarissa, possess at once a certain banality and a certain surprisingly incommensurable feature—in that an arrow sticking in one's heart for all those years suggests an (improbably) chronic state, whereas a clap (as of thunder?) suggests suddenness. However, this contradiction seems to depict a paradoxical truth—that such a regret, while ordinarily in a quiescent state, can at certain cues strike with great suddenness. In Clarissa's words, "suddenly it would come over her, If he were with me now what would he say?—some days, some sights bringing him back to her." In this case, it was Peter's tearful outburst and her response of kissing him that immediately preceded the "clap."

In contrast to the simpler, more matter-of-fact metaphors articulated by Clarissa, the tropes expressed by Peter are more rich, original, and evocative. The first two have in common an image of an irritating and recurring event: time flapping on a mast, and a sleeper jolting against him in a train. So in this novel regret is not only sudden, it is also a recurring irritant. Peter's other metaphors for regret are more agreeable and less stark than any of the others. It is not necessarily unpleasant to gaze into a glassy depth; and to look upon a ghastly beautiful moon from a terrace is ambivalently pleasant. Together they suggest that consciousness (looking) is a positive good, even if the object of consciousness is beautiful only in a ghastly manner.

Other Ironic Metaphors for Regret

Most brief metaphors are not the ideal form in which to express the complex view of regret that is the ironic. Poetry, though it resists paraphrase, is better equipped to do so.

In *Four Quartets* T. S. Eliot expresses ironic regret that is both aware of and yet detached from the inevitable ambiguities, uncertainties, and lost opportunities of life:

> Footfalls echo in the memory
> Down the passage which we did not take
> Toward the door we never opened
> Into the rose-garden. My words echo
> Thus, in your mind.
>   But to what purpose
> Disturbing the dust on a bowl of rose-leaves
> I do not know.[95]

This excerpt manifests a number of elements of the ironic stance. Life is an enormous echoing mansion with so many doors to so many passages that it is impossible to explore them all. Memory is a compound—dust on a bowl of rose-leaves. Given this state of affairs, regret (footfalls echoing in an unexplored passage) is a disturbing, inevitable, possibly futile, though not catastrophic, experience.

A Literary Portrayal of Regret in a Mixed Mode

Anne Tyler's Pulitzer-prize-winning *Breathing Lessons* takes place during one day in the life of a middle-aged couple, Ira and Maggie Moran. In his own eyes, Ira at 50 years old "had never accomplished one single act of consequence."[96] Maggie spends much of the book desperately trying to arrange the reconciliation of her son Jesse and her daughter-in-law Fiona. Both Ira and Maggie have their regrets; but they have very different ways of perceiving the world and thus of dealing with their regrets. In a gender reversal of Clarissa Dalloway and Peter Walsh, Maggie lives out the romantic form of regret and Ira embodies the more "realistic," ironic form.

Even after seven years, Maggie has not accepted her son's failed marriage and her resulting separations from her daughter-in-law and granddaughter. The book's action takes place, significantly, on the eve of her younger child's departure for college, which will result in an empty nest for Maggie and Ira. Rather than sit at home mourning her losses and nursing her regrets (like the Underground Man), Maggie's way is to use her well-furnished fantasy life as a goad to take bold action to restore what is lost and to redeem what is regretted. By intrusively attempting to bring about Jesse and Fiona's reunion, she is acting out her indomitable belief in undoing, restoration, and reconciliation. Maggie's wishful fantasies about repairing her broken world nearly get the best of her and her loved ones.

Ira too has his regrets, notably concerning his failure to have realized his youthful dream to be a doctor. This aspiration of Ira's was sidetracked when, just as Ira had registered at the university, his father suddenly announced that, due to a heart condition, he could no longer continue to work. Ira responds in the desired way by taking over his father's picture-framing business in order to support his father and his two nonfunctioning sisters—Dorrie, who is mentally retarded, and Junie, an agoraphobic. Ira feels trapped, a feeling that is mirrored in the weather during a remembered outing with his family to Baltimore's Harborplace on his only day off:

> the view was nothing but opaque white sheets and a fuzzy-edged *U.S.S. Constellation* riding on a cloud, and Harborplace was a hulking, silent concentration of vapors.
>
> Well, the whole trip ended in disaster, of course. Junie said everything had looked better on TV, and Ira's father said his heart was flapping in his chest, and then Dorrie somehow got her feelings hurt and started crying and had to be taken home before they'd set foot inside a pavilion. Ira couldn't remember now what had hurt her feelings, but what he did remember, so vividly that it darkened even this glaringly sunlit Texaco, was the sensation that had come over him as he stood there between his two sisters. He'd felt suffocated. The fog had made a tiny room surrounding them, an airless, steamy room such as those that house indoor swimming pools. It had muffled every sound but his family's close, oppressively familiar voices. It had wrapped them together, locked them in, while his sisters' hands dragged him down the way drowning victims drag down whoever tries to rescue them. And Ira had thought, *Ah, God, I have been trapped with these people all my life and I am never going to be free.* And he had known then what a failure he'd been, ever since the day he took over his father's business.[97]

Tyler's portrait of Maggie Moran may be about as close as we are going to get in the late-twentieth-century United States to a sympathetic portrayal of a romantic worldview of regret. In Maggie's mind regret is merely a temporary obstacle on the road to eventual triumph, if only the heroine dare to take fate into her own hands. What fuels Maggie is her romantic belief in the possibility of reconciliation, second acts, happy endings. She deeply believes that, because she, Ira, and her children are good persons, therefore their lives *must* turn out happily. In search of these felicitous outcomes, Maggie throws herself into action. The fact that Jesse and Fiona show no interest in reconciliation (independent of her manipulations) does not daunt Maggie, a true believer in her ability to effect romantically discontinuous changes of fortune.

Carefully balancing Maggie's romanticism in this novel is Ira's decidedly nonromantic stance. For Ira, life's central problem is not the romantic one of how to achieve triumphant victory over adversity but the ironic one of how to "gain some perspective on the chaos, ambiguities, and contradictions of human living."[98] His characteristic way of gaining perspective is through emotional distancing and disengagement. Once when he had let Maggie get him all involved and distressed about an incident with their daughter that turned out to be entirely benign, Ira had felt "ridiculous. He'd felt he had spent something scarce and real—hard currency."[99] (The financial metaphor will reappear in Chapter 5 when we take up regret in the context of the technology of decision.) In stark contrast to Maggie, Ira knows in his bones that his and Maggie's miseries represent the usual lot of mixed blessings, compromises, and trade-offs that life has to offer. He knows too that their miseries, as Steiner expresses it, "can neither be fully understood nor overcome."[100]

Ultimately it is not Maggie's romanticism but Ira's ironic acceptance that prevails in the finest part of this book, its tender close. In the last paragraph of *Breathing Lessons* Ira has finally convinced Maggie to cease plotting how to make happen in her children's lives what she wishes. Even as he continues a game of solitaire, Ira holds Maggie while she thinks:

> He had passed that early, superficial stage when any number of moves seemed possible, and now his choices were narrower and he had to show real skill and judgment. She felt a little stir of something that came over her like a flush, a sort of inner buoyancy, and she lifted her face to kiss the warm blade of his cheekbone.[101]

There may exist no unconflicted romantic stance toward regret in these ironic times. After all, it is only a "little stir of something"— no great romantic bolt of lightning—that comes over Maggie. As a couple, Maggie and Ira have perhaps started to abandon the dissociation of thought and feeling with which they have up to now encountered their regret. They seem to have made a good start in the process of fusing thought and emotion, which will eventually bring them to the better state of felt thought.

As sets of deep, fundamental values and beliefs about reality which are often taken for granted, often tacit, these worldviews may have as much or more to do with how we experience regret as do the regretted matters themselves, the subject of the next chapter.

4

Regrets? I've Had a Few: What We Regret Most

Okay. So you overslept this morning. You had no time for breakfast. You missed one bus by seconds and had to wait a half hour for the next in a driving rain. Your work bores you to tears. Your kids are sassy and your spouse preoccupied. If only aging didn't mean creeping weight gain and physical afflictions. You should have gotten that degree. In other words, you've had a few regrets.

Some emotional states and some moods are apparently experienced as objectless feelings, as in "I feel blue [anxious, mad, etc.] but not about anything in particular."[1] But it is probably more usual for feelings, particularly regret, to come with identifiable referents, as in "I regret not having gotten that degree." This chapter is about those referents or objects of regret. In principle, anything at all that anyone cares about can be regretted—meaning that regrets are probably as common, numerous, varied (and chilling?) as the proverbial snowflake. This chapter turns this supposition into two related questions: How widespread an experience is regret? And: What kinds of things do people commonly regret?

Perhaps because of some theorists' tendencies to disparage the particularities of "mere" content (in contrast to supposed universals like "mechanism" or "process"), empirical research on these questions is sparse. Furthermore, even when people are questioned about regret, we may tend to be less than completely honest with ourselves and investigators about something so "negative." But in light of an empirical study that found regret to be the second most common of 20 emotions to come up in everyday conversation,[2] it clearly merits more research attention. In this chapter I draw on every possible source of information, including empirical surveys, fiction, and nonfiction, to sketch out what is known about the varieties of regret. Many of the regrets touched on here will be examined in further depth and from different perspectives in subsequent chapters.

The Incidence and Content of Regret

Though we would like to live without regrets, and sometimes proudly insist that we have none, this is not really possible, if only because we are mortal.

—JAMES BALDWIN

To my knowledge the first systematic effort capable of finding out whether there is empirical support for Baldwin's assumption of the universality of regret occurred in 1949. That year a Gallup poll asked a national sample of adults the following question designed to address their regrets[3] for personal mistakes:

> Everybody makes a mistake now and then. Will you tell me what you consider to be the biggest mistake of your life so far?[4]

In 1953 another Gallup poll asked a national sample of Americans the following less pointed question also designed to address their regrets:

> Generally speaking, if you could live your life over again, would you live it in much the same way as you have, or would you live it differently? If differently: What would you do differently?[5]

A question almost identical to the one posed in the 1953 poll was asked again in the early 1960s of a national sample of adults;[6] in the early 1980s of three different samples of adults by a colleague and myself;[7] and in the late 1980s of a sample of over 300 adults[8].

The proportion of people who say they have some regrets typically ranges between 35 and 65 percent, depending on who is asked, and when. In response to the 1949 poll, 69 percent of the sample specified at least one regret, with only 23 percent saying "Don't know" and only 8 percent saying "No big mistakes, only small ones." A lower 39 percent of the men and 35 percent of the women acknowledged in response to the 1953 poll that they would live their life differently in some way. In response to the 1965 poll, the proportion of the national sample who acknowledged regrets rose nearly to the 1949 level of 64 percent.[9] Fifty-four percent of a sample of adults studied by Jean Manis and myself acknowledged some regrets.[10] (In a pilot study carried out by Richard Kinnier and Arlene Metha, an enormous 97 percent of the 300 adults acknowledged life regrets.[11] However, this sample consisted mostly of graduate students and their friends and relatives, thus limiting its generalizability.)

In all these surveys people's single most common regret centered on their *education*. In 1949 twenty-two percent, in 1953 13.5 percent, and in 1965 43 percent of the national samples said they had not obtained enough education and if they had it to do over, they would get more.[12] Even in quite well-educated samples, from 39 percent[13] to 69 percent[14] mentioned educational regrets.

Educational regrets have also made an appearance or two in literature. In *Breathing Lessons* there is Ira Moran's regret over his failure to have gone on to medical school immediately after high school. The protagonist of Hardy's *Jude the Obscure*, too, regrets a forgone education—as well as the early and unfortunate marriage that precluded the education.

Work-related regrets ran a distant second in two of the national polls and a close third in the other.[15] Eight percent, 9 percent, and 9 percent of the 1949, 1953, and 1965 national samples, respectively, said they had made a poor choice of occupation, and would choose a different occupation if they had it to do over.[16] In the Landman and Manis study, 20 percent of a sample of adults reported work-related regrets, the second most common category after education.[17]

I am aware of only one study that went beyond this general question to inquire about a specific occupation—that is, teaching. Perhaps not surprisingly, given the stresses of teaching and this society's failure to reward it with good salaries or prestige, half of the 691 elementary school teachers surveyed in the early 1980s said they would not become teachers again.[18] One of the more surprising occupational regrets I have ever come across is the one John Adams expressed to his son: "If I were to go over my life again I would be a shoemaker rather than an American statesman."[19]

To a greater extent than men, women in industrialized America have historically had occasion to regret not only which jobs they had but also the fact of working versus not working in a paid occupation. Especially after their childbearing years are over, some women do regret not having worked outside the home. Many of the women in the famous Terman sample of 1000 intellectually gifted individuals (born around 1910) reported in their sixties that if they had it to do over they would change the way they made their decisions about balancing work and family.[20] Although 41 percent of these women described themselves as having been primarily a homemaker, only 29 percent said they would make the same choice again. Instead, they reported that they would pursue meaningful employment outside the home, at least when not raising small children, rather than working primarily as a homemaker or at "just a job." Of course, it should be remembered that these were women who came of age before the women's movement but who were answering the question at the height of the movement and may have been influenced by social factors that shaped both their original choice and their later regrets in the observed directions. However, 61 percent of another sample of 1145 adult women of all ages also expressed regrets about having put off their career.[21] (These women were, however, also questioned at the height of the women's movement, in the late 1970s.)

Work-related regrets appear frequently in literature as well. Think again of Ira Moran's regret about having missed the education that would have afforded him the work life of a physician rather than that of a picture framer *(Breathing Lessons)*. In Henry James's *The Ambassadors*, too, the protagonist regrets, among other things, his paltry accomplishment as editor of the Woollett *Review*. The dying protagonist of Hemingway's "The Snows of Kilimanjaro" bitterly regrets all the literature he had put off writing. Ishiguro's butler-protagonist of *The Remains of the Day* battles a number of work-centered regrets: for having devoted himself to an employer of questionable ethics; for having placed his work above matters of the heart; and for having spent his life in an occupation that protected him from making his own decisions (and mistakes). In Kurosawa's *Ikiru*, the protagonist's regrets stem in part from the *manner* in which he has lived his work life—that is, spending more time avoiding than devoting himself to his work as a public servant.

Not surprisingly, given its importance and the frequency of its collapse, *marriage* emerges as the second or third most common area for regret in the national surveys. Ten percent of the 1949 Gallup sample reported that they had "made mistakes in marriage." Two percent of the men and 6 percent of the women polled in 1953 reported that if they had it to do over, they would avoid a mistake in marriage. Seven percent of those polled in 1965 said they would marry "differently, earlier, later, a different person, wouldn't have married."[22] Twenty percent of the sample of adults questioned by Landman and Manis reported marital regret, with most of them regretting having married too young.[23]

Oddly, regrets about *parenthood* did not figure in any of the national polls. But when Ann Landers asked her readers in 1976 "If you had it all to do over again, would you have children?" an enormous 70 percent of the 10,000 who responded to this wildly nonscientific poll said no.[24] Probably the truth lies somewhere between these two extremes. Fifty-five percent of the group of over 1000 women and 19 percent of the sample of men and women questioned by Landman and Manis reported some parental regrets.[25] In these samples regrets for having had children were rare, but regrets for having had children too early were common. On the other side, a quarter of a sample of 40 childless women reported regret for their childlessness.[26] Finally, contrary to the view of menopause as a regrettable loss of reproductive capacity, an interview study of 60 middle-aged heterosexual women found none of them regretting menopause.[27] Instead, these women said the cessation of menstruation "meant freedom from worry about pregnancy," among other favorable things.[28]

Fifty-five percent of a sample of 44 undergraduates I questioned reported *family*-related regrets, with a quarter of them regretting not having gotten along better with parents or siblings.[29] Eighteen percent regretted not spending more time with their family or not having "appreciated" them more. Eleven percent regretted having given their family a good deal of trouble. Another fairly frequent regret among this sample was their parents' divorces.[30]

Family-related regrets are perennial subjects of fiction and poetry. The regrets of children with respect to their upbringing are a frequent theme in literature, though unheard of in the polls. Marital regrets also show up often in literature. This is the central theme, for example, of Woolf's *Mrs. Dalloway,* as discussed in the previous chapter. The most crucifying regret of Dostoevsky's Underground Man concerns his having driven away Liza, whom he at one time viewed, realistically or not, as a possible marriage partner. Anne Elliot, Jane Austen's heroine in *Persuasion,* also comes to regret an early decision *not* to marry a particular person, and the playing out of this regret is the central issue in this character's life. In George Eliot's *Middlemarch,* Thomas Hardy's *Jude the Obscure,* and Anita Brookner's recent Booker-prize-winning *Lewis Percy,* the plots center on an early marriage that comes to be regretted. So does the dream of a patient of Freud's, as interpreted by Freud and the dreamer herself.[31]

So central is marital regret to the well-being of the married that it reverberates into other areas. It is evident in *Breathing Lessons* that certain strains in Ira and Maggie's pretty-good marriage fuel their continuing regrets over other matters. One senses that if their marriage were more satisfying, Ira could more readily shrug off his occupational regrets and Maggie her empty-nest regrets. At the end, there is a strong sense that their marriage has deepened, and that this will alleviate these other, perhaps displaced, regrets.

Literature shows love-related regret lingering to haunt people well into old age—and even at death's door. In Hemingway's "The Snows of Kilimanjaro" the dying man, Harry, lashes out at his wife, blaming her for his failure to write the literature he now never would. He regrets former wives, their quarrels, and not writing about both. In Tolstoy's "The Death of Ivan Ilyitch" the narrator at first blames his wife and children for his profound deathbed regret for the empty conventionality of his life. Even in old age, the protagonists of Ishiguro's *The Remains of the Day*, Beckett's *Krapp's Last Tape*, and Bergman's *Wild Strawberries* wrestle with regret for having given up the love of their younger years.

Regrets concerning one's children, though perhaps less commonly portrayed in literature than marital regrets, are not unknown. In *Breathing Lessons*, Maggie Moran's regrets center on her children, with a pivotal plot element involving her refusal to accept the divorce of her son. Perhaps even more grievous is Maggie's nearly mute regret regarding her relationship with her teenage daughter, who has for years spent most of her time at the home of a friend's mother whom Maggie resentfully refers to as "Mrs. Perfect." Significantly, this daughter is leaving home for college the day following the novel's action. Like Maggie Moran, the protagonist of *Mrs. Dalloway* suffers twinges of regret for apparently having "lost" her daughter to another woman's influence. One of the most aching regrets of Watanabe in Kurosawa's film *Ikiru* is the fact that his son, to whom he has selflessly devoted himself, fails to return his devotion. The whiskey priest of Graham Greene's *The Power and the Glory* rues his lack of presence and influence in his daughter's life. And of course Lear comes to profoundly regret his decision to disown Cordelia, his only genuinely loyal daughter.

In addition to the big four of education, career, marriage, and children, a variety of *other regrets* have emerged in the existing research. In Kinnier and Metha's sample, after education, most respondents regretted not having been sufficiently assertive (25 percent) or self-disciplined (17 percent), and not having taken more risks (17 percent).[32] Similarly, 8 percent of the 1949 Gallup sample reported that their biggest mistake in life was "lost opportunities, [being] afraid to take a chance"; this regret tied for third place with career mistakes. Other noticeable regrets (reported by 2 to 7 percent of the samples) were for business errors; saving too little money; place of residence; drinking, temper, personality problems; doing too little for others; and not having been more religious.[33]

There is a growing body of research concerning *medical decisions*, particularly the decision to undergo elective surgical sterilization. As some researchers acknowledge, "perhaps the most important of these issues [concerning surgical sterilization] involves the problem of regret."[34] According to reviews of the research,[35,36] most studies show a very low rate of regret (2 to 10 percent) for voluntary sterilization. A typical study found a 6 percent rate of regret (7 of 114 women) for elective female sterilizations.[37] Another found a low 2 percent rate of regret among 139 women questioned 2 to 36 months after laparoscopic tubal division.[38]

The evidence to date does not offer a definitive answer to the question of whether, as James Baldwin assumed, regret is universal. In the 1953 and 1965 national Gallup polls, 60 percent and 31 percent of respondents, respectively, said they would *not* live life any differently.[39] Whether this means they really had no regrets is uncertain, both because they were not directly queried about "regret" and because of the possibility of underreporting due to self-deceiving or self-presentational processes. The apparent discrepancy in the proportions of regret yielded across these two studies is also puzzling. One wonders whether it might reflect in part historical differences in reigning worldview. The particular question posed in both these polls asked respondents to imagine what they would do differently if they had it to do over. Perhaps the significantly higher rate of reporting such thoughts in 1965 than in 1953 grew out of the notorious romanticism of the sixties, with its hope for sudden, even revolutionary, change, and its penchant for fantasy, for questioning authority and the status quo, for imagining states counter to reality. In contrast, the greater *denial* of thoughts about what they would do differently expressed by the 1953 respondents may have been rooted in a more comic worldview, with its more complacent faith in gradual improvement and its relative discomfort with imagining states contrary to life's inevitable disharmonies.

Apart from regret for family of origin, there is another striking difference in what we learn about regret from literature versus research. Death has not once made an appearance as an object of regret in empirical surveys. But literary portrayals of regret occasioned by death seem fairly common: besides the passage from Baldwin quoted above, there are, for example, Bergman's *Wild Strawberries*, Hemingway's "The Snows of Kilimanjaro," Kurosawa's *Ikiru*, Lampedusa's *The Leopard*, and Tolstoy's "The Death of Ivan Ilyitch." Don DeLillo's protagonist in *White Noise* draws an explicit connection between regret and death: "The deepest regret is death. This is all I think about. There is only one issue here. I want to live."[40]

Surely the writers are right that death plays an absolutely central role in the experience of regret. If lives did not end, then mistakes and losses and limitations could always be repaired later. Inasmuch as it is death that renders such matters seriously regrettable, its omission from empirical research seems surprising. Even if those surveyed had not directly experienced its imminence, surely death always reverberates as a call in the background. Perhaps when people enter the role of respondent to scientific surveys, they tend to yield implicitly to the more comic, progressivist, action-oriented worldview of science (and of this culture, so enamoured of Horatio Alger stories), and put aside any propensity to take a tragic view. In contrast, writers of literature, even if not using the tragic genre, may be less likely to entirely suppress in their work their tragic worldview. In any case, this difference in what is learned from science and from literature argues once again for the value of paying attention to both.

Generic Categories of Regret

So far I have in this chapter highlighted the sorts of concrete, specific regrets that most often trouble people. This approach has, I hope, its own intrinsic interest. But there is also something to be said for grouping regrets in more generic categories. Doing so allows us to view regret from a different perspective, as if through a wide-angle lens.

Regrets Categorized by Agency

Regret can be sorted by agency—who or what dishes out the regrettable state of affairs: self, other, or circumstances. The role of personal agency in regret is a contested issue, as discussed in Chapter 2. For some, the proper targets of regret are *only* matters over which one lacks control.[41] For others, regret includes both matters over which one has and one lacks personal control.[42] My own inclination, as argued in the earlier chapter, is that although regret for matters entailing self-agency may prove more intense,[43] regret includes both conditions. I believe that this examination of what people report regretting bears out this conclusion. People do in fact regret matters in which agency is located in the self, others, impersonal circumstance, and some combination of these.

Self as Agent. If I make the mistake of buying a lemon of a used car without first having it checked out by a mechanic and without first checking the repair record of the make and model in question, my regret focuses on myself as agent of this decision. The employer who regretfully has to fire the incompetent employee experiences regret in which the self is the agent.

Literary examples of regret in which the self is agent abound, including: Pip's regrets concerning his ill treatment of his family and his benefactor *(Great Expectations)*; the Underground Man's regrets for having abused and driven away Liza *(Notes from Underground)*; Strether's regrets for having lived an overly constrained youth *(The Ambassadors)*; Clarissa Dalloway's sometime regrets for her choice of marital partner *(Mrs. Dalloway)*; Ira Moran's regrets for his lost dream of becoming a physician *(Breathing Lessons)*; Stevens's regrets for how he has lived his love and work life *(The Remains of the Day)*; and Watanabe's work regrets *(Ikiru)*. All these can be referred to as *agent* regret, inasmuch as they have to do with an undesirable or harmful turn of events brought about by the regretting agent.[44]

Character regret, by contrast, is a matter of being sorry for being a particular kind of person with a particular sort of character.[45] It concerns relatively long-term personal characteristics rather than discrete acts. Character regret overlaps conceptually with *status* regret, defined as regret for one's neglect or for one's state of being (e.g., chronic drug addiction or alcoholism) responsible for some misfortune.[46] Throughout this book I use the more inclusive term, character regret.

Character regret is what is at issue in Woody Allen's quip: "The one regret I have in life is that I'm not someone else." It is regret for having "the wrong stuff." Character regret is the main character in J. M. Barrie's play *Dear Brutus* as well, as expressed in this passage: "What really plays the dickens with us is something in ourselves. Something that makes us go on doing the same sort of fool things, however many chances we get."[47] Likewise, in the preface to *The Ambassadors*, James describes his protagonist, Lambert Strether, as suffering regret "for the injury done his character"[48] by his years of inhibition. In the novel itself Strether makes it clear that this injury was not imposed on him by anyone else but emerged from his own character; he thinks to himself, "He had not had the gift of making the most of what he tried."[49]

My choice of Dostoevsky's *Notes from Underground* as a primary source was based on Amelie Rorty's suggestion that the Underground Man is a prime literary example of character regret.[50] The Underground Man articulates a particularly intransigent version of character regret which entails:

> that you no longer have any way out, that you will never become a different man, that even if there were still time and faith enough to change yourself, you probably would not even wish to change; and if you wished, you would do nothing about it anyway, because, in fact, there is perhaps nothing to change to.[51]

As for empirical research on regret, it appears that most respondents are far less apt in a survey to allude to regrets for *being* a particular kind of person with a particular sort of character (character regret) than regrets for *doing* (or not doing) something (agent regret). Nevertheless, assuming that the respondents were referring to a habitual personal characteristic rather than a rare episode, a few examples of character regret did show up even in the survey studies: regret for personality and behavior problems, temper, lack of assertiveness, lack of self-discipline. The single most frequent instance of possible character regret in the national surveys was a third-place tie (with career regrets) in the 1949 Gallup poll: regret for "being afraid to take a chance." The fact that this category of regret was alternatively phrased in terms arguably more suggestive of agent regret (regret for "lost opportunities") shows the difficulty—without directly asking them—of inferring with precision to what people attribute their regretted decisions and outcomes.

Other as Agent. Not all regretted acts are one's own doing; some are others' doing. When citizens regret the acts of their government, when parents regret the acts of their children, and vice versa, whenever we regret the harmful acts of others, we are evidencing regret focused on another as agent. Beyond the very small number of women who attribute a regretted sterilization to having been pressured by a husband,[52] I have seen no other signs of this category of regret in the existing research. It is in evidence in literature, though. Pip's regret in *Great Expectations*, upon discovering the lowly status of his benefactor, centers on a state of affairs in which someone else is agent, as do the initial complaints against their wives of both Hemingway's and Tolstoy's dying protagonists.

Circumstance as Agent. Sometimes what we regret are matters in which neither we nor another person was an agent, but the "impersonal wind-shift forces of time and chance."[53] Notwithstanding his sardonic insinuation of personal responsibility, the impersonal forces of time are solely to blame in Ionesco's regrets concerning aging: "I can't quite explain to myself how I could allow myself to reach the age of 30, 35, 36. I don't understand how I could have failed to try to prevent this catastrophe."[54] The wind-shift forces of chance are to blame in Pip's fateful encounter with Magwitch, the terminal cancer of Kurosawa's protagonist, and the death on Mount Kilimanjaro of Hemingway's fictional writer.

A methodological caveat bears repeating here. Given the youthfulness of the research, it is as yet difficult to tell whether most survey-revealed regrets concern matters entailing the agency of self, others, circumstances—or some combination or interaction of these. The surveys do tell us that people commonly come to regret an inadequate education and an unsatisfying occupation or marriage. But at this point it remains unknown whether these regrettable decisions are or should be attributed primarily to the respondents themselves, others, or situational factors over which they had no control.

In a way, the phrasing of the research questions used in previous surveys of regret unfairly pulls for self-agency at the expense of others and circumstance: "*Everybody makes* a mistake now and then. What was the biggest mistake of your life?" and "What would *you* do differently?" In addition, this manner of framing the question may reflect the primacy in this culture (and thus in this culture's social scientists) of the idea of self-as-master-of-his-or-her-fate. A more neutral question—for instance, "What do you most regret about your life so far?"—might bring to light a different set of regrets. For example, people may assume personal responsibility for regretted decisions, but may also realize that some portion of accountability lies outside the sphere of their individual agency. Educational opportunities for some individuals are occluded due to *others* (e.g., parents who, like Ira Moran's father in *Breathing Les-*

sons, thwart their children's desires to go to college) or to *circumstances* over which they have no control (e.g., gender, race, economic straits, family imperatives, sociohistorical events, chance events, etc.). People seem aware at least at some level of the contributions of all these (self-as agent, self-as-character, others, and circumstances) to their regrets. In any case, no doubt the stuff of regret is *not* solely "circumstances beyond one's control."

Regrets Categorized by Object

Regrets can be categorized not only in terms of agency but in terms of object, that is, the whom-it-was-done-to or the what-was-done of regret. These differential perspectives yield generic categories of regret that, although different from one another, overlap with the categories just discussed.

Regrets in Which Oneself versus Someone Else Is the Object. Some regrets have oneself as their primary object; others have someone else as their primary object. Regretting the harm your spouse has done to *you* is the first type of regret; regretting the harm you have done to your *spouse* is the second. The predominance of these two types of regret probably varies across individuals and across cultures. As for the latter, research on emotion in general and on guilt (an emotional cousin of regret) in particular suggests that Americans may tend to experience and express more regrets in which the self is the object than non-Western peoples, who may experience and express more regrets in which someone else is the object.[55] Similarly, in non-Western cultures, emotions often point to social interactions, not internal states.[56]

Unhappy Life Events. As discussed in Chapter 2, dictionary definitions of regret tend to include both losing good things and gaining bad things. Although these frequently amount to two sides of the same coin, at times one is highlighted over the other. Losing one's early love, as Peter Walsh did in *Mrs. Dalloway*, better represents a good lost; buying a lemon of a car better represents a misfortune gained.

  In studying regret in college students, I have also seen evidence of both shadings. Among the good things lost as specified by a sample of 149 college students were these: estrangement from members of one's family due to a quarrel; breaking up with a boyfriend or girlfriend; and losing touch with friends. Their regrets for misfortunes gained included: suffering an auto or other type of accident; gaining a lot of weight; having incompatible roommates; and launching a relationship with an insanely possessive guy.

Mistakes. Mistakes—defined as harmful rash, impulsive, or foolish acts—are unhappy life events with a decided tinge of self-recrimination. Mistaken marriages litter life and literature, including those already mentioned in *Middlemarch, Jude the Obscure, Lewis Percy,* "The Snows of Kilimanjaro," and ambivalently, *Mrs. Dalloway.*

Not yet having been married (most of them), the college students I have asked mentioned regret for other mistakes, such as: blowing up with anger at a group of friends; continuing an athletic activity despite an injury; hanging up on someone; and accidentally hurting someone while horsing around. A horrifying real-life example of the latter is the regret of *Naked Lunch* author William S. Burroughs for the accidental fatal shooting of his wife in 1951 when she dared him to shoot a glass off her head while they were both drunk.[57]

Transgressions. Worse than mistakes, transgressions are forbidden, illegal, immoral, or questionably moral acts. The Underground Man's maltreatment of Liza and Pip's maltreatment of Joe, Biddy, and Provis were mistakes—foolish acts that proved harmful. But they were also transgressions in that they were acts whereby the actor knowingly harmed someone who did not deserve to be harmed.

Although guilt may arguably be the emotion more "appropriate" to transgressions, regret is also a frequent reaction to transgressions, according to my conceptual analysis (Chapter 2) and the report of college students. When I asked a group of 149 college students to describe some things they regretted, their catalogue included forbidden acts that they may have also felt guilty about, such as these: purposely frightening a young sibling; starting a fire after ignoring their mother's command to stop playing with matches; calling a parent a nasty name; taking their parents' car for a forbidden spin; vandalizing a car; abusing drugs or alcohol; and cheating on a romantic partner.

Forgone Goods, Missed Opportunities. In a letter to Hugh Walpole, Henry James once wrote: "I think I don't regret a single 'excess' of my responsive youth—I only regret, in my chilled age, certain occasions and possibilities I didn't embrace."[58] In a short story titled "What He Was Like," William Maxwell had a diarist put it in decidedly non-romantic terms: "If I had my life to live over again—but one doesn't. One goes forward instead, dragging a cart piled high with lost opportunities."[59] "Likewise, when people were interviewed about their "experience of time," the single most common reference (82 percent of all responses) was to choices and limits, with the two often linked.[60] We can be only one person, live only one life, take only one road at a time. Still, we can dream. That is why the mere necessity of choosing sometimes elicits regret for that not chosen. Regret is accordingly not limited to matters so definite as misfortunes, mistakes, and transgressions. Shadowy unrealized matters such as forgone goods and missed opportunities also evoke regret.

Opportunities and goods forgone possess varying degrees of actuality. When Ira Moran in *Breathing Lessons* took on the burden of family responsibility and gave up his admission to a university where he had already paid the deposit, he was forgoing a very real opportunity. But even when what is given up is "only" a fantasy, a dream, a ghostly might-have-been, the resulting regret can be as real as the proverbial ton of bricks.

I am reminded of a high school senior who backed out on a planned trip with friends to visit College B after she had accepted admission at College A. She canceled the trip not due to lack of interest in College B or uncertainty about her decision to accept at College A; in fact, she very much wanted to join her friends and to see College B and was ecstatic about going to College A. She made her decision for the express purpose of avoiding a confrontation with regret for a forgone opportunity. Even Paul Newman, who by all accounts seems to have led a charmed life (due in part, as he himself admits, to the lucky accident of having been born with blue rather than brown eyes), expressed regret in his sixties over lost opportunities: "I'll never be a proper father or a great lover or an extraordinary boxer or a capable skier or an astronaut. Those are all things I'm missing."[61]

Sins of Omission. The poem "Something I've Not Done" by W. S. Merwin expresses how something even so apparently insubstantial as inaction can assume the substantiality of a creature that dogs you, climbs on your shoulders, takes away your breath, and demands finally that you add "its story" to your regrets:

Something I've not done
is following me
I haven't done it again and again
so it has many footsteps
like a drumstick that's grown old and never been used

In late afternoon I hear it come closer
at times it climbs out of a sea
onto my shoulders
and I shrug it off
losing one more chance

Every morning
it's drunk up part of my breath for the day
and knows which way
I'm going
and already it's not done there

But once more I say I'll lay hands on it
tomorrow
and add its footsteps to my heart
and its story to my regrets
and its silence to my compass.[62]

College students I have questioned also listed a number of regrets that seem to fit the category of omissions: not studying hard
enough (the single most frequent regret of all in this sample); not
spending enough time with relatives; not trying harder to make
more friends; not having the courage to ask someone out or to de-
fend a friend against attack by others.

An obvious question suggested by this categorization is: Which
is regretted more—action or inaction? This is one question already
addressed by research. Oddly, it is also one of those questions in
which empirical research and folk wisdom have so far yielded different answers.

So far, empirical research has clearly supported the hypothesis
of greater regret (and in two cases also greater rejoicing) following
acts than non-acts, given equal outcomes. At least three different
experiments have found this pattern, including one of my own.[63]
The stories in my study, modeled on vignettes used by Kahneman
and Tversky,[64] concerned: (1) students who either acted or failed
to act to change their section of a college course; (2) workers who
either acted or failed to act to change jobs; and (3) a family who
acted or failed to act to change their vacation plans. In the regret

conditions, the outcomes were negative—a D in the course, a permanent layoff, and 10 days of rain during the vacation, respectively. Participants were asked who felt more regret about their choice, the actor or the non-actor (though of course these were not explicitly so described). For all three situations, most respondents imagined greater regret following action than inaction. On the average, 80 percent of respondents felt that the person who acted would regret a negative outcome more than the one who failed to act[65]— a result that is typical for the action/inaction research so far.[66]

These findings fly in the face of the economic decision model: since the consequences of the two states of affairs (action and inaction) are identical, our appraisal of them also ought to be identical. But the psyche has its own logic that is not the logic of economic decision theory.

Kahneman and Miller have proposed one possible psychological explanation for why action may produce greater regret than inaction.[67] According to this explanation, the intensity of regret for an outcome will depend on the ease with which alternative outcomes are mentally constructed. These authors suggest that it is relatively easy to imagine an alternative to a regretted action (i.e., inaction) that restores the antecedent conditions to a more desirable state. In contrast, given inaction, it is relatively more difficult to imagine the alternative of action. Therefore, the undesirable situation in which the alternative is easier to imagine (that involving action) will be regretted more than the situation in which the alternative is more difficult to imagine (that involving inaction).[68]

An alternative (though still a cognitive) explanation of the findings of greater regret following action than inaction is salience. Acts are often more noticeable, or more salient, than non-acts. The well-documented tendency to overnotice acts and undernotice non-acts[69] may explain the frequently observed tendency to experience greater regret for acts than for non-acts. A third possible explanation centers on our inertia and attachment to the status quo. Keeping the status quo generally requires no action; changing the status quo does. So if we take action and the status quo changes for the worse, our regret is keener than if we had taken no action and the status quo changes for the worse.[70] Whatever the psychological process, research so far finds unfortunate events preceded by action more regrettable than the same events preceded by inaction.

The popular press tells a diametrically opposing story about whether action or inaction is regretted more. A brief article by Carol Tavris published in *Vogue* in 1988 reported that a survey of 48 women found that only one regretted having pursued a life dream, while almost all the women who had not pursued their life dream regretted it.[71] Likewise, a 1985 *Glamour* article titled "The Road Not Taken" declared: "most of us don't regret what we have done so much as what we haven't. . . . I'm sorry there aren't more of me to marry some of the men I've cared about. And there are cities I wanted to live in but haven't, and babies I didn't have, and careers I would have liked to explore."[72] Apparently, the folk psychology in which inaction is intensely regretted is not limited to women. In his 1990 memoir *A Life on the Road*, for example, journalist Charles Kuralt included a chapter titled "Regrets," in which he relates three regrets of his, at least two and arguably all three of which represent regret over actions not taken.

The first regret Kuralt describes is for having sped away from a man he encountered running toward him on a terrifyingly godforsaken road at the top of the Andes. Kuralt drove away, thinking that the man was a gun-wielding bandit; actually the man was a fish-wielding peasant hoping to make a tasty sale. Kuralt realized his mistake just as he was lurching away in his car, but he didn't stop:

> I could have gone back. I could have apologized, and bought the fish . . . the good memories are all of stopping and staying awhile. I realize I've always driven too fast through life, carrying in my baggage too much impatience and apprehension, missing too many chances, passing too many good people in the dust.[73]

The second regret Kuralt recounts is having failed to follow up on the invitation of Bill Magie, a 76-year-old Minnesota north woods guide, to join him in a six-week canoe trip to visit some favorite lakes one last time. A year or two after the invitation, Bill Magie died, never having made that last long trip. Kuralt says:

> I wish with all my heart I had made the long canoe trip with Bill Magie. I can't remember what I was doing from the Fourth of July to the end of August the summer he wanted to go fish every night and listen to the loons and see those distant lakes one more time. What could I have been doing that would have been better than that?[74]

The scene of Kuralt's third regret was a fleabag hotel in West Virginia. On the way to Kuralt's room, the bellboy took Kuralt unasked to another room, where a young, pretty, and very naked woman named Sally offered herself to him. Kuralt declined the offer and went on to his own room. Later that night the fire alarm went off. Kuralt called the desk, only to be told by the manager to go back to sleep, that it was nothing. Soon Sally came running and shouting down the hall, warning the residents to get out, that there was a fire. As he stood outside in the rain waiting for the fire department to extinguish the fire, Kuralt thanked Sally (who was now wrapped in a bedspread) for saving his life. "She smiled. She said, 'Are you still sure you don't want to get under here with me?' " Kuralt reports that he kissed her chastely on the cheek, and left, looking for breakfast. He goes on:

> This was about thirty years ago. Harry Golden, the old editor and author who lived in my hometown, told me when I was a young newspaper reporter, "When you get to be my age, sonny, all you ever think about are the women you could have gone to bed with and didn't." I laughed then.[75]

Kuralt's first example shows how difficult it often is to distinguish between acts and omissions. His words "passing too many good people in the dust" express a regret-for-action; but the words "I could have gone back. I could have apologized, and bought the fish" express a regret-for-omission. Kuralt's last two regrets, however, are clearly for something not done. They are also of interest for suggesting a couple of factors that may specifically give rise to regret for inaction: irreversibility of outcome, especially very serious outcomes like death, and increasing age (or a more distant perspective)[76] of the regretter. The apparent discrepancy between popular and empirical accounts of regret for action versus inaction may be cleared up as further research focuses on factors like these.

Kuralt's Andes regret raises another issue related to action and omission. The reason Kuralt did not stop to check out the man running toward him with something in his hand was because of the perceived risk. Almost immediately, Kuralt regretted having sped away from what turned out to be no risk at all. In the Kinnier and Metha study,[77] as well, it was common for the participants to express regret for not having taken more risks. Regret for being afraid to take a chance or for not having taken more risks might reasonably be thought of as an example of regret for *inaction*, for a sin of omission. A number of the regrets I have placed in other categories above could likewise be framed in terms of omission. For instance, regret for having obtained insufficient education (agent regret) might in some cases be tantamount to regret for "being afraid to take a chance" (or regret for inaction, or even character regret as well). Ionesco shows an intermingling of regret for sins of omission and character regret in the following: "I have burning regrets when, sometimes, I realize that I have tied myself down, that I have bound my hands, put leaden chains on my feet."[78,79]

In summary, it appears that regret is a common, if not a universal, experience. Furthermore, there is remarkable consistency in the regrets of otherwise diverse sets of individuals. Particularly striking is the high incidence of regret for not having continued one's education beyond a particular point, and for marrying and having children too early. It may be that these regrets are as prominent as they are because they prematurely close off a world of other options. In addition, regrets concerning failed or unsatisfying human relationships are unfortunately common.

If Freud was right that our well-being depends preeminently on love and work, then it stands to reason that regret will likely center on love and work gone wrong. For of all that has gone wrong in our lives, we will regret most those things we most care about. To a sizable extent, this survey of regret in literature and science bears out the Freudian prediction. Both literature and empirical research show us regretting matters concerning parents, spouses, children, and other loves. They also show us regretting matters concerning our work, especially the educational path leading to it. But we are also vulnerable to regret over just about anything we care about.

As a result of this exploration, I now read the piece that I referred to on the first page of the Prologue differently than I did the first time I read it. When I first saw it, it spoke to my fears of living life in such a way that I would come to regret my missed opportunities: "I'd try to make more mistakes next time . . . If I had it to do over again, I would go places, do things and travel lighter than I have." Now I know more clearly that it is impossible to escape regret altogether—if not regret for inaction, then regret for action. Now anyone over twelve who claims never to have had any regrets has, I believe, some explaining to do. Have such people made no mistakes? Is there nothing they care about? Have they had all their dreams realized? Are they in a state of massive denial? Are they lying? Have they so firmly resolved their previous regrets that they have forgotten they ever had any? Have they no sense of the tragedy or irony of life?[80] For insofar as time is irreversible and insofar as ambiguity, uncertainty, unresolvable dilemmas, and death are inescapable, regret appears to me the inevitable, universal human experience Baldwin thought it to be.

5

The Logic of Regret: Its Role in Decision Making

An acquaintance who makes his home in the humanities expressed astonishment when he heard me use the phrase that titles my Prologue, "the science and humanity of regret." The humanity of regret he understood. But science of regret? What could that possibly mean? he asked. The answer to this question is to be found in good part in this chapter, which first details major theories of decision making (philosophical, psychological, economic), all of them challenged by the existence of regret. In this chapter I also take up certain serious problems with the standard theory of decision making, plus relevant arguments against the irrationality of regret. Then I suggest how adding regret to decision-making models helps remedy those problems.

Regret in the Classic Decision Models

The Socratic Model

"To know the better is to do the better." "We do what we think is the best thing to do." "The perceived better attracts more than the perceived worse." "No one voluntarily does what she or he believes to be the worse." The principle articulated in these statements, the Socratic principle, has guided certain philosophical perspectives on ethics and decision-making since antiquity. Compare it with this statement: "No one voluntarily acts against his or her current perceived interests." This proposition is *not* the Socratic principle; it is a statement of psychological egoism.[1] In the cynically knowing late-twentieth-century, the latter proposition is likely to strike all but the most militantly optimistic as "patently true"— and the former expressions of the Socratic principle as "patently false."[2]

Paul the Apostle is not alone in finding it self-evident that "The good that I would, I do not; but the evil that I would not, that I do." Nor is it only the world's Hitlers, Idi Amins, and Pol Pots who undermine the plausibility of the Socratic principle. We all violate it. If we do not unflinchingly choose to do the worse, we reluctantly give in to what philosophers call *akratic* acts, acts that due to "weakness of will" go against our better judgment.

We violate the Socratic principle not only when it comes to the moral or "right thing to do" but also when it comes to the pragmatic and purely self-interested matter of choosing what will satisfy us the most. Some of the idle rich regularly choose leisure in hopes of attaining pleasure; but instead they get boredom. Some of the unemployed poor regularly choose addictions or crime, hoping for escape, stimulation, or pleasure; but instead they find they have contributed to their own self-destruction.[3]

For the present purposes, the validity of the Socratic principle concerns me less than the relationship between the Socratic principle and regret. In fact, it is in part the very existence of regret that undermines the Socratic principle. If the Socratic principle is right, then people would never suffer regret. If we always do what we believe to be the good, then it is illogical, even irrational, to feel sorry about anything we do.

But what is meant by *rationality*, a concept notorious for its multiple, surplus, and fuzzy meanings? Helmut Jungermann has cleared away much of the conceptual underbrush by distinguishing three types of rationality: substantive, procedural, and formal.[4] In everyday usage, rationality typically concerns how "realistic" are one's values and beliefs, or how grounded they are in reality; Jungermann calls this *substantive* rationality. Decision theory has more often focused on another sense of the term—*procedural* rationality—defined as the extent to which individuals engage in a diligent and unbiased search for information upon which to base their decisions. Another use of the term (central to disciplines like psychology, philosophy, and economics) centers on the logical coherence or internal consistency of judgments—*formal* rationality. The contributions of each type of rationality to a given judgment or decision do not always relate to one another in a simple manner.

Consider a paranoid schizophrenic's decision to shoot young women with long brown hair—due to their perceived inherent evil as revealed to him by the voice of his dog. This judgment might be high in formal rationality (perfectly consistent with his system of beliefs and values), while simultaneously low in substantive rationality (inconsistent with external reality), and also low in procedural rationality (in his relying on a dog as the sole source of information on this matter).

The judgment facing Hoess at the door to the gas chamber did not lack formal rationality—the extent to which his decision matched his principles or the extent to which he was successfully maximizing his subjectively calculated individual and collective expected utilities. It did and he was. Its defects had more to do with his twisted versions of substantive rationality (what he desired) and procedural rationality (how he made his decision—that is, by blindly deferring to authority and stifling all his "softer emotions").

These distinctions apply not only to psychotics and Nazis. Consider the angry employee who impulsively decides to quit a job. This decision may be high in formal rationality (if it matches his assessment of the best thing to do), and it may be high in substantive rationality (if he has good reason to believe that a better job is in the offing elsewhere). Or the decision may be high in formal rationality (for the above reason) but low in substantive rationality (if he holds an inflated expectation of his capacity to replace the less-than-ideal job with a more ideal one). In either case, if he refuses to put off quitting long enough to obtain an accurate estimate of the likelihood of getting a more satisfactory job, the decision is deficient in procedural rationality. Rationality by any other name is not necessarily rationality.

To return to the topic of regret and the Socratic principle: regret implies, contrary to the Socratic principle, that people sometimes think that they do what is bad, or fail to do what is good. There are two camps on these related issues: those who accept regret and reject the Socratic principle versus those who accept the Socratic principle and reject regret.

Among the latter, philosopher C. G. Luckhardt presents an illustrative example something like the following to support the claim that regret does *not* invalidate the Socratic principle.[5] On his way home from work one Friday evening, Mr. Miller spots in the road a large canvas bag that car after car has been swerving to avoid. He screeches to a stop, and in a hurry to get home on time, he grabs the bag and drives on. At home, he opens the bag and finds $40,000 in cash. Later that night he learns that a local bank has just been robbed of $40,000 and is offering a $10,000 reward for the return of the money. All weekend, this generally decent, honest, and sane fellow ponders whether or not to return the money first thing Monday morning when the bank opens.

Some, like Luckhardt[6] and Hampshire,[7] argue that if, although he is capable of it, Miller fails to return the money on Monday, it is because on Monday he thinks he ought not. If on Monday he also says that he regrets not returning the money, the logical question to be put to Miller is: "Then why don't you return it?"[8] According to Luckhardt, "there seems to be no answer he [Miller] can give"[9]—at least no answer that is formally rational, in the sense of being coherent with his action. Therefore, a reasonable conclusion is that Miller does not really regret his action; he really wants to keep the money. By this reasoning, there is no such thing as coherent and genuine regret for voluntary, concurrent conduct. (With respect to regret for *past* conduct, everyone agrees that it poses no threat to the Socratic principle, because it merely shows that people can change their minds about what is best.) Sartre also attacks the genuineness of regret, asserting that, due to the individual's inescapable responsibility for choice, regret is simply a case of bad faith.[10] In sum, go these lines of argument, the truth of the Socratic principle is secure, because genuine, coherent regret (i.e., regret that entails the admission of willingly acting in a way that one truly knows at that time to be in opposition to the good) simply does not occur in sane persons.

But there is the other camp—those who argue that coherent, genuine regret does exist, and therefore the Socratic principle is wrong. Philosopher William Jacobs provides an illustrative example (suddenly and improbably dated by the recent fall of Communism in the Soviet Union).[11] Natasha (who in the original example is bereft of a surname) is a dedicated Communist from the Soviet Union with a long family history of Communism. She goes abroad for the purpose of selling the crown jewels for famine relief. There she falls in love with a capitalist and, after a struggle with herself, gives him the jewels. She immediately regrets this act, returns to Russia, confesses, and willingly accepts punishment in Siberia.

Contrary to Luckhardt's assertion concerning the case of Miller, there *is* a sensible answer that Miller and Natasha might give someone who demands to know why, if they regret their acts, they don't just do the better thing—namely, "I regret being the kind of person who will not do the better thing." Thus even if a claim of regret for their *act* is incoherent and inauthentic, Miller and Natasha might experience character regret—coherent and genuine regret for who they are.[12] If so, these are paradigmatic examples of akrasia, or weakness of will. Miller and Natasha did not do what they believed *even at that time* was the good. The existence of akrasia and its resultant regret drive a rather large hole in the Socratic principle.[13] Similarly, the phenomenon of cognitive dissonance, which was discussed in an earlier chapter, undermines the Socratic principle: people do things against their better judgment all the time. We smoke, drink, eat to excess even though it is bad for our health and we know it.[14] Common experience then supports regret and fails to support the Socratic principle—as accurate descriptions of the human condition.

So does logic. As Jacobs[15] points out, to deny the possibility of genuine concurrent regret for voluntary acts is to reduce the Socratic principle to a tautology: "If I voluntarily do X, it is because I perceive X to be the good." The previous argument against regret is circular on this count. The circularity stems from the assumption of the primacy of behavior over judgment. (In modern versions of decision theory the blanket term *judgment* is often replaced with separate terms representing the two components of judgment relevant in that theory: *preference* and *beliefs* regarding likely outcomes.) Luckhardt is not alone in this assumption; many modern economists, philosophers, and psychologists share it, viewing behavior (the actual choice) as "revealed preference."

The decision to privilege behavior over judgment is not entirely without merit. If it were not true that people's acts (unless prevented or coerced) can be understood to point to their beliefs or judgments, then "words could always speak louder than actions."[16] However, if behavior *solely defines* judgment, then there is no way to falsify the Socratic (or any other "act-centered") principle.

A model of decision or ethics that hopes to describe the ordinary mortal, rather than a hypothetical "ideally rational" agent, needs not only to distinguish between act and judgment but also between judgments that are action-guiding and those that are not.[17] Consider again the example discussed earlier of the employer who fires an incompetent employee; regrets the act because it devastates the employee; yet would not undo the act, judging it to be the best thing to do.[18] This is not a case of akrasia. This is one of a myriad of decisions involving a *conflict* of judgments. Here the conflict is between an action-guiding judgment (it is right and good to fire her) and a non-action-guiding judgment (I regret firing her because of the harm it does her). As Stocker argues, it is "wrong-headed" to show a "one-eyed attention to what is to be *done.*"[19] Further, it is a "form of crassness . . . which asks only where the action is and gets its answer by looking only at the bottom line."[20]

Decision theory has, in my view, been stunted by the continuing influence of behaviorism in its thinking about such matters. Human beings are more than the sum of their behaviors. A right-headed theory of decision and ethics needs to consider more than behavior. As John Stuart Mill put it in the essay *On Liberty:* "It really is of importance, not only what men do, but also what manner of men they are that do it."[21]

An important implication of this view is that there is not necessarily a *psychological* contradiction between doing X, judging that X is the best thing to do, and judging that doing X is regrettable. Though this represents technically a case of formal irrationality, it is *not* a case of psychological incoherence. Nor is it necessarily a case of spurious regret or bad faith. It is a common instance of psychic conflict, rationally grounded in the very real complexity of the world and in the distinction between action-guiding and non-action-guiding judgment. More generally, genuine regret lodges itself in the spaces between act and character, act and judgment, and action-guiding and non-action-guiding judgment.

In sum, people who are substantively and procedurally rational sometimes fail to act in accordance with what they judge to be good, and sometimes do what they judge to be bad. Though this may be logically inconsistent, it is not necessarily psychologically irrational. We can experience coherent, genuine regret for our acts. We can coherently regret being the kind of person who acts in such and such a way. Or if the judgment about what is to be done is action-guiding and the judgment about what is regrettable is not, regret for the action is neither irrational nor incoherent. Regret is instead a defensible response to a world that inevitably presents decision makers with irreducible conflicts that at times require acting in opposition to one of their various judgments. A better decision model will recognize that neither the world nor most human beings work in obedience to bottom-line, behavior-centered theories.

The Standard Economic Decision Model

To understand modern orthodox decision theory, it helps to understand where it came from. The roots of modern economic decision theory run nearly as deep as those of the Socratic principle, going back at least as far as the philosopher Epicurus (c. 270), who formulated a hedonistic principle that identified the good with the pleasurable. In ethical hedonism, the normative principle is to do what will afford one the greatest pleasure. This idea was modified during the Enlightenment so that the good was no longer equated with pleasure. The central thesis of modern utilitarian economics defines ethical rationality as choosing so as to maximize the good. More specifically, modern utilitarianism (roughly synonymous with "optimal choice" theory, "rational choice" theory, and what I generically refer to as standard or classic decision theory[22]) demands that decisions be based entirely on calculations of *expected consequences*, as opposed to being based on tradition, dogma, rules, obligation, personal responsibility, intentions, or some other principle. In late-twentieth-century America, it has become virtually an article of political and economic faith that the best way to achieve the greatest good for the greatest number is by maximizing individual interests through the competitive free market or other such mechanisms.

Clearly, utility theory, in one or another of its forms, has for centuries played a major role in human thought and practice. All its modern forms are simply variants on a theme. By now utilitarian decision theory has achieved canonical status. In the estimate of a prominent economist-adherent of standard decision theory, this model has "become the dominant, and indeed, almost exclusive model of decision-making under risk in economics, operations research, philosophy, and statistical decision theory."[23] A psychologist-adherent agrees with this assessment and expands the list of disciplines in which the maximization principle plays the central role:

> Not just economics, but all the disciplines dealing with behavior, from political philosophy to behavioral biology, rely increasingly on the idea that humans and other organisms tend to maximize utility, as formalized in modern economic theory. . . . The scattered dissenters to the theory are often viewed as just that—scattered and mere dissenters to an orthodoxy almost as entrenched as a religious dogma.[24]

The more proximal origins of modern decision theory are found in the expected *value* principle: that one ought to choose the option with the highest expected value. Value is defined in objective, usually monetary terms. The expected value (EV) of outcome X is a combined, multiplicative function of the probability of X (p_X) and the monetary value of X (v_X). So in equation format, we can say that the:

Expected value of outcome X = probability of X × Monetary value of X

Or mathematically:
$$EV_X = p_X v_X$$

For example, if someone is asked which he or she would prefer—$6 outright or a lottery ticket with one chance in a thousand of winning $5000, the rational choice according to the EV principle is to take the $6, since the expected value of the lottery ticket is only $5 (0.001 times $5000). But if the choice is between the same ticket and $4, the ticket is the rational choice.[25]

Over the centuries, the assumption of objectivity in judging what is valuable and what is possible has gradually been replaced with the assumption of subjectivity. In the eighteenth century, Bernoulli's expected utility (EU) theory supplanted expected value (EV) theory.[26] Bernoulli replaced the earlier concept of value with the broader and more subjective concept of utility. Utility is "a subjective measure of the attractiveness of a possible outcome to the decision maker(s)."[27] Expected utility is mathematically defined as follows:

$$EU_X = p_X u_X$$

The EU model prescribes that options with the highest expected *utility* are to be chosen. An example of the use of utility rather than monetary value is spelled out below in the decision of Mrs. Russell.

Finally, in the mid-twentieth century, modern utility theory—subjective expected utility (SEU) theory—supplanted the EU model. The centerpiece of the final version of expected utility theory was the concept of subjective probabilities, sometimes called "personal" probabilities.[28] This important change recognizes that, unlike the toss of a coin or a die, many real-life situations involve probabilities that are not objectively knowable. In subjective expected utility theory, then, both probability and utility are defined subjectively. Subjective expected utility theory urges that, in the face of uncertainty, people should choose the option with the higher subjective expected utility. So compellingly rational and seemingly comprehensive is formal SEU theory that the psychologist and Nobel laureate in economics, Herbert Simon, has called it an "Olympian" model[29] and its development one of the "intellectual achievements of the first half of the twentieth century."[30]

Besides the centrality of expected consequences and a behavioral definition of preference, classic decision theory entails a number of other features specified as axiomatic by John von Neumann and Oskar Morgenstern.[31] One of these with direct implications for regret is transitivity. In this context, transitivity concerns the logical ordering or ranking of one's preferences. If I prefer A to B, and B to C, then logically I must prefer A to C. Because the implied relation "is better than" is transitive, it would be illogical and formally irrational (i.e., internally inconsistent) to prefer C to A. However, in the next part of this chapter, we will see that transitivity and other defining features of utility theory are in fact debatable rather than axiomatic.

The choices life confronts us with are rarely so straightforward as the choices between cash and lottery tickets discussed above. How then does SEU theory work in real-life decision making? Consider the decision problem (following an example provided by Hal Arkes and Kenneth Hammond)[32] faced by Mrs. Russell, a thirty-four-year-old woman with a life-threatening health problem who is independently told by three physicians that a difficult operation is available that has an approximately 60 percent chance of curing her and a 40 percent chance of killing her. Without the operation there is an 80 percent chance that her health problem will continue unchanged and a 20 percent chance that she will die in six months.[33] Should she have the operation or not?

This question can be systematically addressed by applying the subjective expected utility model. As defined by decision theory, the decision situation consists of three components. A decision is a "choice between two or more options or *acts*, each of which will produce one of several *outcomes*," depending on the *state of nature* (relevant physical and nonphysical conditions).[34] In this example, there are two possible courses of action, or options: operate and don't operate. There are four identifiable outcomes that could conceivably follow from these courses of action: cure, lingering problem, death with surgery, or death within six months. The probability of each of these outcomes, according to the best medical

knowledge available, is as described before. The patient can fill in
her own subjective utilities for each of these outcomes. Let's say
that when we ask her, Mrs. Russell, after talking it over with herself and her family, decides as follows: there is no (0.00) utility in
death immediately following an operation but some utility (0.10)
to death in six months with no surgery; she assigns moderate utility (0.60) to having the disease linger unchanged; and she assigns
the highest possible utility (1.00) to being cured. The following decision tree reveals the underlying structure to this decision:[35]

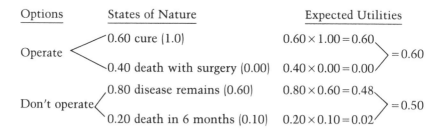

Options	States of Nature	Expected Utilities
Operate	0.60 cure (1.0)	$0.60 \times 1.00 = 0.60$
	0.40 death with surgery (0.00)	$0.40 \times 0.00 = 0.00$ = 0.60
Don't operate	0.80 disease remains (0.60)	$0.80 \times 0.60 = 0.48$
	0.20 death in 6 months (0.10)	$0.20 \times 0.10 = 0.02$ = 0.50

Because it makes explicit the subjective likelihoods and subjective utilities associated with each option, this decision tree also
reveals the formally rational answer to this dilemma. The "operate" option has a higher total subjective expected utility (.60 + .00)
than the "don't operate" option (.48 + .02). Therefore, Mrs. Russell
should have the operation.

This example represents a typical instance of decision analysis,
a relatively new technology of decision making.[36] A decision analyst helps decision makers to apply SEU theory by specifying and
quantifying their own values as well as the best estimates of the
likelihood of alternative possible outcomes. The hope is to assist
people to know what they want and what is possible, so that they
can thereby "do the good that they know," and avoid regret. Enthu-
siasm runs high among decision analysts concerning the potential
of these procedures for improving decisions. But there have also
been rumblings of doubt.

In a recapitulation of the philosophical debates about the Socratic principle and regret, regret throws a monkey wrench into the
works. In this example, if Mrs. Russell has the operation and dies
on the operating table, it would not be too surprising to learn that
her husband and children experience regrets over their decision.
However, they should expect little sympathy from decision analysts, for from their perspective, the decision to operate was clearly

the procedurally and formally rational decision, and therefore regret over an unpredictably unfavorable outcome is simply irrational hindsight. In this view, the tough-minded expected-utility analysis should stay and the tender-minded regret should go. Philosopher Bernard Williams expresses this view (by way of criticizing it) this way: "It may be said that if I am convinced that I acted for the best . . . then it is merely irrational to have any regrets."[37]

But despite the hardheaded assessment of decision analysis, it can be argued on at least two related counts—the existence of non-action-guiding judgment and the inevitability of counterfactual thought—that regret is not clearly irrational in this instance. One line of argument follows Stocker's distinctions between action and judgment and between action-guiding and non-action-guiding judgments.[38] The action-guiding judgment, "operate," is rational in the sense that it was carefully arrived at and formally coherent. If the decision is to operate and Mrs. Russell dies, the family may "feel good" about having chosen that option, knowing that it best represented what they wanted and thought possible. But this judgment could coexist with a number of non-action-guiding judgments based, for example, on counterfactual thought.

The human mind, fortunately not limited by what actually exists, is built in such a way that it draws comparisons between what happens and what might have happened. Therefore, the Russell family's satisfaction might well be dampened by normal human comparisons of reality with imagined alternatives to reality. It is not clearly irrational for the family to regret how unkind was Chance to their loved one in ruthlessly placing her in that group who die in surgery rather than placing her in one of the other groups. The fact that, because Mrs. Russell has died, none of these comparisons and judgments is now capable of guiding further action also does not make them necessarily irrational. They are simply the result of the human ability to extrapolate beyond what is and to imagine what might be—an ability that is neutral with respect to rationality. As contemporary regret theorists hasten to point out, rather than throw out regret in favor of the orthodox prescription, it is salutary to acknowledge the role that regret plays in decision and judgment and to factor it explicitly into the existing models.

Psychological Decision Models

The standard decision models just reviewed (the Socratic and expected-utility principles) have in common a fundamental focus on achieving optimal consequences through acts consistent with one's beliefs and values. Both theories privilege conduct, consequences, and consistency over other matters, such as intention, motivation, interest, desire, and the causal locus (self, other, circumstances) of consequences. Due to the hegemony of the standard models (and their variants), rationality has come to be definitionally equated with formal consistency and maximization of consequences.

Not least among the problems with the standard decision models, however, is their definition of what counts as rational:

> rationality in the sense of value maximization against the background of an agent's beliefs is not the form of all action, nor even all intelligible action. Nor is the correspondingly rational person the form of all people, nor even all intelligible people. Trying to understand people as if they were such rational beings involves inadequate moral psychologies and ignores or misunderstands important and all too common psychological phenomena.[39]

Some adherents of the standard models have implied or explicitly asserted that the only alternatives to these theories are religious dogmatism, prescientific superstition, or anti-intellectual romanticism.[40] There are, however, legitimate competitors to the standard models. To the dismay of many an orthodox decision theorist, Freudian theory and its psychodynamic offshoots have been recommended not only by "outsiders" such as moral philosophers[41] but also by insiders, such as at least one economist-proponent of hard-core decision theory.[42] The fact that psychodynamic theories recognize the role of inner conflict in human decisions makes them cogent alternatives—or at least complements—to the standard models.

Cognitive dissonance theory is an alternative, psychodynamically informed theory of decision making founded on these two ideas: (1) Internal inconsistency (e.g., inconsistency within one's set of beliefs, within one's set of values, or between one's set of beliefs/values and behavior) makes human beings uncomfortable. Like the standard decision theories, we judge such inconsistency to be illogical, and we are uncomfortable with it. Whenever our various attitudes (which include belief and value aspects) or our attitudes and behavior are inconsistent with one another (also whenever we choose between options, and whenever we suffer to gain something), we experience a state of physiological and psychological discomfort or tension called dissonance. (2) This state of tension begs to be resolved into consonance. Consonance is typically arrived at by our changing an attitude to match the attitude-discrepant behavior (or another attitude, a choice, or the cause of the suffering).[43] When Mr. Miller, described above, fails to return the money to the bank, this course of action is inconsistent with his attitude toward larceny and therefore it may predictably evoke cognitive dissonance and a change of attitude consistent with his behavior.

Plainly, the phenomenon of cognitive dissonance undermines the descriptive validity of the Socratic principle. First, it demonstrates that we do act against our better judgment—or at least in contradiction to one of our various judgments and acts. It shows as well that at some level we recognize the logical problem in so doing and attempt to recover logical consistency by psychological maneuvers. In addition, cognitive dissonance theory undermines the assumption that behavior simply and solely defines preferences. Instead, it finds normal, rational human beings to be psychically complex and often internally divided. Indeed, some, like F. Scott Fitzgerald, view such psychic complexity as a distinguishing mark of intelligence: "The test of a first-rate intelligence is the ability to hold two opposed ideas at the same time, and still retain the ability to function."[44]

These features of the theory of cognitive dissonance begin to satisfy the call for models that recognize the "complexities of the psyche," and that recognize that evaluation and other psychological functions, such as motivation, mood, interest, and desire, "need not point in the same direction."[45] Moreover, these other psychological functions (motivation, mood, interest, desire, etc.) ought not be understood as "deflections" from some "normal" state free of motivation, mood, interest, and desire.[46] Assessments of beliefs and values are never free of psychological aspects such as these.

That people do modify their attitudes in the service of dissonance reduction is a well-established fact, having been observed in hundreds of studies.[47] However, not all subjects in dissonance studies alter their attitudes to achieve internal consonance. Instead, some evidence *regret* by reversing their initial choice when given the chance.[48] Regret represents a *failure* to rationalize or justify one's prior conduct or choice. As such, regret challenges the main point of cognitive dissonance theory—its prediction about how dissonance is resolved.

Thus the reality of regret complicates and challenges three important models of decision making—the Socratic principle, standard utility theory, and dissonance theory. Because human beings voluntarily do what they believe to be the worse, fail to make decisions to maximize their expected consequences, and fail to rationalize those conflicted decisions or actions they have taken, human beings are susceptible to regret. In the face of these incontestable realities, it seems rational to scrutinize closely the claim that regret is irrational.

Critique of Decision Theory
With Special Reference to Regret:
Or Why the Classic Decision Model Is
a Bad Model for Decision

In all affairs it's a healthy thing now and then to hang a question mark on the things you have long taken for granted.
—BERTRAND RUSSELL

Because the Socratic principle proves so unconvincing, I now focus on the decision theory dominant today—expected utility theory. This theory has a number of virtues. One is its benevolence, its hope of achieving through application of an evenhanded policy the greatest good for the greatest number. Another is its capacity for helping make sense of difficult decisions by specifying the component beliefs and desires. Lastly, insofar as decision theory succeeds in clarifying the decision-making process, it should reduce the individual's sum total of regret.

Unfortunately, orthodox decision theory also has serious problems. By the 1980s a great deal of empirical evidence had been amassed showing that people do not make their decisions as mandated by orthodox decision theory. At the beginning of the decade, Richard H. Thaler expressed the growing concern about classic decision theory and its construal of rationality this way: "Clearly the relationship between rationality and normative models [i.e., utility models] is a delicate one."[49]

The Impossible Imperatives of Procedural Rationality

Procedural rationality was defined as the use of systematic procedures for information-seeking, learning, remembering, calculating, and drawing inferences in making decisions. Procedural rationality was illustrated in the earlier example in which Mrs. Russell consulted a decision analyst who helped her assign to her options numerical values that accurately reflected her own desires and medicine's best estimates of the relevant probabilities. In addition, she accurately performed the relevant calculations, which revealed that the "operate" option exceeded the "don't-operate" option in expected utilities. In so doing, Mrs. Russell demonstrated an appreciable degree of procedural rationality. She employed smart methods to figure out what she wanted and what was possible and therefore what to choose.

Two related and widely accepted criteria for procedural rationality are: (1) that the decision maker make explicit the grounds for choice—that is, the respective preferences for, and likelihoods of, all reasonable alternative options; and (2) that decisions be made uncontaminated by emotion.[50] Unfortunately, both criteria are problematic. In Chapter 1, I argued for the ubiquity, usefulness, and rationality of emotion. Here I turn to the criterion of explicitness.

Although full explicitness of the grounds for choice is a worthy goal (particularly for important decisions and for formal disciplines like the sciences, philosophy, and the law), it is an unachievable one, for a number of reasons.

First, as Hampshire points out, full accessibility of the bases for choice is *in principle* impossible because of language: by the principle of the "inexhaustibility of description," situations can be described, framed, formulated in an inexhaustible number of ways.[51] It is not feasible to articulate impartially in all conceivable ways all possible courses of action or all possible outcomes entailed in a decision. Instead, we *select* those features that are of greatest interest to us, that are most salient to us, that are socially supported, that we have words for, and so on. But the very manner in which an alternative is linguistically (and thus cognitively) formulated can itself skew a decision. This is something that Tversky and Kahneman's work on framing effects has clearly established: if a choice is framed in terms of losses, most people are willing to take more risk than if the same choice is framed in terms of gains, when most people tend to shy away from risk.[52] Imagine someone receiving a diagnosis of terminal cancer. He might frame his next medical decision as a choice between *action,* trying all possible experimental and exotic "treatments," and *inaction,* seeking only what would result in the least possible suffering before death. Or he might frame his medical decision as a choice between *quantity versus quality* of life. Depending on how he cast his choices, different courses of action would seem rationally to follow.

Though in this example of a life-and-death decision, explicitness is clearly a virtue, there are in other instances advantages to not making your reasoning explicit. Clearly it would make little sense habitually to become lost in thought over piddling decisions like what color shirt to put on in the morning. Furthermore, to take the time to lay out all possible courses of action would not only be inefficient, it could be hazardous—if the decision is what to do when confronted with a grizzly bear in the woods. For the sake of efficiency and of living to make another decision, explicitness should not be a requirement of rationality.[53] For most people, determining why we like this particular person or whether to take this particular job or how we solved a particular problem probably entails both some degree of explicitness and some lack of explicitness. In fact, all complex thought no doubt involves *both* explicit analytic thought and implicit "intuitive" thought, rather than only the former, so-called rational form.[54]

Apart from the impossibility of specifying all courses of action, the requirement to secure valid knowledge of the relevant preferences and probabilities is also impossible. Among the first to identify major violations of these aspects of the procedural rationality prescribed by utility theory were, again, Kahneman and Tversky; in Chapter 7 there is a discussion of several of the ways we tend to misjudge *probabilities*.[55]

Meanwhile many researchers have documented our inability to know what we want—to know our own *preferences*. For one thing, preferences depend on the way in which the question is formulated[56]—for instance, whether it is formulated as a choice between action versus inaction, or between quality versus quantity of life. Preferences also depend on the way in which the answer is elicited, whether by asking the decision maker to choose between options or to adjust the dimensions of two options until the options match, for instance.[57] Besides inconsistency due to these framing and elicitation effects, inconsistency of preferences occurs by virtue of context effects as well as other factors to be discussed in the remainder of this chapter and in Chapter 7. What is relevant here is that all of these thinking patterns fall short of the standard of procedural rationality demanded by utility theory.

A final obstacle to explicitness is the operation of unconscious thought and motivation. If Freud was right about the unconscious, and I think he was, to some extent we actively suppress full knowledge of the reasons for some of our decisions, both as we are making decisions and afterward. One need not accept the romantic's anti-intellectual recommendation implied in the witticism that "Marriage is too important a decision to be left entirely to the conscious mind" to recognize how often unconscious beliefs, needs, motives, and wishes drive decisions. It is not necessary, however, to appeal to the Freudian unconscious in order to argue for the impossibility of full explicitness of the grounds for choice. A great deal of experimental research finds that we are frequently unaware of the reasons for our choices or our actions.[58] We all, for instance, mistakenly think that everyone but us is influenced by advertising; and the advertising industry exploits our lack of self-knowledge to its own profit. Given these facts of human psychology, it is naive to demand that people always know what they want, know what is possible, and then make their decisions accordingly.

Thus a great gap extends between the economic model of decision making and the way humans go about really making their decisions—rendering the model problematic (at least for those of us reluctant to indict human nature as fundamentally irrational). As John von Neumann, one of the systematizers of decision theory, explains:

> The sciences . . . mainly make models. By a model is meant a mathematical construct which, with the addition of certain verbal interpretations, *describes observed phenomena.* The justification of such a mathematical construct is solely and precisely that it is expected to work.[59]

The problem is that the mathematical model with which von Neumann was particularly concerned, expected decision theory, does *not* work—it does not describe observed phenomena. One begins finally to question a model that may or may not reflect what is ideally rational, but that without doubt fails to reflect how mortals of sound mind make decisions.

Herbert Simon coined the term "bounded rationality" as a nutshell summary of some of the realities just discussed.[60] As Simon felicitously expressed it, the classic utility model serves "as a model of the mind of God, but certainly not as a model of the mind of man."[61] Furthermore, this is not a problem fixable by the mind's newest labor-saving device, the computer: according to Simon, the orthodox economic decision model, with its full complement of requirements, "has never been applied, and never can be applied—with or without the largest computers—in the real world."[62]

The False Claim of Neutrality of Ends

Decision theory demands that we choose those ends that best maximize expected utilities, but it claims to be neutral with respect to the specific content of the various ends, goals, or values.[63] Decision theory accommodates quantitative judgments of the intensity of desires ("utilities") but not qualitative judgments of what is better or worse to desire ("values," as understood in the lay sense rather than in the technical sense of decision theory). Decision theory can easily plug into its model a choice between $50 and $200, or a choice between winning $50 with 100 percent probability versus winning $100 with 25 percent probability. But what about the kind of question raised by Sartre, a choice between joining the underground resistance to Nazism versus remaining home to care for one's ill mother? Or the choice between spending one's life as an artist or a geologist? Economic decision theory and the social sciences more generally have tended to shun these qualitative judgments as unscientific because they resist empirical analysis. Or, more accurately, such judgments have been dismissed insofar as they resist empirical analysis.

As one argument goes, Sartre will choose one or the other path. The other individual will choose either the life of the artist or that of a geologist. It may be that these choices are based on implicit reasons emerging from implicit estimates of probabilities and utilities. If so, then one could sit the decision maker down and help him or her make these factors and estimates explicit. Although this might be hard to do, it is possible in principle.[64] I am more persuaded, however, by those who argue that some choices are not amenable to quantitative comparison (incommensurate choices, for example), or if they are, the quantitative analysis does not settle the question (choices involving ambivalence). I will analyze these types of choice in a later section of this chapter.

If the orthodox decision model truly ignored choices between ends, it would be ignoring a significant portion—arguably the far more significant portion—of human decision making. In actuality, modern decision theory is not neutral with respect to ends. Its claim of qualitative neutrality is false. Classic economic decision theory blithely defines maximized consequences as self-evidently a *better end* than other ends. Among the ends implicitly or explicitly assessed by decision theory as inferior to ones that maximize utility is the goal of achieving a balance, a proportion in life, an Aristotelian "golden mean"[65]—which may entail wanting not "the most" but a less than maximum amount of money, fame, glory, love, or any other good. Caring more about the expected consequences of one's own acts than the acts of others (which I shall be discussing in some depth) is also not a legitimate stance according to the standard economic model. However worthy, ends such as these fail to get the vote of decision theory.

Earlier in this chapter, we looked at a version of the standard decision theory that defines preferences behaviorally, as whatever the agent actually chooses. Such a notion can accommodate even the most unlikely choices: to choose A over B is *by definition* to prefer A to B, which is *by definition* to maximize one's expected utilities. But to define and infer utilities entirely on the basis of behavior is not only tautological, it is empirically vacuous, because it is unfalsifiable.[66] Even its adherents have begun to acknowledge the problem of the nonfalsifiability of classic decision theory: "with sufficient ingenuity, one can always find something that a particular decision maker has maximized in a particular situation."[67] Defining preferences behaviorally thus fails to rescue orthodox decision theory from the falsity of its claim of disinterest with respect to choice of ends.[68]

Economic decision theory labels irrational any regret we might suffer after having made qualitative choices like the choice between joining the underground resistance to Nazism versus remaining home to care for one's ill mother and between spending one's life as an artist or a geologist. But, in part because of the falsity of its own position, the classic model merits debate.

The Questionable Assumption of Maximizing Expected Utility

The development of classic decision theory was motivated partly by a hope for a generic policy capable of organizing what Tennyson referred to (in the context of the law) as the "wilderness of single instances." Faced with a thicket of troubling decisions every day, we can be forgiven for wishing for a sharp, all-purpose cutting tool. Modern economic decision theory has advertised the principle of maximizing expected utilities as the tool for all wildernesses. Decision theory expert Robyn Dawes states the classic position this way: "To the degree to which choices are influenced by factors other than considerations of their consequences, they are arbitrary."[69]

To equate rationality with procedural rationality and the goal of maximizing expected utility entails important implications for regret; these, in turn, help to point up the fallacy of this concept of rationality. Orthodox decision theory's stance toward regret is exemplified in the following set of scenarios. Because the formulation and the phrasing can hardly be improved upon, I have quoted at some length from the words of their author, Robyn Dawes:[70]

> 1. "I thought the decision through and I did what I knew I 'shouldn't' have done, and it worked out as badly as I anticipated. For example, I suffered from weakness of the will, drunkenness, or whatever. I am clearly culpable, and I regret the decision.
>
> 2. "I considered the decision inadequately. I 'should' have known it was a bad one; I did the 'right thing' in terms of the factors I considered, but I had at least partial awareness that other factors as well were important, and these factors would have indicated the bad outcome that occurred. I deeply regret not having considered this decision more thoroughly, because if I had, I would have made a different decision.
>
> 3. "I just didn't think about it as a decision at all. ('We've been bombing civilians for some time now, haven't we?') I behaved automatically, and it turned out badly. I may or may not have reached the 'right' decision had I 'thought it out,' but I sincerely regret not having considered it as a decision at all.
>
> 4. "I considered the matter thoroughly and made the best possible choice in terms of all the information available—or potentially available. It just happened to work out badly—for example, as a result of an improbable event. I regret that. (I [Dawes] personally claim that such regret is quite irrational.) I do not, however, regret what I did; there was no good reason to do something else."

From within the context of modern decision theory, regret for decisions taken out of weakness of will (Dawes's first case) is warranted. I agree. As discussed earlier, I may in such cases regret not only the decision but the fact of being the kind of person who made that decision. Regret following decisions made without careful attention to relevant factors (examples 2 and 3) is also warranted. I agree with this also, with all my previously mentioned reservations due to bounded rationality. But for carefully wrought decisions that go wrong, I am not so sure that regret should be condemned as irrational.

It is arguable whether adherence to the mandates of the expected-utility model renders regret nonsensical. First, if one's well-being depends significantly on factors *other* than expected consequences, regret may constitute a coherent response to well-made decisions.

Consider a case of example 4—that is, a variant of the Mayor's Dilemma, a well-known hypothetical moral dilemma. It goes like this.

In 1943 after four German soldiers have been killed by four members of the Greek underground, the Nazis take the assassins prisoner and approach the mayor of the village. The mayor is a principled pacifist, opposed to killing, even in war. The Nazis tell the mayor that in retaliation for the loss of their men, they have rounded up 80 village men who are at this moment complying with orders to dig a large ditch. The next morning all 80 will be ordered into the ditch and executed. When the mayor pleads for the lives of his townspeople, the Nazi officer offers him a deal. The mayor can save the lives of 60 of the 80 men if the next morning he himself shoots to death the four members of the Greek resistance plus 16 villagers. The Nazis have consistently carried out this policy of killing at least five in retaliation for every man they lose, and the mayor knows it. In addition, the Nazis take the mayor into their custody and put him under guard to prevent him from plotting with others a different solution to the dilemma.

With standard decision theory, the choice is between 100 percent probability of 80 deaths versus 100 percent probability of 20 deaths, and the rational decision is for the mayor to put aside his otherwise fine principles and prevent the deaths of the many by killing the few. To hold stubbornly to his pacifism in this situation would amount to indulging his personal squeamishness, thereby causing great misery that could be prevented by a decision based on expected consequences.[71] Furthermore, the mayor should stifle, or at best assign only some small weight to, his anticipated regret, for if the decision maximizes expected consequences, regret is irrational.

However, if we step outside decision theory, the choice looks rather different. From the vantage point of the pacifist's "rule"-based framework dictating "Thou shalt not kill" (except in self-defense, etc.), the mayor's dilemma can be viewed as a problem of responsibility and personal integrity rather than a problem of how to maximize expected consequences. In fact, locus of responsibility is confounded with expected consequences in this particular situation, with the Nazis being proximally responsible for 80 deaths and the mayor for 20. But there is no warrant for equating the consequences of what I do with the consequences of what someone else does.

It is not clear that the mayor should alienate himself from his anticipated regret. To suppress one's genuine, considered commitments would be, as Bernard Williams has stated, to "lose a sense of one's moral identity; to lose, in the most literal way, one's integrity . . . utilitarianism alienates one from one's moral feelings; . . . more basically, it alienates one from one's actions."[72] Why should we require that human beings alienate themselves from their reflected-upon values, principles, or actions—as a criterion of rationality?

This example also demonstrates the fact that in a choice between two evils, regret is simply unavoidable. In fact, decisions among bad choices have been found to yield particularly intense regret.[73] Moreover, it is not only in such extreme circumstances that we confront hopelessly conflicting choices. Mrs. Russell who must choose between death or expensive, risky, and painful surgery; someone who must choose between a painful divorce or the continuation of a seriously damaging marriage; the individual who must choose between caring for a dying parent and a sick child; someone who must choose between staying home to care for an ill mother or leaving home to challenge the murderous rule of a Führer—these are just a few examples in which regret is inevitable.

Unfortunately, then, orthodox decision theory proves not to be the all-purpose tool that it claims. In addition to its failure to decide definitively the best course of action in choices like the Mayor's Dilemma, the principle of maximizing utility can even fail to achieve its own ends on its own terms.

Indeed, the pursuit of formal rationality as defined by standard decision theory can serve demonstrably *irrational* ends, even on its own terms. A good deal of research shows how the attempt to maximize individual utilities can actually minimize collective utilities. It is in my individual interest to drive my own car to work rather than carpool or use public transportation. Driving maximizes my flexibility and autonomy in that I can choose my most convenient departure times independently of others' schedules and needs. However, when most of the inhabitants of a congested city— say, greater Los Angeles—behave in order to maximize their individual utilities on these dimensions, they greatly reduce the habitability of their own air. Formally rational individual decisions can make for group misery.[74]

A third example of the arguable universality of the maximization principle is the decision whether or not to retrieve terrorist-held hostages through an exchange of arms, money, or other concessions. From the point of view of the hostages' families, the utility-maximizing decision is to make whatever exchanges it takes to free their loved ones. But from the point of view of the larger national and world community, the utility-maximizing decision is probably to refuse to make such exchanges—due to the time- and research-honored assumption that rewarding hostage-taking (or anything else) encourages it. (The Mayor's Dilemma could also conceivably be reframed as a hostage situation, which would raise another rationale for refusing to do business with the Nazis.)[75]

In all these examples what makes the application of orthodox decision theory problematic is the existence of conflicting values within and among individuals and between the individual and collective levels. In the Mayor's Dilemma, his belief that *personal* agency for killing is unacceptable proves incompatible with his desire to save as many lives as possible. In the driving and hostage examples, maximizing individual utilities proves incompatible with maximizing the collective utilities of which the individual partakes. Although specific variants of the standard theory are capable of prescribing morally or pragmatically defensible courses of action in one or the other of these problems, to my knowledge there exists no umbrella form that can solve all such problems.

Examples like these also undermine the claim that regret is an irrational response to outcomes that follow carefully made decisions. A mayor capable of carrying out his particular decision with no regrets could be seen as unworthy of his office. Even a saint could be excused for moments of regret for her otherwise "rational" decision to maximize the collective good by using public transportation—like those times she misses a bus and has to wait a half hour in a bone-chilling downpour for the next one. And we hope, for the sake of the global community, that the family is rare to nonexistent that is capable of watching with no regrets as the terrorists who have been paid off to release their own loved one turn around and seize another hostage. Even when my choice is the best one in terms of all the available information concerning expected consequences, regret for a bad outcome may not be irrational.

What we have here is, among other things, a clash of worldviews—in this case, the comic/ironic and the tragic/romantic worldviews. Economic decision theory tells us that although we cannot always know ahead of time what is the best course of action in life, as long as we do our level best to act according to the dictates of expected utility theory, then we will achieve the best of all *possible* outcomes, which we ought to accept with equanimity.

This is essentially a comic view of regret. In contrast, others see certain choices (e.g., the Mayor's Dilemma, the hostage family's dilemma) as brought about by forces that lie outside the governance of reason; as choices unresolvable by the exercise of reason or action; as irremediable dilemmas—and they refuse to accept this state of affairs with equanimity. This is the tragic view. There is no generic decision rule capable of reconciling these incommensurable worldviews, or capable of declaring one valid and the other invalid.

But why should the matter be framed in this either/or, all-or-none manner? Why not speak about more or less regret, about more or less of a self-recriminatory quality to regret? Then it is easy to see why greater regret *is* generally warranted for poorly than for well-made decisions: the former regret is augmented by self-recrimination. But if regret is augmented by self-recrimination, then greater regret for outcomes effected by oneself versus by others may also be warranted, independent of the degree of procedural rationality entailed in the choice.

In summary, a genuinely value-neutral model has no grounds for equating rationality exclusively with consequences in general or with maximized utilities more specifically. It is as "logical" to rank choices in terms of qualitatively better-and-worse ends as in terms of higher-versus-lower expected utilities.[76] As Bernard Williams points out, to the extent that people's well-being depends on nonutilitarian choices, standard decision theory is internally inconsistent to denounce such ends.[77] As I have argued, there are a number of other grounds for challenging the orthodox equation of rationality with the process of maximizing expected consequences. For one thing, many choices that appear irrational when viewed from the standard position can be shown from within *alternative* positions to be not arbitrary and not irrational, but systematic and rational. For another, people's well-being is in fact not universally well served by utilitarian aims. Finally, even if we accept the standard position as the ideal, choices that appear haphazard and irrational under standard utility theory can be seen to make sense when *regret* is added to the calculation of expected consequences, an argument I detail later in this chapter.

The Imperatives of Formal Rationality: The Internal Consistency and Transitivity Axioms

According to classic decision theory, formal rationality (logical coherence or internal consistency) is axiomatically necessary for making decisions rationally. Again, there are sound reasons for prizing internal consistency. Imagine that, after Mrs. Russell's careful decision analysis in which the surgery option was found to yield higher expected utilities than the no-surgery option, she capriciously—out of nothing but a "gut feeling"—decided *not* to have the operation. This decision would lack formal rationality inasmuch as it would contradict her own carefully determined beliefs and desires.

Directly related to the requirement of consistency of choice with belief and preference, decision theory also requires transitivity, or consistency across beliefs and across preferences. By the transitivity principle, once again, if you prefer A to B, and B to C, then logically you must prefer A to C. You would show intransitivity if you then preferred C to A. Transitivity too has been required for formal rationality as defined by orthodox decision theory.

The orthodox decision models also require decision makers to assign multiple probabilities and utilities in a manner that comprehensively orders their multiple preferences. This requirement, called the metricity requirement, consists of the claims:

> that in each situation of choice there is some one value, varying only in quantity, that is common to all the alternatives, and that the rational chooser weighs the alternatives using this single standard.[78,79]

Transitivity and quantitative ordering of preferences are coming under increasing challenge by philosophers, psychologists, and economists, including some adherents of classic decision theory. Whenever the context of a decision changes, whenever the decision maker has several relevant values, ambivalent values, or incommensurate values, the ordering of preferences can rationally change.

Here is an example of how *context* can make for intransitivity:

> When I see fresh peas and corn in the vegetable market, my appetite is whetted for corn over peas. When I see corn and asparagus, I hunger for asparagus over corn. And when I see asparagus and peas, my mouth waters for peas over asparagus.[80]

This ordering clearly lacks transitivity: Asparagus > Corn > Peas > Asparagus. But, as philosopher Elizabeth Anderson points out, preferences among options involving "appetites, habits, and whims" need not show transitivity:[81]

> there is nothing irrational about this ordering. Appetites, attractions, whims, primitive likings, and so forth are not susceptible to any rational criticism whatsoever on purely formal grounds. . . . Any formal pattern of shallow preferences over inconsequential items is ra-

tionally admissible, no matter how bizarre,whimsical, or disorderly it may be. For in matters such as these, the free play of imagination and feeling has full reign.[82]

By the same reasoning, philosopher Amartya Sen, too, refuses to dismiss as irrational this type of inconsistency, pointing out that consistency is a problematic axiom precisely because of our "love of variety . . . and changing tastes."[83] Some adherents of classic decision theory agree on this sort of case, on the grounds that such decisions are unimportant.[84] But it is conceivable that, even when the stakes are high, rationality can coexist with intransitivity.[85]

Apart from context, whenever alternatives are themselves made up of multiple desirable (or multiple undesirable) dimensions— probably more often than not—metricity and transitivity may be mutually hostile imperatives. Consider the following example posed by Amos Tversky, based on the commonplace situation in which an employer has to juggle more than one value in selecting among candidates for a job.[86] The ideal candidate may be intelligent, mature, experienced, creative, socially skilled, geographically mobile, a self-starter, and a good team player. But it would be understandable if the beleaguered employer faced with multiple viable candidates decided to reduce this intransigently multiple array of criteria to, say, two: experience and intelligence. Imagine, following Tversky, that this employer has to decide among three job candidates. Even in this relatively simple case, the procedurally rational employer faces a dauntingly complex task. Here is a listing of the qualifications of three candidates on the two valued dimensions (intelligence and experience); e means some insignificant amount:

Candidate	Intelligence	Experience
A	2e	6 years
B	3e	4 years
C	4e	2 years

The employer is still faced with an intransigent decision. So he refines his strategy for choosing an applicant, as follows: (1) he specifies that he values intelligence more than experience; (2) if two candidates differ only e in intelligence, then the employer considers them equal in intelligence; (3) if the candidates are equivalent in intelligence, then the employer prefers the candidate with more experience.

The employer's method for selecting among job candidates yields an intransitive, though not an irrational, ordering. The employer will prefer A to B because although A and B are equivalently intelligent, A has more experience. By the same reasoning the employer will prefer B to C. Nevertheless, C is preferred to A, because C is significantly (2e) more intelligent than A, and the employer values intelligence over experience. In other words, A > B > C > A, clearly a violation of transitivity. *Plurality of values*, along with the imposition of a single overall metric, has mandated a decision that is irrational if transitivity is considered a necessary feature of formal rationality. But, why call this a case of irrationality? Why not instead call it a case of "rational indeterminacy"[87]—that is, despite its procedural rationality, the strategy is not capable of determining who is the single, unquestionably best candidate.

Aside from context and conflicting values, ambivalence and incommensurability of values further undermine transitivity. Ambivalence means having mixed feelings or values concerning something; we evidence incommensurability of values when we have values that are not capable of being compared with one another. Incommensurate options are options about which "reason has no judgment to make concerning their relative value."[88]

Philosopher Patricia Greenspan defines *ambivalence* as the state of holding "contrary emotions with the same object."[89] Being ambivalent does not mean vacillating between contrary emotions about something, on Monday feeling good about it and on Tuesday feeling bad. In true ambivalence we feel good and bad at the same time. Ambivalence also does not mean indifference. Economist James G. March further explains:

> our deepest preferences tend often to be paired. We find the same outcome both attractive and repulsive, not in the sense that the two sentiments cancel each other and we remain indifferent, but precisely that we simultaneously want and do not want an outcome, experience it as both pleasure and pain, love and hate it.[90]

The earlier examples of Miller and Natasha show ambivalence. Miller simultaneously finds the prospect of keeping the $40,000 attractive and repulsive. Natasha simultaneously wants and does not want to give the crown jewels to the capitalist. More generally, the hypothetical individual in Dawes's first example above could represent ambivalence, both wanting and not wanting the alcohol or whatever. Ambivalence is crucial to my arguments against the claims of economic decision theory, as well as my arguments for the rationality of regret. Therefore, we need an extended examination of ambivalence.

In a deft analysis, Greenspan provides another example of ambivalence: the one raised in Chapter 2 in which you are a rival with a close friend for a job position (say, executive secretary, vice-president, or department chair), and your friend gets it and you don't. It wouldn't be unusual for you in this situation to experience contrary emotions, as Greenspan explains: "I am happy he won (feel good about his winning). I am unhappy he won (feel bad about his winning)."[91] It is not irrational, but appropriate, to experience mixed feelings toward anyone we both identify with and compete with.

We might be able to explain away some cases of so-called ambivalence on the grounds that the contrary emotions really have different objects. This would be valid in some cases, such as these described by philosopher Amelie Rorty:

> a person can, without pathology, consider the negative features of an event so intrinsically bound with desirable features that he does not actively regret the negative features, even though he sees them for what they are . . . (an attitude that many women have toward childbirth, and many parents to the rigors of child-rearing).[92]

This is not case a case of true ambivalence in the strict sense. There are negative features (painful labor, difficult teenage years), but these features are different from the positive features. Regret does not necessarily follow in such cases of mixed emotions, but it does follow from true ambivalence.

We might be tempted to try to explain away every case of ambivalence this way—by declaring that it is not really a case of contrary emotions over the same object but of contrary emotions over *different* objects. Let us return to the case of the individual competing for a job who loses out to a close friend. Isn't this really a case of contrary emotions over different objects: I am happy over his win and unhappy over my loss. No, as Greenspan points out, since his win intrinsically entails my loss, this distinction does not hold. It really is a case of ambivalence, contrary feelings over the same object.

We also might try to deny that this is a case of ambivalence by reducing what we have called "contrary emotions" to "contrary judgments." It *is* more clearly irrational to continue to hold contrary judgments toward the very same object. That is why over time rational persons will do something to resolve the inner conflict—like changing one of the contrary beliefs to match the other (as in dissonance reduction) or like summing the judgments to "form a single 'all things considered' judgment."[93] In this case, the first move might mean coming to an assessment that you are just as happy not to have the headaches of the lost job. The second move might entail coming to an assessment that his winning the position is "on the whole good"[94] (or on the whole bad).

But this case is not about mere judgments, even evaluative judgments. How do we know? For one thing, even after engaging in these processes of qualifying and summing the component judgments, we may still experience mixed emotions, the cheer plus the lump in the throat. They are what is left over after we have reconciled the contrary judgments. Qualifying and summing maneuvers do not modify emotions the same way they modify judgments. Greenspan explains:

> an emotion seems to be appropriate relative to a particular set of grounds, and not necessarily a unified evaluation of one's total body of "evidence." It is enough that it be justified by *some* (adequate) reasons, even if the overall *weight* of one's reasons favors a contrary emotion instead. Thus, emotions may persist, even when they are accompanied by stronger opposing feelings, in a basically rational person."[95]

Emotions, as Greenspan says, have a logic of their own.[96] The logic is not the logic of truth based on the weight of the justifying evidence but the logic of appropriateness given the particular grounds. "An emotion is appropriate as long as there are adequate reasons *for* it, whatever the reasons against it."[97]

There is another sense in which ambivalence is rational. This argument depends on recognizing the close link between emotion and its expression, which is a social and behavioral matter. Greenspan proposes the provocative idea that sustaining ambivalence can actually be *better* than resolving ambivalence. In the case of rivalry with a close friend, for example, resolving the ambivalence could happen in these ways. First, you could come to feel neutral about his win. But that would be to lose something socially and morally valuable—the ability to identify with his interests. Similarly, you could try to suppress your negative feelings about his win. But because that would mean coming to value the win less than before, it would also mean losing something socially and morally valuable—again, the ability to "participate in his emotion, and share his point of view."[98] Or, you could suppress your negative feelings about your own loss. But that would also mean giving up something of value—normal, healthy self-interest. Thus, ambivalence can be more adaptive—more facilitative of genuine social relations—than detachment or resolution. In this case, ambivalence is facilitative of genuine social relations in that it depends on genuine empathy with someone else while simultaneously depending on remaining a person capable of genuine self-interested emotion. Social and interpersonal relations are impoverished to the extent that they are engaged in by someone who does not care, or by someone who is either one-sidedly self-interested or one-sidedly identified with the interests of another.[99]

The upshot of this analysis at this particular point is the conclusion that transitivity does not apply in cases of ambivalence. If the two emotions are really equally strong but opposite, then they cannot be rank ordered. Neither do they cancel each other out, as in indifference. Either emotion has as great a claim as the other (assuming that the relevant probabilities do not differ from one another). Orthodox economic decision theory cannot handle true ambivalence, because it cannot distinguish ambivalence from indifference. In the case of equally strong but opposite emotions (or values, or utilities), the mathematics of the theory would yield the same result as the case of indifference: the two values would erroneously appear to cancel each other out. But ambivalence is emphatically not the same experience as indifference.

Regret represents one important way in which the two experiences differ. When we choose in a state of indifference, meaning we don't care one way or the other, no regret reasonably follows. But when we choose in a state of ambivalence, we care very much both ways. With ambivalence, the choice—either choice—will necessarily entail regret.

Likewise, *incommensurability* of values undermines the transitivity requirement. "A and B are incommensurate if it is neither true that one is better than the other nor true that they are of equal value."

I know a number of people who have endured "commuter marriages" for a year or two; they reluctantly lived apart from someone they loved to accommodate temporary career needs. But if a stranger offered to give these individuals money to leave their partner for a time, they would all be rightly "indignant that someone supposes that they are willing to trade the company of their spouse for money from a stranger."[100] That's because money and love are incommensurables.[101] Incommensurables, because unrankable, cannot be held to the transitivity criterion. Whenever options are incommensurate, transitivity is simply a "non sequitur."[102,103,104]

Moreover, in decisions entailing contests of obligations or incommensurable choices, regret may reasonably follow, whichever alternative is chosen.[105] The choice between caring for a dying parent and a sick child represents a conflict of obligations, as well as a choice between incommensurables. The Mayor's choice is a choice between incommensurables. In such circumstances, as well, regret is unavoidable.

Adam Smith understood something about his version of economic decision theory that we seem to have lost sight of: it is not universally applicable. For example, Smith knew that decision theory does not apply outside the marketplace nor outside a marketplace that is genuinely free and competitive (which is probably to exclude all existing markets).[106] The inappropriateness of standard decision theory in the non-marketplace realms of friendship, love, and other personal relationships stems from the fact of incommensurability and the resulting inability to rank options. The ability to experience genuine interpersonal relationships may itself depend on the ability to appreciate incommensurability—and thus rational intransitivity.[107] In an article contentiously titled "Rational Fools," Amartya Sen goes so far as to declare that "the *purely* economic man is indeed close to being a social moron. Economic theory has been much preoccupied with this rational fool decked in the glory of his *one* all-purpose preference ordering."[108]

To some extent these genteel brawls over the question whether rationality requires internal consistency may also reflect a clash of worldviews. The romantic (and tragic) mentality may never see eye-to-eye with the comic mentality on this issue. Walt Whitman expresses the radically romantic stance toward internal consistency in "Song of Myself": "Do I contradict myself?/ Very well then I contradict myself,/ (I am large, I contain multitudes)."[109] The consistency that the comic view demands as a *sine qua non* for rationality, the romantic scoffs at as "the hobgoblin of small minds" (Emerson).[110]

Conclusions: Why Decision Theory Needs Regret

This conflict of worldviews may be one reason that arguments between proponents and opponents of standard decision theory tend to evoke such strong words. In a classic debate between J. J. C. Smart, a utilitarian, and B. Williams, a nonutilitarian, Smart insinuates that the only alternatives to utilitarianism are "authoritarianism, dogmatism or romanticism."[111] On the other side, Williams refers pejoratively to the "unblinking accountant's eye of the strict utilitarian."[112] Then there is Sen's referring to those who attempt to live by classical decision theory as "rational fools" and "social morons."[113] Dispassionate discourse is hard to come by for those debating worldviews across an uncomprehending abyss.

There is no question that in some instances attempting to approximate the procedures and goals of classic decision models can make for better decisions. There is also no question that, as the narrator in a recent novel by David Slavitt puts it: "too great a reliance on rationality is only another kind of superstition."[114] Based on the analysis presented in this chapter, I offer a slight modification of Slavitt's conclusion: too great a reliance on *a dogmatic, absolutistic, totalistic conception of rationality* is only another kind of superstition.

I have shown how regret derives from a number of ubiquitous aspects of the human condition apart from weakness of will and procedural irrationality, including facts of human psychology like the inexhaustibility of description, counterfactual thought, cognitive limitations, and plurality, ambivalence and incommensurability of value; and facts of the world like chance, scarcity, and the necessity of choosing. For all these reasons, too, the portrait of decision makers painted by standard decision theory has not been matched by the data. Orthodox decision theory fails to describe how people actually make decisions not only because the theory is somehow superior to human cognitive limitations. The theory fails because it is too simple for the complexity of human decisions. Anderson explains:

> the problem with the standard formal theory is that it postulates agents who are just too simple-minded to represent, for normative purposes, the concerns of mature and complex people. It is no surprise that rats and pigeons satisfy the axioms of rational choice almost to perfection, whereas human beings are constantly violating them.[115]

Orthodox decision theory is also too simple for the world. A character in *A Landing on the Sun* by Michael Frayn charmingly expresses this idea:

> . . . happiness is like economics or heat in seawater. You can make the laws of economics work for short periods of time in small models cut off from the rest of the world, just as you can have a hot bath in the sun-warmed pools of seawater left behind on the beach. But as soon as the neat economic model is reconnected with the unstruc-

tured chaos of human affairs, as soon as the tide returns, all gratifying predictivity breaks down, the hot bath disappears at once into the huge reserves of cold in the ocean deeps.[116]

Often "the present world gives us grounds for regret even if we do what is to be done."[117] The "unstructured chaos of human affairs" gives us grounds for regret, even if we live strictly by the laws of economics.

Such careful scholars as Tversky and Kahneman are coming to the reluctant conclusion that "the dream of constructing a theory that is acceptable both descriptively and normatively appears unrealizable."[118] Furthermore, they say:

> the logic of choice does not provide an adequate foundation for a descriptive theory of decision making. We argue that the deviations of actual behavior from the normative model are too widespread to be ignored, too systematic to be dismissed as random error, and too fundamental to be accommodated by relaxing the normative system.[119]

Or to paraphrase Sandra Harding's critique of science,[120] it turns out that orthodox decision theory is a bad model for decision.

What then about that awful wilderness of single instances? Is there any way out? Aristotle thought not—at least not an easy way out using a single all-purpose blade. In the *Nicomachean Ethics* Aristotle asserted that practical reason (of which decision making represents a particular case) cannot be governed by abstract universal principle but only by analysis of the particulars of the concrete case at hand.[121] I agree, but with a qualification. There are some aids available for finding paths in the wilderness—some patterns, some regularities across individual cases. The next two chapters, for example, are full of principles for how to avoid or minimize regret. Although they do not add up to a single all-purpose, universal decision principle, taken together they do represent a variety of useful tools with which to navigate different types of wildernesses.

Further, Aristotle denies the now-orthodox equation of mathematically based theoretical wisdom with practical wisdom, arguing that practical wisdom is not reducible to mathematical abstraction:

> Young people can become mathematicians and geometers and wise in things of that sort; but they do not appear to become people of practical wisdom. The reason is that practical wisdom is of the particular, which becomes graspable through experience, but a young person is not experienced.[122]

To advance the argument against a search for a totalistic decision theory and in favor of more provisional approaches, I need to quote philosopher Martha Nussbaum at length:

> A great part of *rational* deliberation will be concerned with questions about whether a certain course of action here and now really counts as realizing some important value (say, courage or friendship) that is a *prima facie* part of her idea of the good life; . . . . For this sort of question, it seems obvious that there is no mathematical answer; and the only procedure to follow is . . . to imagine all the relevant features as well and fully and concretely as possible, holding them up against whatever intuitions and emotions and plans and imaginings we have brought into the situation or can construct in it. There is really no shortcut at all; or none that is not corruption . . . the content of rational choice must be supplied by nothing less messy than experience and stories of experience. . . . Good deliberation is like theatrical or musical improvisation, where what counts is flexibility, responsiveness, and openness to the external; to rely on an algorithm here is not only insufficient, it is a sign of immaturity and weakness. It is possible to play a jazz solo from a score, making minor alterations for the particular nature of one's instrument. The question is, who would do this, and why? [123]

Although I endorse Nussbaum's assertion that choice is an unavoidably messy business, I don't agree with every detail of this passage. For one thing I don't agree that "there is *obviously* no mathematical answer" to such questions. If that were obvious to me, I would not have spent so much energy taking serious the possibility of mathematical answers. Also, to me the listing is incomplete of what things we should consider when making choices. To the more romantic set of "intuitions and emotions and plans and imaginings" appropriate to Nussbaum's topic—love—I would add, among other things, the more rationalist set of "our best estimates of the relevant probabilities and values." Why not? It couldn't hurt. But I agree with Nussbaum's contention that it also might not help a lot—especially if the choice involves ambivalence or incommensurables.

The intoxicating search for an abstract, impersonal, mathematical decision theory with universal applicability may be an impossible dream. The nature of the world and of our humanity will always play havoc with systems. It is time for a quiet revolution against the scientific doctrine of abstract, impersonal universality. The kind of wisdom that constitutes good decision making is grounded in openness to the particularities of personal experience, the ability to imagine alternatives and to frame them cogently, and enough self-knowledge to recognize those choices we really want. Far from shameful, such flexibility ought to be viewed as something to glory in—just as we glory in the increasing flexibility and decreasing reliance on fixed, hard-wired response that is one of evolution's supreme gifts to *homo sapiens.*

I do not seek to offer an alternative to orthodox economic decision theory. However, I can suggest a few of the features an alternative theory ought to have. A logically, psychologically, and scientifically more defensible approach will seek to model decision making with a human face. It will be grounded on assumptions of contextual rationality[124] and limited rationality.[125] It will recognize the extent to which choice depends on context, understood narrowly as the complex of available alternatives, and understood broadly as the "complex of other claims of the attention of actors and other structures of social and cognitive relations."[126] A better approach to decision making will not dogmatically privilege overt choice, the maximization of expected utility, or internal consistency. It will recognize the limits of logic, and it will recognize that preferences have importance as concerns, values, or "beliefs independent of their immediate action consequences."[127] Finally, a better approach to decision making will, despite our fond wishes, eschew totalistic claims. It will recognize that the best answers to human decision problems are not to be found in general principles but in the particularities of the decision and the decision context, and in the intellectual and emotional flexibility of the decision maker.

Again, none of this means that we should never consider the consequences of actions. Nor does it mean that decisions ought to be based on the romanticism of unreflected emotion or gut feeling. As I have discussed in Chapter 3, romanticism is not the only alternative to what I argue is the essentially comic worldview implied by classic decision theory.

Regret Models

There is no need, nor any way, to justify pervasive features of human thought. But there is a need for an explanation which makes them intelligible.
—JOSEPH RAZ

Recently, a group of researchers asked physicians to make clinical decisions about whether or not to prescribe estrogen for 50-year-old menopausal women described in written case histories.[128] Twelve case descriptions were presented, with three patient factors systematically varied: cancer risk, severity of vasomotor symptoms, and osteoporosis risk. The researchers asked the physicians to specify their subjective probabilities and utilities for each course of action (estrogen, no estrogen). Three categories of outcome were specified: endometrial cancer (concurrently thought to be associated with estrogen treatment), vasomotor symptoms (concurrently thought to be relieved by estrogen treatment), and osteoporosis (concurrently thought to be relieved by estrogen treatment). Although decision analysis based on the physicians' own probabilities and utilities recommended either estrogen treatment or a toss-up, the majority of the physicians recommended *against* estrogen treatment. Decision theory did not predict the actual decisions. Why? Were these physicians irrational?

They were not procedurally irrational; the physicians had explicitly quantified the relevant utilities and probabilities. Nor were they substantively irrational, or misled by false beliefs. In fact, the physicians' probability estimates were "remarkably similar to the published figures" on outcomes.[129] But viewed from within the framework of orthodox decision theory, their decision not to prescribe estrogen treatment appears internally inconsistent with the expected consequences they calculated, hence formally irrational.

Viewed from outside the framework of standard decision theory, however, these decisions become intelligible. In one plausible analysis, it appears that these decisions were designed not to maximize expected utility but to avoid regret. "Although suboptimal with respect to the criterion of expected utility, the observed decisions were consistent with the wish to avoid undesirable consequences in the most important dimension"[130]—that is, life-and-death. The physicians believed that estrogen treatment increased the probability of patients' developing endometrial cancer. Even though they knew that the probability of developing endometrial cancer was low, they decided against estrogen treatment in order to avoid "gambling with death"[131]—an outcome that would yield the maximum regret. The authors conclude:

> It may well be argued . . . that human judgment is influenced by aspects of the task that are excluded by the expected utility model but ought to be included: for example, the attribution of responsibility and anticipation of regret.[132]

A less charitable interpretation of these decisions hinges on lawsuit phobia. The physicians' decisions may have been less informed by their anticipation of regret for a patient's death than by their anticipation of regret for their own legal liability for that death. The ethics of this latter orientation are of course highly questionable, all the more so if one assumes, as the decision analysis did, that the patients would be ill-served by the decision. However, in either case, a decision that appears incoherent within orthodox decision theory is seen as coherent within a theory that takes regret into account.

Not only do intelligible decisions fail to match the imperatives of orthodox decision theory, it is clear that, despite the condemnation of decision theory, the decisions of seemingly rational people quite often include regret. Perhaps because regret is a fact that will not be scorned away, a number of decision formulations have emerged since the 1950s to attempt to take account of it. These include the minimax regret model, the intolerable regret model, and the modified-expected-utility regret model.

The Minimax Regret Model

The earliest regret models proposed that decisions are not always made to maximize utilities, but sometimes to minimize maximum loss—hence the appellation "minimax regret" by which these models are known.[133] The minimax regret principle of decision making is: Choose that option by which, if it turns out to be the wrong one, your maximum loss will be as small as possible.[134] The amount of loss associated with the chosen option is defined as the difference between the best possible payoff and the actual payoff.[135]

How does the minimax regret principle handle the decision faced by Mrs. Russell, as outlined above? First, it begins by specifying the three components of a decision as defined by decision theory: the options or acts, the possible outcomes, and the relevant state of nature (physical and nonphysical conditions).[136] Here is the decision tree for this problem as specified earlier:

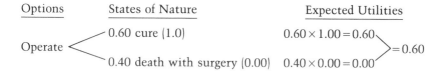

Options	States of Nature	Expected Utilities
Operate	0.60 cure (1.0)	$0.60 \times 1.00 = 0.60$
	0.40 death with surgery (0.00)	$0.40 \times 0.00 = 0.00$

$=0.60$

$$\text{Don't operate}\left\langle\begin{array}{ll}0.80 \text{ disease remains } (0.60) & 0.80\times0.60=0.48 \\ 0.20 \text{ death in 6 months } (0.10) & 0.20\times0.10=0.02\end{array}\right\rangle=0.50$$

The *DECISION* table (or utility table) corresponding to this decision tree follows. In this table the cell entries are the probability-free subjective utilities, as explained earlier.

Options	States of Nature	
Operate	1.00 cure	0.00 death with surgery
Don't operate	0.60 no change	0.10 death in 6 months

Finally, this decision or utility table is translated into regret terms. This entails transforming each raw utility value to a regret/loss value, that is, the difference between the actual payoff and the maximum payoff possible under that state of nature. With respect to Mrs. Russell's decision, the difference between the payoff for a surgical cure (1.00) and the best possible payoff under the non-death state of nature (1.00) is .00, the amount of regret for that cell. The difference between the payoff for no change in the condition due to forgoing surgery (.60) and the best possible payoff under the same state of nature (1.00) is .40, the amount of regret for that cell. And so on. The corresponding *REGRET* table follows:

Options	States of Nature	
Operate	0.00 cure	0.10 death with surgery
Don't operate	0.40 no change	0.00 death in 6 months

The maximum regret for the Operate option is .10, which is clearly less than the .40 maximum regret for the Don't-Operate option. Therefore, under the minimax regret rule that one should choose the option that minimizes the maximum regret, Mrs. Russell should choose the surgery. The utility theory recommends operating also, because this option maximizes Mrs. Russell's expected utility, (.60 + .00) > (.48 + .02). In this case (though not in all), the minimax regret principle urges the same choice as the utility principle, though for different reasons.

The minimax regret principle has its virtues. At least one eminent statistician judged that it "led to some profound theoretical results, especially in sequential analysis, and has greatly unified the whole field of theoretical statistics."[137] Outside of theoretical statistics, minimax regret models prove applicable to a variety of decision problems.

On the positive side, research testing whether people use the minimax regret principle to make risky decisions of a personal nature—for example, whether to borrow on one's life insurance in order to invest in a risky but promising stock—finds that, yes, we do show evidence of using minimax regret principles to make personal life choices. (However, minimax regret is not the uniquely applicable account: the standard expected utility model seems to describe what people do in such situations as well.)[138] A number of studies have found that other sorts of choices, as well, match minimax regret theory.[139]

On the negative side, research has found that people do not use minimax regret principles to decide how to distribute social goods such as income and income tax in a welfare economy.[140] Another negative result for the minimax regret principle was obtained in a study of empirically unusual but experientially commonplace multistage decision problems, that is, problems in which the decision maker is faced with a series of separate decisions, with the probability distribution differing at each stage, contingent on decisions made at preceding stages.[141]

Aside from the empirical failures, the minimax regret principle has limitations of a formal, practical, and psychological nature. A formal problem is that minimax regret models give up something central to expected utility models, namely, probabilities.[142] Another problem is that certain applications of the minimax regret principle produce violations of axiomatic features of utility theory like transitivity,[143] a point I elaborate on later. Besides the formal problems, there is at least one practical problem. In order to compute a loss function, one needs knowledge "not often available to the working statistician"[144] and still less to the person on the street: foreknowledge of the maximum possible and the actual payoffs.

From the point of view of its psychology, the minimax regret principle fails on two counts. First, the minimax regret rule assumes that people's preferences are best represented by an interval scale rather than by a less precise ordinal scale.[145] An interval-scale ranking of 1, 2, 3 requires equal distances between each rank (as the difference between 90 and 80 degrees Fahrenheit is equal to the difference between 80 and 70 degrees Fahrenheit), whereas an ordinal-scale ranking simply means (in the decision context) that 1 is preferred to 2, which is preferred to 3. But an interval scale of preferences requires a far more precise calibration of preferences than that probably performed by most decision makers.

Second, the minimax regret principle fails to describe the psychological state of those decision makers who do not view every decision through the tragic perspective. As Savage describes it, the minimax regret principle is "founded on ultra-pessimism, [in] that it demands that the actor assume the world to be in the worst possible state."[146] The minimax regret strategy has been called the "strategy of the pessimist who thinks, 'No matter what decision I make, the future will be exactly wrong for my decision. If I stay with my old job, the new company will turn out to be a great success. If I go to the new company it will fail. So I had better minimize the maximum regret I can feel for having made the wrong decision.' "[147]

To the extent that decision makers are not fortune-tellers, utter pessimists, or precision preference-instruments, and to the extent that decisions are based on likelihood estimates, minimax regret models miss the mark. Eventually, variants on the original minimax regret model emerged to try to do a better job of modeling people's decisions.

The Intolerable Regret Model

The "intolerable regret"[148] model represents choice as a two-stage process. First, the individual excludes those alternatives associated with intolerable levels of anticipated regret; then the individual selects the maximizing one from the remaining alternatives. In other words, this model of decision making postulates the usual maximization but only after initial attention to future regret. According to this model, people use the anticipation of intolerable regret as a screening device to narrow their range of rational choices. For example, some family members, when confronted with a diagnosis of terminal cancer in a loved one, may immediately rule out the option of seeking palliative treatment only, fearing that upon the death of their loved one, they would be tormented with an intolerable degree of regret for "inaction."[149] Having made this decision, they select what they perceive as the best (utility maximizing) from among the available treatments—say, radiation versus chemotherapy.

The Modern Regret Model

In the 1980s a third type of regret theory was independently formulated by economists David A. Bell[150] and by Graham Loomes and Robert Sugden.[151] These theories reclaimed the framework of expected utility theory and added to the basic model a separate regret factor with its own utility. Minimax regret models had defined regret in terms of value lost. In contrast, these later formulations posited, in Bell's words, that "the disadvantages of regret are traded off against the value of assets received."[152] Thus, these new regret models emphasized the expected value *difference* between the chosen and the rejected options rather than the expected loss associated with the chosen option only.[153,154] In this construal of regret, a choice of A over B implies not only that A is preferred to B but "selecting A and rejecting B is preferable to selecting B and rejecting A."[155] Following is a thorough explication of the reasoning behind modern regret theory by Loomes and Sugden:

> The central idea behind regret theory is that, when making decisions, individuals take into account not only the consequences they might experience as a result of the action chosen, but also how each consequence compares with what they would have experienced under the same state of the world had they chosen differently. . . . The overall level of satisfaction derived is a combination of the basic utility of the consequence actually experienced, and some decrement or increment of utility due to "regret" or "rejoicing". . . . We suggest that individuals choose so as to maximize the mathematical expectation of modified utility.[156]

Significantly, these newer regret theories assume that the value of choosing something depends on its context—on the nature of the things simultaneously rejected.

According to these theories, the modified expected utility of option X is a function of the expected utility of X *plus or minus the amount of regret* for not choosing Y. Regret is defined as the difference between the value of the obtained outcome and that of the alternative not chosen.[157] The term *regret* is used here generically to include both the joy/relief at having made the "right" decision (in which case it is added to the expected utility) as well as the regret at having made the "wrong" decision (in which case it is subtracted from the expected utility). Mathematically, it works like this:

Modified $\text{SEU}_X = \text{SEU}_X \pm \text{Regret}_{\text{Not-}Y}$

Let's return to Mrs. Russell's case and see how the modern regret model predicts her decision. What would a decision analysis
look like that explicitly factored in the (anticipated) regret as defined in modern regret theory? It would parallel the standard decision analysis, as outlined earlier in this chapter, but would add or
subtract a regret value. Because the outcome is as yet uncertain
(probabilistic), Mrs. Russell should employ expected utilities (rather
than raw utilities, as in minimax regret models) to calculate both
the traditional utility component and the regret component of the
equations. The following decision tree reveals the formal underlying structure to this regret-modified decision:

Operate
    (0.60 × 1.0) SEU cure + (0.80 × 0.60) Max. Alternative = +1.08
    (0.40 × .00) SEU death with surgery − (.80 × .60) Max. Alt
    = −0.48

Don't operate
    (0.80 × 0.60) SEU disease unchanged
    − (0.60 × 1.00) Max. Alt = −0.12
    (0.20 × 0.10) SEU death in 6 months
    − (0.60 × 1.00) Max. Alt = −0.58

The combined regret-modified SEU of the Operate option is now:
+.60; for the Don't-Operate option it is −.60. Therefore, the modern regret analysis recommends operating. Through deciding to have
the operation, Mrs. Russell and her family at the same time maximize the likelihood of attaining a desired outcome and minimize
the regret that would follow from recognizing and comparing what
is with what might have been.

Modern regret theories improve upon the pessimism of minimax regret theories by allowing regret to take both positive and
negative values, thus modeling both the unhappy reaction to feeling one has made the wrong decision and the happy reaction to
feeling one has made the right decision.[158] For many, modern regret theories also improve upon the older minimax regret models
by returning to the classic basis of decision—subjective expected
utility—simply adding a regret/rejoicing term to the traditional
equation. Restoring probabilities to the model was especially welcome.

Perhaps the most radical innovation of modern regret theory is an evaluative one: regret theorists argue that neither intransitivity nor regret is necessarily irrational.[159] Now some economists are agreeing with those philosophers who have challenged transitivity as an axiomatic feature of rationality. Modern regret theories in fact frankly predict intransitivity—but nonrandom, systematic intransitivity. Indeed, a number of decisions that appear irrational by virtue of intransitivity when viewed from within classical decision theory can be rationally accounted for by regret.[160] Apart from theoretical analyses, experimental investigations of contemporary regret theory have also yielded empirical support for the systematic but nontransitive preferences predicted by regret theory.[161,162]

My analysis does not stand or fall on the empirical success of these forms of regret theory. In fact, I suspect that, in their return to the basic framework of economic decision theory, these formulations have not gone far enough in a new direction. But regardless of the ultimate success of particular regret theories, they have already improved upon the orthodox models by including a perhaps ubiquitous fact of human decision making. At last scholarship has caught up with the common wisdom:

> Regret is a real phenomenon. It is not clear that it *ought* to be excluded from decision making . . . , for it is something we shall experience just as surely as we experience the other consequences of our decisions.[163]

Conclusions

A better perspective on decision making will recognize that regret is inevitable inasmuch as the following are inevitable: malignant chance, scarcity, choice, weakness of will, counterfactual thought, emotion, cognitive difficulties in estimating preferences and probabilities, intra- and interpersonal plurality, and thus conflict among values and between values and behavior. As Joseph Raz points out in the previous epigraph, inevitable aspects of the human psyche require explanation, not justification. Therefore, a better perspective on decision making will stop declaring regret irrational. Such a perspective will recognize the authority of regret as a legitimate, even useful, component of rational decision making. We will thereby be liberated to proceed to investigate the conditions that distinguish more rational from less rational regret: "What we need is an account of when and, at an extreme, whether we should care about, even to the point of regretting, what could have been or what should have been."[164] In the next chapter and the rest of this volume I abandon that extreme and sterile question of *whether* we should ever regret anything and get on with the more productive questions of what, when, and how.

6

Personal Roots of Regret

What really plays the dickens with us is something in ourselves.
Something that makes us go on doing the same sort of fool things,
however many chances we get.

—J. M. Barrie, *Dear Brutus*

The tragic and ironic worldviews have in common the assumption
that most human conflict and misery are due to personal or internal failings and ambivalences or to uncontrollable external forces.
The tragic flaw in the character of the literary hero, which brings
about the downfall of the hero, exemplifies this assumption. The
romantic and comic worldviews share the assumption that external and controllable forces are what get in the way of human happiness and stability. Likewise, whenever we are called upon to consider the question "What caused X to do Y?" our answers fall for
the most part into the same two categories: internal (personal) and
external (situational) reasons.[i] Accordingly, I have divided the
question of what "causes" regret into two chapters, first exploring
some of the personal characteristics of individuals and then some
of the characteristics of circumstances that help explain when and
why we regret.

I do this for the sake of analytic clarity but with reluctance.
Human reality, especially emotional experience, bridges the banks
of this division; it resides in the transaction between the person

and the environment, and that transaction ends with the essence of each interpenetrating the other. In a very real sense, the internal/external dichotomy is a false one.

Consider, for example, social class. Is this an internal or an external factor? In one sense, it seems clearly an external factor, an accident of circumstance, especially for children. And it is. We have no say in our social class of origin. But then again, surely by the time one is an adult, one's social class has taken on a decidedly personal cast—in the eyes of the world, and often in the eyes of the self too. With respect to the "lower" social orders, this is what Sennett and Cobb[2] meant by the phrase "the hidden injuries of class"—that, for example, not only are working-class and underclass individuals treated with less dignity than individuals of "higher" social classes, but also they tend to internalize the socially defined unworthiness. The converse probably applies to the other social classes as well—with those born with the proverbial silver spoon also tending to internalize their socially defined worthiness. In the profoundly true phrase whose origin I have long forgotten: "socialization [like genetics] goes all the way down."

On the other hand, consider gender. Surely it is an internal factor, a matter of one's personal, private genes. But then again, from the moment the newborn is wrapped in a pink rather than a blue blanket, those genes have social consequences. Certainly by the time one is an adult, one's gender has taken on at least some of the coloring assigned it by one's social norms—in the eyes of the world, and often in the eyes of the self too. So although one's gender is a biological matter, it is inevitably a social construction as well. The same applies to other "personal" factors, such as age, ethnicity, and race; they are at least as much social construction as individual attribute.

There is another sense in which the personal/situational dichotomy fails. The very definition of "person" and thus of the personal is itself socially constructed. In Western cultures independence is generally a central attribute of the mature adult self; here the self, or the person, is defined in isolation from or in opposition to others. In contrast, Eastern cultures generally assume a more interdependent construal of the self, or the person, viewing selfhood as integrally grounded in connection with others. Imagine the plight of the individual—let's call her Jessie—with personal roots in two cultures that differ on this dimension. In one of her cultures Jessie is viewed as clearly separate from her environment and from others, but in her other culture Jessie is viewed as inseparable from her environment and from others. As I have learned through listening to any number of bicultural college students, the difference is real enough to cause some significant strain, especially in conflicts between individual rights and responsibility to others.

Conceptually, the personal/situational dichotomy is a fuzzy set rather than a clear-cut dichotomy. Some factors, like weather, are prototypically situational factors. Some factors, like extraversion, are prototypically personal factors. But many factors, like gender, social class, even weakness of will, show both personal and situational features. Emotions, in particular, are the "product of *transactions* or *relationships* between the person and the environment."[3] For these reasons, you cannot ever really separate antecedents—whether personal or environmental—of emotions from the emotions themselves. The roots and effects of emotions are intrinsic to the emotion. With respect to the subject of this chapter, our personality and our emotions are inextricably intertwined. The fact that, in response to the very same external event, one person experiences the emotion of regret and another exultation serves in part to define who they are. Still, for the sake of bringing a degree of analytic order to this list of root conditions of regret, I reluctantly bow to intellectual tradition.

The conceivable personal "antecedents" of regret are legion.[4] In this book I discuss only a sample, including the following: (a) demographic features such as age and gender; (b) cognitive features such as procedural rationality, dispositional tendencies to engage in rumination and counterfactual thought, and personal values and worldview; (c) emotional factors, such as self-esteem, and states of mixed, ambivalent, or negative emotion; and (d) motivational features like weakness of will and self-deception.

Demographic Sources

Age: The Seasons of Regret

It is striking how often literature portrays regret as a phenomenon of old age and middle age. Psychology seems to agree.

From life-span developmental psychology has emerged the idea of the "life review," the "Janus-like" process of looking ahead (in this case, looking ahead to death) while at the same time looking back over one's past.[5] Developmental psychologist Robert N. Butler asserts that the life review is universal or nearly universal among the aged, and that it demands, among other things, the task of coming to terms with regret.

Butler's formulation is reminiscent of Erik Erikson's[6] view of the centrality in old age of a conflict between despair and integrity. In Erikson's theory of development, until an individual has acknowledged and integrated the less pleasant as well as the more pleasant parts of his or her life, that individual remains unwhole. Personal integrity thus builds on a process of bringing together into the self the wise and the foolish, the strong and the weak, the approved and the regretted aspects of one's self and one's life. On this view, then, regret will be a predominant concern of the aged until they succeed in coming to terms with it.

Recall as well how Baldwin explicitly linked regret with middle age (cf. Chapter 3):

> When more time stretches behind than stretches before one, some assessments, however reluctantly and incompletely, begin to be made. Between what one wishes to become and what one has become there is a momentous gap. . . . Some of us are compelled, around the middle of our lives, to make a study of this baffling geography.[7]

Dostoevsky's Underground Man and Tolstoy's Ivan Ilyitch are in their forties. Tyler's Maggie Moran is forty-eight. James's Lambert Strether, Woolf's Clarissa Dalloway, and Tyler's Ira Moran are all in their fifties. Beckett's Krapp and Bergman's Borg are old, as is Stevens, the protagonist of Ishiguro's novel, *The Remains of the Day*.

The contemporary term, *midlife crisis*, virtually equates acute regret with middle age. As it turns out, this modern equation has a long history. Six hundred years ago, Dante described in *The Divine Comedy* something that sounds very much like a midlife crisis: "In the middle of the journey of our life, I found myself inside a dark forest, for the right way I had completely lost."

If not focusing specifically on middle age or old age, a number of writers have explicitly drawn a link between regret and adulthood in general. Ephron has suggested that writing fiction can give an author "the ultimate shot at revision" of things one might have done differently. To feel the need for revision, one must first regret what is. But "a gift for revision may be a developmental stage . . . that comes along somewhat later, in one's mid-twenties, say," Ephron speculates.[8] Other fiction writers have articulated through their characters a presumed link between regret and adulthood. In her short story "Mariah," Jamaica Kincaid has the 19-year-old protagonist muse: "even I could see that I was too young for . . . real regret."[9] In his journals John Cheever describes a young prostitute in Times Square: "the face seems so immature that she cannot be credited with conscious regrets, but bewilderment, yes. She had, in her bones, expected something very different."[10] In *Winesburg, Ohio*, Sherwood Anderson proposes that it is the experience of regret that definitively separates childhood from adulthood:

> There is a time in the life of every boy when he for the first time takes the backward view of life. Perhaps that is the moment when he crosses the line into manhood. The boy is walking through the street of his town. He is thinking of the future and of the figure he will cut in the world. Ambitions and regrets awake within him. . . . Ghosts of old things creep into his consciousness; the voices outside of himself whisper a message concerning the limitations of life. From being quite sure of himself and his future he becomes not at all sure. . . . The sadness of sophistication has come to the boy. With a little gasp he sees himself as merely a leaf blown by the wind through the streets of his village. He knows that in spite of all the stout talk of his fellows he must live and die in uncertainty, a thing blown by the winds, a thing destined like corn to wilt in the sun.[11]

Here Anderson tells us that regret stirs within us along with the adult recognition that we are "destined like corn to wilt in the sun," that we all must die, usually after physical deterioration. A second insight offered by Anderson is the link between regret and recognizing that we "must live and die in uncertainty, a thing blown by the winds." Both perceptions exemplify the tragic stance toward regret—believing that regret is as inescapable as uncertainty, deterioration, and death, and that these are profoundly insupportable facts.

Whether regret is in fact more common later than earlier in life is, of course, an empirical question. But to beg this question for now: *if* regret is an adult phenomenon, why might this be? Surely Piaget's answer, were he here to ask, would center on the individual's level of cognitive development.[12] The final stage of cognitive development in Piaget's theory is called formal operations, and it entails, among other things, the ability to engage in abstract, hypothetical thought. Formal operations is supposed to appear for the first time in adolescence or early adulthood, if at all. Regret is often associated with the type of hypothetical thought called counterfactual thought, which entails imagining states contrary to fact—what might have been or what might still be. By extension, from within a Piagetian framework, regret will not be expected to make much of an appearance prior to adolescence.

If the cognitive capacity has been in place since adolescence, why is regret so often linked with middle age and old age? Regret in later life might be explained by the greater opportunity to have made mistakes and suffered losses, the narrower range of available choices, and a more desperate yearning to fulfill unrealized possibilities.

The older you are, *the more opportunity you have had* for taking wrong turns, for making profoundly important but misguided decisions. If they are fortunate, children and adolescents are seldom called upon to make important decisions. Although children and adolescents in this culture are permitted more or less leeway in deciding how to spend their allowance or work money, it is still the rare high-schooler who is given carte blanche in decisions of even middling importance—for example, choosing a particular car. The first really important decisions—for example, higher education, occupation, marriage, childrearing—are usually held off until young adulthood. Momentous choices like these then launch a lifetime of significant adult decisions that in the fullness of time may prove mistaken. Major personal crises likely to awaken thoughts of what might have been—such as occupational failure, divorce, loss of or disappointment in one's children, failing health—also tend to have the decency to wait until later adulthood to strike.

In *Breathing Lessons*, Anne Tyler offers the reader a rather subtle answer to the question of why regrets might proliferate with advancing age. Recall her description of fiftysomething Ira as having "passed that early, superficial stage when any number of moves seemed possible . . . *now his choices were narrower.*"[13] Virginia Woolf expresses the same idea through Clarissa Dalloway's musings about herself in her early fifties:

> Oh if she could have had her life over again! she thought . . . She had the oddest sense of being herself invisible; unseen; unknown; *there being no more marrying, no more having of children now, but only this astonishing and rather solemn progress with the rest of them, up Bond Street, this being Mrs. Dalloway; not even Clarissa any more; this being Mrs. Richard Dalloway.*
>
> It was all over for her. The sheet was stretched and the bed narrow. . . .[14]

As evidenced in these passages, the perception of having a narrowed range of choice can be associated with regret for the unrealized potentialities. For some people, this recognition incites redoubled efforts to maintain breathing room or to realize the potentialities. This seems to be the case with many of the men described in the book by Daniel Levinson and others, *Seasons of a Man's Life,* the first rigorous treatment of midlife crisis. Some of these men appear to be rather feverishly pursuing formerly unpursued avenues and formerly undeveloped aspects of the self:

> Every choice I make involves the rejection of many other possibilities. . . . During a transition period—and especially in the Mid-Life Transition—the neglected parts of the self more urgently seek expression.[15]

Psychologist David Gutmann found evidence of a trend in both men and women such that after early parenthood they hope to live out aspects of the self that previously went undeveloped due to the constraints of gender roles. Specifically, men tend to become less aggressive and more nurturant and affiliative over the life span, and women tend to become less affiliative and more agentic and assertive over the life span.[16] In so doing, they may be attempting to medicate their regret for the possibilities earlier unrealized. (Of course, this pattern, characteristic of men and women responding prior to 1975, may or may not survive significant historical changes in gender roles—if and when such changes occur.) This may mean as well that people who live their early adult lives in less sex-typed ways may suffer less sex-role-based regret later. Living out agentic and nurturant roles early may obviate a few so-called midlife crises.

Still, time has a way of dropping more and more *losses* on our doorstep. In *Breathing Lessons,* Tyler's protagonist, Maggie Moran, seems to be suffering from a type of loss that is both stereotypically nurturant and directly linked with advancing age—the "empty nest." Although Maggie has never accepted her son's failed marriage and her resulting separations from her daughter-in-law and granddaughter, what occasions her acute attack of regret over these losses is the imminent departure of her last child for college. The impending empty nest evokes for Maggie a crisis of regret—and desperately assertive measures to resolve her crisis.

Insofar as advancing age brings with it more decisions that end badly, a narrowing of choice due to the role constraints of one's past choices, wishes to pursue unrealized possibilities, and more losses, regret is predictable. Those individuals who accentuate such insights probably lean more toward an ironic or tragic mode of regret than a comic or romantic mode. Someone who recognizes that limitation and loss are inevitable aspects of the human condition, and accepts this recognition with equanimity, will likely experience the less searing, ironic, form of regret. Someone who both possesses this recognition yet rejects it as insupportable will likely experience the more searing, tragic, form of regret.

Regret may or may not depend on a particular age-related level of cognitive or other type of development. But it is definitely not *limited* to those of advanced age. The fictional character of Pip in *Great Expectations* is not alone in suffering regret as a very young man (in his early twenties) for his behavior toward loved ones. When a columnist in *Parade* magazine asked her teenage readers what they most regretted in their lives, they were not at a loss either. One teenager wrote poignantly about his regret for having failed to spend as much time as possible with his mother before her death. Another regretted having gone through a "wild" period around age eleven that caused her parents much distress.[17]

My own research, too, has found regret in young people—that is, college students, most 18 to 20 years of age.[18] One hundred percent of the 149 students I asked in one study listed *at least* one regret—and often as many as five. In response to the question "how often do you regret things," only 8 (7 of them men) of these 149 students answered "almost never." Though most of them wouldn't be caught dead admitting it, I think many adolescents very much regret the loss of childhood. Having to choose a college, a major, or a job frequently entails a battle with regret for those colleges, majors, and jobs that have to be forgone. Unlike Jamaica Kincaid's 19-year-old fictional character, many young people can certainly be credited with real, conscious regrets.

Gender

Stereotypically, women, considered (in this culture) the more emotional gender, might also be expected to be the more regretful gender. Women consistently report more depression and other negative emotions than men.[19] "Regret is a woman's natural food—she thrives upon it," wrote Sir Arthur Wing Pinero.[20] Simone de Beauvoir, writing in *The Second Sex*, agrees that women may be more vulnerable to regret, but finds the source not in their nature, but in their nurture—in their culturally prescribed passivity:

> for woman condemned to passivity, the inscrutable future [and likewise, perhaps, the past] is haunted by phantoms . . . ; being unable to act, she worries . . . in her imagination all possibilities have equal

reality. . . . What she is endeavoring to exorcize in her gloomy rum-
inations is the specter of her own powerlessness.[21]

Whereas thought can be viewed as "experimental action,"[22] in
Beauvoir's account ruminative regret in women *substitutes* for culturally denied action.

At least one empirical study of gender and regret clearly calls
into question the cultural stereotypes. Psychologist Susan B.
Shimanoff[23] used two different methods to explore emotionality in
married couples: (1) self-reports of the perceived frequency of, attitude toward, and expression of regret (and other emotions); and (2)
measurements of the actual expression of regret (and other emotions) in day-to-day conversations. The results were revealing. The
women had a more positive attitude toward and believed that they
expressed more regret than the men. But in fact there was no gender difference in the expression of regret (or in the degree of emotional expression, more generally). In the words of the author, "the
reported differences reflect stereotypical assessments rather than
actual differences."[24] This and similar findings of the power of gender stereotypes of emotionality[25] imply that the study of gender
and regret may prove especially tricky.

In response to the 1953 Gallup poll discussed in Chapter 4
(whose results were reported separately for men and women), there
appears to be no overall gender difference: 39 percent of the men
and 35 percent of the women reported regret.[26] The Kinnier and
Metha sample also showed no overall difference by gender in reporting having regrets of some kind.[27]

As for specific regrets, there appear to be no gender differences
in the Gallup sample, with the possible exception of marital and
career regrets. Six percent of the women versus 2 percent of the
men reported regret for a "mistake in marriage"; conversely, 9 percent of the men versus 3 percent of the women reported regret for
a career choice.[28] Only one of the seven regrets cited by more than
15 percent of the age or gender groups studied by Kinnier and Metha
showed a significant gender difference: 20 percent of the men and
only 10 percent of the women reported regretting not having spent
more quality time with family.[29] In both surveys the differences
between the sexes were exceptions to the rule of similarity.

Research with college students has yielded similar results. A
recent study of regret by Calvin Chin in a sample of 98 college
students found no difference in the degree of self-reported regret of
the men and women.[30] In response to a question very like that

originally asked by Gallup, the men and women in a sample of 44 undergraduates I studied were equally likely to acknowledge some regret or other. The only area showing a gender difference was that of family, with the young women reporting more family regrets than the young men. The most common family-related regrets concerned not getting along well with parents or siblings.[31]

A different sample of 149 undergraduates I have studied also yielded mixed gender results. The young women reported a significantly greater number of family-related regrets than the young men. However, men and women reported equal numbers of educational, job-related, and risk-related regrets, and equal totals.[32]

The previously discussed research by Gutmann[33] suggests that in middle adulthood men and women may be equally beset by regrets over undeveloped aspects of the self, though the content of these regrets might be mirror images of one another. Middle-aged men appear more likely to regret their past failures with relationships and women their past failures to take action to effect desired results. Two findings observed by Kinnier and Metha[34] provide relevant empirical evidence: men were twice as likely as women to regret not spending time with family; and middle-aged and older respondents were significantly more likely to report this regret than younger respondents. Recalling as well the greater tendency among young (college-age) women than among young men to report family-oriented regret, it appears that age and gender may both play a role in the experience of certain regrets (chiefly familial ones). But so far, men's and women's regrets appear more similar than dissimilar in incidence and content.

Social Position

Social class as an internalized aspect of one's self-concept[35] could shape regret in a number of ways. For instance, the individual who holds a strong assumption that we are the masters of our fate (a worldview characteristic of modern Western cultures)—and who occupies a position near the bottom of the social hierarchy—may be expected to experience both more regret and a different quality of regret than someone at the top. A plausible hypothesis is that socioeconomic status will be inversely related to regret: the lower one's social status, the more regret—because the greater and more significant one's deprivation. Objective deprivation may also be less important than subjective factors like the perceived degree of deprivation relative to others.[36]

In addition, insofar as the individual internalizes the societal denigration associated with low social status, it seems likely that in this culture the regret of the societally less privileged may tend to take on a characterological form; that is, such individuals may consider them*selves* to blame for what has gone wrong in their lives to a greater extent than do individuals from higher strata of society. Those from the lower social classes may tend to think something like: "I've been laid off because I'm just not up to par" rather than "I've been laid off because of a downturn in the economy."

We know that personal ("It's *my* fault"), global ("I can't do *anything* right"), and stable ("I'll *never* be able to get my life together") explanations of negative events tend to produce greater depression than explanations focusing on situational, specific, and temporary factors.[37] Similarly, class-based regret may lead to greater hopelessness insofar as it is grounded in negative explanations like these. Such regret may even prove tragic in its self-fulfilling expectation of unhappy endings.

Dostoevsky's Underground Man shows this pattern. He gluts himself on regret. The regretted acts result in large part from his shame over his lack of position in society. His regretful state is sustained by the enormous discrepancy between his ideals and his socially degraded reality. Finally, his experience of regret takes on a deeply tragic cast in which he despairs of the possibility of resolution.

Cognitive Sources

Procedural Irrationality

In addition to the demographic characteristics of age, gender, and social class, a number of cognitive characteristics undoubtedly influence regret. Economic decision theory suggests an important one: procedural rationality. Those who habitually neglect the canons of good decision making may find themselves habitually suffering regret for hasty and poorly made decisions. Failing to seek out a reasonable amount of good information regarding the likelihood of alternative outcomes, failing to analyze or recognize what one really wants, or disregarding such knowledge in favor of one's "gut" reactions—all these forms of procedural irrationality are recipes for regret. But some people may show exemplary procedural rationality in their consumer decisions and abysmal procedural rationality in their love decisions, or vice versa. Such a pattern would suggest that procedural rationality is less a stable and consistent disposition of the person than something that varies with the situation. Under this as-yet-untested assumption, I examine procedural irrationality in greater detail in the next chapter.

Dispositional Counterfactual Thought and Rumination

People also show different propensities to engage in *rumination*— deliberately mulling over things or brooding about them. For example, compared to extraverts, introverts are more reflective and pay more attention to the inner world.[38] Research on a personality trait called "negative affectivity"—the tendency to experience aversive emotional states (in which category regret fits)—finds that individuals high in negative affectivity are more introspective than those lower in negative affectivity.[39] It appears that some of the well-known gender difference in depression may be due to women's greater degree of rumination, which tends to heighten depression.[40] In view of these and similar avenues of research, another plausible hypothesis about the relationship between personality and regret is that introverts and other habitual ruminators will experience more regret than extraverts and other types of personalities who avoid rumination.

The second hypothesis has in fact been tested. Recently, Calvin Chin carried out a study in which he measured the degree of ruminativeness and of regret of 98 University of Michigan students. The results supported the hypothesis that the more ruminative we are, the more regret we are likely to report. (The women were not found to be more ruminative than the men in this study.)[41]

Among the kinds of thinking likely to be done by someone who broods is counterfactual thinking, or thinking about what might have been. In J. M. Barrie's play *Dear Brutus*, a mischievous old man orchestrates a Midsummer Eve foray into the forest of second chances. He has carefully selected his unwitting victims on the basis of their decided penchant for imagining what might have been. Only the one character not given to might-have-beens escapes the humbling trance. (Barrie's play avoided predictable gender stereotyping, in that the only individual *not* plagued with regret is a woman.)

Surely Barrie's intuition was right that not everyone is equally predisposed to engage in the activity of imagining what might have been. If so, not everyone is equally predisposed to the regret presumably associated with counterfactual thought.

In principle, we might be expected to imagine less ideal conditions than we actually experience (e.g., "If only I hadn't met X, think what happiness I would have missed") just as often as *more* ideal conditions ("If only I hadn't met X, think what misery I would have avoided"). Counterfactual thoughts about less-ideal states are probably associated with joy or relief, and counterfactual thoughts about more-ideal states with regret. However, research consistently finds an asymmetry on this and related dimensions, such that losses loom larger than equivalent gains in people's hearts and minds.[42] In the light of the known psychological disparity between our reactions to losses and gains, it seems safe to assume that (everything else being equal) the more rumination, the more attention to loss, and thus the more regret.

Assuming that counterfactual thought consists at least partially of imagination, it is a reasonable (and testable) hypothesis that the greater the personal proclivity for counterfactual thought, the more regret. This idea informs a literary critic's description of the fictional characters of author Bobbie Ann Mason: "She [Bobbie Ann Mason] portrays the disquieted lives of men and women not blessed with much money or education or luck, but cursed with enough sensitivity and imagination to allow them to suffer regrets."[43] This observation of Quammen's also implicitly poses a counter-hypothesis to one I proposed above—that is, Quammen implies that the incidence of regret, like imagination and counterfactual thought, might distribute itself rather evenhandedly across socioeconomic and social class lines.

At the extreme of the rumination continuum lies obsessive (i.e., involuntary, uncontrollable, and irrational) brooding. For obsessive ruminators, the process of making decisions is always fraught with regret. As psychological decision experts Irving Janis and Leon Mann assert, "[c]ompulsive [roughly synonymous with "obsessive"] personalities . . . continue to have doubts about the unknown risks inherent in every decision."[44]

Freud's patient known as the Rat Man (described in Chapter 2) exemplifies obsessional rumination and counterfactual thought.[45] Dostoevsky's Underground Man could be a fictional cousin of the Rat Man (indeed, the Underground Man compares himself explicitly to a mouse gnawing at itself in its underground hole). The Underground Man's self-chosen solitude is taken up entirely by dark brooding in which he endlessly (and fruitlessly) lives and re-lives regret.

On the face of it, Ishiguro's protagonist, Stevens, in *The Remains of the Day* falls on the opposite side of the continuum. He diligently avoids thinking by filling up his time with work. Indeed, Stevens's work has a distinctly compulsive cast to it, going so far as to displace attention to his dying father and the woman who loves him. Yet Stevens may be using work as a strategy for avoiding a natural-born ruminator's constant doubts about every decision. His early decision to become a butler allowed him to duck other life decisions, trivial and serious, all of which were left to his employer. Then through compulsive work, Stevens was able to suppress awareness of his regrets—until the first vacation of his life cornered him with his regret for precisely this lifelong escape from freedom. This fictional rendering also indirectly corroborates Butler's proposal that one reason for the putative universality of a life review process among the aged is that retirement eliminates the deployment of work as a defense against reflection.[46]

It would appear that those who spend more time and energy thinking in general, and thinking counterfactual thoughts specifically (such as introverts, habitual ruminators, and obsessives), are in for more regret than their less reflective peers.

Personal Values

Regret has little respect for rule books, etiquette manuals, lists of commandments, or economic models. Like other emotions (as well as other psychological processes in general), regret depends less on universal, objective assessments than on personal values and norms. Anything that one cares about or that conflicts with one's values or falls below one's standards may produce regret. Inasmuch as norms and values lack universality, it would be foolish to attempt to formulate universal propositions as to what is a "proper" occasion for regret.[47] One individual regrets the very "injury to character" in having even considered joining his friends in a successful plot to rob a bank, and another regrets not having joined his friends in the successful robbery. The only certainty is that one of the incorrigible costs of caring about something (whether money, one's own character, or anything else) is vulnerability to the experience of regret.

Inasmuch as regret is at times a "moral sentiment" (along with guilt, remorse, pride, etc.), certain of our bedrock values are particularly relevant to it. For example, regret is utterly unjustifiable to the thoroughgoing determinist or thoroughgoing believer in predestination or fate. If our choices are wholly determined, then regret makes no sense. But regret does make sense to the semi-determinist that I suspect most of us are. We do believe in regularities of nature, including some regularities of "human nature." But we also believe that human choice is not entirely determined (though the consequences of our choices may be).[48] As William James points out, to the extent that our worldview is less than thoroughly deterministic, that we think we "could have done otherwise," we lay ourselves open to the experience of regret for outcomes of which we are or were an agent.[49,50]

Emotional Sources

Self-esteem

Psychologists Robert A. Josephs, Richard Larrick, Claude Steele, and Richard Nisbett[51] have hypothesized that people with low self-esteem will suffer more regret than people with high self-esteem. The reasoning is based on Steele's notion of self-esteem as a system of resources functioning to maintain one's self-regard.[52] When individuals with high self-esteem suffer the mistakes, losses, and other forms of misfortune that occasion regret, the threat to their self-esteem is minimal, in that they know they can fall back on other personal resources yielding compensatory positive outcomes. But individuals with low self-esteem lack this conviction; therefore, regret oppresses them. As a result, people low in self-esteem appear to make more choices to reduce their anticipated regret than do people high in self-esteem. For example, compared with those higher in self-esteem, people with lower self-esteem were found by these researchers to prefer choices without feedback about the alternative outcome. For these individuals, ignorance—of the other outcome—is bliss.[53]

Mixed Emotions and Ambivalence

Mixed emotions and ambivalence are, I have suggested in Chapter 5, the norm rather than an "abnormal" or pathological state of affairs. There I also argued that while mixed emotions need not lead to regret, genuine ambivalence (equally intense and opposing emotions about the very same object) does necessarily lead to regret.

In one study, women who later regretted their decision to have elective sterilization recalled having felt more ambivalent about sterilization at the time of the decision than those without later regrets.[54] Though it is possible that this finding may have been distorted by retrospective bias, it is a hypothesis worth looking into with methods better designed to address it.

We know that being in a good mood over one matter seems to "recruit" other rosy thoughts and feelings, resulting in maintenance of the original good mood.[55] Recent research has persuasively concluded that those who accurately acknowledge personal shortcomings, unpleasant realities, and lack of personal control tend to show a constellation of distressing emotions, particularly depression.[56] People who score high in neuroticism also seem significantly more reactive to negative events than non-neurotics.[57] Emotions often occur in positive or negative clusters rather than in isolation.[58] The negative emotions of anger, depression, and anxiety or shame and depression typically occur together, or are reported as occurring together.[59] In light of such findings, it would not be surprising if regret were associated with dysphoric moods and emotional distress, at least in the short run.

A history of psychological distress does appear to distinguish people at high risk from those at low risk for regret following elective sterilization. In one study, 75 percent of the regretful women and only 5 percent of the satisfied women reported significant emotional distress the year prior to a tubal ligation.[60] Two other studies corroborate and extend this result.[61] In addition, some habitually troubled women may compound the usual decision difficulties by making sterilization decisions at times when they are especially vulnerable—for example, during pregnancy or in the postpartum period.[62] This may explain the finding of more regret among postpartum than nonpostpartum sterilizees. Or it may be that post-sterilization regret is simply a concomitant of the greater depression sometimes experienced in the postpartum period, even by otherwise untroubled women.[63]

The available empirical evidence supports the intuition that regret does possess unpleasant psychological concomitants, including poor psychological and emotional adjustment. In a study in which 40 emotionally disturbed criminal offenders were asked to explain their criminal acts, those whose explanations included higher levels of feelings of "remorse, regret, need for punishment"[64] also had higher levels of depression and neuroticism. A study in which 120 cancer patients were interviewed and tested during the first

100 days following diagnosis found that patients with more intense regret about the past showed higher levels of emotional distress than patients without so much regret.[65]

Again, emotional distress may not only "cause" regret, but the influence may flow in the other direction as well: regret may "cause" emotional distress. Alternatively, regret and emotional distress may more often simply be concomitants, with neither "causing" the other.

For J. M. Barrie in *Dear Brutus*, the implicit assumption is that it is the sadness that evokes regret: he defines "might-have-beens" as "shades made of sad folk's thoughts." On the other hand, many of us assume that to regret is to lay ourselves open to a world of distress. Lampedusa expressed this folk theory regarding the downward pull of regret in *The Leopard*, when he wrote: "And now that he [Don Fabrizio, the Prince of Salina] had begun regretting the past, he would find himself, in moments of worst humor, slithering quite a way down that perilous slope."

But in all previous research, the question of causal direction remains clouded. In fact, none of the studies establishes whether regret functions as a "cause" or an "effect" of emotional disturbance—or simply an outgrowth of emotionally disturbing situations. Nor do these studies conclusively establish whether "normal" people in "normal" circumstances with more intense regret show evidence of more emotional distress or maladjustment than such people with less regret. Some of my research suggests that regret and other emotional distress coincide—at least in the short run.[66] Even so, it is not yet known whether the presumed association between regret and other dark feelings lasts over the long run—although longitudinal research I have collaborated on suggests it may not.[67]

Motivational Sources

Weakness of Will

The individual struggling unsuccessfully with an addiction may be said to manifest akrasia, or acting against one's better judgment due to "weakness of will." Such an individual typically vacillates between resolve and weakness of will, with episodes of backsliding followed by piercing regret (and often remorse, shame, guilt, and self-loathing, as well). In his journals of the 1960s John Cheever

recorded this sort of struggle with alcoholism. Although he loathed
the idea of drinking before noon, day after day he recorded in his
journals morning surrenders to the whiskey hidden in the pantry. In
one particularly dreadful passage Cheever provides a blow-by-blow
account of himself desperately monitoring the comings and goings
of his wife from the kitchen for an excruciating hour beginning
at 9:30 when he wanted a drink but did not want (at least on the
conscious level) his wife to see him drinking. Finally with horror
he watches her set up the ironing board in the kitchen; he writes:

> This oughtn't to take more than five minutes, but five minutes was
> more than I could wait, and in full view of my wife, and the world, I
> went into the pantry and mixed a drink. It was eighteen minutes to
> eleven.[68]

Elsewhere Cheever describes these kinds of lapses specifically in
terms of weakness of will:

> There is a path through the woods that I can take this rainy morning;
> but instead I will take the path to the pantry and mix a Martini. Look,
> look, then, here is a weak man, a man without character.[69]

As discussed earlier, akrasia is a formula for regret. "While regret
is not necessary for every case of akrasis, it is characteristic for the
akrates to regret what he has done."[70] Insofar as individuals differ
in weakness of will, they will also differ in the frequency with
which they experience regret. Likewise, in those particular spheres
that individuals suffer weakness of will, they will be more likely
to experience regret.

Self-deception

It does not take a doctrinaire Freudian to recognize that the real
reasons for a decision sometimes escape the conscious awareness
of the decision maker. Even researchers thoroughly disinclined to
a Freudian worldview have amassed convincing evidence that people often fail to recognize the bases of their decisions and judgments.[71] Still, self-deception motivated by self-protectiveness seems
a human force to be reckoned with. To the extent that we make
decisions in the dark, we place ourselves at risk for later regret.

Research clearly finds, for example, that the best predictor of
an unregretted sterilization is choosing it out of a genuine conviction that one has all the children one wants.[72] But a given individ-

ual may report this as his or her reason, not consciously acknowledging other reasons. Some people with marital problems may seek sterilization as an unrealistic solution to the marital problems. Some people may seek sterilization primarily out of a need to exercise control in a marital war. For some the decision represents a symbolic rejection of their partner. Or themselves. In any case, if someone chooses sterilization as a reproductive "solution" to a non-reproductive problem, he or she is vulnerable to later regret—particularly if divorce and remarriage eventually eliminate the real problem.

Self-knowledge is probably another component of psychological "sensitivity"—as in the fictional characters described earlier as "cursed with enough sensitivity . . . to allow them to suffer regrets." Because self-knowledge is not inevitable, but a task, there are degrees of self-knowledge and therefore degrees of awareness of regret: individuals may be conscious of feeling regret, vaguely conscious of regret but unaware of precisely what it is that they regret, or unaware of regret. Dostoevsky's Underground Man, for instance, is all too aware of his regret and of exactly what he regrets. Ira in *Breathing Lessons* seems most of the time only vaguely aware of what he regrets. Stevens in *The Remains of the Day* is unaware (until the end) of personal regret.[73] Research on the personality trait of "negative affectivity," already discussed, finds that individuals who score higher on this tendency to experience unpleasant emotional states are more honest with themselves about their own failures and shortcomings than individuals who score lower on negative affectivity.[74] By extension (given equivalent levels of failure, loss, mistakes, and so forth), individuals with more self-knowledge ought to be expected to experience more postdecision regret at the conscious level.

The failed side of self-knowledge is self-deception. As those like Freud and Sartre[75] have pointed out, most of us militantly avoid knowing unpleasant things about ourselves and our lives:

> we try to hide anguish from ourselves; we apprehend our particular possible [i.e., our present and the actual] by avoiding considering all other possibles [i.e., our past and what might have been].[76]

In the interests of self-protectiveness, we may deny regret, hide it from ourselves, cover it with what Nietzsche called the "veil of the past,"[77] or self-servingly distort the underlying memories. In Chapter 8 I discuss in detail various defensive strategies people

commonly employ to ward off regret. For now, it is of interest to
note simply that individuals differ in their ability and inclination
to ward off the self-knowledge that implicates regret.

Again, lack of self-knowledge need not be a static characteristic
of the individual, as it was for Dostoevsky's Underground Man and
Beckett's Krapp. Fictional characters like Ivan Ilyitch (Tolstoy), Dr.
Borg (Bergman), and Stevens (Ishiguro) illustrate how initial states
of self-deception can evolve to later states of self-knowledge.
Therefore, the presumed connections between self-knowledge and
regret are probably time-limited and limited by the nature of the
regret and the regretter.

In fact, as Erikson proposed (and as will be discussed in greater
detail in Chapter 8), over time, given genuine resolution, the greater
one's self-knowledge, the *less* one's regret. Take character regret,
for example. If over time one alters one's character in the desired
direction, then greater self-knowledge may yield less regret than it
did earlier. This seems to be the case with Dr. Borg in Bergman's
film, *Wild Strawberries*, as analyzed by Erik Erikson.[78] In reaction
to his bleak regret over a lost love, Borg had allowed himself to
harden into a state of embittered retreat from intimacy. Late in
life, after a crucial confrontation with Marianne, his daughter-in-
law, he permits himself to re-do some of his previous mistakes by
showing care for Marianne and his son. As a result, he is no longer
a prisoner of unacknowledged regret. Through a belatedly lived experience of regret, he has at last transcended it.

However, if one does not make desired changes, self-knowledge
and regret may continue to go hand in hand, as they do in the
Underground Man. A more ironic variant of this pattern is exemplified by the insight expressed in J. M. Barrie's *Dear Brutus* that
serves as the epigraph of this chapter.[79] To the extent that we do
go on doing the same sort of fool things, and know it, we will go
on experiencing regret. This is perhaps the quintessential statement of the tragic (and ironic) sense of regret: that human conflict
and misery is due primarily to unalterable personal, internal failings.

In conclusion, literature and the limited body of available research
reveal aspects of the person that place one at greater risk for regret.
Increasing age, procedural irrationality, ruminativeness, low self-
esteem, ambivalence, chronic emotional distress, and weakness of
will appear significantly linked with the experience of regret. It is
also possible, but as yet not established or not tested, that regret

may be associated with gender, self-knowledge, and other personal characteristics. Yet, despite our staunch cultural inclination to look for causes inside the individual, the comic and romantic world-views are partly right—some of our regret is due to factors outside ourselves.

7

Occasions of Regret

Although we commonly think of emotion as bubbling up from the most private wellsprings of the individual, external circumstances significantly shape emotion as well. External, or situational, factors influence the quality of regret, how intensely it is experienced, and when it is experienced and expressed. Moreover, because emotion consists of a transaction between a person and his or her circumstances, it does not really make sense to try to separate them. In the interests of analytic clarity, in this chapter I am treating external circumstances as separable, but I do so in an "as-if" manner. The comic and romantic constructions of regret view controllable, external factors as primarily responsible for frustrating human happiness, and the exercise of reason and action as the primary antidotes. Among the external, situational factors shaping regret are the large influences of culture and the more minute influences having to do with the context of decisions, the antecedents of decisions, and the regretted outcomes themselves.

Situational Sources of Regret

Cultural Regulation of Regret

Culture and historicity significantly color the individual's experience and expression of emotions.[1] Here are a few examples. In cultures that consider anger unacceptably immature—for example, in

Tahiti and in the Utka Eskimo tribe—it is nonexistent in adults.[2] Whereas in the United States we have literally codified the pursuit of happiness, on the South Pacific island of Ifaluk, "happiness is viewed as amoral, if not immoral."[3] For the Ifaluk peoples, happiness is an immature emotion that needs to be socialized away; children are happy; the mature person is calm, gentle, and nurturing. In a related vein, when a Japanese acquaintance arrived in the United States, his first impression of his highly educated associates was that they were disconcertingly unintelligent. Later, he understood his mistake. These Americans relished the exercise of wit, and laughed and joked around a lot. Because in his culture indiscriminate levity betokens a certain intellectual dimness, he had jumped to an erroneous conclusion. No, emotion is not a purely private, individual matter, but is to a considerable extent culturally and historically constituted.

Like emotion in general, regret too comes equipped with "feeling rules,"[4] or cultural norms prescribing when it is "unfounded or required, appropriate or unreasonable."[5] Indeed, due to its significant cognitive component, regret may be even more responsive to cultural prescriptions than other emotions, such as fear.

Item: Five hundred twenty passengers die in a 1985 Japan Airlines plane crash. The president of Japan Airlines expresses deep regret and resigns his position. Top airline executives personally visit every family who lost a relative, to express their deep regret.

Item: On July 3, 1988, the *Vincennes*, a U.S. warship, accidentally shoots down an Iranian aircraft, killing 290 civilians. Afterward, President Reagan and other military and government leaders express official regret. However, in the eyes of many observers, including Walter Shapiro, who wrote in the July 18 issue of *Time* magazine, the regret has a notably lukewarm, "yes-but" character, stressing the United States' innocence of malicious intent and Iran's contribution to the tragedy through its bellicose conduct in the Persian Gulf. Many American citizens seem to share the government's attitude. Less than two weeks after the event, the president of the PTA in Toledo suggests in an interview on National Public Radio that perhaps Iran had loaded the plane with already-dead bodies and aimed it at the Navy ship with the intent either to destroy the ship or to cause the ship to shoot at it, thereby undermining the United States in world opinion.

Despite the common element in these stories of accidental deaths due to aircraft mishaps, there is an important difference. The typical American reaction to the Persian Gulf deaths was muted, qualified regret, if any; the reaction of the president and other officials of the Japanese airline was intense, unqualified regret. As is not uncommon in Japan and other Eastern cultures, the Japanese officials not only expressed formal regret in words but took action to express their sense of responsibility for the tragedy. I believe that this discrepancy cannot be entirely explained by the arguably differential ease of empathizing with victims from one's own country versus victims from another, even an unfriendly, country. How often does an American executive resign in regret for the lethal mistakes of his or her company? The discrepancy may tell us something significant about the cultural constitution of regret.

As alluded to in Chapter 1, one possible reason for the horrified fascination with regret in America is our horrified fascination with uncertainty, randomness, chance. From the point of view of the United States, there was a strong element of chance in the *Vincennes* incident; it was partly a matter of bad luck that we mistook that particular plane for a warplane and successfully fired upon it. Everyone just happened to be in the wrong place at the wrong time. The ways of chance (the more Western concept) and of fate (the more Eastern concept) are fascinating—in part because they are terrifying.

But the same terror that we find fascinating finally causes us to repudiate regret. In the West we refuse to accept fate as an explanatory concept, we only reluctantly accept chance as an explanatory concept, and we want to reject regret for those events that appear outside of human control. This may account for the predominance of questions about how the expensive, technologically sophisticated U.S. military radar system could have misperceived the large, ascending civilian plane for a small, descending fighter plane. The question of whether fate/chance could have gotten the better of scientific know-how is a most disturbing question for us.

Perhaps even more discomfiting are those occasions when regret clearly requires the admission of personal responsibility or blame. Of course, no one enjoys admitting to poor judgment, but this is where the cultural differences seem most pronounced. The conduct of the president of Japan Airlines following the crash was not atypical for Japan, but would be quite unusual in the West. More generally, culture surely influences the willingness to publicly acknowledge responsibility through overt expressions of regret.

This apparent difference in the expression and perhaps the experience of regret may be grounded in cultural differences in conceptions of the self and identity. In one study, American participants reported that their self changes only 5 percent to 10 percent in different situations, but Japanese participants reported that their self changes 90 percent to 99 percent across different situations.[6] Americans have more of a sense of the adult self as crystallized and unchanging, whereas the Japanese have more of a sense of the adult self as fluid and adapting to one's social roles. Consequently, when Americans do something regrettable, their whole sense of self is shaken—because they tend to assume that their "whole identity is characterized by the one bad thing they did and they are someone they don't want to be."[7] In this connection, *Time*'s commentator speculated:

> America's tongue-tied denial [of regret and responsibility for shooting down the civilian Iranian plane] may be rooted in the way the destruction of Flight 655 brutally conflicts with the nation's self-image. Americans do not see themselves as trigger-happy gunslingers. . . . Terrorists are supposed to be the ones who cause death in the air.[8]

This may be one reason for the American reluctance to experience or express regret: in this culture to acknowledge regret is tantamount to admitting fundamental and unchangeable personal unworthiness. In contrast, for individuals from other cultures to acknowledge regret effects a lesser blow to their self-regard. It merely indicates trouble in one social role. To the extent that the sense of self consists of a sense of oneself-in-many-social-roles, the bulk of self-esteem remains undamaged.

To some extent Japanese and Americans possess reverse-image norms of how socially embedded the mature individual ought to be:

> In Japan, the infant is seen more as a separate biological organism who from the beginning, in order to develop, needs to be drawn into increasingly interdependent relations with others. In America, the infant is seen more as a dependent biological organism who, in order to develop, needs to be made increasingly independent of others.[9]

(Actually, the American view appears to be a minority view among the world's cultures.)[10] As psychologists Hazel Markus and Shinobu Kitayama have found, these divergent construals of the self as *independent* versus *interdependent* do shape emotional experience.[11]

In order to manage the complex network of social and interpersonal duties and obligations that fundamentally define selfhood in Japan, a complex set of social norms has evolved. Thus, when a Japanese does something that harms someone else, he or she is expected to express personal regret and to act upon that regret in some concrete way. That is why, after the jet crashed killing several hundred people, not only did the airline president resign in regret but executives from Japan Airlines paid personal visits to every family who had lost a family member, to apologize and express their regret. In contrast, in the United States, where the adult is viewed more as a rugged individual sufficient unto him- or herself, regret seems more a private than an interpersonal or collective experience. As for the *expression* of regret, American pragmatism may account for some of the American reluctance, as a colleague of mine explains:

> it is probably strategically unwise to admit responsibility even if it is obvious, because this admission could increase one's [legal] liability. Furthermore, I don't think that Americans feel that apology is worth very much after causing harm—this relates to the pragmatic orientation of American ethics. For the Japanese, the psychological pain and regret on the part of the harm-giver is a major part of the retribution for the wrong.[12]

Finally, recall the 1984 survey discussed in Chapter 1 that found that only 1 percent of 12,000 almost entirely American respondents described themselves as oriented toward the past.[13] The authors of this survey speculate that this percentage would be significantly higher in other cultures.

It stands to reason, then, that different orientations toward the past, along with different orientations toward fate, chance, selfhood, responsibility, and pragmatics, might underlie differences in cultural norms toward the experience and expression of regret.

The Decision Context: Threats to Procedural Rationality

A reiteration of a definition is in order. Procedural rationality includes: a reasoned effort to anticipate the likely consequences of acts or decisions; a reasoned effort to know what we want; and a reasonable effort to seek out all the available information pertinent to those judgments. For the most part, decisions deficient in procedural rationality are more likely to be regretted than procedurally rational decisions.[14] Regret is colored by external features of the decision context that in turn influence each of these elements of procedural rationality.

UNCERTAINTY OF PROBABILITIES

If only because of human fallibility in guessing the likelihood of future consequences, regret is inevitable. Psychological research has discovered a number of situations in which people tend to misjudge probabilities. First, we frequently misjudge the probability of future random events, treating random events as if they had memory of the past. Decision expert Robyn Dawes provides a delightful example of this problem, called the gambler's fallacy. He cites a "Dear Abby" letter in which the writer laments the fact that she has just given birth to her eighth child, her eighth girl. She can't understand how this happened, since the doctor had told her that "the law of averages were [sic] in our favor 100 to 1."[15] As Dawes explains, although it is true that the probability of having eight consecutive daughters is minuscule (about $1/2^8 = 1/256$), the probability of having another daughter after seven previous daughters is quite high (about 1/2). "Like coins, sperm have no memories," wryly concludes Dawes.[16] Not only gamblers and family planners, but all decision makers who misjudge the likelihood of random events place themselves at risk for making decisions they later regret.

Second, probability estimates often go wrong by being too closely tied to an initial estimate. This has been called the "anchoring" error by psychological researchers Daniel Kahneman, Paul Slovic, and Amos Tversky. For example, when individuals who erroneously believe that the probability of a plane crash is .70 are informed that the probability is actually closer to .10, they tend to underadjust the initial estimate and end up with a guess that the probability of a plane crash is, say, a still uncomfortable .50.[17] Individuals who, due to this particular error, have spent a lifetime avoiding trips requiring air travel may eventually come to regret these decisions.

Third, probability judgments can be off by being based on readily accessible examples gleaned from a biased sample. Suppose that after these individuals afflicted with unwarranted fear of flying have (under)adjusted to .50 their initial probability of a plane crashing, a string of four plane crashes occurs in five months. The ease of coming up with images of these very vivid examples may lead such individuals to readjust their probability estimates back up to .70, or even higher. Kahneman, Slovic, and Tversky call this the availability fallacy, in that the misjudgment of probabilities is based on a biased sample of readily available examples.[18]

Fourth, probability estimates often go astray when we base them on superficial resemblances to prototypical instances rather than on base rates (the actual statistical frequency of an event or characteristic in a population). Kahneman, Slovic, and Tversky called this the "representativeness" error, due to its overweighting of representative examples or scenarios.[19] For example, a physician may be led astray by a pattern of symptoms that resembles a common disease but even more closely matches a rare disease. If the physician focuses only on how representative the symptoms are of the rare disease and ignores the overall probabilities, he or she may tend to wrongly diagnose the disease.[20] Regrettable decisions stem in part from these and other pervasive problems in estimating the likelihood of outcomes.

JUSTIFIABILITY OF DECISIONS

Recall that at least one definition of regret includes the feature of self-recrimination.[21] Although I do not view self-recrimination as a necessary feature of regret, I agree that insofar as our decisions are not easily justifiable in terms of the estimated likelihood of particular consequences, they put us at risk for this particularly vexing form of regret.

As economist Robert Sugden points out, most people will experience more regret if they ignore an expert's advice to bet on a particular horse and it wins than if they follow the expert's advice not to bet on a particular horse and it wins.[22] In such instances, even given equal monetary losses, self-recrimination magnifies the regret likely felt by the bettor who ignores the expert advice.

According to economists Hersh Shefrin and Meir Statman,[23] it is a fact that stockholders get smaller returns from growing, visibly profitable companies than from static companies frequently perceived by the uninitiated as "dogs." Yet, many people are more comfortable buying stocks in the highly visible companies. This has to do with self-recriminatory regret, explain Shefrin and Statman:

> If you buy Continental Illinois and it goes down in price, you'll blame yourself. "How could I be so stupid?" you'll say. . . . However, if IBM stock drops, you'll look at the misfortune as an act of God.[24]

Thus, tacit or conscious fear of self-recriminatory regret may drive decisions in the first place. If not, then postdecision regret for decisions counter to the backing of authority, or otherwise unjust-ifiable, may hit harder than regret for more defensible decisions.

UNCERTAINTY OF PREFERENCES

Standard economic decision theory demands not only that people ground their decisions on good estimates of the likelihood of future consequences but also on good estimates of their own preferences (see Chapter 5). As James March points out, decision theory tradi-tionally assumes that preferences are absolute, relevant to the given decision, stable, consistent with one another, precise, and exoge-nous (unaffected by the choices they mandate).[25] In fact, prefer-ences behave notoriously badly in terms of these very characteris-tics. Indeed, preferences are frequently not absolute, but are instead assessed relative to other preferences; they are not brought to bear when making a specific choice; they are unstable over time, incon-sistent with one another, ambiguous, conflicted, incommensura-ble, and themselves affected by prior choices and their conse-quences.

Preferences are relative and contextual rather than absolute for a number of reasons, including the scarcity of desired resources, the sheer number of viable alternatives, and the nature of the set of alternatives as a whole.

The Relative Nature of Preference: Scarcity of Desired Resources. As we have already seen, there are misfortunes for which the agent or decision maker is not to blame, which are nonetheless regrettable. One such category is those decisions significantly influenced by scarcity—of time, money, personal resources, and so on. An inde-pendently wealthy person can afford to act on his or her true pref-erence when faced with a choice between taking time off work to be with a hospitalized partner (and losing a job) or not taking time off work (and keeping the job). The person who, due to scarcity of money, cannot afford to lose the job is at risk for regret whichever course of action he or she takes.

An implication of this fact is that one's social and economic position in society will shape one's experience of regret—its fre-quency, content, and mode (tragic, comic, romantic, or ironic). A pertinent testable hypothesis is that those faced with greater scar-city of resources—that is, those of lower social status—will expe-rience more regret. Furthermore, the less "realistic" the potential for gaining a piece of a limited pie, the more corrosively hopeless—

perhaps tragic (in the sense spelled out in Chapter 3)—the tenor of the regret. Again, research on relative deprivation suggests that it will not be the objective level of deprivation per se but the subjective sense of how deprived one is compared to others that will influence the degree of regret.[26] This means, for example, that someone who works for a company with an across-the-board freeze on raises will probably experience less regret (and other emotions) than someone who alone among his co-workers failed to get a raise.

Empirical research provides support for the presumed role of scarcity in regret. Most women who obtain elective sterilizations remain happy with their decision. But, as discussed in Chapter 4, those who base this decision on financial scarcity are at risk for later regret. One study found, for example, that compared with the vast majority of women who were satisfied with their earlier tubal division, those few women with later regret or ambivalence were more likely to report that their decision had been driven by financial circumstances rather than having been made solely on the basis of having enough children.[27] Assuming that these reports were not distorted by retrospective bias, these findings support the idea that scarcity engenders regret.[28]

The Relative Nature of Preference: Number of Viable Options. Preference can also depend on something so simple as the number of viable alternatives.[29] If the choice is between a trip to Jamaica or the equivalent in money, your preference may be different than if your choice is between a wardrobe, a luxury car, a trip to Jamaica, or the equivalent in money.

A corollary of this sort of relativity of preference is that regret may threaten decisions with multiple attractive alternatives more than decisions offering only one or a more limited set of alternatives. To minimize regret from this source, some shoppers purposely limit their shopping trips to one or two stores rather than go to the mega-mall teeming with a bewildering array of attractive choices—each with its attendant opportunities for regret.

Ideally, the tantalizing or tormenting awareness of multiple alternatives would lead us to carefully weigh such decisions, precisely because we can so vividly imagine regret for the roads not taken. If so, regret may be minimized.[30] But "at the extreme, a decision maker who has severe problems with regret may sometimes prefer to have only a single alternative offered than a choice among two or more," hypothesizes David Bell, an author of modern regret theory.[31] Ironically, then, the greater the number of appealing choices, the greater the opportunity for regret—though probably without the tragic overtones of regret that results from a restricted choice.

The Relative Nature of Preference: Desirability of Set of Choices. The conclusions of the last two sections appear to pose a contradiction—greater regret for a restricted number of options *and* greater regret for a larger number of options. The contradiction is resolvable, however. It may be less the relative desirability of individual choices or the sheer number of options than the attractiveness of the set of available choices *taken as a whole* that affects regret. Research finds that decisions among sets of wholly *negative* choices tend to produce particularly intense and long-lasting regret.[32] Decisions among particularly attractive options also make for regret, although less intense.

Research also reveals exactly what sorts of thoughts underlie the experience of regret in these respective situations. In a study by Robert Wicklund,[33] the (all male) subjects had to choose one among a set of eight items (e.g., a desk lamp, wallet, cigarette lighter, shaving bag, cologne, camera flash, umbrella, and bar aids). When all the items were attractive (as rated by prior pilot testing), regret arose mostly from the process of bolstering the perceived attractiveness of the *rejected* alternatives. When all the items were unattractive, regret involved mostly the process of disparaging the attractiveness of the *chosen* alternative.

Irrelevance of Preference to Choice. Given the difficulty of ascertaining the "truth" about anything internal (including preferences, desires, and values), many economists, psychologists, and others who study decision-making have decided to rely on something overt—the actual decision—as the "objective" indicator of preference. As we've seen before, standard economic decision theories equate preference with choice. Yet, everyone knows that our actual decisions and actual choices do not always reflect what we most deeply care about or want.

This disjunction stems in part from the nature of time and its relationship to human wanting. Beliefs and preferences can be momentary; but caring about something occurs over an extended period of time. Similarly, a choice is a momentary act, and thus may or may not reflect what we deeply want or care about:

> Since the making of a decision requires only a moment, the fact that a person decides to care about something cannot be tantamount to his caring about it. . . . This would hardly be worth pointing out except that an exaggerated significance is sometimes ascribed to decisions, as well as to choices and other similar "acts of will."[34]

That a worker opts to keep the job rather than lose it by taking time off to be with a sick partner does not necessarily mean that he or she *prefers* being at work. The choice may or may not reflect what the worker most cares about. That someone has indulged in still another drinking binge does not necessarily mean that he prefers alcoholism over sobriety. Nor does the fact that he voluntarily enters an alcohol rehab program necessarily mean that his preference is to abandon alcoholism. For human beings, a momentary choice cannot stand in once and for all for an enduring preference—a truth perhaps informing AA's motto: One day at a time.

External as well as internal factors may underlie the irrelevance of preference to actual choice. Instances of regret after succumbing to social pressure despite the claims of one's better judgment are legion, and not only among terminally insecure adolescents. Even if one's preferences remained firm in the face of actual choice and social pressure, this imperfect world presents its own limits in the form of unavailable circumstances. Although the worker might prefer to live in a world in which one did not have to work for a living, and although the alcoholic might prefer to live in a world in which alcohol is nonexistent, those preferences are not available choices.

Whatever its cause, the fact of a frequent disjunction between momentary choice and long-term preference need not imply that we (as theorists or as actual decision makers) ought to discount entirely the momentary choice. Some momentary decisions (e.g., those requiring long-term commitments or carrying dire consequences) are loaded with significance. A decision maker cognizant of the significance of a particular decision and capable of anticipating later regret may at the moment of decision rationally choose to put aside a previous judgment. Here are some reasons why:

> Not only does making a choice imply greater commitment and conflict than does making a judgment; it also tends to bring responsibility and regret strongly into consideration. These factors may cause the decision maker to ignore his or her previous judgment when the choice point arrives.[35]

One senses, for example, that Virginia Woolf's Clarissa Dalloway may have originally favored Peter Walsh over Richard Dalloway. However, when it came time to make a long-term commitment, she chose Dalloway. Perhaps this choice was driven by her anticipation of less regret in the long run for having given up the less stable, more stimulating Walsh than for having given up the more stable, less stimulating Dalloway. If so, then the choice, though not reflective of one strong preference, was rationally reflective of another.

External factors (such as pressures to conform and scarcity or unavailability of the desired resources), as well as internal factors (perhaps "weakness of will," perhaps insight into one's long-term desires), can and do render some of one's preferences at times irrelevant to one's choice.

Instability of Preference. Standard decision theory's axiomatic requirement for temporal stability and internal consistency of human preference has proved itself an impossible dream (see Chapter 5 for a more extensive discussion). Because of our very human "love of variety . . . and changing tastes,"[36] as well as our very human desire at least occasionally to indulge mere whims,[37] instability of preference is to be expected. Some decision theorists grant as much with respect to unimportant choices.[38] As I argue in the next sections, instability of preference and internal inconsistency concerning even highly important decisions are also to be expected, something so far not acknowledged by decision theory. Three grounds for instability and inconsistency of preference are conflict among values, incommensurability of values, and change of values as a result of choice itself.

CONFLICT AMONG ALTERNATIVES AND VALUES. Assuming for the moment that happiness is what is to be maximized by rational choice, a nonexhaustive set of strategies for distributing happiness equitably are these: making some people very happy and others slightly less happy, versus making everyone happier but no one very happy, versus a high probability of making everyone a little happier, versus a low probability of making everyone a lot happier. If I were to ask a classroom full of my university students which of these strategies should be implemented in their dorm room, in their family, in their neighborhood, in the country, in the world, I envision radical and intense disagreement. Moreover, I imagine that the students, and others, might disagree not only among themselves but also within themselves.

Therefore, I find it astonishing that in a discussion of these classic examples, a defender of orthodox decision theory, J. J. C. Smart, has declared that "there are not in fact many cases in which such a disagreement could arise."[39] Nor is Smart alone; much of classical decision theory has either ignored or shrugged off the role of conflict in decision making. Yet the parents torn between the sick child and work; someone torn between drinking or not; the individual torn between two lovers—all dramatize a common state of conflict between alternatives.

Many decision conflicts stem from the inescapable fact that "good and bad features co-vary over alternatives. For example, better quality is accompanied by higher cost, higher profit by greater risk."[40] Orthodox decision theory prescribes that in such situations one should simply analyze the trade-offs, and agree to give up one value in favor of another. But this injunction ignores the psychological fact that "people find it difficult to make trade-offs, even under conditions that apparently favor doing so."[41]

Furthermore, certain decision conflicts; because they entail ambivalent emotions or incommensurable values, definitively resist resolution through trade-off. Recall that incommensurable options are those that are not rankable using logic; and this is not because the options are a matter of indifference or of equality to the decision maker.[42] One of the examples of incommensurability already presented is the famous example of the young person's choice between leaving home to join the underground resistance to the Nazis versus staying home to care for an ill mother. Only commensurable values can be compared with one another and therefore traded off against each other. The existence of choices about which "reason has no judgment to make concerning their relative value"[43] means that in some circumstances regret may be unavoidable.

Choices among incommensurables and choices requiring trade-offs of conflicting values will frequently (if not always) evoke regret, whatever the choice—due to the undeniable advantages of the rejected alternative and the undeniable disadvantages of the chosen alternative. Such regret is not as easily dismissed as some decision theorists would like. Thus, in Woolf's novel, Clarissa Dalloway attempts to justify to herself her decision to marry Richard Dalloway rather than Peter Walsh by reminding herself that although she has given up the emotional intensity of life with Peter, she has gained the emotional stability of life with Richard. But the reader keenly senses how tenuous is this attempt at accepting the trade-off. After all, Richard Dalloway and Peter Walsh amount to more than the sum of their characteristics; a choice between them is a choice between incommensurables.

Besides conflict within a single individual, conflict of preferences among individuals is ubiquitous. Even if society agrees that it needs to improve the general well-being by building more prisons, factories, low-income houses, or roads, it may disagree violently about whose backyard to put them in.

Recently a number of scholars, including philosophers and economists, have begun to recognize the fact that conflict is the usual state of affairs, rather than an aberration.[44] An important implication is that regret is the usual state of affairs rather than an aberration.

INFLUENCE OF PRIOR CHOICE ON PREFERENCE. During the U.S.-led war against Iraq in 1991 the number of U.S. military reservists requesting conscientious-objector status and even deserting the military rose dramatically from a baseline rate of a couple of hundred per year to many thousands.[45] Some observers objected to this trend on the grounds that the reservists knew what they were getting into when they joined. Some of the dissenting soldiers, however, reasoned differently. As they saw it, their original choice to join the military had, first of all, carried only a low probability of combat, as (except for the incursion into Grenada) it had been 20 years since the United States had fought a war and over 45 years since the United States had fought a declared war. But more important, their decision to join the military had led to experiences, notably basic training and perhaps participation in the U.S. invasion of Panama, that moved them to reevaluate the role of the military and their role in it. Their change of heart, however, seemed to require no major change of conduct—until U.S. troops were sent to the Middle East to launch an all-out attack on Iraq. At the point when these individuals were called up to fight this war, they were put in a position where they might be required to kill. At this point, some of them found that their values had changed, and the change was due to their prior decision to enlist in the military and what they had learned as a direct result of that decision. As this example shows, aside from mere whim, change of taste, desire for novelty, or conflict among difficult trade-offs and incommensurable choices, another basis for instability of preferences is their capacity to be affected by prior choices and the unforeseeable consequences of those choices.

Some influential researchers in economic and psychological decision theory have begun to perceive the incorrigibility of preference as a serious threat to classic decision theory. The psychologists Tversky, Sattath, and Slovic acknowledge: "In the absence of well-defined preferences, the foundations of choice theory and decision analysis are called into question."[46] At the very least, insofar as our preferences suffer from one or more of these threats to their discernment, the likelihood of regret increases.

According to the classic formulation of economic decision theory, the chief ingredients of a procedurally rational decision are knowledge of probabilities and knowledge of one's preferences. Unfortunately, in real life, decisions rarely come equipped with known probabilities and preferences. Hence the ubiquity of regret following such inevitably imperfect decision making.

AVAILABILITY OF RELEVANT INFORMATION CONCERNING PROBABILITY AND PREFERENCE

Decision problems posed within the framework of economic decision theory have tended to be cast as monetary gambles on games of pure chance in which both the probabilities and utilities are known or knowable. In real life, however, decisions are often messier and more difficult, because of multiple uncertainties—including uncertainty about exactly which probabilities and preferences are relevant, as well as uncertainty concerning how to quantify those probabilities and preferences recognized as relevant.

A consumer puts himself at risk for regret in buying a car off the used-car lot without checking ahead of time the repair information that he knows could be found in publications like *Consumer Reports*. In contrast, the hypothetical consumer who buys the same car at the same price after having factored in all the available information that it is reasonable to seek can anticipate less regret than the other consumer—even if in both cases the car dies in two weeks. Empirical evidence confirms the intuition that most people correctly anticipate greater regret when they make decisions without (rather than with) the benefit of information they know to be available about potential consequences.[47]

Empirical studies of specific life decisions further support the presumed implications of this aspect of procedural irrationality for later regret. Compared with a group of women satisfied with their decision to undergo elective sterilization, the regretful women had made their decision more hastily and without reconsidering it.[48] Moreover, the women with later regrets were more likely than the nonregretful women to report having made the decision less than freely; instead, they reported that they had been inadequately informed about the decision and had felt pressured by their physician or husband. The authors of this study agree that many of the regretful women had in fact been pressured by their husbands: "many of these women [were] involved in marriages where power is expressed in terms of control over childbearing."[49] This result may be related to the finding of greater regret among women whose husbands had a vasectomy than among women who chose a tubal ligation—apparently due to the former women feeling less in charge of the decision.[50]

Findings such as these seem to suggest, among other things, that couples ought to try to sit down and thoroughly discuss decisions involving both parties. Unfortunately, at least one study casts doubt on the common wisdom that more "communication" always makes for better decisions. One study found that a great deal of discussion between spouses, when the husband had a high educational level, was associated with greater ambivalence before the decision,[51] which has been associated with greater regret later.[52] The authors of this study speculated that, at least in this instance, "more discussion implies difficulty in making a decision rather than thorough and effective decision-making."[53] It may be that the greater ambivalence of women with more highly educated husbands arose out of a sense of having had their information search limited by a husband mutually perceived as holding the intellectual upper hand.

At its best, knowing that additional relevant information is available has the effect of putting the brakes on sufficiently to enable the decision maker to seek out the available information—precisely in order to avoid later regret. At its worst, especially with the excessively ruminative decision makers discussed in the previous chapter, this knowledge can paralyze.[54]

In sum, it is clear that regret integrally depends on aspects of the context, including anything that influences what we think we want, what we think possible, and what kind of search we engage in to find out what we want and what is possible.

Characteristics of Antecedents of the Decision

Characteristics of the decision context that undermine our ability to make informed decisions are not alone in precipitating regret. In addition, certain characteristics of the course of action taken—such as its usualness and salience—can be expected to give rise to more or less regret.

EXCEPTIONAL ANTECEDENTS

The distinction between the usual and the unusual has been called by Cynthia Ozick one of the "most natural divisions the mind is subject to."[55] According to Ozick, we respond to the *unusual* by

> paying attention to it . . . it seizes us so undividedly, it declares itself so dazzlingly or killingly, it is so deafening with its LOOK! SEE! NOTICE! PAY ATTENTION! that the only answer we can give is to look, see, notice, and pay attention. . . . The Extraordinary does not let you shrug your shoulders and walk away.[56]

In contrast, the *usual* is taken-for-granted, safe, almost invisible:

> The Ordinary lets us live out our humanity, it doesn't scare us, it doesn't excite us, it doesn't distract us—it brings us the safe return of the school bus every day.[57]

Imagine a driver who for once breaks his rule of never picking up hitchhikers and is then robbed by that hitchhiker. Now imagine a driver who frequently picks up hitchhikers and is robbed by one.[58] Given equivalently nasty outcomes, which driver will likely feel more regret for picking up that hitchhiker?

Building on this sort of question, Kahneman and Tversky predicted that exceptional, nonroutine, unusual conditions preceding a misfortune would prove mentally more mutable than usual ones and therefore would elicit greater regret. In a series of experiments designed to test this prediction,[59] they presented subjects with brief written scenarios about a hypothetical Mr. Jones who is killed in an automobile accident on his way home from work. The usualness of one of two elements of each scenario was varied: subjects were told either that Mr. Jones had taken an unusual (or usual) route home or had left the office at an unusual (or usual) time. After reading a version of this scenario, subjects were asked to complete an "if-only" stem from the perspective of Mr. Jones's friends or family. The experimental instructions read as follows:

> As commonly happens in such situations, the Jones family and their friends often thought and often said, "If only . . . " during the days that followed the accident. How did they continue this thought? Please write one or more likely completions.

In the original study and my replication of it, most people altered the events by imagining a more *usual* scenario—that is, by altering the unusual element (time or route) rather than some other aspect of the situation.[60]

This pattern can be explained in terms of the ease of mental simulation of alternatives to reality. Given an unfortunate event or outcome, people seem more inclined to mentally undo it by constructing more readily imaginable (usual) antecedent events rather than less readily imaginable (unusual) ones.[61] It is easier for the driver who never picks up hitchhikers to mentally undo his unfortunate change of heart than for the driver who frequently picks up hitchhikers to mentally undo his act of taking pity on still another one.

Whatever the mechanism (the attention-getting nature of unusual events, the ease of imagining more routine events, or something else entirely), research suggests that the less routine the antecedents of malign consequences, the greater the regret. So, given equivalently nasty robberies, the driver for whom it is not routine to pick up hitchhikers will likely experience greater regret than the driver for whom it is routine.

SALIENT ANTECEDENTS

Acts, events, and positive instances are also more attention-getting than non-acts, non-events, and negative instances. Beliefs in things like ESP are probably based to a large extent on this fact. We'll recall those two dramatic occasions when a clairvoyant sense of something amiss with a relative received confirmation, but forget the dozens or even hundreds of times when such feelings went unconfirmed. The confirmations become events and the disconfirmations non-events; the events declare themselves "dazzlingly, killingly" while the non-events escape our notice. (Sherlock Holmes's astute inference as to who-done-it, based on his observation of a non-event—the dog that did *not* bark in the night—is a widely cited literary illustration of an *exception* to the rule of undernoticing non-events.)

Empirical evidence of this effect comes from experiments in which subjects are exposed to both occurrences and nonoccurrences in order to observe how people generally form concepts, solve problems, or distinguish between two stimuli. Experiments, for example, in which subjects are presented with both positive instances (sparrows are birds) and negative instances (bats are *not* birds) to use to form a concept or distinguish between two stimuli regularly find that we underuse negative instances.[62] The effect also operates on a more personal level. It appears that people's inferences about their own attitudes (when these are weak or ambiguous) depend more on their own acts than their non-acts.[63] Cognitive limitations may underlie the tendency to overlook nonoccurrences. Because nonoccurrences are less salient than occurrences, they tend to be less available for further processing during thinking or problem solving.[64] Whatever the specific mechanism, the tendency to overnotice acts and undernotice non-acts may explain the pattern of greater regret for acts than for non-acts, as discussed in Chapter 4. In general, when things go awry we tend to focus our regret on those antecedent features of decisions that are more noticeable or more easily wished away.

Characteristics of Decision Outcomes

Besides the previously discussed antecedents of the outcome, there are aspects of the outcome itself—other than its degree of undesirability—that make for greater or lesser degrees of regret. Among these are the imminence and irreversibility of the outcome, knowledge of alternative outcomes, psychological proximity to better outcomes, and interpersonal effects of outcomes.

IMMINENCE OF OUTCOME

Regret surely breathes harder down the neck of most students as they decide to put off a planned study session for an exam tomorrow than for an exam a month from now. Regret undoubtedly looms larger for the middle-aged addicted smoker with a chronic cough than the teenager taking her first drag from a cigarette. In general, people are notoriously better at anticipating their potential regret over a decision with imminent rather than remote negative consequences.[65]

IRREVERSIBILITY OF OUTCOME

The observation that "You can't turn back the clock" is often linked with a conclusion that therefore regret makes no sense. "Things without all remedy should be without regard," declared Lady Macbeth in an effort to quell her husband's well-merited guilt over the murder of Duncan. As I have argued, regret has a way of rudely ignoring such advice. In fact, the notion that regret for irreversible outcomes burns hotter than regret for reversible outcomes seems a good candidate for the status of truism. However, it is one of the many questions concerning regret yet to be empirically tested.

Literature has this to say on the question. In *The Remains of the Day*, it is not until Stevens is confronted with the irreversibility of a significant decision in his life that he suffers an attack of conscious and intense regret. The death of his fantasy of regaining Miss Kenton/Mrs. Benn precipitates his awareness of how very much he has lost. In *Breathing Lessons*, as well, it may be the irreversibility of Maggie's impending empty nest that sends her off half-cocked to try to salvage her son's marriage, and, not coincidentally, to try to move her granddaughter into her own home. Plainly, as discussed below, the ultimate irreversible outcome, death, can occasion the ultimate in regret. The regret of Ivan Ilyitch, as portrayed in Tolstoy's story "The Death of Ivan Ilyitch," is so excruciating precisely because it is too late to reverse the conventional and empty life he now rues.

KNOWLEDGE OF ALTERNATIVE OUTCOMES

"I don't even *want* to know how it could have turned out." This statement implicitly acknowledges how painful it can be to know, rather than not to know for sure, that a regrettable reality could have been better. My own research[66] and that of others[67] suggest that when bad things happen, most people spontaneously *imagine* a more positive alternative outcome, and this process magnifies their regret. However, decisions that confront the decision maker with *knowledge* of a better alternative outcome probably have even greater potential for regret than those in which the decision maker is left in a state of uncertainty. This intuition—a finding I stumbled across while looking for something else—may explain the lack of popularity of a new test capable of removing the uncertainty in the minds of children of parents with Huntington's disease (each of whom has a 50 percent chance of developing the disease). Some individuals may reason that the awful uncertainty is more tolerable than knowing for sure that they have this progressive, incurable disease.[68]

In fact, the regret accrued in knowing exactly how much better off one might have been can more than offset the pleasure of a happy event. This is well illustrated in the following example:

> Mr. A is waiting in line at a movie theater. When he gets to the ticket window he is told that as the 100,000th customer of the theater he has just won $100.

> Mr. B. is waiting in line at a different theater. The man in front of him wins $1000 for being the 1,000,000th customer of the theater. Mr. B wins $150.[69]

When asked whether they would rather be Mr. A or Mr. B, some people actually say they would rather be Mr. A. Except for regret, this "illogical" response makes no sense. Even though he won $50 less than Mr. B, Mr. A has come away with a free and clear $100. In contrast, Mr. B's pleasure is reduced by regret based on knowing what nearly was his: his regret-modified net utility is a dismal $150 minus $1000.

How distressing it is knowing what might have been depends not only on *what* might have been, but on *who* knows it. As discussed in the previous chapter, recent research suggests that particular personality traits, such as low self-esteem, may render some individuals more vulnerable than others to regret due to knowledge of what might have been.[70]

PSYCHOLOGICAL PROXIMITY TO BETTER OUTCOMES

The example of the two movie-goers shows something else besides the relative bliss associated with ignorance of what might have been. Psychologically speaking, it is clearly *not* true that a miss is as good as a mile. Whatever the context, the regret of the "1,000,001th customer" is, logically or not, likely to prove more intense than the regret of someone who didn't come close.[71]

Kahneman and Tversky provided a persuasive demonstration of this phenomenon when they asked research subjects who would be more upset: Mr. C who arrived at the airport 30 minutes late for his flight to discover that his flight had left right on time, or Mr. T who also arrived 30 minutes late to discover that his flight had left just five minutes before. A full 96 percent of their sample believed that Mr. T would be more upset than Mr. C.[72] Both effects— greater regret for known outcomes and for near-hits—demonstrate again the fact that regret is not an absolute, but a relative and contextual matter.

In conclusion, regret ought not be viewed as a purely private emotion. The experience and expression of regret depend on a number of external factors, including cultural norms, as well as characteristics of the decision-making context, of the outcome's antecedents, and of the outcome itself.

A Time To Regret

Fortunately for our sanity, regret tends to be something that comes and goes, not a chronic state. Furthermore, it seems more likely to come at some times and in some circumstances than at others—especially occasions in which sorry consequences force themselves upon us, during leisure time, when reminiscing on the past, when we are in a sad mood or life crisis, or when death is imminent.

"Facing the Music"

An ad for Waterman pens (with the punch line "There are some decisions one never lives to regret") shows a man ruefully admitting: "I bought stocks like they were going out of style. And they were." Similarly, when I asked a sample of 149 college students when in their daily lives they were most aware of regret, the third most frequent answer (12 percent of all responses) concerned times when the negative consequences of their choices directly confronted them. One said "when consequences loom"; many mentioned specific occasions central to the life of a college sample—especially exam time and "when I do badly on papers I put little effort into."[73] The distressing thing about "the morning after" is the eyeball-to-eyeball confrontation with sorry consequences. These examples point to surely one of the most prevalent occasions for regret: whenever we are forced to confront undesirable outcomes of our own decisions. These examples highlight regret upon the occasion of recognizing that one has harmed oneself. Others could be marshaled that show regret upon recognizing that one has harmed another: "I bought stocks with my trustee's money like they were going out of style. And they were"; "I regret disappointing my parents and wasting their money by putting forth little effort in college"; and "The morning after, I regretted having misled him/her to expect a long-term relationship with me."

Independent of whether the harm accrues to oneself or others, occasions in which we are inescapably confronted with unpleasant consequences of our acts will likely give rise to regret.

Psychological Distance from the Status Quo

For Henry James's protagonist, Strether, in *The Ambassadors*, regret that had remained tacit became fully conscious upon his gaining distance from America. Living in Paris evoked poignant regrets for his lost youth, regrets that he had repressed in Woollett, Massachusetts:

> He felt, strangely, as sad as if he had come for some wrong, and yet as excited as if he had come for some freedom. But the freedom was what was most in the place and the hour; *it was the freedom that most brought him round again to the youth of his own that he had long ago missed.* . . . the main truth of the actual appeal of everything was none the less that every thing represented the substance of his loss, put it within reach, within touch, made it, to a degree it had never been, an affair of the senses. That was what it became for him at this singular time, the youth he had long ago missed—a queer, concrete presence, full of mystery, yet full of reality, which he could handle, taste, smell, the deep breathing of which he could positively hear. It was in the outside air as well as within; it was in the long watch from the balcony, in the summer night of the wide, late life of Paris, the unceasing soft, quick rumble below of the lighted carriages that, in the press, always suggested the gamblers he had seen of old at Monte Carlo pushing up to the tables.[74]

In this passage James helps to illuminate what it is about certain kinds of distance that brings to the fore unacknowledged regret: "it was the freedom that most brought him round again to the youth of his own that he had long ago missed."

First, there were his observations and perceptions of others' "freedom." The sight of lighted carriages rumbling through the city late on a summer's night evoked fantasies of the stimulating life that Strether might have lived had he not settled for stodgy Woollett. "Gamblers he had seen of old at Monte Carlo pushing up to the tables," Parisian nightlife, and other sensual summer nights—vivid images of people taking pleasure and taking risks—evoked by contrast his own austerely circumspect youth.

Alternatively, Strether's own experience of freedom from daily distractions may have occasioned his regret. Preoccupation with the bustling dailiness of life helps keep thoughts and feelings like regret at bay. A breach from the quotidian, on the other hand, simultaneously offers rest and recreation plus the unwelcome intrusion of regret. This latter fact helps explain why weekends, leisure time, vacations, and travel have the perverse power to distress.

There is more to be learned on this score from Kazuo Ishiguro's wise book, *The Remains of the Day*. It is mostly this second form of freedom, offered to the traveler—freedom from the distraction of work—that finally breaks through the protagonist's (Stevens) considerable defenses in *The Remains of the Day*. Stevens has lived his whole life in the conviction that two qualities make for a "great" butler, which he desperately hopes he has been: (1) "dignity," which he defines as an extreme of self-restraint; and (2) serving a "distinguished" house, which he defines as a morally upright house, one engaged in "furthering the progress of humanity."[75] For 30 years Stevens served in the house of Lord Darlington, who has since died. Now he has a new, American employer, Mr. Farraday. In dutiful obedience to his new employer, Stevens reluctantly embarks on a driving vacation in the summer of 1956. Ishiguro's brilliant portrayal of the process of regret slowly surfacing into the consciousness of a singularly well-defended individual merits our close study.

Before the holiday, Stevens employs flat-out denial to deceive himself as to two major truths about his life, one concerning love and the other work. First, the reader understands that Stevens not-quite-consciously loves the former head housekeeper at Lord Darlington's. But he denies her unavailability by continuing to think of her as Miss Kenton, when she has in fact been Mrs. Benn for years. Second, Stevens denies his doubts about his work life. Defensively, he assures his employer, Mr. Farraday, (as well as himself) that his life of service to Lord Darlington has been supremely satisfying and worthwhile (so much so that he has not felt the need to get out and see the rest of his country): "It has been my privilege to see the best of England over the years, sir, within these very walls."[76]

On day 2, Stevens is still reaching to convince himself that he has spent his life in service to a great man: "Let me say that Lord Darlington was a gentleman of great moral stature. . . . Nothing could be less accurate than to suggest that I regret my association with such a gentleman."[77]

On day 3 he inches closer to the truth, acknowledging his reservations about Lord Darlington's moral stature, but not acknowledging personal regret for his lifelong association with this man: "It is hardly my fault if his lordship's life and work have turned out today to look, at best, a sad waste—and it is quite illogical that I should feel any regret or shame on my own account."[78] Of course, in the light of Stevens's own definition of what makes for a great butler, feelings of regret and shame on his part are *perfectly* logical.

Later he begins to allow himself to question this professional ideal of his, particularly the element of self-restraint. He is haunted by a number of past incidents in which his conception of professional correctness had led him to behave with inhuman coldness to Miss Kenton. At one point, he had abruptly ended their habitual evening meetings over cocoa, despite (or because of) the deep personal satisfaction the meetings had afforded both of them. On another occasion, even though he knew she had just received distressing word of her aunt's death, he maintained his usual air of cold correctness with Miss Kenton. Now on his holiday he gains partial insight into his mistakes and his loss, but remains defensive, employing the perennial strategies of rationalization and brute suppression of distressing thoughts:

> But what is the sense in forever speculating what might have happened had such and such a moment turned out differently? One could presumably drive oneself to distraction in this way. In any case, while it is all very well to talk of "turning points," one can surely only recognize such moments in retrospect. . . . There was surely nothing to indicate at the time that such evidently small incidents would render whole dreams forever irredeemable.
>
> But I see I am becoming unduly introspective, and in a rather morose sort of way at that.[79]

In response to a pre-trip letter from Mrs. Benn in which she informs Stevens that she has separated from her husband, Stevens decides to meet with her and invite her to return to the staff. The reader knows that this is Stevens's last-ditch attempt to draw Miss Kenton/Mrs. Benn back into his life. Stevens and Mrs. Benn meet on the sixth day of the trip. He learns that she has a daughter, is expecting a grandchild, and has again returned to her husband, whom she has left more than once. When Stevens ventures that she has not been entirely happy, she simultaneously denies it and quite directly acknowledges that she wonders whether she would have been happier with Stevens:

> But that doesn't mean to say, of course, there aren't occasions now and then—extremely desolate occasions—when you think to yourself: "What a terrible mistake I've made with my life." And you get to thinking about a different life, a *better* life you might have had. For instance, I get to thinking about a life I might have had with you, Mr. Stevens. And I suppose that's when I get angry over some trivial little thing and leave. But each time I do so, I realize before long—my right-

ful place is with my husband. After all, there's no turning back the clock now. One can't be forever dwelling on what might have been.[80]

At her musing that she might have had a better life with Stevens, Stevens suppresses his earth-stopping grief; characteristically, he remains the very soul of reserve. He calls upon the familiar strategy of warding off regret by keying in on the acceptable aspects of his life and quashing attention to what might have been:

> You're very correct, Mrs. Benn. As you say, it is too late to turn back the clock. . . . We must each of us, as you point out, be grateful for what we *do* have.[81]

At last, two days later, Stevens experiences his sorrowful epiphany of regret. He is on a pier with a number of other people waiting for the sun to set and for the pier lights to be turned on; when the lights go on, everyone cheers. A retired butler nearby strikes up a conversation with Stevens; they share notes about butlering. Stevens expresses the awful truth of his past and present:

> The fact is, of course . . . I gave my best to Lord Darlington. I gave him the very best I had to give, and now—well—I find I do not have a great deal more left to give.[82]

At this point, Stevens's previous standard of personal excellence— summed up in his term "dignity"—collapses, and finally he breaks down:

> Lord Darlington wasn't a bad man. He wasn't a bad man at all. And at least he had the privilege of being able to say at the end of his life that he made his own mistakes. . . . He chose a certain path in life, it proved to be a misguided one, but there, he chose it, he can say that at least. As for myself, I cannot even claim that. You see, I *trusted.* . . . I trusted I was doing something worthwhile. I can't even say I made my own mistakes. Really—one has to ask oneself—what dignity is there in that?[83]

From literary works like *The Ambassadors* and *The Remains of the Day* we learn that the physical and psychological distance associated with leisure, travel, and vacations can serve to arouse regret, and that they do so in part by confronting us with novel stimuli, perceptions, and experiences that break down our usual defenses while at the same time showing us what might have been. Leisure, travel, and vacations have the potential to arouse regret also by showing us more clearly what is. Travel is, after all, notorious for its ability to give us "perspective." While enmeshed in the demands of daily life, we are often preoccupied with trying to accommodate ourselves to circumstances so close that they remain virtually invisible to us. Distance shifts perception from a self-oriented focus to a self-in-the-situation focus, a shift that can show up malign circumstances for what they are. Strether's experience of Parisian nightlife, risk-taking, and "freedom" helped him to see clearly not only Paris's cosmopolitan attractions but also Woollett's pinched provincialisms. Stevens's experience of the "undignified" but warmly human world outside of Darlington Hall helped him finally to grasp the attractions of other ways of life and the malignancies of his own life.

External Reminders

Of course regret does not strike only away from home. The second most common impetus for regret in the daily lives of college students I have queried is an external cue or reminder of the regretted object (13 percent of 214 responses). A student who regretted having given up piano, for instance, reported experiencing regret whenever he sees someone else play or whenever he is asked to play. Several students whose major regret concerned a lost love mentioned that their regret flared up whenever they saw the former love or other happy couples.

In *Ulysses* James Joyce identifies a bewilderingly diverse list of times, places, and circumstances capable of evoking regret:

> There are sins or (let us call them as the world calls them) evil memories which are hidden away by man in the darkest places of the heart but they abide there and wait. . . . Yet a chance word will call them forth suddenly and they will rise up to confront him in the most various circumstances, a vision or a dream, or while timbrel and harp soothe his senses or amid the cool silver tranquility of the evening or at the feast at midnight when he is now filled with wine.[84]

In Virginia Woolf's novel, similarly evanescent things precipitated Clarissa Dalloway's regrets: "suddenly it would come over her, If he were with me now what would he say?—some days, some sights bringing him back to her."

Woolf makes the proximal occasion of Clarissa Dalloway's attack of acute regret the visit in the flesh of Peter Walsh, the suitor she had long ago rejected. When Clarissa and Peter reminisce about their past, he breaks into tears and she kisses him. It is only then that she experiences the full impact of her loss:

> all in a clap it came over her, If I had married him, this gaiety would have been mine all day!
>
> It was all over for her. The sheet was stretched and the bed narrow. . . . He has left me; I am alone for ever, she thought, folding her hands upon her knee. . . . Take me with you, Clarissa thought impulsively, as if he were starting directly upon some great voyage.

For Peter Walsh, too, seeing Clarissa Dalloway brought regret that he could not shake off:

> He only felt, after seeing her that morning, among her scissors and silks, making ready for the party, unable to get away from the thought of her; she kept coming back and back like a sleeper jolting against him in a railway carriage.

A "chance word" (Joyce), "some days, some sights" (Woolf), and certainly an actual encounter with the object of one's regrets (Woolf)—almost any personally meaningful reminder of a loss can arouse regret.

Other Unpleasant Mood States

As we have already seen, emotional distress can be looked at as a longstanding characteristic of an individual, a trait. But emotional distress can also be a state, a temporary experience occasioned by specific and temporary circumstances. Just as the warm glow of a good mood induced by a happy event overflows the boundaries of its source and spreads itself over all of one's life,[85] so does the grey dullness of a bad mood. In fact, my college student sample frequently identified bad moods and bad times as prime occasions for regret. Eleven percent of 149 students I questioned said they tend to feel regret when they are sad, down, or depressed. Another six percent of the sample mentioned that painful or stressful times also seem to be regretful times.[86]

Times Free for Reflection

I have already discussed the possible role of personality and how ruminativeness may dispose someone to regret. But independent of personal predispositions, particular situations also lend themselves to greater reflectiveness. The college students I studied listed a va-

riety of occasions of regret that have as a common denominator
the availability of time for reflection: namely, whenever they are
reflecting on life, the past, the future, or simply "things" (10 percent of all responses); when they are alone (9 percent of all responses); and when they are not busy (4 percent). A few of these
undergraduates also mentioned early morning, a time of day that
is for most of them usually free of distractions and busyness (in
fact, free from full waking consciousness!). Besides these, by far the
single most frequently reported time for regret was evening or
nighttime (19 percent of responses). Here they concur with at least
three literary figures: with Dickens, who set Pip's might-have-beens
when he "woke up in the night"; with Joyce's thoughts about the
power of the "cool silver tranquility of the evening" and "[the feast
at] midnight" to arouse regret; and with Charles Kuralt's observations that "Sometimes at night before sleeping, little regrets come
back to me."

Remembrance of Things Past

Though memory does not always evoke regret, regret is frequently
associated with memory. Butler's notion of the life review rein-
forces the frequent association between regret in old age and reflecting on the past.[87] However, college students too report that for
them a prime occasion for regret is any time they reflect on the
past. Evidently regardless of age, whenever we look back on our
life, we heighten the potential for regret.

In *Mrs. Dalloway*, the eponymous protagonist loses her characteristic composure only upon reminiscing with Peter Walsh about
their past closeness. For Peter Walsh, too, the old wound of his
ever-present regret over Clarissa's rejection is torn open when he
and Clarissa reminisce together.

When speaking with Mrs. Benn about what might have been
for them, Stevens's lifetime of inhibition holds him back from expressing his profound regret for the loss (*The Remains of the Day*).
He remains composed until the very end of the holiday during which
he has opened himself progressively more and more to the experience of regret. At long last, in his pier-side review of his past,
Stevens weeps with regret.

Intimations of Mortality

"Death is that possibility that invades my present, truncates my
future, and monumentalizes my past." In this paraphrase of Hei-

degger on death, Krell[88] points to the imperious manner in which the fact of mortality suffuses all of life—its past, present, and future. Of particular interest to this discussion is the way that people seem impelled to examine their past when death is perceived as imminent.

In his celebrated short story, "The Death of Ivan Ilyitch," Tolstoy chronicles a dying man's process of reviewing his life and wrestling with excruciating regret. During the last three weeks of his life, Ivan Ilyitch struggles to understand why it is that the thought of his conventionally respectable adult life fills him with uncomprehending disgust and regret. At first Ivan Ilyitch discharges his seething emotions onto his wife, son, and daughter, refusing to see any of them and recoiling in disgust when they press themselves on him. Bewildered by his own rage, he eventually asks himself whether it is he, not they, who might be to blame for his turmoil:

> "Can it be that I did not live as I ought?" . . . immediately he put away this sole explanation of the enigma of life and death as something absolutely impossible.[89]

He is torn between thinking that perhaps he did not live as he ought and refusing this thought, for three days shrieking in protest: "I won't!" Finally, two hours before his death, Ivan Ilyitch can no longer avoid facing regret: " 'Yes, all was wrong,' he said to himself; 'but that is nothing.' " At that moment Ivan Ilyitch's son enters the room, takes his hand, kisses it, and dissolves in tears. At this point in his death throes Ivan Ilyitch experiences an epiphany:

> It was at this very same time that Ivan Ilyitch fell through, saw the light, and it was revealed to him that his life had not been as it ought, but that still it was possible to repair it.[90]

The furious self-preoccupation falls away. Ivan Ilyitch turns to his son and his wife, and he feels pity for them. He says to his wife:

> "I am sorry . . . and for thee" . . . He wanted to say also, "Prosti—Forgive," but he said, "Propusti—Let it pass."[91]

No longer fearing death, within moments Ivan Ilyitch dies, at peace. The fact of imminent death brought about a crisis of regret that Ivan Ilyitch at last resolved through acts of consciousness and acts of pity for his loved ones.

In Kurosawa's film *Ikiru* a diagnosis of terminal cancer launches the protagonist, Mr. Watanabe, on a similar war with regret over the emptiness of his life. This protagonist, however, is allotted months rather than days to work through his regret. His turning point occurs when he decides it is not too late to change his former approach to his work. Instead of continuing to waste his days assiduously trying to avoid work, he devotes himself singlemindedly to a project to transform a piece of fallow city land to a children's playground. Through reparative action in the world, the protagonist succeeds in transcending regret before death.

Hemingway's "The Snows of Kilimanjaro," too, centers on a deathbed confrontation with regret. As gangrene poisons his body, regret for all the stories this writer "had saved to write until he knew enough to write them well"[92] poisons his spirit. In his delirium he hallucinates past events from his life that when he wakes he regrets not having written about. He vacillates between lashing out at his wife and blaming himself for the dissipated years spent avoiding writing. Unlike the protagonist of Tolstoy's and Kurosawa's more romantic stories, this protagonist undergoes no epiphany and no sudden transformation. In a state of inner warfare, caught between quarreling with his wife and resolving not to quarrel with her, between regret and resolving not to regret, he dies. Only a waiting predatory hyena notes the moment of his passing.

Once in a while, a real-life deathwatch struggle with regret becomes public. This was the case with Lee Atwater, the chairman of the Republican National Committee and campaign manager for George Bush's 1988 campaign. Following immediately upon the heels of these achievements in 1990, at age 39 Atwater learned he was dying of an inoperable brain tumor. He died at the end of March 1991. In a magazine article that appeared a month before his death, Atwater wrote about how he was attempting to "come to terms with some [of his] less than virtuous acts."[93] He described his belated apology to a South Carolina Democrat whose history of electroshock therapy he had opportunistically exposed during a campaign in 1980. Atwater also publicly stated that he was sorry for aspects of the extremely negative campaign he had waged in 1988 for George Bush against Michael Dukakis, repudiating his pit-bull behavior toward Dukakis as "nakedly cruel."[94] Atwater explained:

> I've come a long way since the day I told George Bush that his "kinder, gentler" theme was a nice thought, but it wouldn't win us any votes. I used to say that the President might be kinder and gentler, but I wasn't going to be. How wrong I was.[95]

Apparently, Tolstoy's romantic vision of the deathbed resolution of regret is realizable in fact as well as fiction. In its obscurity, gravity, uncontrollability, and irremediability, awareness of death qualifies as the quintessentially tragic antecedent of regret.

To the extent that these external factors are controllable, one is disposed to a more comic mode of experiencing regret. If all the ways we fail to figure out what we want and what is possible are reparable by the exercise of reason, then a more comic view of regret (such as that of classic decision theory) follows. To the extent that these factors evade personal control, as in situations with an intransigent scarcity of desired resources, or devoid of good options, the experience of regret may take on an unavoidably tragic cast.

As we have seen in this chapter and the one before it, a host of occasions, as well as a host of precipitating conditions, both internal and external, serve to evoke regret. Once regret has declared itself, our next concern is what to do with it.

8

Transformation of Regret

How is regret transformed over time? As mentioned earlier, empirical research on regret has only recently made its debut. Investigations of regret as a historical, dynamic process—investigations capable of answering the vital question of how it is transformed—are nonexistent. Although in principle autobiographies might serve as valuable sources of such material, with the exception of T. E. Lawrence's *Seven Pillars of Wisdom* (with its equal parts of regret and guilt), I am unfamiliar with autobiographies that illuminate regret as temporal process.[1]

However, there are rich psychological theories of development, coping, and psychotherapy that offer promising insights pertinent to this question. Novels, too, are particularly good at portraying the extended periods necessary for the unfolding and transformation of regret. In this chapter I draw on both types of sources to explore the question of how best to accomplish the transformation of regret.

The Psychology of Transformation

Stress, Coping, and Transformation

Resolution and transformation are cousins to coping, which has been defined as the "constantly changing cognitive and behavioral efforts to manage specific external and/or internal demands that are appraised as taxing or exceeding the resources of the person." [2] Regret might be viewed as an internal demand that most people would appraise as taxing their resources—as, in a word, stressful. As such, regret calls for some coping strategies. For guidance as to how to resolve regret, it makes good sense, then, to turn to the research on stress and coping.

Empirical research on stress and coping supports the idea that people are not simply the passive victims of their emotions (as implied in that synonym for the *emotions, passions*). Instead, we more or less actively construct, maintain, and transform our emotions.[3] (This, of course, is not to imply that the processes of constructing, maintaining, and transforming emotions always occur with full awareness.) There is considerable evidence, for example, that once we have attained the blessed state of being in a good mood, we will do a variety of things to sustain that state.[4] Compared to a control group, more people in a good mood offer help to others in need—if the nature of the help is likely to sustain rather than to threaten the good mood.[5] Probably even more urgently, people regularly take active measures to rid themselves of bad moods and unpleasant emotions. To describe this process I have intentionally chosen to use a word—*transformation*—that (unlike *management* or *regulation*) does not connote dampening or stifling emotions.

The earliest efforts to explore coping prompted psychologists to propose stages in the process, or traits in the person—to explain the observed differences over time and among individuals. The popular press continues to favor stage theories, with their orderly succession of phases. In one well-known stage theory, we see denial and isolation, anger, bargaining with fate, depression, and acceptance[6]; in another, shock, attention, action, detachment, autonomy, and connection.[7] Trait approaches have sought to predict people's coping as a function of their personal predispositions such as: repression versus sensitization[8]; hysterical versus obsessive cognitive styles[9]; and more recently Type A versus Type B personality[10]; as well as others discussed in Chapter 6. But, by now, the weaknesses of stage and trait theories of coping have been pretty well established. The way people actually go about trying to cope with stress (such as regret) proves far less sequential and more contextually variable than most stage or trait theories would predict.[11]

There are any number of worthwhile models of coping.[12] However, I shall focus on catalogs of coping strategies that prove particularly useful in explaining the several roads to the transformation of regret.

One of the best-known theories proposes a tripartite scheme, distinguishing among appraisal-focused, emotion-focused, and problem-focused modes of coping.[13] Others use different language to describe analogous processes: (1) cognitive reappraisal; (2) mood management (through distraction, expression, self-reward, alcohol, and other pharmacological intake); and (3) problem-directed action.[14] Whatever their labels, these three elements of coping map reasonably well onto the concepts of thought, feeling, and behavior.

Appraisal-focused coping entails efforts to think differently about a stressor. One widely studied appraisal-focused strategy is cognitive restructuring, or redefining the situation—for example, seeing it not as a threat but as a challenge.[15] With respect to regret, an individual relying on cognitive restructuring might strive to think something like "It was a mistake. But it was a reasonably good decision given what I knew then. Now let's see how I can turn my mistake to my advantage." *Emotion-focused* coping puts a premium on managing—usually by avoiding or dampening—one's feelings; this involves, for example, engaging in wishful thinking or simply suppressing negative feelings. Studiously avoiding the experience of regret and repeating to oneself sentiments like "It's stupid to feel bad about that. It's history" are emotion-focused strategies of coping with regret. *Problem-focused* coping is defined as making attempts to manage, change, or (if all else fails) withdraw from the source of the stress—for example, by defining the problem, generating alternative possible solutions, systematically assessing each alternative, making a rational choice among alternatives, and acting. This triumvirate has sometimes been joined by a fourth category of mood-regulating activities: *affiliation* with others—seeking out others with whom to distract or enjoy ourselves, with whom to vent our feelings, or with whom to discuss and assess the problem.[16]

Which coping strategy proves most effective at reducing stress depends partly on the match between the characteristics of the stressor and the mode of coping. For example, when a regrettable situation is changeable, then problem-focused strategies are primarily called for. In contrast, when no action is possible that would change a regrettable situation, then the problem-focused mode of coping would make a poor match, but the other three modes might relieve the regret. Emotion-focused avoidance seems adaptive with certain aspects of a stressful situation, but not with the whole. Thus denial of the fact of having cancer appears to be a worse coping strategy than denial of the implications of having cancer (imminent death). In addition, emotion-focused avoidance and denial may be noninjurious early (e.g., immediately upon learning that one has cancer), but not if early action is called for (e.g., during a heart attack) and not as a long-term habit. In general, effective coping depends on the ability to select wisely from a range of coping strategies.[17]

Numerous research studies have supported the hypothesized role of cognitive appraisal in reducing unpleasant emotions. For example, one study tried to alleviate public-speaking phobias through cognitive processing consisting of examining the source of one's beliefs about public speaking. Compared to a control group and a catharsis group (in which subjects were instructed to try to relive a fearful public-speaking experience, concentrating on their emotional reactions), the cognitive processing group showed a significant reduction of fear when placed in a public-speaking situation, as assessed by physiological and self-report measures.[18] The authors of this research speculate that "forcing subjects to focus on the bases of their beliefs may produce an awareness of the illogicality of the process . . . thereby reducing the affect."[19] This is the central tenet of a number of schools of therapy, especially rational-emotive therapy[20] and cognitive therapy.[21]

Although cognitive appraisal, reappraisal, or reframing appears to be the most common method of self-medication,[22] it isn't always the best medicine. Neither is the method of mood management that amounts to squelching unpleasant emotions. Thomas Borkovec and his colleagues recently discovered that chronic worriers and people with anxiety disorders differ from people without undue anxiety in that they do too *much* thinking and too *little* feeling of their fears.[23] When subjects with and without public-speaking phobias were asked to imagine themselves talking in public and to try to *feel* the anxiety, surprisingly the dispositionally nonanxious group showed a marked physical (cardiovascular) response, but the anxious group showed practically no physical response. This counterintuitive finding has prognostic significance: for according to Borkovec and Inz, "studies have found that the physical response is a positive sign that the emotional information is being processed"—and "the more we can call up an affect . . . the more likely we can change."[24] Borkovec and Inz go so far as to refer to the activity of experiencing the negative emotion as "the miracle" ingredient responsible for helping relieve people of acute anxieties and chronic worrying.

By extension, it seems likely that relief from regret may also depend on the ability and willingness to call up and to experience the emotional aspects of regret as fully as possible. This is, of course, a controversial proposition. It is controversial not only from within a stress-and-coping framework with its suspiciousness of emotion but more generally within this culture. It merits a brief foray into some of the principal elements of the controversy.

Most of us have to some extent absorbed the advice to let it all hang out lest you explode. This advice may be traced to the Freudian concepts of psychic hydraulics, catharsis, and abreaction. The *hydraulic* metaphor suggests that discharging emotion works like a safety valve, releasing something that would otherwise build up and explode, or implode. *Catharsis* is the ancient and related idea that emotions are purged through their expression. According to Aristotle, emotional involvement in the dramatic portrayal of tragedy produces catharsis, or purging, of the emotions of fear and pity. The Freudian theory was that, as I discussed earlier, repressed emotions (and other psychic processes) do not just magically disappear. If they are not permitted overt expression (or are not otherwise resolved), they will find covert means of expression, through slips of the tongue, dreams, and symptoms, for example. One psychoanalytic technique used for helping people become master of their emotions, then, rather than to continue to be mastered by them, is the use of *abreaction* in the context of analytic sessions. Abreaction is the unrestrained experience of emotion, or reliving a past trauma with all its attendant emotion. The psychoanalytic theory of treatment was imported into the culture in the form of the Freudian-sounding advice not to repress your emotions but to express them, and to do so intensely.

However, permission for emotional expressiveness has always faced off uneasily across from its opposite number—civilization's command to control our emotions. A good part of the process of socializing children, after all, concerns teaching them this. Culture has issued us a double-bind, then: telling us to express emotion and simultaneously forbidding it.

There is another strand to this complicated mesh. Soon after the middle of this century, much of scientific psychology had become disaffected with the perceived excesses of Freudian theory, and sought to empirically disprove it. A debased version of the catharsis/abreaction notion proved an easy target. Psychological research soon demonstrated that expressing anger is as likely to increase anger as to reduce it.[25] Everyday experience, too, confirms that the uncontrolled expression of emotion often takes a situation from bad to worse. Exploding with one's partner or boss can escalate a flash of anger into massive all-out war. Such observations and research have been cited to disprove Freudian theory and to advise against venting emotion. Carol Tavris's influential book, *Anger, the Misunderstood Emotion*, is perhaps the best-known instance.[26]

So by now we have a double dose of the recommendation to stifle emotion—the prohibitions of civilization have now apparently been buttressed by the prohibitions of science. Both urge us to avoid or ignore or suppress or stifle or explain away unpleasant feelings. Conquest of emotion is the heart of the advice. I believe that this counsel is based on at least three errors: a misguided equation of emotion with excessive emotion, a misguided equation of the context of everyday life with the context of psychotherapy, and a misguided dissociation of emotion and thought.

First, emotion is not abreaction. Of course, we know that. Yet, we need never even have heard of abreaction to find ourselves thinking of emotion as almost inevitably done to excess. Countless degrees of emotional expression lie between the extreme of unrestrained expression of emotion and the other extreme of its suppression. It is unproductive to continue to pose the issue in the overly black-and-white form that it often takes. The truth is that the unrestrained experience and expression of emotion is exactly what is needed at one moment, its suppression is exactly what is needed at another moment, and something partway between these extremes is exactly what is needed most of the time. Our fear of explosive emotion too often leads us to reject emotion altogether.

Second, the interpersonal context of psychotherapy is different from the interpersonal context of everyday life. One significant difference is the presence and purpose of the therapist in one setting but not in the other. What is appropriate in the consultation room is not necessarily appropriate in the home or on the job. Much of the modern "scientific" call to suppress emotion is simply irrelevant to the point that Freud intended. Just as Freud never recommended that people should go around acting out sexually wherever and whenever they feel like it, neither did he ever recommend that people go around emotionally venting wherever and whenever they feel like it. The Freudian notion was that it might be useful in the privacy of the consultation room. When it comes to psychotherapy—or other private, temporary, and strategic contexts—permitting oneself to feel and to express full-blown emotion *can* eventually lead to its reduction.

But as Freud well knew, it is not the ventilation of emotion per se that is therapeutic, but what happens to it next—the fusion of intellectual insight with emotional experience that goes by the name of "working-through" (which I discuss in some detail in the next section). Countless degrees of intellective elaboration and reframing lie between the extremes of blind ventilation and intellectualized suppression of emotion. In fact, much research, as well as psychodynamic theory, find that the full experience of unpleasant emotion is a necessary moment on the way to its transformation. How interesting that a poet, T. S. Eliot, came upon the same insight as Freud: the first step with emotion is surrender, not conquest. What happens later, in therapy and in a sagacious life, is the marriage of mind and emotion, the reunification of sensibility. Reflecting upon one's fully experienced emotion is a moment on the way to its transformation.

At this point it may help us to reconsider what can be learned from the "ghost" metaphor for regret used by so many writers (e.g., Sherwood Anderson, J. M. Barrie, Henry James, Maxine Kumin, and M. Scheler). Is it better to ignore or confront ghosts? In Maxine Kumin's "History Lesson," the poet clearly tells us not to flee from the ghosts of regret but to confront them, and (shifting metaphors) to cultivate regret, at least for a season:

> That a man may be free of his ghosts
> he must return to them like a garden.
> He must put his hands in the sweet rot
> uprooting the turnips, washing them
> tying them into bundles
> and shouldering the whole load to market.[27]

Yes. Those able to tolerate for a time putting their hands in the sweet rot of regret stand a better chance of being free of it in the long run than those unable or unwilling to do so. The one who flees, to use Scheler's words once again, becomes an "eternal fugitive from the past," thereby sinking "deeper and deeper into the dead arms of that very past." This claim (and not the misinterpreted version of the catharsis principle) is fundamental to a second theoretical approach, the psychoanalytic, applicable to the transformation of regret.

The Freudian Perspective on Transformation

In "Mourning and Melancholia"[28] and elsewhere, Freud offers formulations relevant to regret, including descriptions of normal and neurotic sadness, and prescriptions for how to resolve these baneful states.

"Working-through"—meaning going beyond intellectual insight to something like "lived experience"—constitutes an essential element of psychoanalytic treatment. An extended definition of working-through follows:

> the repetition of all the details of the emotional pattern, including abreaction [the free expression of repressed emotions] and insight, during analysis, when the ego's defense measures are gradually reduced. It consists of experiencing and understanding each aspect of the neurosis as it is revealed under treatment and as the patient's resistance to self-expression diminishes.[29]

At least one modern psychoanalytic psychologist has explicitly taken the intellective/emotional concept of working-through one step further—into the realm of behavior, asserting: "Anyone who collects insights step-by-step, but does not do anything with them— that is, does not *use* them by casting around for and adopting behavioral change—is not engaged in the serious labor of working through."[30]

There are similarities between the elements of working-through and the four major strategies identified by the coping research: insight is parallel to cognitive appraisal, abreaction to emotion management, behavior change to problem-focused coping, and the therapeutic relationship to affiliation. More broadly, there is explicit agreement on the need for working-through. Emotion researcher Nico Frijda, for example, echoes Freud when he asserts that "disengagement from concerns requires some sort of work."[31]

However, there are profound differences. First, in the psychoanalytic approach, although insight does entail an intellectual component, it does not entail using the intellect to quash emotional conflict. Second, as discussed in the previous section, the kind of emotional experience prescribed by Freud—that is, free and full expression within the treatment context—diametrically opposes the prescription to minimize emotion often implied by researchers of stress. Third, behavioral changes likely to follow from psychoanalytic treatment are in principle neutral—in contrast to a certain slant in the stress-and-coping perspective toward adjusting to the strictures of society. Fourth, the interpersonal role of the psychoanalytic therapist is not to distract, mollify, or even necessarily to "support" the patient (as in affiliation), but to facilitate the individual's struggle to overcome resistance to insight, emotional experience, and behavior change.

In addition to the concept of working-through, the Freudian perspective offers a valuable distinction between normal grief (mourning) and neurotic depression (melancholia). Mourning or grief is a normal, profoundly painful but temporary state of dejection occurring in reaction to the loss of a loved one, or some other personally important loss.[32] Freud describes "the work of mourning" (like all working-through) as a painful task that of necessity takes time—because it requires bringing up "each single one of the memories and hopes which bound the libido to the object,"[33] "hypercathecting" (fully and emotionally experiencing) each of these memories and hopes, and finally parting from them. The work of mourning rests on a foundation of confrontation, not suppression— an idea expressed in this adage attributed to Baal Shem-Tov, the founder of Hasidism: "In remembrance resides the secret of redemption." According to Freud, the process of working-through mourning absorbs an enormous amount of psychic energy—a fact that accounts for the abrogation of interest in the outside world and the general inhibition characteristic of mourning.

In contrast, melancholia, or neurotic depression, is characterized not only by dejection, self-preoccupation, and inhibition of activity and of the capacity to love, but also by other qualities not typically experienced in mourning—notably, abject self-denigration.[34] The main difference between normal grief and neurotic depression, then, is the self-recrimination that characterizes neurotic depression. Frequently, though not always, neurotic depression differs from normal grief in that the source of the sorrow remains opaque to the depressed individual.

But the tremendous energy required by the working-through process does not explain the fact or the clamorousness of the self-abasement of neurotic depression. This requires an understanding of the dynamic etiology of neurotic depression. In the psychoanalytic account of neurotic depression, self-abasement arises from the psychic experience of the loss as a loss in one's self, entailing a loss of self-respect. But why would anyone suffering diminished self-respect so shamelessly proclaim that fact? According to Freud, the curiously open and insistent nature of the self-accusation arises from the fact that the accusations actually apply not to oneself, but to someone or something else—"some person whom the patient loves, has loved or ought to love,"[35] or some circumstance "of being wounded, hurt, neglected, out of favour, or disappointed."[36] In other words, the "self-reproaches are reproaches against a loved object which have been shifted on to the patient's own ego,"[37] and "the conflict between the ego and the loved person [is] transformed into a cleavage between the criticizing faculty of the ego and the ego as altered by the identification" with the disappointing love object.[38] Hence the idea of depression as anger turned inward. Furthermore, this represents another difference between normal and neurotic depression: the latter is characterized by sometimes unconscious, usually disavowed emotional ambivalence toward someone else. But what is gained by this dismaying displacement of anger inward? Freud explains: "by taking flight into the ego love escapes annihilation."[39] In other words, neurotic depression permits one simultaneously to mourn a loss and to obviate the loss. Someone you carry around in your psyche is not truly gone.

The work of normal mourning involves gradually coming to accept the reality of the loss, ending in a transfer of one's interest from the lost object onto the rest of the world. But for neurotic depression, which is marked as well by ambivalence (love and anger), working-through is more problematic, since it entails overcoming unconscious resistance to acknowledging and experiencing the ambivalence. The work of neurotic depression ends either when "the fury has spent itself or [when] the object is abandoned as no longer of value."[40] That is, neurotic depression is resolved when the feelings have been fully and conclusively experienced and either accepted or genuinely rejected.

Like the psychoanalytic formulation of working-through, the distinction between mourning and melancholia can be extended to regret. When individuals acknowledge to themselves their mistakes, transgressions, lost opportunities, or other losses, a normal reaction is not only temporary sadness but also regret, the painful state of feeling sorry about these states of affairs and about the context in which they occurred. Regret usually includes a comparison of "what is" with "what might have been" and often a wish to undo "what is." Normal regret can be worked through by repeated bouts of emotional engagement with reality *and* with the ghosts of what might have been. Ideally, these bouts will not occur only within the head of the individual, but interpersonally.

I think at this point of a man I met once in a local deli. When he overheard someone else ask me about how this book was going, he engaged me in conversation about it. Almost immediately, he told me that he is a transvestite and that he is writing a book about it. After we talked for quite a while, I felt bold enough to ask him whether he had any regrets. "Every day!" he shot back. "Every time I put my clothes on" (referring to his male clothes). His regret was obviously intense. But he was functioning nevertheless, and in the process of writing a book about his experience. How was it that he was doing all right, despite experiencing intense regret every day, more than every day? He mentioned that it was a support group that saved his life. Privately, I noticed also that he was not dining alone, but with a young woman. I suspect that his engagement with others does save him, as well as his considerable powers of reflection and expression. For all of us, it is such interactions between interior and exterior, between what is and what might be, between self and others, that eventually bring us to accept regretted realities and free our psychic energies to range elsewhere.

As with neurotic sadness, the course of *neurotic* regret is complicated. Neurotic regret occurs when the source of regret goes unacknowledged, or when it involves unacknowledged ambivalence or marked self-hatred, or both. In this case, the first task is to overcome the resistance to acknowledging the source of regret. Then, the ambivalence must be acknowledged and worked through, meaning that both the negative (anger) and the positive (love) feelings must be fully experienced (in Freudian language "hyper-cathected"). Finally, the element of pathological self-hatred must be resolved by sustaining the anger with oneself and with the other over the loss, mistake, and so on, until either "the fury has spent itself"[41] or the misfortune is perceived as not worthy of one's continued regret. If part or all of this painful process is bypassed, then the individual will be left with gnawing, persistent regret.

An Object-Relations Perspective on Transformation

The standard Freudian perspective on the human reaction to unwanted psychic and external events has been modified by a number of theorists, including object-relations theorists. In general the object-relations school delves further back in personal history than Freud—that is, back to infancy—to locate the source of later mental conflict. More to the point, object relations theory provides an account of adult mental life as grounded in one's unconscious perceptions of the particularities of one's relationships with important others (object relations) rather than on the unilateral and universal instinctual impulses (erotic and aggressive) posited by Freud. With respect to the present concerns, Melanie Klein's concept of reparation adds an important facet to a psychodynamic model of the resolution of regret.

According to Klein,[42] because no human parent is ubiquitous, omniscient, or all-giving, every infant inexorably encounters frustrating or unsatisfying circumstances. The infant's wish does not always immediately produce breast or bottle; the toddler's desire to urinate and defecate at will is foiled by the parent who insists that the toddler limit the times and places for these activities; sometimes a parent has the gall to leave an infant with someone else for a time. Progressive psychological development depends on the successful transfiguration of one's anger, sadness, and regret over these untoward states of affairs. According to Klein, resolution entails negotiating three stages: (1) an anger phase, in which the infant projects his own anger and aggression onto the parents, imagining that they hate him; (2) a depression phase, in which the infant mourns the absence of wished-for psychic goods; and finally (3) a reparation stage, in which the individual "achieves integration concurrently with good object relations and thereby repairs what had gone wrong in his life."[43] Melanie Klein's pertinent insight is that the sorrow of regret represents a developmental improvement over blaming others for one's unhappiness.

Like the Freudian process of working through mourning, the process of reparation is founded on a base of acknowledging and experiencing conflicting emotions. A successful reparatory process ends with the acceptance of reality, with all its good and bad, limits, loss, separations, and deprivations. Reparation can take either of two specific forms analogous to those identified by Freud: reconciliation or detachment. But, as Klein explains, true reparation and thus true resolution can be short-circuited by "defensive" reparation, in which (1) the anger and depression are suppressed, repressed, bypassed; or (2) there is an attempt quickly, magically, once and for all to undo the loss. The concept of reparation brings to the Freudian concept of working-through a greater emphasis on the interpersonal nature of the final resolution of internal conflict. Reparation takes resolution outside the confines of the head and heart of the individual (as in the coping literature) and outside the confines of the therapy room (as in Freudian transference) into the wider world of others.

This differential emphasis is highlighted in Hannah Segal's[44] thoughts on resolution through aesthetic sublimation. For Segal, aesthetic creativity rests on a hybrid Freudian/Kleinian process of working through mourning. In this spirit Segal[45] quotes Rilke: "Beauty is nothing but the beginning of terror that we are still just able to bear." According to Segal,[46] artists create worlds of their own in order to "find an equivalent for life." More explicitly pertinent to regret is Segal's analysis of Proust. "According to Proust, an artist is compelled to create by his need to recover his lost past," says Segal.[47] In the artist's creation the final stage of reparation is accomplished: "all his lost, destroyed, and loved objects are being brought back to life."[48] Moreover, artistic creation depends directly on the work of mourning and working-through. Artistic blocks may result from the failure to experience loss and to accomplish the work of mourning. In contrast, "according to Proust, it is only the lost past and the lost or dead object that can be made into a work of art. . . . It is only when the loss has been acknowledged and the mourning experienced that re-creation can take place."[49] Some have interpreted Thomas Hardy's poems about his deceased wife as a creative effort symbolically to repair his loss through use of the trope of prosopopoeia, or ascribing life to the dead.[50]

The following poem, "History as the Painter Bonnard" by Jane Hirshfield, gives beautiful expression to the interpersonal emphasis of the object-relations school, Klein's notion of the value of regret, and Segal's notion of repairing regret through artistic creation and revision:

Because nothing is ever finished
the painter would shuffle, *bonnarding,*
into galleries, museums, even the homes of his patrons,
with hidden palette and brush:
overscribble drapery and table with milk jug or fattened pear,
the clabbered, ripening colors of second sight.

Though he knew with time the pentimenti rise—
half-visible, half brine-swept fish, their plunged shapes
pocking the mind—toward the end, only revision mattered:
to look again, more deeply, harder, clearer,
the one redemption granted us to ask.

This, we say, is what we meant to say. This. This.
—as the kiss, the sorrowful murmur,
may cover a child's bruises, if not retract the blow.
While a woman in Prague asks softly, in good English,
for the camera, "But who will give us back these twenty years?"

Ah love, o history, forgive
the squandered light and flung-down rags of chances,
old choices drifted terribly awry.

And world, self-portrait never right, receive this gift—
shuffling, spattered, stubborn,
something nameless opens in the heart: to touch
with soft-bent sable, ground-earth pigment, seed-clear oil,
the rounding, bright-fleshed present, if not the past.

The kissed child puts his hand at last back into his mother's,
though it is not the same;
her fine face neither right nor wrong, only thoroughly his.[51]

It is not only the artist who is driven to shuffle around trying to repair what has gone wrong. Anyone whose choices have "drifted terribly awry" may find himself or herself impelled by the possibility of revision, repair, even redemption through human touch and re-touching.

Transformation in Erikson's Model of Psychosocial Development

According to Erik Erikson's ego analytic theory of adult development over the life span, full human development is contingent upon successful resolution of eight "crises."[52] The infant, for example, struggles between trust and mistrust, with successful resolution yielding hope. The adolescent attempts to forge a personal identity. The task in early adulthood is to negotiate the conflict between isolation and intimacy in favor of intimacy with others. In middle adulthood, the individual must struggle to overcome self-absorption, replacing it with generativity or care for others, particularly the young. The final task of the individual is to come to terms with regret and despair, thereby achieving what Erikson calls *integrity*. In this account, integrity and wisdom presuppose the process of bringing together the good and the bad, the wise and the foolish, the strong and the weak facets of oneself and one's life. Wisdom emerges like a phoenix from the ashes of regret and despair.

In an interview-based study of regret versus ego integrity in eight elderly individuals, Christie Carlson discovered at least one living exemplar of the Eriksonian path to the resolution of regret, one Mrs. E. When Carlson asked Mrs. E. if there were things she often thought about that she wished she had done differently in her life, Mrs. E. laughed and said:

> Oh, yes. I've made mistakes, of course. When you come to grips with life, you come to feel you have to do certain things. You have to face

things and master adversity when it comes. You probably won't always do things in just the right way, but you have to be willing to accept that you're likely to make some mistakes along the way.[53]

Empirical support for Erikson's proposed association of integrity—and a crisis of regret—with old age has been found in studies such as one that asked people from three stages of life to describe or to project (prospectively or retrospectively) their own experience of integrity.[54] Young (average age of 20), middle-aged (average age of 48), and elderly (average age of 69) individuals were asked to what extent 16 items designed to measure integrity applied to them concurrently, prospectively, or retrospectively. The items inquired about matters such as: accepting one's personal life as something that had to be; reviewing one's past life as appropriate and meaningful; resolving past conflicts and feelings of regret. Among the items specifically targeting regret were: "In general, I would say I have few regrets about my past life"; "If I had to do it all over again, there are very few things about my life that I would change"; "All in all, I am comfortable with the choices I made regarding my life's work." The Eriksonian predictions were confirmed: the integrity scores were higher for the old-age focus than for either of the younger temporal focuses. A more direct test of Erikson's model found that a sample of elderly individuals (average age of 72) who were identified by their peers as "wise" scored significantly higher on the measure of ego integrity—hence lower in regret—than a comparison group.[55]

Literary Exemplars of the Transformation of Regret

Of course not everyone achieves a state of wisdom, whether in old age or earlier, which entails a genuine resolution of regret. Like almost anything human, regret may change in either a regressive or a progressive direction. A regressive form of dealing with regret might recall the lines of Langston Hughes: it is "what happens to the dream deferred"; it dries up "like a raisin in the sun." A progressive transformation of regret might mirror the lines of Jane Hirshfield: "to look again, more deeply, harder, clearer/the one redemption granted us to ask." Here I take up literary examples to illustrate a process of regret that moves in successive steps from regret submerged to regret unresolved to regret partially resolved to regret redone and repaired, and finally to regret transcended.

Regressive Forms of Managing Regret

The various defense mechanisms,[56] some of which I have already discussed, provide a useful framework for organizing the many ways *not* to deal with regret. Especially insofar as regret stirs up anxiety concerning disavowed impulses, wishes, or acts, it may elicit psychological maneuvers designed to reduce the anxiety—among them defensive denial, suppression, repression, undoing, rationalization, intellectualization, and regressive fantasy.

One of the more primitive defenses is brute denial. Strictly speaking, in denial the individual negates the evidence of his or her senses, rejecting external reality. However, denial can be understood more broadly to include denial of information, of threatening information, of personal relevance, of urgency, of vulnerability, of responsibility, of emotion, and of emotional relevance.[57] Literature provides many examples of the denial of regret, and we sample a few here.

Repression is the unconscious act of barring unwanted psychic material (e.g., impulses, wishes, memories) from awareness. Suppression is the conscious act of barring unwanted psychic material from awareness. It is suppression that Lady Macbeth recommends to her guilty husband when she tells him that "Things without all remedy should be without regard." King Lear, wracked with regret over Goneril's and Regan's treachery toward him and over his foolish treatment of Cordelia, desperately turns to suppression: "No, no, no. That way madness lies. I will think on't no more."

Frequently individuals employ more than one defensive tactic to shield themselves from the psychic threat entailed in regret. Literary examples abound. James Joyce was describing the combined use of defensive suppression, repression, and denial in this passage from *Ulysses*:

> There are sins or (let us call them as the world calls them) evil memories which are hidden away by man in the darkest places of the heart [repression and/or suppression]. . . . He may suffer their memory to grow dim [suppression], let them be as though they had not been and all but persuade himself that they were not or at least were otherwise [denial].[58]

In "The Snows of Kilimanjaro,"[59] Hemingway tells the story of a dying writer hounded by regret for literature he has put off writing and now would never write. Against this background of regret, the protagonist recalls having used the defenses of suppression and denial in the past, defenses that *in extremis* have failed him: "You kept from thinking and it was all marvellous." Hemingway articulates the self-protective functions of denial of emotional vulnerability[60] in particular: "He had been contemptuous of those who wrecked. . . . He could beat anything, he thought, because nothing could hurt him if he did not care."[61]

In Tolstoy's "The Death of Ivan Ilyitch," another dying protagonist defensively denies and suppresses regret:

> when the thought occurred to him, as it had often occurred to him, that all this came from the fact that he had not lived as he should, he instantly remembered all the correctness of his life [denial], and he drove away this strange thought. . . . "I must not think about these things; it is too painful," said Ivan Ilyitch to himself [suppression].[62]

In the following passage, as well, Ivan Ilyitch calls upon denial and suppression to evade regret:

> "Can it be that I did not live as I ought?" . . . immediately he put away [suppression] this sole explanation of the enigma of life and death as something absolutely impossible [denial].[63]

Denial, suppression, and repression can be thought of as forms of pulling the wool over our eyes so as not to see the fearsome shadows of regret menacing in the dark. But these strategies can never rid us of the source of these shadows. Employing defense mechanisms to cope with regret works only in the short run. In the long run, relying on defense mechanisms is counterproductive. To add another metaphor: "It is the non-localized hurts that do the damage," writes William Stafford in the poem "Letter."[64] Defense mechanisms impair the positive transformation of regret by keeping hurts non-localized. Recognition and acknowledgment of regret is the necessary first step toward its positive transformation.

Regret Acknowledged

J. M. Barrie's play *Dear Brutus* depicts two of the next steps in the process toward resolution of regret—acknowledging regret and one's contribution to regret. After having served as involuntary subjects in a naughty "experiment" that required them to actualize their might-have-beens, the players in *Dear Brutus* come to the sobering realization that they have made no more of their second chances than they had of their first. Each one recognizes that it was not chance, fate, or circumstances that had thwarted them, but something in themselves that makes them go on making the same sort of mistakes—"however many chances we get."[65] Purdie, for instance, who had previously used his regret over his choice of spouse to justify his extramarital dalliances, comes to the realization that: "I say, I believe I am not a deeply passionate chap at all; I believe I am just . . . a philanderer!"[66] Similarly, one of the characters points out that Mrs. Dearth, who had also made a miserable marriage, "would always choose the wrong man, good man or bad man, but the wrong man for her."[67] This insight, of course, underlies the play's Shakespearean title: "The fault, dear Brutus, is not in our stars,/ But in ourselves . . ."

There are certain hazards in this skeptical attitude toward second chances—notably acquiescence in the individual or societal status quo. This is in fact reflected in Barrie's comfortingly aristocratic assumption that Matey, the butler, was destined by nature for a life of thievery and domestic service—a social position in which he supposedly felt ever so much more "comfortable" than he did in his second chance as a man of wealth and position.

Even on the individual level, the end of the process ought not be resignation, which the psychologist Nico Frijda defines as "goal abandonment when the underlying concern is still alive."[68] At the extreme, resignation can amount to an acceptance of one's vileness: "I am what I am—a thoroughly and immutably despicable travesty of a human being. Period." This resembles the fatalistic thought that Camus leaves with readers in *The Fall*. Following the narrator's failure to do anything to save a young woman who committed suicide by jumping into the Seine, he obsesses over the realization that he is not innocent. The last words of *The Fall* express both regret for his inaction and fatalistic acceptance of the probability that he would make the same mistake a second time:

> "O young woman, throw yourself into the water again so that I may a second time have the chance of saving both of us!" A second time, eh, what a risky suggestion! Just suppose, *cher maître*, that we should be taken literally? We'd have to go through with it. Brr . . . ! The water's so cold! But let's not worry! It's too late now. It will always be too late. Fortunately![69]

Self-knowledge and acceptance of our personal contribution to our regrets need not end with facile but culpable self-acceptance or detached, fatalistic, resigned acceptance of circumstances. The transformational processes may culminate in a rather different sort of resolution of regret. However, it is also possible to take the first step, to localize the hurt in Stafford's words, and even to take the next steps of acknowledging personal responsibility, and still fail to complete the journey—as can be seen in the next literary examples from *Notes from Underground* and *Mrs. Dalloway.*

Sham-Resolution of Regret Through "Acceptance": Notes from Underground

The protagonist of Dostoevsky's *Notes from Underground* does not forestall regret through denial, repression, or suppression. Instead, he not only acknowledges regret; he positively dwells on it. Yet all this attention to his regret proves fruitless, in part because he substitutes for genuine progressive resolution other defensive maneuvers—namely, undoing, rationalization, intellectualization, and regressive fantasy.

Within a psychoanalytic framework, undoing is a defense mechanism whereby "something positive is done which, actually or magically, is the opposite of something which, again actually or in imagination, was done before."[70] After the murders Lady Macbeth urges not only suppression but also undoing upon her husband: "a little water clears us of this deed." Her own compulsive handwashing in sleep exemplifies the process of attempting magically to expunge something that was actually done. The protagonist of *Notes from Underground* tries to convince himself that he can undo (not psychically, but in actuality) one of his two major regrets—for having made a perfect ass of himself with his "friends." At the conscious level, the Underground Man intends to undo his offensive behavior with Simonov by a confession and apology. Actually, he writes Simonov a letter consisting of equal parts apology and self-justification. In this letter he claims: "I took the blame for everything upon myself,"[71] in the next breath rationalizing his conduct by appealing to his having been drunk.

The Underground Man makes heavy use of rationalization, as well, in an effort to ward off his second thoughts over having initiated a friendship with Liza. He grows terrified that if she comes to know him, she will devalue him for his lowly financial and social position. In response to his welter of agonizing feelings, he tells himself on the one hand that he is not good enough for her, and then again that she is not good enough for him. With these thoughts he tries to explain away the regret. Later, immediately after he has finally driven Liza away forever, he attempts to undo his mistake by running to find her. However, this regret also resists undoing, in actuality and psychically. Therefore, he again calls upon self-contradictory rationalizations: he tries to convince himself both that his insulting Liza amounted to her purification and that to have married her would have amounted to her defilement.

Unable either to undo or rationalize away his profound unhappiness, he arms himself with the defense he is best at—intellectualization, or reframing a painful reality in abstract, emotionally distanced terms. Here, for example, he intellectualizes his misery: "which is better—cheap happiness, or noble suffering?"[72] His uncompromising insistence on confronting the "truth" at the cost of his social and emotional equilibrium represents another example of the use of intellectualization to deal with regret: "how preferable it is to understand everything, to be aware of everything, of all impossibilities and stone walls, and yet refuse to reconcile yourself to a single one of those impossibilities and walls."[73] The following analysis of fixation applies almost uncannily to this character: "in forever seeking a perfectibility . . . that is not and can never be possessed, this person continues to refuse any compromise with life on its own realistic basis in the present."[74] The unmitigated black-and-white view that is characteristic of both the tragic and the romantic visions proves his undoing. Refusing either to accept or to alter his life, he fails Erikson's last test (as he has failed the earlier one of intimacy versus isolation)—the test pitting integrity over and against regret and despair.

Similarly, he refuses to settle for a conventionally easy answer to the question of who is to blame for his mistakes: "you are somehow to blame even for the stone wall, although, again, it is entirely obvious that you are not to blame at all."[75] On the one hand, he accepts responsibility for the past, and defines the act of confessing in writing these Notes as "corrective punishment."[76] However, as is also the case with the protagonist of *The Fall*, confession proves a static, rather than a progressive, solution to regret, due perhaps to the solipsistic nature of these particular confessions.

On the other hand, in a satirical parody of the scientific determinism of Dostoevsky's day,[77] the Underground Man disavows any personal responsibility whatsoever, asserting that he is not to blame for the stone wall, and claiming that his stunted life is only an extreme form of all lives—"We are stillborn."[78] Such cognitive complexity might have been marshaled in the service of wisdom; but this protagonist uses cognitive complexity merely to shield himself from feeling. As a result, his regret over Liza remains a static thing. He continues doing what he has always done; he attempts to escape into ideas and books from the hellish isolation that is his life.

Finally, the Underground Man "copes" with regret by indulging in romantic, regressive fantasies of rescue and sudden glory: "But I had a way out, which reconciled everything: escape into the 'lofty and the beautiful'—in my dreams, of course. I was a terrible dreamer."[79]

Dostoevsky's protagonist goes so far in his intellectualization that he claims to find pleasure in regret and in the idea that it "cannot be otherwise." If we take his words at face value, we might describe the protagonist as having attained resolution of regret through acceptance. The Underground Man's sense that it "cannot be otherwise" bears some resemblance to Erikson's view of integrity as entailing a sense that one's life course had a certain inevitability. But it doesn't take intensive psychoanalytic training to perceive this particular state as a false resolution. Tragically, the Underground Man convinces himself that it is impossible to change, too late to change. Thereafter, he need only lie back and fatalistically "accept" his "fate" rather than sustain the difficult struggle for genuine dignity in a world that devalues him—and whose devaluation he has too uncritically internalized.

From a purely psychological point of view then, the Underground Man exemplifies what Freud might call neurotic regret. Indeed, the Underground Man calls himself "sick." Along with the usual characteristics of "abrogation of interest in the outside world, loss of the capacity to love, and inhibition of all activity," his regret reeks with pathological self-reproach. With respect to "working-through" regret, he has taken the first step, in that he does acknowledge the fact that he is regretful. But the obsessive rethinking of his regrets serves only the regressive function of allowing him simultaneously to mourn and deny his loss. It may also serve as an attempt to bypass the mourning process and simply to club regret into submission with the brute force of intellect.

The Underground Man has taken even the second step toward resolution, acknowledging his own contribution to his rueful state. But he has not taken the next step of the "working-through" process: he has not acknowledged his ambivalence concerning the possibility of being a party to satisfying social and personal relationships. He does allow himself to experience the anger with himself and others over his mistakes and losses; but he militantly wards off the desire and sadness that must also be fully experienced. Rather than recognizing and resolving the ambivalence of his feelings for Liza, he swings wildly between extremes of idealization of her and contempt for her. He fails as well to resolve the element of self-hatred poisoning his regret. Instead, he swings wildly between self-denigration and self-apotheosis, never fusing these into a redeeming, complex view.

Because he bypasses essential aspects of the working-through process, he is left with a sterile personal ideology and endless, morbid regret. Given his proclivity for thought over either action or emotion, the protagonist is someone who has "become so immersed in a private, eternal life of the mind that potentially enriching interpersonal experiences [notably with Liza] pass by."[80] In brief, in terms of the stress-and-coping literature, the Underground Man has overused appraisal-focused modes of coping, and underused problem-focused and affiliative modes. In psychodynamic terms, this protagonist exemplifies a failure of working-through: his "insight" consists mostly of intellectualization; his emotion work is halfhearted and half-done; and he translates none of it into conduct.

But all these analyses one-sidedly center on the individual. In each of them the plight of the Underground Man is viewed as a personal failure to resolve his regret and change his life. A more comprehensive psychological analysis, however, would locate part of the responsibility for this tragic failure in society.[81] His problem is to some extent societal repression—that is, the power of society to seriously stunt individual development through the social devaluation of individuals because of their social class.

The lowly social position of this protagonist and his shame over his status contribute significantly to his inability to envision or to effect a meaningful future for himself. Shame concerning his station in life moves him to behave in an overly sensitive and overly guarded manner to try to protect the tattered remnants of his injured dignity. This shame eventually leads him to withdraw to his underground mouse hole, where tragically regret "ramifies like a fungus . . . in the dark." Social repression leads in his case to an intellectualized refusal of resignation, along with an unfortunate social withdrawal that precludes the successful transformation of regret. The protagonist of *Notes from Underground* shows a corrosively tragic variety of regret stemming from the perception of an intransigent discrepancy between personal dreams and social reality.

Partial Resolutions of Regret: Mrs. Dalloway

Unlike the tragic devolution portrayed in *Notes from Underground, Mrs. Dalloway* charts the progress of romantic and ironic struggles with regret. This novel also presents an extravagantly comprehensive catalog of transactions that human beings can and do carry on with regret. Woolf portrays through the characters of Clarissa Dalloway and Peter Walsh these methods of dealing with regret: undoing, denying, suppressing, and experiencing the regret; justifying the chosen alternative and denigrating the rejected alternative; and attempting to take full pleasure in the actual choice. This novel thus contributes a great deal to understanding the potential for carrying the transformation of regret beyond those self-protective postures just examined. Yet ultimately even here the transformation of regret remains incomplete.

Experiencing Regret. Unlike the Underground Man, Peter Walsh permits himself to fully experience the emotion of regret, not merely the intellectual judgments that only partially define regret. In fact, Peter is something of a virtuoso at experiencing the emotion of regret. There are scenes; there are tears. After Peter tells Clarissa that he is in love with Daisy, "to his utter surprise, suddenly thrown by those uncontrollable forces through the air, he burst into tears; wept; wept without the least shame, sitting on the sofa, the tears running down his cheeks."[82]

This is when Clarissa takes his hand and kisses him; Elizabeth comes in and Clarissa introduces her daughter to Peter with a flourish of false cheer. Afterward, Peter leaves, annoyed by her superficiality and yet utterly devastated by his loss:

> and then it's all up, it's all up, he thought, looking rather drearily into the glassy depths, and wondering whether by calling at that hour he had annoyed her; overcome with shame suddenly at having been a fool; wept; been emotional; told her everything, as usual, as usual. . . .
>
> As a cloud crosses the sun, silence falls on London; and falls on the mind. Effort ceases. Time flaps on the mast. There we stop; there we stand. Rigid, the skeleton of habit alone upholds the human frame. Where there is nothing, Peter Walsh said to himself; feeling hollowed out, utterly empty within. *Clarissa refused me, he thought. He stood there thinking, Clarissa refused me.*[83]

Once again, after a brief, embarrassed wish to undo his outburst, Peter allows himself to suffer the full brunt of the pain of his regret. Thus he positions himself at the starting point for a genuine struggle with regret.

Denying Regret. Yet at other times Peter Walsh regresses to more primitive reactions to regret. He shows several varieties of denial when at her party he watches Clarissa enter the room and thinks:

> *No, no, no! He was not in love with her any more!* He only felt, after seeing her that morning, among her scissors and silks, making ready for the party, unable to get away from the thought of her; she kept coming back and back like a sleeper jolting against him in a railway carriage; *which was not being in love, of course;* it was thinking of her, criticising her, starting again, after thirty years, trying to explain her.[84]

The vehemence of Peter's "No, no, no!" is telling. He is self-protectively attempting to deny the reality of his regret by emphatically saying it isn't so; it "was not being in love, of course." Furthermore, he is attempting to deny the urgency and emotionality of his reaction: "He only felt . . . unable to get away from the thought of her . . . which was not being in love, of course; it was thinking of her, criticizing her . . . trying to explain her."

Suppression. Rather than experiencing her regret painfully and immediately, or alternately attempting to deny it, as Peter does, Clarissa more often tries to bypass regret. Her favored way of doing this is by avoiding the reminders. Thus, even though Bourton, the summer house where her romance with Peter took place, is still in her family, Clarissa Dalloway has rigorously avoided ever returning.

Rationalization: Justifying the Alternative Chosen. An earlier chapter showed Clarissa attempting to justify, rationalize, even idealize her marriage with Dalloway, by reminding herself of its positive aspects of tranquility and "space":

> *So she would still find herself arguing in St. James's Park, still making out that she had been right—and she had too— not to marry him. For in marriage a little licence, a little independence there must be between people living together day in day out in the same house; which Richard gave her, and she him.* (Where was he this morning for instance? Some committee, she never asked what.) *But with Peter*

everything had to be shared; everything gone into. And it was intolerable.[85]

In the language of cognitive dissonance theory, this is called "bolstering," or emphasizing the desirable aspects of one's choices.[86] This is often what we are up to when cognitive dissonance impels us to transmute an original attitude into a different one congruent with our conduct.

Rationalization: Denigrating the Lost Opportunity. The last passage also reveals the other prong of the pitchfork of rationalization, minimizing the attractiveness of the unrealized alternative. Clarissa Dalloway repudiates the thought of life with Peter Walsh, focusing particularly on his alleged emotional intrusiveness: "But with Peter everything had to be shared; everything gone into. And it was intolerable."[87]

The results of an experimental study of rationalization as a reaction to regret receive literary corroboration here. Like the experimental subjects,[88] Clarissa Dalloway proves more convincing, and thus more self-convincing, in repudiating the unchosen alternative (Peter Walsh) than in bolstering the chosen alternative (Richard Dalloway). Moreover, one senses that the particular dimension on which Clarissa Dalloway chooses to focus her rationalizing efforts—emotional autonomy versus emotional engagement with another—is a critically *important* dimension for her, another resemblance to the empirical results. But this dimension is at the same time a locus of extreme ambivalence: she desperately wants emotional engagement at the same time that she fears it. Her actual marital choice better reflects her conscious fear of emotional engagement than her less conscious yearning for it. Therefore, she puts more effort into repudiating what she unconsciously wants than into celebrating the second-best that she chose.

Peter, too, engages in repeated efforts to justify, and explain away, his regretted fate. A few hours after he has left her in the morning, Peter receives Clarissa's "Heavenly-to-see-you!" note, and he understands that she too is beset with might-have-beens about their possible life together:

> She had felt a great deal; had for a moment, when she kissed his hand, regretted, envied him even, remembered possibly (for he saw her look it) something he had said—how they would change the world if she married him perhaps; whereas, it was this; it was middle age; it was mediocrity; then forced herself with her indomitable vitality to put all

that aside, there being in her a thread of life which for toughness, endurance, power to overcome obstacles, and carry her triumphantly through he had never known the like of. Yes; but there would come a reaction directly he left the room. She would be frightfully sorry for him; she would think what in the world she could do to give him pleasure (short always of the one thing) and he could see her with the tears running down her cheeks going to her writing-table and dashing off that one line which he was to find greeting him . . . "heavenly to see you!" And she meant it.

Peter Walsh had now unlaced his boots.

But it would not have been a success, their marriage (emphasis added).

Part of his reaction to comprehending that both he and Clarissa are suffering regret is to admire her ability to "put all that aside." Likewise, he attempts to bully his own feelings into submission by brute "rationality," concluding that, despite their mutual attraction, their marriage would have been a mistake. This process is advanced by belittling Clarissa: her life without him is a "mediocrity," he thinks; and "she had the makings of the perfect hostess," he tells her scornfully. He further censures her as worldly and frivolous, and as having taken on the "public-spirited, British Empire, tariff-reform, governing-class spirit" of her husband.

In addition, both Clarissa and Peter react to regret with *second-order* sour grapes—by denigrating the other's choice. When Peter confronts Clarissa with the fact that he is in love with Daisy (a married woman with two children), she responds at first with jealousy and then by deprecating this woman she has never met, prejudging her as a person who had undoubtedly fooled and flattered Peter. This process helps her to justify her own rejection of Peter: "Thank Heaven she [Clarissa] had refused to marry him!" she thinks.[89]

Similarly, Peter belittles Dalloway (through Hugh Whitbread), as well as Dalloway's marriage. First, he deprecates Clarissa's old friend Hugh, whom Clarissa admires for his unselfish devotion to his mother and ailing wife. Peter describes Hugh this way: "he had no heart, no brain, nothing but the manners and breeding of an English gentleman"[90] —an indictment that sounds suspiciously like displaced criticism of Richard Dalloway, the more immediate cause of Peter's pain.

Peter also casts aspersions directly on Clarissa and Richard's marriage:

> With twice his wits, she had to see things through his eyes—one of the tragedies of married life. With a mind of her own, she must always be quoting Richard—as if one couldn't know to a tittle what Richard thought by reading the *Morning Post* of a morning! These parties for example were all for him, or for her idea of him.[91]

All these first- and second-order criticisms nicely illustrate sour grapes, a time-honored mode of alleviating regret for things one does not have.

Amor Fati: Attempting to Fully Appreciate One's Reality. Edith Wharton once wrote:

> In spite of illness, in spite even of the archenemy sorrow, one can remain alive long past the usual date of disintegration if one is un-afraid of change, insatiable in intellectual curiosity, interested in big things, and happy in small ways.

Wharton's list comprises a recipe for *amor fati,* loving one's fate without resignation. In *Mrs. Dalloway* Woolf has Peter Walsh at-tempt to console himself for the loss of Clarissa through a con-scious effort to be "happy in small ways," or to experience as fully as possible the small joys, particularly the impersonal joys, still available to him:

> The compensation of growing old, Peter Walsh thought, coming out of Regent's Park, and holding his hat in hand, was simply this; that the passions remain as strong as ever, but one has gained—at last!—the power which adds the supreme flavour to existence,—the power of taking hold of experience, of turning it round, slowly, in the light.
>
> A terrible confession it was (he put his hat on again), but now, at the age of fifty-three one scarcely needed people any more. *Life itself, every moment of it, every drop of it, here, this instant, now, in the sun, in Regent's Park, was enough. Too much indeed. A whole life-time was too short to bring out, now that one had acquired the power, the full flavour; to extract every ounce of pleasure, every shade of meaning; which both were so much more solid than they used to be, so much less personal.* It was impossible that he should ever suffer again as Clarissa had made him suffer.[92]

This passage echoes Henry James's Strether and Ishiguro's Stevens, whose responses to regret center on striving to expand the capacity for sensory and social apprehension, to live the rest of life as fully and as humanly as possible. However, the concluding reference here—to a flight from people and from the lacerating suffering oc-casioned by people—gives the reader pause.

Walking in the very same park, Clarissa too cultivates the capacity to take pleasure in every detail of life in the present, at the same time suppressing thoughts of the past:

> But every one remembered; what she loved was this, here, now, in front of her; the fat lady in the cab. Did it matter then, she asked herself, walking towards Bond Street, did it matter that she must inevitably cease completely; all this must go on without her; did she resent it; or did it not become consoling to believe that death ended absolutely?[93]

Clarissa's effort to transcend regret proves at least as unpersuasive as Peter's. She ends by reflecting on death and whether it is rational to regret the loss of one's life, or whether it is not more rational to welcome death as the ultimate consolation.

Viewed from the object-relations perspectives of Klein and Segal, Clarissa Dalloway and Peter Walsh appear not to have discovered significant ways to resolve regret by repairing their losses. The closest they come to reparation is through cultivating an appreciation for the small pleasures open to them.

From an Eriksonian framework, neither protagonist has successfully resolved the crisis of middle age. Peter Walsh seems to have largely failed to develop a capacity for generatively nurturing others. This is all the sadder because he seems to have had the potential for generativity: he is often described as "kind"; he is seen comforting a crying child in Regent's Park; and he thinks to himself that he understands and likes young people. Even less generativity is displayed by Clarissa. Even though she prides herself on having helped young people "who were grateful to her,"[94] we are often told she is cold and we see her avoid real human warmth at almost every opportunity.

The research on coping would reveal Clarissa Dalloway and Peter Walsh as limited in their ability to cope, in that they rigidly fall back on appraisal-focused and emotion-focused modes for managing regret. In addition, Clarissa Dalloway makes use of affiliation, but a distinctly shallow form of it. She throws all those parties mostly for the purposes of distraction and (if we are to believe Peter) of pleasing her husband, rather than for the purpose of gaining insight into her predicament by communing with friends. In part the failure of these characters to resolve their regret may be due to their rather rigid reliance on a favored coping strategy (or two) rather than on a judicious blending of several. Clarissa Dalloway works very hard at suppressing feelings of all kinds, especially love[95] and hatred.[96] The coping research might recommend that she try as a first step to experience her *emotion* fully; as a condition for resolution, she may need to hit rock bottom emotionally. In contrast, coping research might recommend to Peter Walsh that he try as a first step to *think* a bit more. For both, the task is ultimately to bring the two—thought and feeling—together in their experience.

From the perspective of the Freudian concept of working-through, Clarissa Dalloway represents in one sense an upscale, highly socialized counterpart and in another sense a reverse image of the Underground Man. First the similarities. She, too, acknowledges regret—although as infrequently and as superficially as possible. And like the Underground Man, she fails to face the ambivalence complicating her regret, especially her ambivalence about the road she did take—her marriage to Richard Dalloway. Because she wards off the pain of fully experiencing either her sorrow at the loss of Peter or her desolation and anger at Richard's inability to "touch" her, she never completely works through these feelings.

The earlier analysis of ambivalence also suggests that "resolving" her ambivalence is not necessarily the best thing to do.[97] It clearly is not desirable to strive for a desire-less state of complete detachment—not to care. That is no route to becoming a fully developed human being. Neither is it necessarily a good thing to strive to reconcile her contrary feelings. To curb her genuine desire for emotional engagement with her partner would be to deny something good in herself; to curb her genuine desire for a measure of emotional distance from her partner would also be to deny something good in herself. Rather than "resolve" the ambivalence through favoring one over the other, it might be a better thing to learn to sustain both desires.

But in several ways her experience of regret is the reverse image of that of the protagonist of *Notes from Underground*. First, in contrast to the straightforwardness of the Underground Man's regret, hers manifests itself in conscious satisfaction that combines with vague dissatisfactions and longings for death. Second, whereas the Underground Man allows himself fewer sad feelings than angry ones, she allows herself no angry feelings, only vaguely sad ones. Anger is clearly there, but she is always vigilant to suppress it: "never to be quite secure, for at any moment the brute would be stirring, this hatred . . . this hatred!"[98] Her ability to "put all that aside" may reflect her sociohistorical position as an upper-class Victorian British woman—just as the Underground Man's anger may reflect his sociohistorical position as a nineteenth-century, lower-class Russian man. Third, rather than choosing the Underground

Man's withdrawal from the external world, she attempts to console herself with a rather frenetically active (though hollow) social life—a "solution" more accessible to her because of her more privileged position in society. Nor does she engage in the self-recrimination characteristic of the Underground Man. This too may reflect her freedom from those "hidden injuries of class"[99]—such as internalization of societal denigration of the impoverished—suffered by the Underground Man.

To a greater extent than Clarissa Dalloway, Peter Walsh freely acknowledges regret over his loss, without obsessively ruminating over it, as does the Underground Man. Moreover, he lays himself open to feeling his loss; he freely weeps for it. Finally, he acknowledges his ambivalence—that on the one hand Clarissa has become something of a shallow socialite but on the other hand he still loves her. Nor does he show the constant self-reproach or wholesale withdrawal from personal relationships of the Underground Man. Still, he has to some extent withdrawn psychically from the peopled world, attempting to find consolation in safer, nonpersonal experience. Even his "intended" may or may not be accessible to him—at the moment she is married to someone else.

Mrs. Dalloway renders in lavish detail the efforts of two individuals of considerable psychological, social, and financial resources to resolve their regret. Both put up a struggle. But in the end both fail to transcend regret. Rather than genuine resolution we find at best lonely resignation. Thus, *Mrs. Dalloway* disturbs and destabilizes the reader, leading the reader in true ironic fashion to admire and to question the adequacy of *both* styles of regret portrayed, the romantic (Peter Walsh) and the ironic (Clarissa Dalloway).

Having examined a number of examples of regret unsatisfactorily resolved, I now discuss four literary examples of more compelling transformations of regret: *The Ambassadors, Great Expectations, Ikiru,* and *Breathing Lessons.* In these, we see a progressive movement toward a more and more exemplary transformation of regret.

Regret Re-done: The Ambassadors

According to James himself, the principal question of interest in *The Ambassadors* is what Strether does with his regret over not having fully "lived" his youth. In this literary portrait regrettable mistakes are perceived from a comic perspective as something largely

resolvable through action (as elaborated in Chapter 3). James identifies two related ways in which one might transcend regret—not
by undoing but by *redoing*—through both vicarious and direct
experience. In the following passage Strether expresses the first
idea:

> I began to be young, or at least to get the benefit of it, the moment I
> met you [Maria Gostrey] at Chester, and that's what has been taking
> place ever since. I never had the benefit at the proper time, which
> comes to saying that I never had the thing itself. I'm having the ben-
> efit at this moment; I had it the other day when I said to Chad "Wait"
> [i.e., don't return to Woollett, to your mother, just yet]; I shall have it
> still again when Sarah Pocock arrives. It's a benefit that would make
> a poor show for many people; and I don't know who else but you and
> I, frankly, could begin to see in it what I feel. I don't get drunk; I don't
> pursue the ladies; I don't spend money; I don't even write sonnets.
> But, nevertheless, I'm making up late for what I didn't have early. I
> cultivate my little benefit in my own little way. It amuses me more
> than anything that has happened to me in all my life. They may say
> what they like—*it's my surrender, it's my tribute, to youth. One puts
> that in where one can—it has to come in somewhere, if only out of
> the lives, the conditions, the feelings of other persons. Chad gives me
> the sense of it . . . and she [Madame de Vionnet] does the same. . . .
> The point is that they're mine. Yes, they're my youth, since somehow,
> at the right time, nothing else ever was.*[100]

In this passage Strether speaks about making up for lost time by
living vicariously, through the lives of Chad and Madame Marie de
Vionnet. Not only does Strether refuse his ambassadorial "duty" to
persuade Chad to leave Madame de Vionnet, Strether becomes their
champion. From an Eriksonian perspective,[101] Strether could be described as making up for his lost youth by living generatively, supporting the young.

James's second answer to the problem of regret is revealed
through his portrayal of a superficially quite trivial consumer regret—that for a painting of a scene in the French countryside,
a Lambinet. Strether had wished to purchase the Lambinet years
before in Boston, but had passed it up then, feeling he couldn't afford it:

> He *had* dreamed—had turned and twisted possibilities for an hour: it
> had been the only adventure of his life in connection with the pur-
> chase of a work of art. . . . The little Lambinet abode with him as
> the material acquisition that, in all his time, he had most sharply
> failed of.[102]

While in France, Strether effects a satisfying transformation of this regret. One day he takes a train and decides to ride and ride until he feels like getting out, which he does:

> It will be felt of him that he could amuse himself, at his age, with very small things if it be again noted that his appointment was only with a faded Boston enthusiasm. He had not gone far without the quick confidence that it would be quite sufficiently kept. The oblong gilt frame disposed its enclosing lines; the poplars and willows, the reeds and river—a river of which he didn't know, and didn't want to know, the name—fell into a composition, full of felicity, within them; the sky was silver and turquoise and varnish; the village on the left was white and the church on the right was gray; it was all there, in short— it was what he wanted: it was Tremont Street, it was France, it was Lambinet. Moreover he was freely walking about in it.[103]

One thinks here of George Herbert's "living well is the best revenge." Or, more gently, living well is the best remedy. Perhaps even better than possessing the forgone painting, Strether possesses the reality: "he was freely walking about in it"—that is, the lovely French countryside. Not only has he transcended his regret over his lost youth through taking vicarious pleasure in the lives of worthy others, but (like Peter Walsh and Clarissa Dalloway in *Mrs. Dalloway*) he has learned to take full pleasure in the present in the "very small things" in his own life, in the freedom open to him in his maturity.

In Paris, he develops his capacity to surrender to beauty and to unconventional decency, without ascribing base motives to himself or others. He finds that he has the capacity to enjoy the company of lovely, cultivated women, women he admires and adores, and who admire and adore him. Woollett (Massachusetts), on the other hand, in the person of Sarah and her mother, remains unable to, or willfully chooses not to, comprehend or appreciate the beauty and dignity of such relationships. The generic solution to the problem of Strether's regrets consists of re-doing his past life of constraint in the present—through an expansion of sensation, of experience, and of human sympathy. In France, Strether gets another chance to get it right.

Still, in the end there remain intimations of perhaps yet-incomplete resolution. First, his trip to the picturesque countryside is in the end marred when Strether accidentally encounters Chad and Madame de Vionnet together in the boat. At this point, Strether seems to bump up against certain limits of his human sympathies.

He is forced to an understanding that he had never really allowed himself before—namely, the exact nature of the relationship in question. Despite his newfound urbanity, Strether is shocked. Strether here shows himself still tied to the norms of Woollett, Massachusetts.[104]

Second, in the end, Strether abandons Maria Gostrey, who seems willing and able to accompany Strether on another step toward resolution—through a loving, intimate relationship.[105] Moreover, his stated reason for leaving her—"to be right," not to have gained anything for himself—seems to echo the sanctimonious censoriousness of Woollett, Massachusetts, rather than to sound a new, more expansive note.

Both reactions demonstrate a less-than-perfect state of transformation of Strether's regret for not having "lived." Although he acquits himself very well with respect to Mrs. Newsome's odious demands, the full fruition of personal transformation seems held back by his own character and perhaps by his parochial background.

Regret Repaired: Great Expectations

Great Expectations delineates a romantic mentality toward regret, viewing life as a quest in which mistakes are capable of being suddenly and decisively repaired, mostly through the application of heroic action. Midway through the novel Pip comes to regret his past neglect of Joe and Biddy. He considers undoing this neglect by returning to them. But he rejects this alternative partly because he prefers to stay in London where he can more easily maintain his new social pretenses, and partly because he knows that past behavior resists undoing:

> I would not have gone back to Joe now, I would not have gone back to Biddy now, for any consideration: simply, I suppose, because my sense of my own worthless conduct to them was greater than every consideration. No wisdom on earth could have given me the comfort that I should have derived from their simplicity and fidelity; but *I could never, never, never, undo what I had done.*[106]

As for Pip's initial dismay concerning the identity of his benefactor, the criminal Provis (alias Magwitch), he eventually rejects the premise on which it is based. In the end, despite the world's view of Provis's worth, Pip has developed genuine admiration for Provis:

For now my repugnance to him had all melted away, and in the hunted wounded shackled creature who held my hand in his, I only saw a man who had meant to be my benefactor, and who had felt affectionately, gratefully, and generously, towards me with great constancy through a series of years. I only saw in him a much better man than I had been to Joe.[107]

This change in his feelings for and relation to Provis represents the critical event in the redemption of Pip. In behaving in a filial manner to Provis, his second "father," Pip not only symbolically repairs the damage he has done in neglecting Joe, his first "father," he also actually repairs the damage to his own character. At the same time, he behaves in such a way as to bring a measure of human warmth into Provis's wretched life. These acts represent a significant improvement over the tortured retreat of the Underground Man and the lonely resignation found at the end of *Mrs. Dalloway*.

Pip's progress through regret and its vicissitudes in *Great Expectations* is better described by Klein's model than by the other three previously discussed. Although Pip apparently skips the first stage of resolution as described by Melanie Klein,[108] the anger stage, he does progress through the rest of the stages. He mourns the absence of wished-for goods—a loving and "good" (i.e., conventionally respectable) benefactor. And most important, he succeeds in *repairing* to some extent what had gone wrong in his life. Through his filial relationship with Provis, Pip repairs the damage previously done to Provis, to Joe and Biddy, and to his own character as well.

Regret Transcended: Ikiru *and* Breathing Lessons

In *Ikiru* ("To live"), a 1952 movie written and directed by Akira Kurosawa, the protagonist takes a somewhat different route from regret to transcendence—one through reparative social action. After the death of his wife thirty years earlier, Mr. Watanabe has been little more than a walking corpse. In fact, a co-worker has nicknamed him "The Mummy." When his wife died, he decided to forgo remarriage in order to devote his life to his motherless son. But as an adult, the son is devoid of gratitude or affection toward his father. Meanwhile, Mr. Watanabe has continued his lifelong job as Chief of the Citizens' Section of City Hall. There, along with all the other bureaucratic time-servers, he assiduously avoids any real work on behalf of the public he by rights serves.

When he learns that he has stomach cancer and less than a year to live, Mr. Watanabe determines to learn to live. He tries dissipation, but finds it ultimately unsatisfying. Then he pursues a lively, kind young woman from work, whose companionship makes him feel alive; but she eventually rejects his overtures. Finally, after some uncharacteristic time AWOL, he returns to work and devotes himself singlemindedly to the task of fulfilling the request of a group of citizens to turn a mudhole of a city corner into a children's playground. With new assertiveness, Mr. Watanabe overturns every bureaucratic obstacle and succeeds in having the playground built. He dies, following a scene in which we see him contentedly swinging in the newly built park, singing the following plaintively tragic song in the snow:

> Life is so short.
> Fall in love, dear maiden.
> While your lips are still red;
> Before you can no longer love—
> For there will be no tomorrow.
>
> Life is so short.
> Fall in love, dear maiden,
> While your hair is still black.
> Before your heart stops,
> For there will be no more tomorrow.[109]

The coping strategy of cognitive reappraisal makes no appearance in *Ikiru*; even at the end Watanabe appraises his earlier regrets as regrets. *Ikiru* clearly shows the ineffectiveness of attempting to cope with regret through distraction, self-reward, and escape through alcohol. It also shows the limits of private human relationships in resolving regret. This protagonist chooses problem-directed action to begin to transform his regret for an empty life. He finally realizes that there is something he can still change about his regrettable life—the degree of devotion with which he attends to the needs of others as part of his job. As a consequence, he takes direct action to solve this part of his existential problem.

In Erikson's terms, Mr. Watanabe succeeds in overcoming the midlife struggle against stagnation through redirecting onto his larger social milieu the caring that had fallen on fallow soil with respect to his own son. The neighborhood children become the recipients of his newfound efforts to carry out his job with devotion to others' needs.

At the same time that he transcends through generativity his twofold regret (over his son's ingratitude and his own wasted work life), he also transcends regret through Kleinian reparation. He earns the respect of the neighborhood and even of his lazy co-workers, as well as new self-respect, by succeeding in having the park built— thereby repairing what had gone wrong in his life. One can almost imagine hearing him whisper in the park—his gift to the world— the words of Jane Hirshfield's poem about reparation:

> Ah love, o history, forgive
> the squandered light and flung-down rags of chances,
> old choices drifted terribly awry.
> And world, self-portrait never right, receive this gift . . .

Recall that in *Breathing Lessons* the protagonists, Ira and Maggie Moran, are besieged with regret—Ira for the forgone opportunity to become a physician, and both Maggie and Ira for the disharmonies in the lives of their children and in their own married life. Ira plays out an ironic frame of mind toward regret, determined to view mistakes and losses with detached acceptance, as inevitable in an imperfect world. Maggie, in turn, manifests the romantic outlook, viewing mistakes and losses emotionally as obstacles that must be overcome through an exuberant fantasy life and heroic action.

In Ira's response to his regret for having given up his chance to be a physician in favor of caring for his needy family, there is a progression from less resolution to more resolution over the course of his fictional life. Immediately after the fiasco at Harborplace, for which he was partially responsible, having refused to humor his sister Dorrie's fantasy that Elvis lives, he puts an arm around both sisters (Dorrie and Junie), hugs them, and is filled with love for them all:

> He had known then what the true waste was; Lord yes. It was not his having to support these people but his failure to notice how he loved them. . . .
>
> *But then the feeling had faded (probably the very next instant, when Junie started begging to leave) and he forgot what he had learned.*[110]

I suspect that Ira so easily "forgot what he had learned" because the resolution was premature and therefore vulnerable. In response to his flash of regret and resentment, a more "moral" side of Ira's psyche makes its protest heard. It is hard to say to what extent the feeling of love described here is the real thing versus the result of the defense mechanism of reaction formation, whereby one produces the conscious experience of an emotion (in this case, love) that is the opposite of a disavowed one (in this case, resentment).

The flimsiness of Ira's early attempt to resolve this particular regret may also account for the continuity of familial regret in his life. At the moment his son is a failed rock star, his daughter something of a rejecting prig, and his wife an impetuous busybody. No wonder he has his regrets. Counterfactual thoughts and justifications tumble one on top of another in his mind:

> Maybe if he hadn't gotten married. Or at least not had children. But that was too great a price to pay. . . . Well, if he had put his sister Dorrie in an institution . . . and told his father, "I will no longer provide your support." . . . And made his other sister venture into the world to find employment.[111]

Later still, Maggie bursts into tears over the emptiness of her home, and Ira startles her by putting his "elbows on the table and lower[ing] his head into his hands."[112] At first, she doesn't understand Ira's gesture of despair. Then it strikes her:

> He was just as sad as Maggie was, and for just the same reasons. He was lonely and tired and lacking in hope and his son had not turned out well and his daughter didn't think much of him, and he still couldn't figure where he had gone wrong.
>
> He let his head fall against her shoulder. His hair was thick and rough, strung through with threads of gray that she had never noticed before, that pierced her heart in a way that her own few gray hairs never had. She hugged him tightly and nuzzled her face against his cheekbone. She said, "It will be all right. It will be all right."[113]

At this point Ira achieves possibly all the resolution to be hoped for in his life—he feels his sorrow, his wife shares it with him, and he is loved, regrets and all.

Despite the deep significance of this moment for both of them, neither has turned over a new leaf. Still Ira's and Maggie's characteristic strategies for managing distressing emotion work at cross purposes. He remains the voice of the reality principle, bursting the bubbles of her fantasies, forcing unwanted truths upon her. When, at the end, Maggie is still clinging to the unrealistic wish to bring her granddaughter to live with them for the "better schools," Ira firmly vetoes the idea. Finally, she stops arguing. In the last paragraph of the book, Ira holds Maggie (even as he continues his game of solitaire), and she thinks:

He had passed that early, superficial stage when any number of moves seemed possible, and now his choices were narrower and he had to show real skill and judgment. She felt a little stir of something that came over her like a flush, a sort of inner buoyancy, and she lifted her face to kiss the warm blade of his cheekbone.[114]

One senses that perhaps at last Maggie has joined Ira in accepting life's limits and losses—without surrendering either to resignation or despair. I imagine her giving up her frenetic drive to change what she does not like about her life and coming to relish the consolations life has offered her, especially the tremendous comfort of loving and being loved. Unlike the Underground Man, who keeps himself entirely and defiantly alone with his regrets, and unlike Clarissa Dalloway and Peter Walsh, with their unwilling and lonely resignation, Maggie and Ira are alone *together.* Unlike Maggie's just-widowed best friend, Maggie and Ira are "in this together."[115] Unlike the Underground Man, Peter Walsh, Clarissa Dalloway, and Lambert Strether, these protagonists have not forsworn others as sources of genuine intimate joy. Nor, unlike Clarissa Dalloway, have they taken refuge in wishes for death as the ultimate silencer of clamorous regret. Ira and Maggie Moran have taken the transformation of regret nearly to its human limits.

These last two literary examples show their protagonists moving away from an experience of regret in which thought and feeling were dissociated toward an experience in which they are united. T. S. Eliot proposed that this process of uniting thought and feeling had the potential of producing superior poetry.[116] To unite the thought and feeling of regret is, in my view, to make a kind of living poetry of the raw material of one's life. These stories also have in common the golden thread of reciprocal relationships with others. The resolution of regret in each case is not a purely private matter but something that takes the individual outside him- or herself—back to the world of others. For the stoic Ira Moran, the path to transcending regret entailed breaking down and weeping in the presence of his wife. For the overly in-charge Maggie Moran, it meant giving up and giving in to quiet acceptance. And it meant paying heed to her husband's emotional needs rather than only her own. For Watanabe, transcending regret entailed going against the stream of his quiet sadness to become active and engaged in the world. "It is this backward motion . . . /Against the stream, that most we see ourselves in. /It is most us," Frost wrote.

9

The Contrary Wisdom of Regret

Dreams go by contraries.
—JAMES JOYCE, *Ulysses*

It must be the brook
Can trust itself to go by
contraries . . .
—ROBERT FROST, "West-Running Brook"

To say more than human things
   with human voice,
That cannot be; to say human
   things with more
Than human voice, that, also
   cannot be;
To speak humanly from the
   height or from the depth
Of human things, that is
   acutest speech.
—WALLACE STEVENS, "Chocorua to Its Neighbor"

These pages have told many different stories about regret. The stories have come from widely varied places on either side of the abyss separating science and the humanities, from mathematical models of economic and psychological decision theory to novels and poems.

The stories have been told from the comic, romantic, tragic, and ironic perspectives. They have addressed the wistful question of the simply curious: "What sorts of things do most people regret?" And the urgent question of the tormented: "What can be done about this regret of mine?" Now it is time to ask whether there is coherence in this Rashomon-like array of stories about regret. A look backward through this book could yield, I suppose, something like deconstruction's critical nihilism. It could support a conclusion that the text of regret, like literary texts, offers no single, fixed meaning but multiple and conflicting meanings—and therefore, that the text of regret is inherently indeterminate and meaningless. This is not the conclusion I draw from my look back.

True, regret can lay claim to no single, fixed set of laws that universally describes its nature or its natural history. But it is not the case that one perspective is just as good (or as bad) as another. It is not the case that regret remains indeterminate. Or meaningless. There *is* a coherent, though not a simple, linear story to be told about regret. The analogy of the Rashomon-like story captures the elements of the subjectivity, variegatedness, and ongoingness of regret. Yet the analogy fails to reveal another deeply true characteristic of regret—how it can both preserve and transcend the past. The analogy of a multilayered oil painting better captures this feature (while concealing the temporal dynamics). Like the sixty-plus-layered portrait hanging on my wall, regret is composed of multiple and diverse layers that together add up to a complexly structured whole.

Even better than the analogies of Rashomon or a many-layered oil painting is that of the dialectic. In this chapter I explore a dialectical perspective on what I consider one of the single most important questions about regret—namely, how it, and thereby, the self, might best be transformed. I shall then apply the dialectical method to the task of advancing an enlarged, integrative understanding of regret as concept and experience.

Dialectical Transformations of Regret

In the last chapter, I invoked models of development, coping, and psychotherapy in an effort to understand the varieties of transformation of regret. Dialectical models offer another[1] description of the process of resolution and transformation. Each of the following genres of the dialectic—the Socratic dialectical method, Hegel's dialectical theory, and Stanley Fish's principle of literary reading as a dialectical process—contributes something important and unique to the goal of understanding the process of transforming regret, and thereby oneself.

In the *Republic*, Plato draws a portrait of the dialectic as a method of inquiry. The Socratic dialectical method is defined as a:

> method of question and answer which Plato inherited from Socrates, the respondent putting forward his "hypothetical" attempts at definition, the questioner demanding an "account" of his meaning and subjecting his suggestions to examination and refutation (elenchus) and so leading him on to amend them.[2]

The goal of the dialectic is thus to approach truth through discussion and debate of various views, each of which contributes to, yet is eventually abandoned for, a better view. In the Allegory of the Cave, the method is presented as analogous to the gradual enlightenment of a prisoner who has been held captive in a dark cave all his life and who therefore mistakes shadows for reality. Upon release from the cave, the former cave-prisoner is able at first only to gaze upon the muted light reflected in water from living creatures, then at the light of the moon and the stars, and eventually at the world as bathed in the dazzling light of the Sun.

The *Phaedrus* has been called the "supreme example of the dialectical mode in operation."[3] It proceeds through a series of hypotheses or propositions about, among other things, the nature of speech and writing. It addresses in turn specific questions about what distinguishes good from bad rhetoric and writing. For example, truthful but plain or badly formed speech is bad, because it is not persuasive; but then again, vivid, persuasive speech can be bad, because it is not entirely truthful. The dialogue ends with Socrates appearing to denounce all speech and all writing. But then again, since the denouncement itself takes a linguistic form, perhaps it too needs to be questioned . . . .

As analyzed by literary critic Stanley Fish,[4] the *Phaedrus* proceeds by presenting a series of ostensibly true propositions, each of which is then challenged, so that at the end the reader has been brought to a position that is different from and better than any explicitly presented in the text. The *Phaedrus* presents not a linear argument but a back-and-forth process eventuating in a self-generating change of vision; in Fish's words, a dialectical presentation "is the vehicle of its own abandonment." Fish sees this process as resembling that described by Wittgenstein in the *Tractatus*, where each reader is urged to "throw away the ladder after he has climbed up it"[5]; with this trope Wittgenstein makes the dialectical claim that once readers understand his propositions, they will have transcended them.

The gradational nature of the dialectical method relies critically on the process of constantly questioning assumptions:

> it treats its assumptions not as first principles, but as *hypotheses* in the literal sense, things "laid down" like a flight of steps up which it may mount all the way to something that is not hypothetical, the first principle of all.[6]

Surprisingly, though, the intellective climb of the dialectic ends not at the top step, but with a descent. The individual, after "having grasped this [the first principle], may turn back and, holding on to the consequences which depend upon it, *descend* at last to a conclusion."[7] So Wittgenstein's analogy fails, after all; the thing to do is not to kick the ladder away after using it to climb to the top, but to keep the ladder for climbing down again. According to the original formulation of the dialectic, after apprehending the first principle, the enlightened individual is to return to the world of decision and action—back to the world of others—except that the one who returns is a changed person.

Not only thought in general but also literary experience in particular can be viewed as a potentially dialectical process. Literary texts (analogous to the Socratic staircase and Wittgenstein's ladder) have the potential to operate, according to Stanley Fish, as "self-consuming artifacts," which upon being read dialectically "use [themselves] up."[8] Dialectically read texts consume themselves in the sense that the process of reading dialectically has so altered the reader that a later reading of the same text means something different from the earlier reading.

Fish analyzes the *Phaedrus* then as a dialectical text that succeeds insofar as it destroys itself. More generally, all dialectical texts function as self-consuming artifacts by bringing the reader to a new place grounded on the reader's both incorporating and going beyond the arguments presented in the text. Fish identifies "contradictions [and] moments of blurring" as particular features of a text that make it dialectical, in that contradictions and moments of blurring "become invitations to examine closely premises too easily acquiesced in."[9] The process of reading dialectically—whether it is *Notes from Underground* or our own life—is also described by

Fish as frequently a salutary though emotionally shattering experience. Here again, the unification of thought and emotion is a transformative experience.

In *Phenomenology of Spirit* Hegel[10] applies the dialectic to the formulation of a model of, among other things, human development and, more generally, historical development. Webster's *Third New International Unabridged Dictionary* defines the Hegelian dialectic as a:

> logical development progressing from less to more comprehensive levels that on its subjective side is the passage of thought from a thesis through an antithesis to a synthesis that in turn becomes a thesis for further progressions ultimately culminating in the absolute idea and on its objective side is an analogous development in the process of history and the cosmos.

For Hegel the process of becoming a full human being (the "subjective side" of the dialectic) consists of a process of canceling, yet preserving, previous stages.

How one knows reality, for instance, develops in a dialectical fashion, according to Hegel. The individual begins at the position Hegel calls "sense-certainty"—that is, the epistemologically naive conviction that knowledge of the sense world is immediately given, much as a photograph seems to provide an immediate, faithful copy of a portion of the world. But this original conviction of unproblematic knowledge through sensation is eventually superseded by the recognition that knowledge of the world is in fact less passive and "less purely immediate than it at first seemed."[11] This realization leads to the moment Hegel calls "perception," in which the individual recognizes that while it is true that perception is based on an "assemblage of [sensory] properties" of the object, it is also true that the individual actively *constructs* a meaningful synthesis out of these separate sensory properties.[12] Not that something is constructed out of whole cloth; the perceptions of "normal" (say, nonpsychotic) people are constructed within the constraints of reality. But what is perceived is constructed by us based in part on our particular interests, expectations, wishes, needs, social norms, and prior knowledge of the world. We use the evidence of the senses to *make* sense of the world. Developmentally, therefore, the sensation/perception distinction is first accepted, only to be understood as a necessary but false distinction.[13]

Similarly, other dualities—subject versus object, essence versus appearance, the unchangeable versus the variable in human personality, self versus other—are first distinguished, and then recognized as false. In the Hegelian system, the summit of human development—which he calls "Spirit"—is approached through a series of such alienations and negations, with each successive position superseding yet preserving previous positions. Hegel explains:

> By this alienation it creates for itself the possibility of a higher existence, if only it could take back again into itself its alienated object, than if it had remained undisturbed within the immediacy of being—because Spirit is all the greater, the greater the opposition from which it has returned into itself; but it creates this opposition for itself by setting aside its immediate unity, and by alienating its being-for-self. However, if such a consciousness does not reflect on itself, the intermediate position, or middle term, which it occupies is an unhappy void, since what should fill and fulfill it has been turned into a fixed extreme.[14]

The dialectical process applies also to the practical world of everyday affairs. This is depicted both in Hegel and at the end of Plato's Allegory of the Cave. For Plato the ideal commonwealth is one governed by philosopher-kings. The philosopher, lover of wisdom, is one who has first been released from the darkness of the cave and has finally beheld the world in the full radiance of sunlight. Such a fortunate individual understandably prefers to linger in the higher realm of the light and resists the thought of returning to the darkness of the cave. Nevertheless, Plato insists, this individual must be prevailed upon to "come down again to the prisoners"[15]—for the "acutest speech," says Wallace Stevens, is "to speak humanly from the/ height or from the depth / Of human things."

All this is by way of introducing an argument for a dialectical view of the problem of how to transform regret. I am using the term *dialectic* in the sense of a process of development that proceeds by weighing and bringing together contradictory elements; in the sense that Fish envisioned of a dynamic, self-destroying, yet self-creating process; and in Joyce's and Frost's sense of going forward by going backward, "going by contraries." Unlike the formal dialectics, my sense of the dialectic excludes (provisionally, of course!) the possibility of ever achieving an *absolute*. On this account, the transformation of regret depends on an ongoing process of dialectically reading the text of one's life, especially its sad parts. A cornerstone of a dialectical understanding of regret is the idea that before one can possibly cope with, work through, resolve, or transcend regret, one must first experience fully the painful fact of regret itself. It will not do in the long run to deny regret, or to hold it at arm's length with face averted. Only by first "setting aside [one's] immediate unity" (Hegel), and then by reflecting on the dissociated fragments of one's self, is eventual resolution possible. Deliberate, reflective destabilization precedes and generates later resolution. In this manner regret is potentially a "self-consuming artifact," a human experience that succeeds insofar as it uses itself up.

To show how the dialectic can offer solutions to the problem of regret, I shall now apply it to two of the literary illustrations of the transformation of regret presented in the preceding chapter. Although it could be applied to any and all of the literary examples I have discussed, I shall here focus on *Ikiru* and *Breathing Lessons* because I believe they afford a particularly clear view of the transcendent features of the transformation of regret.

In his belated search for how to live, the first thing the protagonist of *Ikiru* has to do is set aside his "immediate unity" (Hegel)— what a pallid phrase for Watanabe's experience. When he really sees his sad life for what it is and learns that he is about to die, he hits bottom. He stops going to work. He tries one blind alley after another to distract himself from his pain and to try to find his way again. Eventually he works out a way to transform his regret. Here is a dialectical and many-layered retelling of Watanabe's story.

In Baldwin's terms, first Watanabe stands at the jaws of the "momentous gap" between what he wishes to have become and what he has actually become. Then he uses this grim recognition as a last opportunity to "create" something of value. In Hegelian language, Watanabe successively disturbs and "alienates his being-for-self," looks upon the wretched pieces of his life and self, and embarks on successive attempts to put himself back together. In Rosenwald and Wiersma's formulation,[16] to transform his regret Watanabe converts a perplexity into a problem. That is, he converts his psychological state of confused, resigned suffering into the recognition that he has a choice among alternatives. He briefly tries the usual distractions—wine, women, and song—eventually bumping up against the limitations of each of these as solutions to the problem of regret. Ultimately he finds a solution surprisingly near at hand—in his work. In Platonic language, Watanabe mounts the flight of steps toward a first principle; then "having grasped [it he] turn[s] back, and holding on to the consequences which depend on it, descend[s] at last to a conclusion." The principle that Watanabe finally grasps is that meaning can be found in work, and that it is not too late for him. With his new insight, he at last returns to his desk, a changed man, a man resolved to create meaning where there was none. The particularities of his descent entail Watanabe's efforts to transform a piece of blighted city slum into a children's playground. In Hegelian language, he takes on a being-for-others, which eventuates in meaningful selfhood. In his own world, Watanabe has at last made of himself something of a philosopher-king (Plato), a beautiful soul (Hegel), a nonbaffled geographer of the momentous gap between what he meant to become and what he is (Baldwin). He dies honored by others and at peace with himself and his life.

Anne Tyler's *Breathing Lessons* chronicles a similar dialectical transformation of regret. At the delicate moment when Maggie and Ira weep, first separately, then together, they succeed in putting aside their "immediate unity" (Hegel), allowing regret to work its painful cure by tearing them apart as individuals and as a couple. Their heroism lies in their fortitude in rising from this nadir. Maggie and Ira eventually transcend the loneliness of their regret by coming to stand together on common ground. Maggie finally gives up her desperate fantasy of repeopling her empty nest; Ira consoles her by "settl[ing] her next to him." They discover themselves by discovering the other.

Common to both stories is the Socratic process of first surrendering to regret and then transcending regret through a descent—a descent to that firmly human level where human beings interact with other human beings living their own particularized human lives. Like the protagonist of Sherwood Anderson's *Winesburg, Ohio*, these protagonists have put themselves in a position where they achieve the comfort of observing: "I have come to this lonely place and here is this other." In the words of Wallace Stevens, the protagonists have at last come to experience "humanly . . . from the depth/Of human things." A dialectical analysis suggests that regret (like all things human) is transcended not by reaching for some supra-human plane but by allowing oneself to become fully human.[17]

Dialectical Understanding of Regret

The notion of the dialectic reveals some of the most important features of regret. It also provides a method particularly well-suited for enlarging the understanding of the experience and concept of regret as begun in earlier chapters. Setting aside its "immediate unity," regret too can benefit from being first "broken down" into its dualistic components of reason and emotion, interiority and exteriority, past and present, actual and possible—before it is put back together into a coherent, though multilayered, whole in which these dichotomies are negated yet preserved.

Regret and the Dissociation of Reason and Emotion

The distinction between reason and emotion is frequently used as a club with which to assault regret. However, dialectical procedures help us with our earlier considerations. They help forge a less skewed understanding of the union of reason and emotion within regret.

Regret as Emotion. Rooted as it is in the Norse word *grata* (to weep), regret is etymologically very much a matter of emotion. To say "I regret" implies that I am experiencing some greater or lesser degree of sorrow, grief, psychic distress. Furthermore, regret is always about something we take personally—often something directly pertinent to our own character or conduct and thus our self-regard—but, at minimum, something we care about. Human beings are built in such a way that we are emotional about ourselves and about what we care about. The very nature of human psychology explains regret's irreducibility to a reasoned calculation.

The character of Peter Walsh in Virginia Woolf's *Mrs. Dalloway* delineates well the more specifically emotional side of regret. In contrast with Clarissa Dalloway, who succeeds most of the time in keeping the emotion of regret at bay, Peter Walsh is battered by it. When the two of them reminisce together about the time when he had wished to marry her, Peter experiences regret with a force as intense as grief: "it almost broke my heart too, he thought; and was overcome with his own grief. . . . I was more unhappy than I've ever been." At this moment under the influence of Peter's emotion, the always-composed Clarissa Dalloway succumbs to the pain. When she asks him whether he remembers the lake, she experiences the "pressure of an emotion which caught her heart, made the muscles of her throat stiff, and contracted her lips in a spasm as she said 'lake' "—before she struggles to regain control of herself.

In one sense Dostoevsky's protagonist of *Notes from Underground* also manifests regret-as-emotion. The day after issuing his invitation to Liza, he finds that "her memory tormented me with special force." He could "not calm down":

> As the evening advanced and the dusk gathered, my emotions, and with them my thoughts, kept changing and growing ever more confused. Something would not die down within me, in the depths of my heart and my conscience; it refused to die down and scalded me with anguish.

This no description of cold cognition. This is a description of warm, indeed "scalding," emotion. Even after fifteen years, his memory of Liza and of his impulse to save her (and himself) torments the Underground Man. Moreover, he refuses to retreat from this pain into defensively ironic detachment: instead he describes himself as a non-self-deceived mouse who forever "slip[s] back ignominiously into its hole with a smile of feigned contempt *in which it doesn't itself believe.*"

The Underground Man explicitly and forcefully allies himself with desire and emotion over and against reason, notably in a long diatribe against the Socratic principle that people do regrettable things only out of ignorance of their own best interests. He insists instead that people at times do regrettable things not blindly, but deliberately, simply to assert the validity of individual desire over the claims of impersonal, utilitarian rationality. When the Underground Man cries "but reason is no more than reason," it is the the cry of the romantic for the authority of desire against the tyranny of reason. He goes so far as to romanticize regret (and a gang of related emotions, such as guilt, self-loathing, and disgust) as a pleasurable emotion: "I would feel a certain hidden, morbid, nasty little pleasure. . . . "

Refutation of Regret as Simply Emotion. Though *Notes from Underground* tells a primarily tragic tale, the Underground Man also articulates the absolutistic romantic mentality that splits emotion and reason, idealizing emotion and damning reason. This, I believe, is where the Underground Man (and every unmitigated romantic) goes wrong. He transforms, or attempts to transform, the painful emotion of regret into a morbidly "pleasurable" emotion. He fairly wallows in it. In this half of his divided psyche, the Underground Man personifies the self-indulgent, anti-intellectual "irrationality" that emotion in general—and regret in particular—is often accused of.[18]

It is this hyper-emotional form of regret that is most often condemned not only by decision theorists but also by the person-on-the-street—and by writers whose targeted audience is the person-on-the-street. In the self-help book *Woulda, Coulda, Shoulda: Overcoming Regrets, Mistakes, and Missed Opportunities*,[19] some of the authors' most virulent warnings apply to what they call "emotional reasoning"—for example, "I know I can never be happy. I just feel it. I just know." Love songs are famous for taking a defiantly emotional stance toward regret. There is the old song that goes: "Maybe I'll give, and maybe I'll get. Maybe I'll live a life of regret. Nevertheless I'm in love with you." There is the new song from *A Chorus Line* that goes: "Won't forget, can't regret, what I did for love." As these examples demonstrate, regret that is univocally emotional *is* irrational—or at minimum nonrational. In such situations the advice of psychological and economic decision theory is well taken. To help avoid decisions that one will sooner or later regret, perhaps the song writer should have written: "Is this really love, or something else—infatuation, lust, neediness, narcissistic self-aggrandizement, power-seeking?" Or "Am I absolutely sure that this person is worth a *life of regret?*" But, then, these wouldn't be love songs. Nevertheless, particularly when the decision is an important one, people whose regret is one-dimensionally emotional may need to do a little less feeling and a lot more thinking.

Regret as Reason. Regret has historically been dismissed within psychological and economic decision theory as an irrational, emotional indulgence. And, as I have just argued, in some forms it is precisely that. However, since the early 1980s a new attitude toward regret has been whispered in the halls of reason. Modern regret theories rooted in economics have begun to argue and to marshal empirical support for the claim that regret is not only *not* irrational, but that factoring in regret can make sense of common patterns of decision that heretofore wrongly appeared irrational.

Dostoevsky's Underground Man is a fictional epitome of someone with a highly emotional experience of regret. Yet, in another sense Dostoevsky's complex protagonist illustrates an experience of regret that is highly intellective. This character has chosen a life "underground," where, like a mouse gnawing at himself, he obsessively mulls over the two major regrets in his life. Unlike the one-sidedly emotional individual, the Underground Man values "truth" above all ("How preferable it is to understand everything, to be

aware of everything"), illustrating, as well, one of the preferred solutions of the tragic mentality—reflective thought.

To regret is to reason. Regret is a form of inductive reason in
that it proceeds from the given to the not-given, comparing what
is (a particular "given") with what might have been. Regret is a
form of critical reason in its origins and its outcome: it is a "direct
consequence of the [intellective] capacity to recognize and to name
differences . . . and the capacity to conceive multiple alternatives."[20] And it is an evaluation, a judgment, an evaluative judgment that something has in some way gone wrong. Regret cannot
fairly be dismissed as *nothing but* emotion.

Refutation of Regret as Simply Reason. The task of analyzing regret by breaking it down into emotional and intellective components is complicated by the fact that in this culture reason and
emotion have already been radically split, and split in an ambivalently asymmetrical manner.

The Western mind tends to frame the matter as a clear-cut dichotomy: reason *versus* emotion. This is not the case in all cultures. The language of the Ifaluk, for example, fuses thought and
emotion, rather than splitting them, using a single word *nunuwan*
to signify the experience of thought and emotion together.[21] Moreover, in Western culture emotion is devalued as "the irrational, the
uncontrollable, the vulnerable, and the female."[22] In a recent interview, a young Michigan writer, Mary Gaitskill, recalled this disparaging attitude toward emotion among her girlhood peers. "The
worst thing they could think up to call [an unpopular girl] was
'Emotional'—'Oh, god, Emotional, that was so stupid!' they'd say.
That characterized their mentality. You were not supposed to feel
at all."[23] In this culture, to be called emotional is to be attacked.

In the university classroom, I have numerous times witnessed
the prevailing cultural hostility toward emotion. To introduce the
topic of emotion, I typically ask my students, first, to think of
someone they know whom they would describe as "emotional";
next, I ask each student to provide at least one trait adjective (other
than "emotional") that describes the person he or she is thinking
of, and I write every adjective on the board. Afterward, I ask for a
show of hands as to how many of the students had in mind a male
and how many a female. Out of the approximately 30 students in
each class, typically only two or three choose a male as their prototypical "emotional" person. This part of the demonstration lends

informal support to the above claim that in our folk theories of emotion we identify emotion with the female.

An alternative explanation is, of course, that the students' responses reflect not a cultural construction, but a reality of nature, that females are in fact and by nature more emotional than males. This account, however, is belied by research that finds an absence of neonatal gender differences in emotionality, and evidence of the operation of cultural norms in creating differences by adulthood.[24] As for regret, the explanation by nature is belied by the paucity of observed gender differences.[25]

The cultural *devaluation* of emotion is revealed in a second segment of this classroom exercise—when we code each of the trait adjectives for its social desirability and compare the number of desirable, undesirable, and neutral adjectives. (For those descriptors that are not unambiguously desirable or undesirable, I ask the authors which sense they had in mind.) Desirable descriptors typically include adjectives like: loving, caring, outgoing, thoughtful. Examples of undesirable descriptors include: fickle, nervous, moody, short-tempered, flaky, irrational, selfish, egocentric, not too bright, and unstable. Neutral or ambiguous descriptors include: analytical, sensitive, and whimsical. When I conduct this exercise, I find that the undesirable far outnumber the other two categories of descriptors of "emotional" individuals, typically by a ratio of something like 23 (undesirable) to 3 (desirable) to 4 (neutral or ambiguous). In this culture to be thought emotional is to be disparaged.

Yet the reason versus emotion duality is not the simple (if biased) duality it may at first appear to be. It is actually a complicated, internally contradictory matter. The ambivalence lurking within it could conceivably be coaxed out by pulling a similar stunt with the term "unemotional." Although I have not tried this myself, it seems likely that "unemotional" is no compliment either,[26] except from a hyper-rationalist perspective. But from another perspective, it may be an insult, amounting to reviling someone as cold, inhuman, estranged from self and others. "[T]he emotional is, for individual Americans, simultaneously good and bad, antithought and against estrangement, core of the self and residual effect," says anthropologist Catherine Lutz.[27] The ambivalence revealed by the disjunctive connotations of *reason* and *emotion* represents, Lutz points out, "both a cultural contradiction and a necessary feature of any dualism whose simplicities cannot hold in the face of the demands social processes will put on it."[28] This is one of those moments of blurring and contradiction that I believe begs for a dialectical critique of assumptions.

Lutz is right that the reason versus emotion dualism is an overly simplistic construction undercut by social processes. It is undercut by something else as well—by psychological experience. It is "sick" to lack reason and it is "sick" to lack emotion—and we (most of us) know it. However, in this culture and time the denunciation of irrationality has been hammered home to a greater extent than the denunciation of unemotionality. For that reason, the dangers of hyper-rationality discussed in earlier chapters requires reinforcement.

Recall that one of the earliest of the Western models of decision making was the Socratic principle, which asserted that to know the good is to do the good, or that human beings fail to do the good only out of ignorance of the good. Recall too the abundant evidence disconfirming this idea. Dostoevsky's Underground Man is but one fictional personification of the failure—in fact, the deliberate rejection—of the Socratic principle. But the Socratic principle fails in real life as well as in fictional lives. For the truth is that human beings are only *partly* rational. What is more, it is entirely fitting and proper that humans beings are only partly rational.

The one-sidedly rational individual—recall Rudolph Hoess from Chapter 1—is less than a full human being. Apparently, even a genius like Wittgenstein can find himself bewildered by life if all he has is rationality with which to meet it. Bruce Duffy describes Wittgenstein (and his family) in *The World As I Found It: A Novel* as utterly stymied over the failure of logic to dismiss his grief over the suicides of his two brothers:

> Yet, in their minds, Wittgenstein and his siblings would periodically revert to these magical half-conscious wishes that said *if only* and *had not* and if one could only make these things that *ought* but *aren't* and *can't* and *never will be.*
>
> Wittgenstein would not soon, or perhaps ever, disentangle the grammar of these illogical propositions.[29]

In *War and Peace* Tolstoy implies that hyper-rationality may function at times as a bulwark against feeling. The sister of the scholarly Prince Andrew (who has been unnerved by precipitous feelings of love for Natasha) notices how stiltedly Prince Andrew is speaking: "with extreme logic, as if punishing someone for those secret illogical emotions that stirred within him. At such moments Princess Mary would think how intellectual work dries men up."[30] An alternative inference, and one implied by Tolstoy, is that someone (male *or* female) might choose hyper-intellectuality *in order to* dry up his or her feeling.

I like to imagine Dostoevsky's Underground Man venturing out of his mouse hole to "do lunch" with the fictionalized Wittgenstein and Prince Andrew, straightening them out on this point with his critique of reason: "You see, gentlemen, reason is unquestionably a fine thing, but reason is no more than reason . . . . "

People like the desiccated Prince Andrew and the uncharacteristically baffled Wittgenstein could benefit from appreciating the authority of emotion. Again, what I am asserting is not the anti-intellectual elevation of gut feeling. Emotion is not to be fomented or stifled—but (and here the double meaning as verb and adjective is intended) cultivated.

A Dialectical Synthesis of Regret as Reasoned Emotion and Felt Thought. From a dialectical perspective, this exercise in formulating and refuting hypotheses (Plato) and in "passing through" fictional words (Fish) concerning regret-as-emotion and regret-as-reason ought to culminate in a new reading (Fish) such that the words now mean something different. I believe it does. This dialectical analysis suggests that, for regret (as more generally), the reason-versus-emotion dichotomy is descriptively and prescriptively both false and true. It is a false dichotomy in that for human beings the activity of reasoning about anything we care about necessarily engages emotion, and the activity of feeling necessarily engages reason. It is a true dichotomy because emotion is no more reducible to reason than reason is to emotion. It would be an error to omit one or the other, or to privilege one over the other. A full understanding and experience of regret thus both accommodates and transcends the reason/emotion dualism. Regret, fully experienced, is a matter of thought and feeling united. T. S. Eliot's approving words describing[31] Coleridge's elucidation of human imagination apply as well to regret: "judgment ever awake . . . [united with] feeling profound or vehement."[32]

Regret and the Dissociation of Interiority and Exteriority

The distinction between interior and exterior, or between psychic and overt acts, is frequently deployed as another club with which to attack regret. As I have earlier discussed, regret is repudiated in many folk psychologies as well as in classic formal decision theory on the grounds of its presumed power to immobilize the individual in a quagmire of interiority.[33] "What use is it to focus on what you should have done then as opposed to what you *can do* now?" ask the authors of *Woulda, Coulda, Shoulda: Overcoming Regrets, Mistakes, and Missed Opportunities.*[34] This rhetorical question draws its persuasive power in part from its implicit orientation toward action and its denigration of reflection. On this dimension, Spinoza doubled the opprobrium typically heaped upon regret when he declared that it makes us "twice impotent." The cult of exteriority is as hard on regret as is the cult of unidimensional rationality.

Of course, regret-bashers are right: regret *is* a largely interior matter—a matter of thinking and feeling. But they are wrong if they therefore assume regret to be in principle incompatible with or inimical to decision and action. It is true that, for a character like Dostoevsky's Underground Man, regret appears paralyzing. But a second look shows that it is in fact this character's refusal fully to experience his regret that is paralyzing him. The Underground Man's problem is that he co-opts his own interiority with defensive intellective maneuvers like rationalization and intellectualization. This is how he renders himself "twice impotent." Consider, in contrast, three other fictional characters detailed in this volume: Pip *(Great Expectations)*, Maggie Moran *(Breathing Lessons)*, and Mr. Watanabe *(Ikiru)*. In these cases (as in some of my own research),[35] the process of giving free rein to regret eventuates over time in decisive action.

Leaving the realm of fiction, consider a man of action *and* reflection, someone like the legendary T. E. Lawrence. Interest in the life of Lawrence seems almost limitless. His autobiographical account of his exploits in the Middle East, *Revolt in the Desert* (an abridgement of his massive *Seven Pillars of Wisdom*), was published in March 1927 by Cape Publishers in England and Doran in New York. According to John E. Mack's Pulitzer-prize-winning biography of Lawrence, in less than four months (by the end of June) it had sold 3,000 copies in England and 120,000 in America.[36] Cape's profits for 1927 shot up from £2,000 to £28,000, a dramatic success due almost singlehandedly to sales of *Revolt in the Desert.* A new wave of adulation followed the 1962 film version of his life, *Lawrence of Arabia.* Although I have no comparative figures on the popular appeal of autobiographies by a similar man of action like

General Douglas MacArthur or a similar man of reflection like Thomas Merton, I suspect that much of the fascination with Lawrence stems from our recognition that, in contrast to the typical man of action, this was a fuller human being, precisely because he also was a man with an exquisitely developed inner life (and the ability to write well about both). Neither exteriority alone nor interiority alone makes for as fully realized a human being as their conjunction in the same individual.

That human affairs consist of both exteriority and interiority is in part a consequence of the fact that decent human life is, as philosopher Michael Stocker puts it "a mixture of both the practical and the ideal."[37] The following example of Stocker's makes this point well. Consider a man who has squandered all his money. Ideally, he ought to pay his debts now. Nevertheless, he cannot. Some would argue that because it is impossible for him to repay his debts now, any regret on his part is irrational. Most versions of utilitarianism argue this. But this is to unreasonably privilege the exterior—the overt act. A theory that recognizes the merit of regret in this case, even though action is impossible, also recognizes the vital role of interiority in who we are, as well as the ultimate significance of who we are, an insight well expressed by J. S. Mill in *On Liberty*: "It really is of importance, not only what men do, but also what manner of men they are that do it."[38]

In sum, a dialectical analysis finds that, for regret, the interior-exterior duality is both true and false. The distinction is true in that interior states are not ontologically synonymous with exterior states. (As an obliquely related piece of collegiate graffiti explains: "If you doubt the existence of the real world, bang your head against this wall.") Yet it is descriptively and prescriptively a false dichotomy in that for developed human beings inner states are as much "social artifacts" as exterior acts[39]; acts of consciousness are as much acts as are overt behaviors; and acts of consciousness can prove as significant as overt acts. There is no warrant to omit one or the other, or to privilege one over the other. A full understanding and experience of regret both accommodates and collapses the interiority/exteriority dualism. Regret, properly understood, is a matter of bringing the outer world inside for a closer look, before returning again to the outer world.

Regret and the Dissociation of Past and Present

"What use is it to focus on what you should have done *then* as opposed to what you can do *now*?"[40] This previously quoted question consists of two different implicit distinctions—that between interiority and exteriority just mentioned, and that between past and present. But as I have discussed earlier in this volume, the past/present duality is another distinction pertinent to regret that is both true and false. It is literally true that yesterday is not the same as today; and yesterday can never be undone. But the past/present dichotomy is also false. Epistemologically, the past is not so much discovered as constructed. The past is constructed in the light of the present—in the light of the concerns, hopes, and standards of the present, as well as in the hindsight of actual outcomes. Experientially, for human beings, who live not only on the literal plane but also on the symbolic plane, the past lives on in the present. Faulkner's assertion could easily have come from the pen of Freud: "The past isn't dead. It's not even past." Therefore, a full understanding and experience of regret both accommodates and collapses the past/present duality. Regret, properly understood, is the past alive in the present.

Regret and the Dissociation of Possible and Actual

Finally, regret comes about through comparing the actual with the possible. This is not to say, as Beauvoir did, that in our imagination every possibility has *equal* reality: some are clearly only a ghost of a chance, and we know it. Still, some possibilities *will* assert themselves as substantial forces to be reckoned with. Some of those things we have not done *will* show up on our doorstep demanding that their story be added to our regrets. It's no good telling us that because the possible is unreal it makes no sense to contrast it with what is real. This advice is too literal-minded for the human psyche. We *will* envision the possible, especially when the actual fails to satisfy our hopes and dreams. To do so is partly what makes us human. To do so is what makes us change for the better. It is a good thing that the human mind is not limited by what actually exists. It is in this capacity to care enough about the particularities of experience to bother to imagine alternatives to reality that we accomplish the task of becoming fully human. Therefore, a full understanding and experience of regret both accommodates and collapses the actual/possible duality. Regret is the possible pressing its hopeful claims upon the actual.

This dialectical process of "going by contraries" reveals again the rich complexity of regret. Both as concept and as human experience, regret is *best* apprehended as an emotion informed by reflective intelligence, as an interior matter with implications for exteriority, as a look at the past capable of informing and energizing the present, and as the insistence of the possible upon a hearing in the world of the actual. The portrait that emerges is a many-layered one given depth and resonance and radiance by the preservation of multiple and variegated layers.

Still, the portrait of regret is not complete. Other relevant distinctions discussed in previous chapters can benefit from dialectical scrutiny—notably the four worldviews of regret.

The Romantic, Comic, Tragic, and Ironic Attitudes Toward Regret: To Go By Contraries

I believe that the repudiation of regret so characteristic of much Western folk psychology and formal theory originates to a large extent in a recoil from the romantic and tragic worldviews and a flight to the comic and, more recently, the ironic worldviews.

Romanticism promises many good things but at a price that the modern and postmodern sensibility finds too dear. It promises heroic individuality, certainty, and hope—but at the cost of the submission of one's self and one's reason to absolutistic dualities and orthodoxies. One of the dangers of unalloyed romanticism is, as Voltaire knew, that "the best is the enemy of the good." In the romantic mentality if this is not a mansion I am living in, then it must be a chicken coop; if my life is not a triumph, it must be a complete and utter failure; if I am not a hero, then I am a nothing. Such thinking can promote the self-destructive withdrawal and despair of an Underground Man—or worse. To reject romanticism is in part to reject the absolutistic worldview and its potentially catastrophic consequences. To reject regret as irrationally emotional, and to link regret with impotence, is to reject two of the three romantic solutions for dealing with the disharmonies of life—fantasy and emotion—in favor of the solution preferred by the comic stance—reasoned action.

The tragic worldview, a harsher mistress than the romantic, promises the astringent comfort of certainty along with the cold light of "truth." But again, many moderns find the price too high, particularly the submission of their critical faculties to absolutistic orthodoxies. From another perspective, many moderns object to the tragic mentality as an affront to action and an affront to the future. To reject regret as navel-gazing is to reject the tragic stance's radical interiority as a solution to the central disharmonies of life. To reject regret as overly "negative" is to reject the nonprogressivist assumption of the tragic stance, along with its view of time as linear and thus irreversible. To reject the possibility of irremediable regret is to reject the tragic expectation of disastrously unhappy endings.

Much of popular culture and Western intellectual fashion has turned its back on the romantic and tragic visions and embraced the comic vision.[41] Rejecting the idea of the the past as unchangeable and thus regret as tragically irremediable, the comic mentality asserts the opposite. Rather than willingly allow oneself to slide down that perilous slope into the "might-have-been trap,"[42] the individual armed with the comic attitude simply refuses to step within miles of that slope. The Enlightenment school of thought as well as modern scientism share central hallmarks of the comic vision, including the guiding convictions that: (1) "in reason can be found a universally applicable standard for judging validity and worth";[43] (2) the tyranny of superstition, convention, and absolutistic dogma can and ought to be overthrown unilaterally by reason; (3) reflection is a waste of time unless it directly mobilizes action; and (4) if propositions (1), (2), and (3) govern human affairs, progress will inevitably follow.

The tenets of classic economic and psychological decision theory fit this description as well. Classic decision theory has assumed the definability and solubility of problems. It has insisted on nonemotional reason as *the* standard for judging decisions. And it has proposed that if only some umbrella model of rational choice (usually some variant of the expected-utility model) were universally applied, human choice would be virtually infinitely improved.

One metaphor for regret associated with the comic vision is the financial metaphor articulated in *Breathing Lessons* when Ira Moran reflects on an episode in which he lost his usual cool and allowed himself to get emotionally upset: afterward, he had felt "ridiculous. He'd felt he had spent something scarce and real—hard currency." The popular recommendation to be careful how you "invest" your time and energy—including psychic energy—also stems from the financial metaphor. In the comic worldview a resolutely dispassionate cost-benefit analysis is *the* answer to unbalanced accounts. The thing to do is to apply rational thought (often as set down in the expected-utility model) to balance the accounts. Orthodox decision theory has further assumed that balance is restorable without much difficulty—because conflict, ambivalence, and incommensurability are assumed to play only a minor role, if any.

In this view, emotion in general and regret in particular are foolish wastes of hard currency.

In the other influential comic metaphor for regret, the human information-processing machine is out of order, causing wasted energy and inefficient operation. Its solution is to scrape all that sticky emotion off the machine to free the machine once more to do its putatively all-important task—namely, to process information with minimal waste. Its answer to the problem of decision regret is to stop emotion—with brute force, if necessary—from gumming up the works, to apply reason alone to estimate probabilities and preferences, to act on these calculations alone, and then to accept without emotion the product cranked out by the information-processing machine and by life.

At bottom both metaphors are economic. Unlike other possible metaphors for regret—a judgment-processor, a font of wisdom, a journey to enlightenment, a "momentous gap," a dialectical liberation from/descent back to the peopled world, a dream or a brook that goes by contraries—these comic metaphors for regret focus on shrewd spending—of money, time, energy, emotion, resources in general. In the world of the information-processing machine and the balance sheet, life is a market, and regret has no place in the market. Both metaphors are based on economic metaphors for the mind prevalent today, but with roots deep in the Enlightenment.

Criticisms of the economic definition of emotion have deep roots, as well, extending back as far as Rousseau's strikingly timely critique written in the eighteenth century:

> In a social system animated by competition for property, the human personality was metamorphosed into a form of capital. Here it was rational to invest oneself only in properties that would produce the highest return. Personal feeling was a handicap since it distracted the individual from calculating his best interest and might pull him along economically counterproductive paths.[44]

Whatever its cogency, such criticism has generally been outshouted.

The Enlightenment installed impersonal reason in place of personal feeling as *the* answer to the perplexities of human existence. The Enlightenment rejected blind faith in superstition, tradition, and dogma—in favor of blind faith in reason.

But the truth is, once again, that "too great a reliance on rationality is only another kind of superstition." Platonically universal, axiomatic, solely reason-based formulations cannot be sustained in the face of human reality. Regret (as virtually all things human) depends on the hopes, values, and mores of individuals and societies, matters that are notoriously and irreducibly particular, non-axiomatic, and personal. As Aristotle insisted, in practical reason it is the discernment of particulars, not impersonal principle—still less algorithmic principle—that is required. Philosopher Martha Nussbaum explains that whenever we have a difficult decision to make, one in which possible regret looms:

> the only procedure to follow is . . . to imagine all the relevant features as well and fully and concretely as possible, holding them up against whatever intuitions and emotions and plans and imaginings we have brought into the situation or can construct in it. There really is no shortcut.[45]

Where the Enlightenment and modern scientism went wrong, then, was not so much in adopting the comic worldview but in pairing it with the worst of the romantic worldview—its absolutism.

Although the comic is now, I believe, the intellectually and scientifically prevailing stance toward regret, one can make out on the horizon the glimmerings of a change of sensibility, perhaps even a paradigm shift—toward the ironic. Signs of an ironic mentality in the twentieth century have materialized in science, literature, and popular culture. Ironic formulations in science include the new rationalism called "bounded rationality," as well as fuzzy logic, chaos theory, and quantum theory. It is worth taking a look at each of these in turn.

Within psychology and economics, the influence of classic decision theory, originally based on a model of an absolutistically "ideal" decision maker seeking always to maximize his or her wants, has been significantly challenged by Herbert Simon's notions of bounded rationality and satisficing. To acknowledge bounded rationality is to acknowledge that human reason is inevitably limited—by the intractable difficulty of estimating likelihoods and preferences, by reality constraints such as intractable scarcities of available resources and of time in which to make decisions, by intractably conflicting desires, and so on. The related concept of satisficing posits that when we make decisions we generally are not in fact maximizing, but satisficing—doing as well as we *reasonably* can within the very real constraints of rationality and reality. Since Simon, the decision models have been considerably scaled down from their romantically "Olympian"[46] heights to a level cognizant of limitation, uncertainty, and ambiguity—all elements of an ironic sensibility.

Late in his life Wittgenstein introduced the notion of fuzzy logic, arguing that certain concepts elude clear definition in the classical sense of a delimited set of *defining* features and can only be defined in terms of "characteristic" features—"'characteristic' because they recur often (not always)."[47] "Game" is such a concept. Any game shares some but not all features with other games, but no defining feature is shared by all games. The edges separating game from nongame are blurred.[48] A particular game can at best be defined in terms of its family resemblance to an indefinite set of features shared by most but not all games. Fuzzy logic represents real-world events as ironically uncertain, continuous, and ambiguous rather than precise, all-or-nothing, either-or in nature.

Linguists have applied the notion of fuzzy logic to the analysis of certain features of language. For example, as Lakoff[49] points out, terms like "tall" and "middle-aged" are fuzzy concepts, with no clear boundaries separating them from concepts like "short" and "young." Thus, a 39-year-old might be classified as middle-aged, though less prototypically middle-aged than a 50-year-old. Hedges— terms like "very," "sort of," "strictly speaking," "technically," and "par excellence"—represent an entire class of linguistic terms not definable in classical, criterial terms. Hedges linguistically illustrate the ironic proposition that "sentences will very often be neither true, nor false, nor nonsensical, but rather true to a certain extent and false to a certain extent, true in certain respects and false in other respects."[50]

About 25 years ago, the concept of fuzzy logic was applied to theoretical mathematics by Lotfi Zadeh, who coined the term "fuzzy sets." Zadeh urged the elimination of precise, absolutistic measurements of speed, recommending instead, for instance, that a set of speed measurements could "be lumped together and called slow"[51]—simplifying mathematical computations. It was expected that fuzzy logic would prove most applicable to "systems in which *human judgment and emotions* play a certain role"[52]—especially law and psychology. The challenge of fuzzy logic to the precision and rule-governedness of probability theory[53] appears particularly applicable to human judgment and emotion—and to the place of regret in decision theory—though to my knowledge this particular application has yet to be made.

The psychologist Eleanor Rosch's extension of these ideas to the notion of fuzzy conceptual sets[54] has been widely applied within other areas of psychology. The notion has been used in the analysis of personality traits and diagnostic psychiatric categories,[55] and also emotion.[56] We know, for example, that not everyone agrees on the questions of whether pride or surprise are emotions; thus emotion, too, appears to be a concept with fuzzy boundaries. Similarly, as shown in Chapter 2, regret itself is an emotion with more or less fuzzy boundaries separating it from others like sadness, disappointment, remorse, and guilt.

Chaos theory represents a third scientific movement with decided elements of the ironic sensibility. From its birth around 1960, chaos theorists (or more broadly and less dramatically, scholars of nonlinear dynamics) have shown a "taste for randomness and complexity, for jagged edges and sudden leaps"[57]—a sensibility that initially aroused disdain and even hostility in other scientists. Chaos theorists took as their central problem the complexity of nature. This led them to tackle questions previously considered intractable and thus scientifically uninteresting, like: how smoke rises, how fluids eddy and flow, the erratic structure of coastlines, the rise and fall of insect populations and human epidemics, and the kinds of chaotic (that's right, chaotic, not regular) patterns characterizing healthy hearts and brains.[58] Chaos theory has pointed up the overly simplistic nature of a number of earlier beliefs. It has discovered, for example, that contextual factors can amplify initially small uncertainties into tremendously complicated, chaotic-looking uncertainties that nevertheless are not random. This central idea, called "sensitive dependence on initial conditions," has been explained with respect to weather "only half-jokingly" as the Butterfly Effect—"the notion that a butterfly stirring the air today in Peking can transform storm systems next month in New York."[59] Apparently some artificial-intelligence researchers have also embraced chaos theory for its attention to:

> the kind of infinitely self-referential quality that seems so central to the mind's ability to bloom with ideas, decisions, emotions, and all the other artifacts of consciousness. With or without chaos, serious cognitive scientists can no longer model the mind as a static structure.[60]

Finally, there is quantum theory, which has been described as a "beautiful mathematical structure that became the most revolutionary, broad-ranging, and successful of modern theories."[61] I will leave the specifics of this theory to the physicists, but suffice it to say that among the most revolutionary aspects of quantum theory are its central features of "subjectivism,"[62] "uncertainty, indeterminism, and mystery."[63] Its development during the first half of the twentieth century by physicists such as Planck, Bohr, and Heisenberg was in large part a response to the failure of experimental data to match the deterministic predictions of the special theory of relativity. Even scientists who are acutely uncomfortable with the subjectivism, uncertainty, and indeterminism of quantum theory have had to admit their admiration for its seemingly almost limitless predictive power.[64]

Signs of an ironic sensibility show up in literature as well, in certain of the works I have here discussed, including *Mrs. Dalloway*, *The Fall*, and *Breathing Lessons*. Each of these novels presents a more or less (more in *The Fall* and *Mrs. Dalloway*; less in *Breathing Lessons*) ironic vision of life as a matter of limitation, compromise, ambiguity, and uncertainty—and thus ambivalence and regret. And of course the idea of indeterminacy is central to the recently dominant deconstructionist theories of literary critiism.

All these approaches evidence a new appreciation of the assumptions of the ironic worldview—complexity, irregularity, ambiguity, subjectivity, limitation, and uncertainty. If many human concepts and experiences obey the principles of fuzzy logic, if our best efforts sometimes produce rational indeterminacy, if minuscule contextual factors can produce massively chaotic-looking outcomes, if the neat and trim principle of utility-maximization has failed us, then perhaps the search for an omnibus decision principle that would render regret moot is an impossible dream. If reason is limited, then blind faith in reason is itself irrational. It is not too soon to ask then whether the ironic mentality offers the answer to the human problem that is regret. To do so, I want to take another, harder look at the ironic mentality.

In an analysis of television, Mark Crispin Miller, the author of *Boxed In: The Culture of TV*, shows that the rationalist recoil against romanticism and tragedy can lead not only to the comic elements just discussed, but also to irony:

> [In *1984* the weapons of the Party are] the weapons of pure irony, which is necessarily the attitudinal vehicle and expression of Enlightenment. Analogous to Enlightenment and fostered by it, pure irony denudes the world of every value, devastating—with just a little smile and deft repetition—whatever person, concept, feeling, belief, or tradition it encounters, until there is nothing left but the urge to ironize.[65]

In a review, titled "Deride and Conquer," of Miller's book, Jackson Lears extends Miller's analysis:

> The cultural style that has emerged in the past decade or so, one that celebrates irony as a way of life, could plausibly be called postmodern. The postmodern hero is street-smart and adwise; he sees through everything; decodes everything, mostly for fun; and is always protected by his ironic detachment.[66]

An ironic stance specifically toward regret is articulated in a recently translated avant-garde novel, *Hourglass,* by Yugoslavian author Danilo Kis:

> One way of solving the problem of existence is to come close enough to the things and beings that have struck us as beautiful and mysterious to discover that they are without mystery and without beauty; this is one form of hygiene that we may choose; it may not be very commendable but it gives us a certain peace of mind and makes life easier for us—because *it enables us to regret nothing,* for it convinces us that we have attained the best possible ends and that this best did not amount to much, and to make our peace with death.[67]

Such critiques uncover serious flaws in unadulterated irony. The form of irony that amounts only to "corrosive knowingness" in league with self-protective "smirk"[68] is not, I think, our best answer to regret.

Contradictions like these invite us to re-enter the dialectic. Perhaps another go-round might reveal an alternative form of the ironic stance that would prove more bracing than corrosive. In an intellectual history of the concept of maturity, Christie Kiefer[69] offers, I believe, the outlines of such an alternative. In Kiefer's sketch irony is characterized not only by the awareness of pervasive unreliability, limitation, complexity, uncertainty, absurdity, but also by transcendence of this awareness—through the recognition that we may nevertheless need to hold onto some logically suspect "language, ideas, and identities"[70]—because they're all we have. Even if they are not demonstrably true, even if they are illusions, or to put it more harshly, "lies," certain ideas function, in Ibsen's phrasing, as *"saving"* lies. This notion echoes the views of three great philosophical prophets of a transcendently ironic stance—Kant, Nietzsche, and Vaihinger.

Kant defended certain moral and religious beliefs—such as belief in the existence of a Supreme Being, a soul, free will, immortality, and a realm of morality—insofar as these are held lightly as

"useful fictions" and not ossified into dogma.[71] Nietzsche defended
the rationality of nonreligious "regulative fictions," in particular
the illusion of free choice.[72] Vaihinger developed these ideas into a
philosophical system he termed the "philosophy of 'as if'."[73] The
"as if" for Vaihinger are fabricated concepts, products of the imagination, or useful fictions—which we clearly recognize to be fabri-
cations, productions, and fictions, even while we choose to make
use of them. As he points out, we regularly treat mathematical
symbols "as if" they had the value of the actual numbers they represent, and money "as if" it had the value of actual amounts of
gold. It is useful to do so. It is useful, as well, to treat other fictions
as if they were real. Whereas someone who really subscribed to the
idea that free choice is illusory (such as a thoroughgoing determinist) would have no reason to act, or to act morally, someone who
chose to treat free choice "as if" it were real would be liberated
from paralysis and amorality. The philosophy of "as if" offers a
valuable improvement on a destructively literal form of the ironic
stance toward regret. Ironically, regret itself has this "as-if" quality, inasmuch as it entails comparing reality with some fabricated,
or imagined, better state of affairs.

   This analysis, as well as the logic of the dialectic itself, implies
that it is best not to limit oneself to only one among these four
alternative stances toward regret. To insist upon complexity is no
dodge. Instead of one-dimensional answers, what is needed are syn-
cretic *sets* of worldviews. Furthermore, I think that *different* sets
are best suited for different individuals, different contexts, different
times, different worlds.

   The comic view of bettering the world through reasoned action, prediction, and control (as epitomized in science) did (and still
does) represent an antidote to romantic, pre-Enlightenment absolutism, superstition, fatalism, and blind faith. However, as I have
argued, taken alone, the comic stance is flawed by overweening
optimism and blind faith in reason.

   The comic vision of predictability, controllability, definability,
unemotional rationality, and inevitable improvement may also
benefit from being tempered with the tragic vision of the inevitability of conflict and suffering. Death and other disasters demand
it. Life *is* unruly, unpredictable, and unreasonable; catastrophe comes
in at least as many forms as triumph. Yet the tragic vision also
needs to be tempered with the comic vision of predictability, controllability, definability, and possible improvement.[74] The need for
courage to live demands it.

Ironic appreciation of indeterminacy did (and still does) represent a reasonable reaction to post-Enlightenment recognitions of the failure of science to rescue us from all that is not amenable to human action, reason, prediction, and control. However, ironic detachment is not an appropriate response to such an intolerable world as, say, the Holocaust. There, romantic heroism is needed to temper an accurate but overly quietistic view of life as inevitably ("Ho hum") a mix of good and evil. In today's cynical world, where emotion is looked on as nothing but irrational and self-indulgent, a movement toward romantic idealism and passion may be just what is needed to pull us out of the quicksand of knowing apathy. Whereas in the ironic worldview the fact of death renders life absurd, in the romantic worldview the fact of death renders life monumental. Unalloyed irony ultimately fails anyone with the (admittedly premodern) conviction that life and individuals are important.

Still, it is possible to take oneself *too* seriously. This is another reason that a combination of the romantic and the ironic stances may prove better than either taken alone. This is particularly true when considering one's stance toward one's *own* importance. This Jewish proverb nicely expresses what I mean: "Everyone should carry two pieces of paper, one in each pocket. On one sheet should be written: 'The whole universe was created just for me.' On the other: 'I am but dust and ashes.'" The ironic worldview comes equipped to serve as an antidote for those who through a romantic worldview take themselves too seriously. The confluence of irony and romanticism is better than either one by itself.

Again, my claim is that there is no universally best way of approaching regret. This claim need not, however, abandon us to the formalist's nightmare of a "wilderness of single instances." There are paths in this forest. It's just that which set of paths is best depends on where you're starting from.

Starting at his unrelievedly romantic/tragic position, Dostoevsky's Underground Man would have been well served by complicating himself by welcoming a measure of irony to his vision of regret. Ironic acceptance of (*not* resignation to) the inevitability of falling short of his utopian ideal would have allowed him to transcend despair. An adoption of "as-if" thinking could have lifted his paralysis, mobilizing him to work "as if" the ideal were realizable. This form of irony would nicely fulfill Gramsci's counsel of "pessimism of the intellect; optimism of the will." Moreover, this form of irony would not require us to "deny [our] pain. It simply demands a more complicated vision, one in which a condition or event

is not either good or bad but is, rather, both good and bad, not
sequentially but simultaneously."[75]

On the other hand, those starting from a position of ironic detachment can benefit from complicating themselves by adding romantic emotional engagement. Someone as well-defended as Clarissa Dalloway would be well served by a dose of undefended
romanticism to her excessively ironic vision of regret. She could
have retained her keen awareness of life's necessary limitations,
ambiguities, and compromises. At the same time, a degree of romantic respect for her own feelings as well as a measure of an "as-
if" affirmation of the possibility of redemption might have allowed
her to transcend her state of vague yearning and misty despair. In
fact, these are exactly the saving elements that Maggie Moran
brought to her marriage with Ira. Just as Maggie had something to
learn from ironic Ira about the limits of emotion and action, Ira
had something equally important to learn from romantic Maggie—
that "a person who cares about something thereby incurs certain
costs, connected with the effort which investing himself requires
and with the vulnerability to disappointment and to other losses
which it imposes."[76] Regret is one of those costs of caring.

I do not mean to imply that this is easy. Becoming the kind of
person in whom the romantic and ironic, the comic and tragic,
emotion and reason are not dissociated is, I assume, not easy—but
a momentous task.

I personally believe that one of the most defensible positions
for my time and place is a hybrid mentality—ironic romanticism,
or if you prefer, romantic irony—arrived at and constantly re-
negotiated through a dialectical process. This perspective would
preserve a number of elements of irony: its responsiveness to the
inevitability of dilemma, compromise, ambiguity, limitation, and
uncertainty; its ascription of conflict and misery in part to uncontrollable, arbitrary forces; and its acceptance of the literal impossibility of perfection. But this perspective would reject the kind of
ironic emotional disengagement that "enables us to regret nothing"
(Kis). Although it may sometimes be possible (and perhaps in extreme circumstances rational) to minimize regret by reducing desire to a minimum, this is hardly ideal. Nor does the ironic attitude require us to drown ideals—even romantically utopian ideals—
in a sea of relativism. Rather, a better ironic stance will be one
tempered by romantic "as-if" affirmation of, say, more or less cogent (though seldom absolutistically *certain*) distinctions between

right and wrong, true and false, good and evil. Such as-if affirmation should provide a useful antidote to hot-tub-and-crystals quietism, streetsmart-and-adwise disengagement, and despairing resignation alike. Such as-if affirmation should also prove useful in fostering ameliorative action by individuals and groups. After all, solutions to many regrets (like those of the Underground Man, Mrs. Dalloway, and the Morans) are not merely in the head but are also sociopolitical in nature. Ultimately, such as-if affirmation has the potential to foster genuine transcendence of life's inevitable regret.

In the face of regret, the romantic ironist is both chastened and engaged. The romantic ironist engages in a struggle which acknowledges the force of regret rather than defensively denying or evading it. Yet the romantic ironist is not so easily defeated in this struggle, armed as she is with a nonresigned expectation of regret grounded in a nonresigned expectation of conflict, loss, limits, mistakes, and bad luck. Finally, in the spirit of the dialectic, the romantic ironist is always alert to contradictions and moments of blurring that suggest it is time to question once again the present accommodation. It is always about going forward by going backward, "going by contraries."

We don't have to imprison regret in the rationalist cell for fear of its otherwise falling prey to romanticism. It is better to think of and to experience regret as a dialectical process that develops in a particular individual living out a particular history in a particular context with particular opportunities and limitations. This way of thinking of and experiencing regret robs us of the comfort of a blanket set of general principles. But it gives more than it takes away. "The more . . . ambivalences you can hold in your head, the better off you are, intellectually and emotionally."[77] Yes. Being fully human means feeling and thinking; it means having mixed feelings; it means experiencing the fullness of felt thought and reasoned emotion.

How fascinating that Joyce and Frost arrived at the same saving insight, the wisdom of trusting oneself to "go by contraries," like dreams, like the West-Running Brook of Frost's poem. Like regret. Frost's poem, written in the form of a dialogue between a couple, works because it touches us both through our heart and our head— as regret works when it is a matter of both the heart and the head:

> "What does it think it's doing running west
> When all the other country brooks flow east

To reach the ocean? It must be the brook
Can trust itself to go by contraries
The way I can with you—and you with me"

. . . .

"That wave's been standing off this jut of shore—"
(The black stream, catching on a sunken rock,
Flung backward on itself in one white wave,
And the white water rode the black forever,

. . . .

"Speaking of contraries, see how the brook
In that white wave runs counter to itself.
It is from that in water we were from
Long, long before we were from any creature.
Here we, in our impatience of the steps,
Get back to the beginning of beginnings,
The stream of everything that runs away.
Some say existence like a Pirouot
And Pirouette, forever in one place,
Stands still and dances, but it runs away,
It seriously, sadly, runs away
To fill the abyss' void with emptiness.
It flows beside us in this water brook,
But it flows over us. It flows between us
To separate us for a panic moment.
It flows between us, over us, and *with* us.
And it is time, strength, tone, light, life, and love—
And even substance lapsing unsubstantial;
The universal cataract of death
That spends to nothingness—and unresisted,
Save by some strange resistance in itself,
Not just a swerving, but a throwing back,
As if *regret* were in it and were sacred. . . ."[78]

Notes

Prologue: The Science and Humanity of Regret

1. Bruner, J. (1986). *Actual minds, possible worlds.* Cambridge, Mass.: Harvard University Press.

2. Nussbaum, M. C. (1990). *Love's knowledge.* New York: Oxford University Press, p. 6.

3. O'Brien, C. C. (1988, Nov. 24). Keeping up with the Shaws. *New York Review of Books*, p. 6.

4. Huxley, A. (1963). *Literature and science.* New Haven, Conn.: Leete's Island Books, p. 55.

5. Even though interdisciplinary work (like regret itself) remains somewhat unfashionable, I am certainly not alone in prizing it. Psychologist William Bevan has urged his discipline and mine that: "[i]t would do us all good to loosen up and look around, not only to our closer relatives in the biological sciences and in the social sciences, but to the humanities as well." Philosopher Bernard Williams has called for scholarly commerce specifically between moral philosophy and psychology. Economist James March has recommended that economics turn to ethics, criticism, and aesthetics for consultation in revising the standard economic decision theory, which has proved empirically unsupported. Even more disconcerting to many of his colleagues in economic and psychological decision theory, March has proposed looking to Freud for help in understanding the "complicated contradiction between conscience and self-interest." Generally speaking, my interdisciplinary scholarship is animated by the hope articulated by Richard Rorty: that "in the process of playing vocabularies and

277

cultures off against each other, we produce new and better ways of talking and acting." (See Bevan, W. [1991]. Contemporary psychology: A tour inside the onion. *American Psychologist, 46,* 475–483, p. 479; March, J. G. [1978]. Bounded rationality, ambiguity, and the engineering of choice. *The Bell Journal of Economics, 9,* 587–608, p. 603; Rorty, R. [1982]. *Consequences of pragmatism [Essays: 1972–1980].* Minneapolis: University of Minnesota Press, p. xxxvii; Williams, B. A. O. [1965]. Ethical consistency. *Aristotelian Society, 39,* 103–124.)

6. Donoghue, D. (1981). *Ferocious alphabets.* Boston: Little, Brown, p. 101.

7. Trilling, L. (1953). *The liberal imagination.* Garden City, NY: Anchor Books, p. xiii.

8. Cited in Nagel, T. (1993, March 4). The mind wins! [Review of *The rediscovery of the mind*]. *New York Review of Books,* p. 39.

9. Ackerman, D. (1990). *A natural history of the senses.* New York: Random House, p. 277.

10. Bruner, p. 50.

11. Ackerman, p. 277.

12. Cited in Sandelands, L. E. (1988). The concept of work feeling. *Journal for the Theory of Social Behaviour, 18,* p. 455.

13. Huxley, p. 32.

14. Ryle, cited in Geertz, C. (1973). *The interpretation of cultures.* New York: Basic Books, p. 6.

15. Geertz, C. (1973). *The interpretation of cultures.* New York: Basic Books, p. 28.

16. Geertz, p. 7.

17. Landau, M. (1984). Human evolution as narrative. *American Scientist, 72,* 262–268.

18. Atwood, M. (1991, Fall). Northrop Frye remembered. *Michigan Quarterly Review,* p. 648.

19. Kenny, D. (1979). Correlation and causality. New York: Wiley, p. 5.

20. Lakoff, G., & Johnson, M. (1980). *Metaphors we live by.* Chicago: The University of Chicago Press; and Olney, J. (1972). *Metaphors of self.* Princeton, NJ: Princeton University Press.

21. See Chapter 3 for elaboration on each of these metaphors.

22. I am thinking of the wealth of cross-historical and cross-cultural evidence that undermines the essentialist understanding of the human psyche and behavior implied by the phrase "human nature."

23. Nussbaum, p. 7.

24. Booth, W. (1988). *The company we keep: An ethics of fiction.* Berkeley: University of California Press, p. 260.

25. Morse Peckham, cited in Booth, p. 497.

26. Calvino, I. (1988). *Six memos for the next millennium.* Cambridge, Mass.: Harvard University Press, p. 112.

1. The Uses of Regret

1. Kahneman, D., & Tversky, A. (1982b). The simulation heuristic. In D. Kahneman, P. Slovic, & A. Tversky (Eds.), *Judgment under uncertainty: Heuristics and biases.* New York: Cambridge University Press, p. 206.

2. Bedford, E. (1956–1957). Emotions. *Proceedings of the Aristotelian Society.* London: Harrison & Sons.

3. Hampshire, S. (1960). *Thought and action.* New York: Viking, p. 241.

4. Kahneman & Tversky, p. 206.

5. Bell, D. E. (1980). Explaining utility theory paradoxes by decision regret. *Proceedings of the fourth international conference on multiple criteria decision making.* University of Delaware, Newark. August 10–15, 1980. New York: Springer-Verlag, 1981; Bell, D. E. (1982). Regret in decision making under uncertainty. *Operations Research, 30,* 961–981; Loomes, G., & Sugden, R. (1982). Regret theory: An alternative theory of rational choice under uncertainty. *The Economic Journal, 92,* 805–824; Loomes, G., & Sugden, R. (1987). Testing for regret and disappointment in choice under uncertainty. *The Economic Journal, 97,* 118–129.

6. Savage, L. J. (1951). The theory of statistical decision. *Journal of the American Statistical Association, 46,* 55–67.

7. Taylor, G. (1985). *Pride, shame and guilt: Emotions of self-assessment.* New York: Clarendon Press, Oxford University Press.

8. Festinger, L. (1957). *A theory of cognitive dissonance.* Evanston, Ill.: Row, Peterson, p. 270.

9. Rorty, A. O. (Ed.) (1980). *Explaining emotions.* Berkeley: University of California Press, p. 501.

10. R. Dawes, personal communication, July 24, 1991.

11. Hershey, J. C., & Baron, J. (1987). Clinical reasoning and cognitive processes. *Medical Decision Making, 7,* p. 207.

12. Ionesco, E. (1940–41/1971). *Present past, past present: A personal memoir* (H. R. Lane, Trans.). New York: Grove, p. 30.

13. Plato. (1952). *The Republic.* Great Books of the Western World. R. M. Hutchins, Ed. Chicago: Encyclopaedia Britannica, Book IV, p. 354.

14. Plato, pp. 353–354.

15. Aristotle. (1935). *Nicomachean ethics* (P. Wheelwright, Ed. and Trans.). New York: Odyssey Press, p. 179.

16. Nisbett, R., & Ross, L. (1980). *Human inference: Strategies and shortcomings of social judgment.* Englewood Cliffs, New Jersey: Prentice-Hall.

17. Freeman, A., & DeWolf, R. (1989). *Woulda, coulda, shoulda: Overcoming regrets, mistakes, and missed opportunities.* New York: HarperPerennial.

18. As I completed my book, this book on regret came out: C. Klein

and R. Gotti (1992) *Overcoming regret: Lessons from the roads not taken.* New York: Bantam.

19. Shea, J. (1989, January 13). Without a radio, Shea takes a final look at life. *Michigan Daily/Weekend,* p. 10.

20. Chapman, R. L. (1992, February 23). Letters. *New York Times Book Review,* p. 34.

21. Brinkley, A. (1990, October 14). A savage and demeaning ritual [Review of *Pledging allegiance*]. *New York Times Book Review,* p. 28.

22. Gonzales, A., & Zimbardo, P. G. (1985, March). Time in perspective. *Psychology Today,* pp. 21–26.

23. Dawes, R. M. (1988). *Rational choice in an uncertain world.* San Diego: Harcourt Brace Jovanovich, p. 24.

24. deSousa, R. (1987). *The rationality of emotions.* Cambridge, Mass.: MIT Press, p. 221.

25. Staw, B. M. (1976). Knee-deep in the big muddy: A study of escalating commitment to a chosen course of action. *Organizational Behavior and Human Performance, 16,* 27–44.

26. Dawes, p. 31.

27. deSousa, p. 221.

28. Dawes, p. 291.

29. John Dewey very elegantly makes this point and others more directly pertinent to the place of time in selfhood in: Dewey, J. (1960). Time and individuality. *On experience, nature, and freedom* (R. Bernstein, Ed.) (pp. 224–243). Indianapolis, Ind.: Bobbs-Merrill.

30. Dawes, p. 31.

31. Romaker, R.S. (1991, December 2). U-M memories. *Ann Arbor News,* C1.

32. Mansfield, K. In *Correct Quotes.* Software. Novato, Calif.:WordStar Intl. Inc., 1990–91.

33. Bishop, E. (1980). *The complete poems 1927–1979.* New York: Farrar, Straus and Giroux.

34. Kempton, M. (1992, April 23). Brother, can you spare a dime? *New York Review of Books,* p. 55.

35. Discomfort with the thought of being a loser may have caused at least one of our politicians to unwittingly rewrite Santayana's famous warning: "Those who cannot remember the past are condemned to repeat it." In October 1989, Michigan's governor panned (sight unseen) the movie *Roger and Me,* which portrays in decidedly pessimistic tints the impact of General Motors' layoffs on the Michigan city of Flint. The governor was quoted as stating that it is best to focus on the future and "not dwell on the friction or conflict of the past. If a person dwells too much on the past [sic] they're [sic] doomed to repeat it," he said. (See Foren, J. [1989, October 5]. Governor raps Flint movie without seeing it. *Ann Arbor News*).

36. Price, E. (1979). *Leave your self alone.* Grand Rapids, Mich.: Zondervan.

37. Hogarth, R. (1986). *Judgment and choice* (2nd ed.). New York: Wiley; Janis, I. L., & Mann, L. (1977). Anticipatory regret. In *Decision making: A psychological analysis of conflict, choice, and commitment* (pp. 219–242). New York: Free Press.

38. Ephron, N. (1986, November 2). Revision and life: Take it from the top—again. *New York Times Book Review*, p. 7.

39. Lowry, M. (1947/1971). *Under the volcano.* New York: New American Library.

40. Rorty, A.

41. See, for example, the following: Abramson, L. Y., Metalsky, G. I, & Alloy, L. B. (1989). Hopelessness depression: A theory-based subtype. *Psychological Review, 96,* 358–372; Abramson, L. Y., Seligman, M.E. P., & Teasdale, J. (1978). Learned helplessness in humans: Critique and reformulation. *Journal of Abnormal Psychology, 87,* 49–74; Alloy, L. B., & Abramson, L. Y. (1979). Judgment of contingency in depressed and nondepressed students: Sadder but wiser? *Journal of Experimental Psychology: General, 108,* 441–485; Alloy, L. B., & Abramson, L. Y. (1982). Learned helplessness, depression, and the illusion of control. *Journal of Personality and Social Psychology, 42,* 1114–1126; Lewinsohn, P. M., Mischel, W., Chaplin, W., & Barton, R. (1980). Social competence and depression: The role of illusory self-perceptions. *Journal of Abnormal Psychology, 89,* 203–212; Peterson, C. (1991). *Health and optimism.* New York: Free Press; Peterson, C., & Seligman, M.E.P. (1984). Causal explanations as a risk factor for depression: Theory and evidence. *Psychological Review, 91,* 347–374; Watson, D., & Clark, L. A. (1984). Negative affectivity: The disposition to experience aversive emotional states. *Psychological Bulletin, 96,* 465–490.

42. Gudjonsson, G. H. (1984). Attribution of blame for criminal acts and its relationship with personality. *Personality and Individual Differences, 5* (1), 53–58; Weisman, A.D., & Worden, J. W. (1976–77). The existential plight in cancer: Significance of the first 100 days. *International Journal of Psychiatry in Medicine, 7,* 1–15; Landman, J., Vandewater, E., Stewart, A., & Malley, J. (Under review). Missed opportunities: Ramifications of counterfactual thought.

43. Taylor, G.

44. Wideman, J. E. (1984). *Brothers and keepers.* New York: Holt, Rinehart & Winston, p. 152.

45. This is not to say that obsessively regretful thought always proves deleterious. What grand work of art or science was ever produced without some degree of obsessive thinking about how to improve upon what had been regrettably only mediocre? But eventually thought ought to facilitate decision and action, when these are possible.

46. Landman, J., Pais, D., & Nykiel, C. (in preparation, 1993). Regret in young adults.

47. Ibsen, H. (1884/1954). *The wild duck.* In *Three plays* (U. Ellis-Fermor, Trans.). Baltimore: Penguin, p. 219.

48. Frankfurt, H. G. (1988). *The importance of what we care about: Philosophical essays.* New York: Cambridge University Press; Frijda, N.H. (1986). *The emotions.* Cambridge: Cambridge University Press; Klinger, E. (1975). The consequences of commitment to and disengagement from incentives. *Psychological Review, 82,* 1–25.

49. Solomon, R. C. (1976). *The passions: The myth and nature of human emotion.* Notre Dame, Ind: The University of Notre Dame Press.

50. Hellman, L. (1976). *Scoundrel time.* Boston: Little, Brown, pp. 42–43.

51. No comment. (1991, May). *The Progressive,* p. 10.

52. See Taylor, G.

53. Freeman & DeWolf, p. 85.

54. Dostoevsky, F. (1864/1981). *Notes from underground.* New York: Bantam, p. 7.

55. Dickinson, E. (1983). *The complete poems of Emily Dickinson* (T. H. Johnson, Ed). Cambridge, Mass.: Harvard University Press, p. 365.

56. Baumbach, J. (1989, February 5). Amorality on the rampage [Review of *The Hungry Girls*]. *New York Times Book Review,* p. 36.

57. Davis, F. (1979). *Yearning for yesterday: A sociology of nostalgia.* New York: The Free Press.

58. Proust, M. (1948). *Pleasures and regrets* (L. Varese, Trans.). New York: Lear/Crown, p. 360.

59. Sartre, J.-P. (1956). *Being and nothingness* (H. E. Barnes, Trans.). New York: Washington Square Books, p. 637.

60. Sartre, p. 649.

61. Fussell, P. (1983, September). The critic as human being. [Review of *Characters and their landscapes*]. *Atlantic,* p. 122.

62. Ashbery, J. (1970). *The double dream of spring.* New York: E. P. Dutton, p. 90.

63. James, W. (1890). *The principles of psychology* (Vol. I). New York: Henry Holt, p. 127.

64. Freud, S. (1930). *Civilization and its discontents* (J. Strachey, Trans). New York: Norton, 1961, p. 16.

65. Freud, S. (1915). Repression. In *General psychological theory: Papers on metapsychology.* New York: Collier, p. 107.

66. Hampshire, S. (1983). *Morality and conflict.* Cambridge, Mass.: Harvard University Press, p. 137.

67. The commandant at Auschwitz was Rudolph Hoess (Höss) who should not be confused with Rudolf Hess, Hitler's Deputy Party Leader of the National Socialist Party who died in the late-eighties at Spandau Prison.

68. Dawes, R. M. (1981). Plato vs. Russell: Hoess and the relevance of cognitive psychology. Tech. Report No. 43. Institute for Social Science Research, Eugene, Ore.: The University of Oregon, p. 2.

69. Dawes, Plato vs. Russell, pp. 1–2, emphasis added.

70. Oatley, K. (1992). *Best laid schemes: The psychology of emotions.* New York: Cambridge University Press.

71. Arnold, M. B. (1960). *Emotion and personality.* New York: Columbia University Press; Ellsworth, P. C., & Smith, C. A. (1988). From appraisal to emotion: Differences among unpleasant feelings. *Motivation and Emotion, 12*, 271–302; Folkman, S., & Lazarus, R. S. (1985). If it changes it must be a process: Study of emotion and coping during three stages of a college examination. *Journal of Personality and Social Psychology, 48*, 150–170; Frijda, N. H. (1986). *The emotions.* Cambridge: Cambridge University Press; Frijda, N. H. (1987). Emotion, cognitive structure, and action tendency. *Cognition and Emotion, 1*, 115–143; Frijda, N. H. (1988). The laws of emotion. *American Psychologist, 43*, 349–358; Lazarus, R. S. (1982). Thoughts on the relations between emotion and cognition. *American Psychologist, 37*, 1019–1024; Lazarus, R. S. (1991). *Emotion and adaptation.* New York: Oxford University Press; Oatley, K. (1992). *Best laid schemes: The psychology of emotions.* New York: Cambridge University Press; Plutchik, R. (1980). *Emotion: A psychoevolutionary synthesis.* New York: Harper & Row; Roseman, I. (1979, September). *Cognitive aspects of emotion and emotional behavior.* Paper presented at the meeting of the American Psychological Association, New York City; Roseman, I. J. (1991). Appraisal determinants of discrete emotions. *Cognition and Emotion, 5*, 161–200; Scherer, K. R., & Ekman, P. (Eds.) (1984). *Approaches to emotion.* Hillsdale, NJ: Erlbaum; Smith, C. A., & Ellsworth, P. C. (1985). Patterns of cognitive appraisal in emotion. *Journal of Personality and Social Psychology, 48*, 813–838; Smith, C. A., & Ellsworth, P. C. (1987). Patterns of appraisal and emotion related to taking an exam. *Journal of Personality and Social Psychology, 52*, 475–488.

72. Hampshire, p. 162.

73. Plato, Book IV, p. 424; italics are mine.

74. Frank, R. H. (1988). *Passions within reason: The strategic role of the emotions.* New York: Norton.

75. Frank, p. ix.

76. Frank, p. 4.

77. Frank, p. xi.

78. Frank, p. x.

79. Hampshire, S. (1960). *Thought and action.* New York: Viking, p. 241.

80. Frank.

81. Janis & Mann.

82. Alloy & Abramson, Judgment of contingency; Lewinsohn, Mischel, Chaplin, & Barton.

83. Fiedler, K. (1988). Emotional mood, cognitive style, and behavior regulation. In K. Fiedler & J. Forgas (Eds.), *Affect, cognition, and social behavior* (pp. 100–119). Toronto: Hogrefe International; Schwarz, N. (1990). Feelings as information: Informational and motivational functions of affective states, pp. 527–561. In E. T. Higgins & R. M. Sorrentino (Eds.), *Handbook of motivation and cognition: Foundations of social behavior*, Vol 2. New York: Guilford; Schwarz, N., Bless, H., & Bohner, G. (1991). Mood and persuasion: Affective states influence the processing of persuasive communications, pp. 161–199. In M. P. Zanna (Ed.), *Advances in experimental social psychology*, Vol. 24. San Diego, Calif.: Academic Press; Sinclair, R. C. (1988). Mood, categorization breadth, and performance appraisal: The effects of order of information acquisition and affective state on halo, accuracy, information retrieval, and evaluations. *Organizational Behavior and Human Decision Processes, 42,* 22–46.

84. Schwarz, Bless, & Bohner.

85. Kahneman, D., & Miller, D. T. (1986). Norm theory: Comparing reality to its alternatives. *Psychological Review, 93,* p. 137.

86. Sartre, p. 626.

87. But to correct in the future the very same things that went wrong in the past is not the only possible benefit of a regretful study of the past. This is probably not the function of much regret in the elderly (Sidney Gendin, personal communication). Nor was it the function of the profound deathbed regret experienced by Tolstoy's protagonist, Ivan Ilyitch.

88. Gordon, S. L. (1990). Social structural effects on emotions. In T. D. Kemper (Ed.). *Research agendas in the sociology of emotions* (pp. 145–179). Albany: State University of New York Press.

89. Crosby, F. (1982). *Relative deprivation and working women.* New York: Oxford University Press; Guimond, S., & Dube-Simard, L. (1983). Relative deprivation theory and the Quebec nationalist movement: The cognition-emotion distinction and the personal-group deprivation issue. *Journal of Personality and Social Psychology, 44,* 526–535; Gurin, P. (1987). The political implications of women's statuses. In F. Crosby (Ed.), *Spouse, parent, worker: On gender and multiple roles* (pp. 165–196). New Haven: Yale University Press.

90. Landman, *et al.,* under review; Johnson, M. K., & Sherman, S. J. (1990). Constructing and reconstructing the past and the future in the present. In E. T. Higgins, & R. M. Sorrentino (Eds.), *Handbook of motivation and cognition: Foundations of social behavior* (Vol. 2), pp. 482–526. New York: Guilford; Markman, K. D., Gavanski, I., Sherman, S. J., & McMullen, M. N. (1993). The mental simulation of better and worse possible worlds. *Journal of Experimental Social Psychology, 29,* 87–109; Ruvolo,

A. P., & Markus, H. R. (1992). Possible selves and performance: The power of self-relevant imagery. *Social Cognition, 10,* 95–124.

91. Abigail Stewart, Elizabeth Vandewater, Janet Malley, and I are in the process of conducting research whose preliminary results appear to show the galvanizing effects of regret. For the well-educated middle-class women in this sample, short-term emotional costs of regret appear to have eventuated in longer-term gains of important life changes. It looks as if these women were able to translate their regrets about the past into goals, and then to translate those goals into real life changes.

92. Taylor, S. E. (1983). Adjustment to threatening events: A theory of cognitive adaptation. *American Psychologist, 38,* 1161–1173; Taylor, S. E., & Brown, J. D. (1988). Illusions and well-being: Some social psychological contributions to a theory of mental health. *Psychological Bulletin, 103,* 193–210.

93. Gordon; Rawls, J. (1963). The sense of justice. In H. Morris (Ed.), *Guilt and shame.* Basic Problems in Philosophy Series. Belmont, Calif.: Wadsworth, 1971; Smith, A. (1759/1793). *The theory of moral sentiments* (Vol I). Basil: J. J. Tourneisen.

94. DeMott, B. (1982, March 14). [Review of *Dinner at the Homesick Restaurant*]. *New York Times Book Review.*

95. Kierkegaard said this: "It is perfectly true, as philosophers say, that life must be understood backwards. But they forget the other proposition, that it must be lived forwards" (Kierkegaard, S. [1967]. *The Journals of Soren Kierkegaard: A selection.* A. Dru (Ed. & Trans.). Bloomington, Ind.: Indiana University Press.

96. Frost, R. (1977). *North to Boston.* New York: Dodd, Mead.

97. Ionesco, p. 30, emphasis added.

98. Adelson, J. (1983, Fall). The self and memory in *1984. American Educator,* p. 42.

99. Crossman, R. (1949). *The God that failed: Why six great writers rejected Communism.* New York: Harper, p. 162.

100. Rawls, p. 141.

101. Gaylin, W. (1979, January). On feeling guilty. *Atlantic,* p. 82.

102. Cited in Lukacs, J. (1968/1985). *Historical consciousness or The remembered past.* New York: Schocken, p. xxviii.

103. Stocker, M. (1987). Moral conflicts: What they are and what they show. *Pacific Philosophical Quarterly, 68,* 104–123.

104. Taylor, G., p. 99.

105. Parfit, D. (1984). *Reasons and persons.* New York: Clarendon/Oxford, p. 169.

106. Stocker, p. 114.

107. Butler, S. (1927). *Erewhon: or Over the range.* New York: The Modern Library.

108. Platonov, A. (1975). *The Foundation Pit.* (M. Ginsburg, Trans.). New York: E. P. Dutton, p. 56.

109. Gordon.

110. Frank.

111. Cassill, R. V. (1970). Symposium: The writer's situation. In T. Solotaroff (Ed.), *New American Review*, Number 9, p. 71.

112. Morris, J. N. (1966). *Versions of the self.* New York: Basic Books, p. 219.

113. Kundera, M. (1981). *The book of laughter and forgetting.* New York: Penguin, p. 158.

114. Orwell, G. (1949). *1984.* New York: Signet, 1983, p. 164.

115. Rosenwald, G. C., & Wiersma, J. (1983). Women, career changes, and the new self. *Psychiatry, 46,* 213–229.

116. Rosenwald & Wiersma, p. 216.

117. Rosenwald & Wiersma, p. 217.

118. Rowenwald & Wiersma.

119. Rosenwald & Wiersma, p. 224.

120. Scheler, cited in Rosenwald & Wiersma, p. 217.

121. Lasch, C. (1979). *The culture of narcissism.* New York: Warner, p. 26.

122. Smith, A.

123. Spinoza, B. (1952). Ethics. In R. M Hutchins, (Ed.), *Great books of the Western World.* Vol. 31. Chicago: Encyclopaedia Britannica.

124. Nietzsche, F. (1887/1974). *The gay science.* (W. Kaufmann, Trans.). New York: Vintage Books.

125. Freud, *Civilization.*

126. Forster, E. M. (1924). *A passage to India.* New York: Harvest, p. 51.

127. Morrow, L. (1983, May 23). The morals of remembering. *Time,* p. 88.

128. Gordon; Harré, R. (Ed.) (1986). *The social construction of emotions.* Oxford: Basil Blackwell.

129. Keillor, G. (1983, July 11). The current crisis in remorse. *The New Yorker,* p. 36.

2. What We Talk About When We Talk About Regret

1. This contrast was highlighted for me by Fred Davis's (1979) book *Yearning for Yesterday: A Sociology of Nostalgia.* New York: The Free Press. There he defines nostalgia as: "a positively toned evocation of a lived past in the context of some negative feeling toward present or impending circumstance...that subjective state which harbors the...belief that THINGS WERE BETTER (MORE BEAUTIFUL) (HEALTHIER) (HAPPIER) (MORE CIVILIZED) (MORE EXCITING) THEN THAN NOW" (p. 18, capitals in original).

2. Knowing what I know of his life, I imagine that the late Raymond

Carver must have had his regrets. It is with deep respect that I have appropriated and modified his title for this chapter.

3. Bedford, E. (1956–1957). Emotions. *Proceedings of the Aristotelian Society.* London: Harrison & Sons, p. 299.

4. Hampshire, S. (1960). *Thought and action.* New York: Viking, p. 241.

5. Goodman, N. (1973). *Fact, fiction, and forecast* (3rd ed.). Indianapolis: Bobbs-Merrill.

6. Goodman; Kripke, S. A. (1980). *Naming and necessity.* Cambridge, Mass.: Harvard University Press; Lewis, D. K. (1973). *Counterfactuals.* Cambridge, Mass.: Harvard University Press.

7. Kripke.

8. Hart, H. L. A., & Honoré, A. M. (1959). *Causation in the law.* London: Oxford/Clarendon Press, p. 15.

9. Kahneman, D., & Tversky, A. (1982b). The simulation heuristic. In D. Kahneman, P. Slovic, & A. Tversky (Eds.), *Judgment under uncertainty: Heuristics and biases.* New York: Cambridge University Press.

10. Kahneman & Tversky, p. 206.

11. Kahneman, D., & Tversky, A. (1982a). The psychology of preferences. *Scientific American, 246,* 160–173.

12. Bell, D. E. (1980). Explaining utility theory paradoxes by decision regret. *Proceedings of the fourth international conference on multiple criteria decision making.* University of Delaware, Newark. August 10–15, 1980. New York: Springer-Verlag, 1981; Bell, D. E. (1982). Regret in decision making under uncertainty. *Operations Research, 30,* 961–981; Loomes, G., & Sugden, R. (1982). Regret theory: An alternative theory of rational choice under uncertainty. *The Economic Journal, 92,* 805–824; Sage, A. P., & White, E. B. (1983). Decision and information structures in regret models of judgment and choice, *IEEE, SMC-13,* 136–145; Schoeffler, M. S. (1962). Prediction of some stochastic events: A regret equalization model. *Journal of Experimental Psychology, 64,* 615–622.

13. Bell, Explaining utility; Bell, Regret; Loomes & Sugden.

14. Sugden, R. (1985). Regret, recrimination and rationality. *Theory and Decision, 19,* p. 77.

15. Sugden, p. 79.

16. Ellsworth, P. C., & Smith, C. A. (1988). From appraisal to emotion: Differences among unpleasant feelings. *Motivation and Emotion, 12,* 271–302; Fehr, B., & Russell, J. A. (1985). The concept of emotion viewed from a prototype perspective. *Journal of Experimental Psychology: General, 113,* 464–486; Folkman, S., & Lazarus, R. S. (1985). If it changes it must be a process: Study of emotion and coping during three stages of a college examination. *Journal of Personality and Social Psychology, 48,* 150–170; Frijda, N. H. (1986). *The emotions.* Cambridge: Cambridge University Press; Frijda, N.H. (1987). Emotion, cognitive structure, and action tendency. *Cognition and Emotion, 1,* 115–143; Frijda, N. H. (1988). The laws

of emotion. *American Psychologist, 43,* 349–358; Kemper, T. D. (Ed.) (1990). *Research agendas in the sociology of emotions.* Albany: State University of New York Press; Lazarus, R. S. (1982). Thoughts on the relations between emotion and cognition. *American Psychologist, 37,* 1019–1024; Lazarus, R. S. (1991). *Emotion and adaptation.* New York: Oxford University Press; Ortony, A., Clore, G., & Collins, A. (1988). *The cognitive structure of emotions.* New York: Cambridge University Press; Smith, C. A., & Ellsworth, P. C. (1985). Patterns of cognitive appraisal in emotion. *Journal of Personality and Social Psychology, 48,* 813–838; Smith, C. A., & Ellsworth, P. C. (1987). Patterns of appraisal and emotion related to taking an exam. *Journal of Personality and Social Psychology, 52,* 475–488; Russell, J. A. (1978). Evidence of convergent validity on the dimensions of affect. *Journal of Personality and Social Psychology, 36,* 1152–1168; Russell, D., & McAuley, E. (1986). Causal attributions, causal dimensions, and affective reactions to success and failure. *Journal of Personality and Social Psychology, 50,* 1174–1185; Russell, J.A., & Mehrabian, A. (1977). Evidence for a three-factor theory of emotions. *Journal of Research in Personality, 11,* 273–294; Stipek, D., Weiner, B., & Li, K. (1989). Testing some attribution-emotion relations in the People's Republic of China. *Journal of Personality and Social Psychology, 56,* 109–116; Weiner, B. (1985). An attributional theory of achievement motivation and emotion. *Psychological Review, 92,* 548–573.

17. Roseman, I. (1979, September). *Cognitive aspects of emotion and emotional behavior.* Paper presented at the meeting of the American Psychological Association, New York City; Roseman, I. J. (1991). Appraisal determinants of discrete emotions. *Cognition and Emotion, 5,* 161–200; Roseman, I. J., Spindel, M. S., & Jose, P. E. (1990). Appraisals of emotion-eliciting events: Testing a theory of discrete emotions. *Journal of Personality and Social Psychology, 59,* 899–915.

18. Roseman, *Cognitive aspects;* Roseman, appraisal determinants; Roseman, Spindel, & Jose.

19. Roseman, Spindel, & Jose.

20. Festinger, L. (1957). *A theory of cognitive dissonance.* Evanston, Ill: Row, Peterson; Festinger, L. (1964). *Conflict, decision, and dissonance.* Stanford, Cal: Stanford University Press.

21. Croyle, R.T., & Cooper, J. (1983). Dissonance arousal: Physiological evidence. *Journal of Personality and Social Psychology, 45,* 782–791.

22. Festinger, L., & Walster, E. (1964). Post-decision regret and decision reversal. In Festinger, *Conflict, decision, and dissonance* (pp. 112–127).

23. An alternative to the dissonance-based explanation of choice reversal is psychological reactance, or the reassertion of freedom threatened by having to make a choice. See: Abelson, R. P., & Levi, A. (1985). Decision making and decision theory. In G. Lindzey & E. Aronson (Eds.), *Handbook of Social Psychology, Vol. I: Theory and Method* (pp. 231–309).

New York: Random House.; Brehm, J. W., & Wicklund, R. A. (1970). Regret and dissonance reduction as a function of postdecision salience of dissonant information. *Journal of Personality and Social Psychology, 14,* 1–7; Wicklund, R. A. (1970). Prechoice preference reversal as a result of threat to decision freedom. *Journal of Personality and Social Psychology, 14,* 8–17. In either case, the experience of regret is not called into question, just the underlying "causal" processes.

24. Festinger, *A theory,* p. 270.

25. Festinger, *Conflict, decision, and dissonance.*

26. Hampshire, S. (1983). *Morality and conflict.* Cambridge, MA: Harvard University Press.

27. Hampshire, p. 145.

28. Van Amerongen, J. (1989, March 12). "The Neighborhood" Cartoon. *Ann Arbor News.*

29. Kleinginna, P. R., & Kleinginna, A. M. (1981). A categorized list of emotion definitions, with suggestions for a consensual definition. *Motivation and Emotion, 5,* p. 355.

30. Woolf, V. (1925). *Mrs. Dalloway.* New York: Harcourt, Brace, & World, p. 63.

31. Sartre, J.-P. (1948). *The emotions: Outline of a theory.* New York: Philosophical Library, p. 51.

32. For an extended discussion of ambivalence, using this example, see Chapter 5, and Greenspan, P. S. (1980). A case of mixed feelings: Ambivalence and the logic of emotion. In A. O. Rorty (Ed.), *Explaining emotions* (pp. 223–250). Berkeley: University of California Press.

33. Rorty, A. O. (Ed.) (1980). *Explaining emotions.* Berkeley: University of California Press, p. 496.

34. Kahneman & Tversky, The simulation heuristic.

35. Roseman, *Cognitive aspects*; Roseman, Appraisal determinants; Roseman, Spindel, & Jose; Russell & Mehrabian; Shimanoff, S. B. (1984). Commonly named emotions in everyday conversations. *Perceptual and Motor Skills, 58,* 514; Storm, C., & Storm, T. (1987). A taxonomic study of the vocabulary of emotions. *Journal of Personality and Social Psychology, 53,* 805–816.

36. Storm & Storm.

37. Russell & Mehrabian.

38. Frijda, *The emotions,* p. 256.

39. Frijda, The laws, p. 351.

40. Others who have highlighted the central role of personal concerns and goals in emotion include the following: Frankfurt, H. G. (1988). *The importance of what we care about: Philosophical essays.* New York: Cambridge University Press; Gray, J. A. (1971). *The psychology of fear and stress.* London: Weidenfeld & Nicholson; Gray, J. A. (1982). *The neuropsychology of anxiety: An enquiry into the functions of the septohippocampal system.* Oxford: Oxford University Press; Klinger, E. (1975). The con-

sequences of commitment to and disengagement from incentives. *Psychological Review, 82,* 1–25; Mowrer, O. H. (1960). *Learning theory and behavior.* New York: Wiley; Oatley, K. (1992). *Best laid schemes: The psychology of emotions.* New York: Cambridge University Press; Pribram, K. H. (1971). *Languages of the brain: Experimental paradoxes and principles of neuropsychology.* Englewood Cliffs, NJ: Prentice-Hall.

41. Rorty, A.; Silber, J. R. (1967). Being and doing: A study of status responsibility and voluntary responsibility. *University of Chicago Law Review, 35,* 47–91.

42. James, W. (1890). *The principles of psychology* (Vol. I). New York: Henry Holt, p. 323.

43. Kernberg, O. (1975). *Borderline conditions and pathological narcissism.* New York: Jason Aronson, p. 315, emphasis added.

44. Markus, H., & Nurius, P. (1986). Possible selves. *American Psychologist, 41,* 954-969.

45. Markus & Nurius.

46. Roseman, Appraisal determinants.

47. I am grateful to Joan Bossert for pointing out to me the parallels between my view of regret as felt thought and the ideas Eliot expressed in this essay. See Eliot, T. S. (1950). Tradition and the individual talent. In *Selected essays* (pp. 3–11). New York: Harcourt, Brace and Co.

48. I thank George Bornstein for referring me to this essay. See Eliot, T. S. (1975). The metaphysical poets. *Selected prose of T. S. Eliot* (F. Kermode, Ed.) (pp. 59–67). New York: Harcourt Brace Jovanovich; Farrar, Straus and Giroux, p. 64.

49. Eliot, *Selected prose,* p. 65.

50. Stocker, M. (1979). Desiring the bad: An essay in moral psychology. *The Journal of Philosophy, 76,* p. 753.

51. Zajonc, R. B. (1980). Cognition and social cognition: A historical perspective. In L. Festinger (Ed.), *Retrospections on social psychology.* New York: Oxford University Press.

52. Festinger, *A theory,* p. 270.

53. Festinger, *Conflict, decision, and dissonance.*

54. Brehm & Wicklund.

55. Wicklund, R. A., & Brehm, J. W. (1976). *Perspectives on cognitive dissonance.* New York: Wiley.

56. Sugden.

57. Williams, B. A. O. (1976). Moral luck. *Aristotelian Society, 50,* 115–136.

58. For technical details, see Loomes, G., & Sugden, R. (1987). Testing for regret and disappointment in choice under uncertainty. *The Economic Journal, 97,* 118–129; and Loomes, G. (1988). Further evidence of the impact of regret and disappointment in choice under uncertainty. *Economica, 55,* 47–62.

59. Storm & Storm.

60. Storm & Storm.

61. Roseman, *Cognitive aspects*; Roseman, Appraisal determinants.

62. Davis.

63. Laplanche, J., & Pontalis, J.-B. (1973). *The language of psycho-analysis.* (D. Nicholson-Smith, Trans.). New York: Norton, p. 477.

64. Freud, S. (1909). *Three case histories.* New York: Collier, 1963, p. 50.

65. Freud, A. (1936). *The ego and the mechanisms of defense* (revised edition). New York: International Universities Press.

66. Freud, S. *Three case histories.*

67. Freud, S., *Three case histories,* p. 153.

68. Fenichel, O. (1945). *The psychoanalytic theory of neurosis.* New York: Norton.

69. I can't resist adding to the discussion of undoing a wonderful word I recently came across: to *penelopize,* meaning to do and undo over and over.

70. Festinger, *A theory.*

71. Festinger, *A theory.*

72. Kahneman & Tversky, The simulation heuristic.

73. Rorty, A., p. 497.

74. Zajonc.

75. But see Sandelands' illuminating discussion of similar questions with respect to thoughts and feelings about work: Sandelands, L. E. (1988). The concept of work feeling. *Journal for the Theory of Social Behaviour, 18,* 437–457.

76. Rorty, A., p. 495.

77. Taylor, G. (1985). *Pride, shame and guilt: Emotions of self-assessment.* New York: Clarendon Press, Oxford University Press, p. 99.

78. Heat-Moon, W.L. (1991, September). PrairyErth: Portraits from Chase County, Kansas. *Atlantic,* p. 69.

79. Heat-Moon, p. 70.

80. Storm & Storm.

81. Montaigne, M. de. (1580/1936). Of repentance. *The essays of Michel de Montaigne* (J. Zeitlin, Trans.). Vol III. New York: Knopf, p. 23.

82. Solomon, R. C. (1976). *The passions: The myth and nature of human emotion.* Notre Dame, Ind.: The University of Notre Dame Press, p. 349.

83. Thalberg, I. (1963). Remorse. *Mind, 72,* 545–555.

84. Taylor, G., p. 98.

85. Roseman, Spindel, & Jose.

86. Roseman, Appraisal determinants.

87. Thalberg.

88. See also Taylor, G.

89. Thalberg, p. 547.

90. Montaigne, p. 23.

91. Freud, S. (1930). *Civilization and its discontents.* (J. Strachey, Trans). New York: Norton, 1961, p. 84.

92. Thalberg, p. 546, emphasis in original.

93. Thalberg, p. 547.

94. Tangney, J. P. (1992). Situational determinants of shame and guilt in young adulthood. *Personality and Social Psychology Bulletin, 18*, p. 199.

95. Russell & Mehrabian.

96. I thank Sidney Gendin for this example.

97. Fingarette, H. (1967). Real guilt and neurotic guilt. In H. Morris (Ed.), *Guilt and shame.* Belmont, Calif.: Wadsworth, 1971; Lewis, H. D. (1947). The problem of guilt. *Explanation in history and philosophy. Aristotelian Society Proceedings,* Vol. 21. London: Harrison & Sons; Roseman, *Cognitive aspects*; Roseman, Appraisal determinants; Roseman, Spindel, & Jose.

98. Jaspers, K. (1947). Differentiation of German guilt. In H. Morris.

99. Arendt, H. (1964/1985). *Eichmann in Jerusalem: A report on the banality of evil.* New York: Penguin.

100. Fingarette; Harvey, J. W. (1947). The problem of guilt. *Explanation in history and philosophy. Aristotelian Society Proceedings.* Supplementary Volume 21. London: Harrison & Sons; Lewis, H. D.; Taylor, G.

101. Tangney; Wicker, F. W., Payne, G. C., & Morgan, R. D. (1983). Participant descriptions of guilt and shame. *Motivation and Emotion, 7,* 25–39.

102. Wicker, Payne, & Morgan.

103. Interestingly, the answer to the question of what specific categories of transgressions most often elicit guilt differs across cultures. For Americans, violating a legal or moral precept is the most commonly reported cause of guilt; for Chinese, hurting others emotionally is (See Stipek, Weiner, & Li).

104. Roseman, *Cognitive aspects,* p. 10, n. 10.

105. Solomon, R. C. (1976). *The passions: The myth and nature of human emotion.* Notre Dame, Ind.: The University of Notre Dame Press.

106. Solomon.

107. Ellsworth & Smith; Folkman & Lazarus; Izard, C. E. (1972). *Patterns of emotions.* New York: Academic Press; Izard, C. E. (1977). *Human emotions.* New York: Plenum; Scherer, K. R., & Ekman, P. (Eds.). (1984). *Approaches to emotion.* Hillsdale, NJ: Erlbaum; Schwartz, G. A., & Weinberger, D. A. (1980). Patterns of emotional responses to affective situation: Relations among happiness, sadness, anger, fear, depression, and anxiety. *Motivation and Emotion, 4,* 175–191; Smith & Ellsworth.

108. Diener, E., & Emmons, R. A. (1985). The independence of positive and negative affect. *Journal of Personality and Social Psychology, 47,* 1105–1117; Ellsworth & Smith; Polivy, J. (1981). On the induction of emotion in the laboratory: Discrete moods or multiple affect states? *Journal of Personality and Social Psychology, 41,* 803–817.

109. Lewis, H. B. (1971). *Shame and guilt in neurosis.* New York: International Universities Press.

3. Worldviews of Regret: A Literary Framework

1. I do not intend to categorize these authors' (James, Dickens, Dostoevsky, Woolf, Tyler) generic stance as comic, romantic, tragic, or ironic—only the specific work at hand. Moreover, although I believe that a single stance predominates in each of these novels (with the exception of *Breathing Lessons,* which embodies equal parts of two stances), traces of more than one of these stances can be found in each novel.

2. I selected these particular texts through a mixture of serendipity and appeal to experts. Friends in the English department at the University of Michigan recommended *Great Expectations* and *Mrs. Dalloway* as focusing on a theme of regret. A chapter on regret by Amelie Rorty (1980) directed me to *Notes from Underground* as exemplifying character regret. Following a talk I gave on some of my empirical research on regret, a graduate student in psychology suggested I take a look at regret in *Breathing Lessons.* The names of my benefactors appear in the Acknowledgments. I am also indebted to Robert Butler's chapter on the life review for referring me to a number of other works in which regret plays a major role, including Beckett's *Krapp's Last Tape,* Hemingway's "The Snows of Kilimanjaro," Henry James's "The Beast in the Jungle," and Lampedusa's *The Leopard.* For the life of me I cannot remember what or who pointed me toward Henry James's *The Ambassadors;* perhaps I happened upon it myself?

3. A word about method. In one sense my method of using literature is every bit as innocent of the modern literary movements such as structuralism and deconstruction as it may appear to the initiated. That is, I am engaging in the old-fashioned activity of reading literary works as if they have determinate meanings. In two other senses, my method is not quite as innocent or naive as it may appear. First, I am aware that I am reading through my own subjective lens; I agree with modern reader-response theorists that there is no other way to read. Clearly, the role of my interest in *regret* has shaped my readings of these works. In true postmodern fashion, I do not assume that mine are the *only* defensible meanings determinable through readings of these works. Readers without my motivating interest have read and will read the same works differently than I have. My regret-focused readings are undoubtedly shaped by other subjective factors—especially my own personal and social history. This does not mean either that my readings therefore lack value to anyone else, or that one reading is "just as good as" any other reading. This is also not to negate the purely aesthetic value of these works. I also do not mean to deny the possible specific contribution of literary style to knowledge, although this is something I pass over, except for the fact of doing it honor through

direct quotation. In sum, in this volume I am addressing literature in a frankly instrumental, frankly subjective, frankly constructed mode as a rich source of insight into regret.

4. Frye, N. (1957). *Anatomy of criticism: Four essays.* Princeton, NJ: Princeton University Press.

5. Steiner, G. (1961). *The death of tragedy.* New York: Hill and Wang.

6. Schafer, R. (1976). *A new language for psychoanalysis.* New Haven, Conn.: Yale University Press, p. 23.

7. Schafer, p. 55.

8. Schafer, p. 26.

9. McAdams, D. P. (1985). *Power, intimacy, and the life story: Personological inquiries into identity.* Homewood, Ill.: Dorsey Press.

10. Meehl, P.E. (1979). A funny thing happened to us on the way to the latent entities. *Journal of Personality Assessment, 43,* 564–581; Mendelsohn, G., Weiss, D., & Feimer, N. (1982). Conceptual and empirical analysis of the typological implications of patterns of socialization and femininity. *Journal of Personality and Social Psychology, 42,* 1157–1170.

11. Mendelsohn, Weiss, & Feimer, p. 1167.

12. For a model of the empirical testing of these stances with respect to the psychological constructs of intimacy and power, see McAdams.

13. McAdams, p. 92.

14. McAdams, p. 92.

15. Schafer, p. 36.

16. Schafer, p. 35.

17. Schafer, p. 35.

18. Schafer, p. 35.

19. McAdams, p. 92.

20. Steiner, pp. 6–8.

21. Schafer, p. 36.

22. Schafer, p. 35.

23. Schafer, p. 35.

24. Schafer, p. 35.

25. McAdams, p. 93.

26. Steiner, pp. 6–8.

27. Schafer, p. 46.

28. Pip is not the only character in *Great Expectations* afflicted with regret for past acts. Miss Havisham, for example, hideously wastes her own life and deforms that of her charge, Estella, by giving herself up to vengeful fury for having been abandoned on her wedding day. Eventually, though, Miss Havisham comes to regret the fact that she has succeeded in creating in Estella a monster devoid of human feelings, even toward Miss Havisham herself. Miss Havisham could be viewed as almost a stock personification of regret without transcendence. For the present purposes, however, it is sufficient to focus on Pip's regret.

29. Dickens, C. (1861/1978). *Great expectations.* New York: Oxford University Press, p. 125.

30. Dickens, p. 258.

31. Dickens, p. 340.

32. Broyard, A. (1988, May 15). All the comforts of Dickens. *New York Times Book Review*, p. 13.

33. Baldwin's passage is cited in Levinson, D. (with C. N. Darrow, E. B. Klein, M. H. Levinson, B. McKee). (1978). *The seasons of a man's life.* New York: Knopf, p. 250.

34. To my astonishment, I retrospectively stumbled upon some validation for my associating a bridge with Baldwin's chasm. In his story "Sonny's Blues," Baldwin himself connects the images of chasm and bridge. He writes: "The seven years' difference in our ages lay between us like a chasm: I wondered if these years would ever operate between us as a
bridge."

35. James, H. (1903/1963). *The ambassadors.* New York: Heritage Press, p. vi.

36. James, H., p. 55.

37. James, H., p. 41.

38. James, H., p. 54.

39. James, H., p. 54.

40. Rorty, A. O. (Ed.) (1980). *Explaining emotions.* Berkeley: University of California Press.

41. Schafer, p. 29.

42. I thank Sidney Warshausky for this insight.

43. Ephron, N. (1986, November 2). Revision and life: Take it from the top—again. *New York Times Book Review*, p. 7.

44. Dostoevsky, F. (1864/1981). *Notes from underground.* New York: Bantam, p. 152.

45. Rorty, A.

46. Dostoevsky, p. 127.

47. Dostoevsky, p. 128.

48. Dostoevsky, p. 147.

49. Dostoevsky, p. 12.

50. Dostoevsky, p. 10.

51. Dostoevsky, p. 7.

52. Dostoevsky, p. 11.

53. The Socratic principle is discussed in detail in Chapter 5.

54. Dostoevsky, p. 21.

55. Dostoevsky, p. 31.

56. Dostoevsky, p. 7.

57. Dostoevsky, p. 7.

58. Dostoevsky, p. 14.

59. Frank, J. (1986). *Dostoevsky: The stir of liberation, 1860–1865.* Princeton, NJ: Princeton University Press.

60. Dostoevsky, p. 13.

61. Dostoevsky, p. 65.

62. According to J. Frank, Dostoevsky was parodying the social romanticism of his day via the well-known fantasy of rescuing the good-hearted prostitute.

63. This is not to deny the importance of Dostoevsky's critique of the science-based belief in a rational, materialistic, deterministic trajectory toward utopian progress. This critique is exemplified in the Underground Man's rejection of the Crystal Palace—understood as an actual edifice constructed to celebrate this trajectory for the London World's Fair in 1851. For a thorough discussion of this aspect of the Crystal-Palace reference, see J. Frank.

64. Dostoevsky, p. 14.

65. This requires, however, a qualification, for the protagonist never holds on for long to this self-serving conviction, but instead slides over into self-lacerating recognition of the internal origins of his fate: "you are somehow even to blame for the stone wall." This complex position arises from Dostoevsky's bouncing back and forth between a critique of the variety of scientistic determinism that denies "free will" and his recognition of the limitations of free will (See J. Frank). But sensitivity to the limits of free will is a hallmark of both the ironic and the tragic worldviews. We see further manifestations of a primarily ironic and tragic disposition in the narrator's acute responsiveness to human dilemmas, paradoxes, ambiguities, and uncertainties, as evidenced by his tortured explanations of how he takes perverse pleasure in his miserable regrets, for example.

66. Barrie, J. M. (1922). *Dear Brutus: A comedy in three acts.* New York: Scribner's, p. 77.

67. Barrie, p. 78.

68. Hemingway, E. (1963). *The snows of Kilimanjaro and other stories.* Middlesex, England: Penguin Books, p. 9.

69. Hemingway, p. 15.

70. Smith, T. R. (Ed.) (1919). *Baudelaire: His prose and poetry* (F. P. Sturm, Trans.). New York: Modern Poetry.

71. Dickinson, E. (1983). *The complete poems of Emily Dickinson* (T. H. Johnson, Ed). Cambridge, Mass.: Harvard University Press, p. 365.

72. Beckett, S. (1958/1984). *Krapp's last tape.* In *Collected shorter plays: Samuel Beckett.* New York: Grove Press, p. 62.

73. Beckett, p. 63.

74. Dinesen, I. (1937). *Out of Africa.* New York: Vintage, 1985, p. 231.

75. Wideman, J. E. (1984). *Brothers and keepers.* New York: Holt, Rinehart & Winston, p. 152.

76. Lampedusa, G. di. (1960). *The Leopard* (A. Colquhoun, Trans.). New York: Pantheon, p. 116.

77. Galassi, J. (1984, October). Still life. *Atlantic,* p. 90.

78. I am grateful to Jonathan Galassi for taking the time to share with me his own thoughts on the role of regret in "Still Life" (personal communication, October 2, 1992).

79. Woolf, V. (1925). *Mrs. Dalloway*. New York: Harcourt, Brace, & World, p. 9.

80. Woolf, p. 114.

81. Woolf, p. 14.

82. Woolf, p. 70.

83. Woolf, p. 71.

84. Woolf, pp. 62–63.

85. Woolf, p. 63.

86. Woolf, p. 64.

87. Schafer, p. 35.

88. Schafer, p. 36.

89. Woolf, p. 10.

90. Woolf, p. 70.

91. Woolf, p. 115.

92. Woolf, p. 73.

93. Woolf, p. 73.

94. Woolf, p. 62.

95. Eliot, T. S. (1952). *The complete poems and plays: 1909–1950*. New York: Brace & World, 1971, p. 117.

96. Tyler, A. (1988). *Breathing lessons*. New York: Knopf, p. 125.

97. Tyler, p. 166, emphasis in original.

98. McAdams, p. 93.

99. Tyler, p. 129.

100. Steiner, p. 8.

101. Tyler, p. 327.

4. Regrets? I've Had a Few: What We Regret Most

1. Sandelands, L. E. (1988). The concept of work feeling. *Journal for the Theory of Social Behaviour, 18,* 437–457.

2. Shimanoff, S. B. (1984). Commonly named emotions in everyday conversations. *Perceptual and Motor Skills, 58,* 514.

3. Elsewhere I have suggested that although these survey questions were intended to elicit regrets, they are better understood as having elicited counterfactual thoughts, or thoughts about possible but unactualized states (See Landman, J., Vandewater, E., Stewart, A., & Malley, J. [Under review]. Missed opportunities: Ramifications of counterfactual thought). First, the questions do not directly inquire about regret per se. Second, the questions do not appear to address specifically the rather painful psychological state that is regret. It is conceivable that people might idly speculate what would have happened had they done something different, while experiencing little or no regret regarding what they did. This seems to be the case with a character in a recent short story by Allen Barnett: "I don't have any regrets, but sometimes I wonder if you had come to New York when I asked you to, if things would be different now" (cited by Wolitzer,

M. [1990, July 15]. Review of *The body and its dangers. New York Times Book Review*, p. 17]. Still, these questions do seem to get at something rather close to regret, defined as distress over a desire unfulfilled or an action performed or not performed.

4. Erskine, H. (1973). The polls: Hopes, fears, and regrets. *Public Opinion Quarterly, 37,* 132–145.

5. Erskine.

6. Erskine.

7. Landman, J., & Manis, J. D. (1992). What might have been: Counterfactual thought concerning personal decisions. *British Journal of Psychology, 83,* 473–477.

8. Kinnier, R. T., & Metha, A. T. (1989). Regrets and priorities at three stages of life. *Counseling and Values, 33,* 182–193.

9. Erskine.

10. Landman & Manis, J.

11. Kinnier & Metha.

12. Erskine.

13. Kinnier & Mehta.

14. Landman & Manis, J.

15. Erskine.

16. Erskine.

17. Landman & Manis, J.

18. Moracco, J. C., D'Arienzo, R. V., & Danford, D. (1983). Comparison of perceived occupational stress between teachers who are contented and discontented in their career choices. *The Vocational Guidance Quarterly, 32,* 44–51.

19. Wills, G. (1983, February 20). An American family [Review of *Descent from glory*]. *New York Times Book Review*, p. 1.

20. Sears, P. S. (1979). The Terman genetic studies of genius, 1922–1972. In A. H. Passow (Ed.), *The gifted and the talented: Their education and development.* The 78th Yearbook of the National Society for the Study of Education, Part I. Chicago: University of Chicago Press.

21. Landman & Manis, J.

22. Erskine.

23. Landman & Manis, J.

24. Brans, J., & Taylor Smith, M. (1987). *Mother, I have something to tell you.* New York: Doubleday.

25. Landman & Manis, J.

26. Loewenstein, S. F., Bloch, N. E., Campion, J., Epstein, J. S., & Salvatore, M. (1981). A study of satisfactions and stresses of single women in midlife. *Sex Roles, 7,* 1127–1141.

27. Berkun, C. S. (1986). In behalf of women over 40: Understanding the importance of the menopause. *Social Work, 31* (5), 378–384.

28. Berkun, p. 382.

29. Landman & Manis, J.

30. Landman & Manis, J.

31. Freud, S. (1907). The manifest content of dreams and the latent dream-thoughts. *Introductory lectures on psychoanalysis*. (J. Strachey, Ed. & Trans.). New York: Norton, 1966.

32. Kinnier & Metha.

33. Erskine.

34. Miller, W. B., & Shain, R. N. (1985). Married women and contraceptive sterilization: Factors that contribute to pre-surgical ambivalence. *Journal of Biosocial Sciences, 17*, p. 471.

35. Romans-Clarkson, S. E., & Gillett, W. R. (1987). Women who regret their sterilization: Developmental considerations. *Journal of Psychosomatic Obstetrics and Gynaecology, 7*, 9–17.

36. Shain, R. N., Miller, W. P., & Holden, A. E. C. (1984). The decision to terminate childbearing: Differences in preoperative ambivalence between tubal ligation women and vasectomy wives. *Social Biology, 31* (1–2), 40–58.

37. Cooper, J. E., Bledin, K. D., Brice, B., & Mackenzie, S. (1985). Effects of female sterilization: One year follow-up in a prospective controlled study of psychological and psychiatric outcome. *Journal of Psychosomatic Research, 29*, 13–22.

38. Kopit, S., & Barnes, A. B. (1976). Patients' response to tubal division. *Journal of American Medical Association, 236*, 2761–2763.

39. Erskine.

40. DeLillo, D. (1986). *White noise.* New York: Penguin, p. 283.

41. Montaigne, M. de. (1580/1936). Of repentance. *The essays of Michel de Montaigne.* J. Zeitlin (Trans.). Vol III. New York: Knopf; Solomon, R. C. (1976). *The passions: The myth and nature of human emotion.* Notre Dame, Ind.: The University of Notre Dame Press.

42. Roseman, I. J., Spindel, M. S., & Jose, P. E. (1990). Appraisals of emotion-eliciting events: Testing a theory of discrete emotions. *Journal of Personality and Social Psychology, 59*, 899–915; Taylor, G. (1985). *Pride, shame and guilt: Emotions of self-assessment.* New York: Clarendon Press, Oxford University Press; Thalberg, I. (1963). Remorse. *Mind, 72*, 545–555.

43. Roseman, I. J. (1991). Appraisal determinants of discrete emotions. *Cognition and Emotion, 5*, 161–200.

44. Rorty, A. O. (Ed.) (1980). *Explaining emotions.* Berkeley: University of California Press.

45. Rorty, A.

46. Silber, J. R. (1967). Being and doing: A study of status responsibility and voluntary responsibility. *University of Chicago Law Review, 35*, 47–91.

47. Barrie, J. M. (1922). *Dear Brutus: A comedy in three acts.* New York: Scribner's, p. 109.

48. James, H. (1903/1963). *The ambassadors.* New York: Heritage Press, p. vi.

49. James, H., p. 54.

50. Rorty, A.

51. Dostoevsky, F. (1864/1981). *Notes from underground.* New York: Bantam, p. 7.

52. Ballou, J., & Bryson, J. (1983). The doing and undoing of surgical sterilization: A psychosocial profile of the tubal reimplantation patient. *Psychiatry, 46,* 161–171.

53. Rorty, A.

54. Ionesco, E. (1940–41/1971). *Present past, past present: A personal memoir* (H. R. Lane, Trans.). New York: Grove, p. 30.

55. Markus, H. R., & Kitayama, S. (1991). Culture and the self: Implications for cognition, emotion, and motivation. *Psychological Review, 98,* 224–253; and Stipek, D., Weiner, B., & Li, K. (1989). Testing some attribution-emotion relations in the People's Republic of China. *Journal of Personality and Social Psychology, 56,* 109–116.

56. Gordon, S. L. (1990). Social structural effects on emotions. In T. D. Kemper (Ed.). *Research agendas in the sociology of emotions* (pp. 145–179). Albany: State University of New York Press.

57. Price, M. H. (1992, February 9). Author reflects on screen adaptation of his novel. *Ann Arbor News,* E5.

58. Bartlett, J. (1980). *Familiar quotations.* E. M. Beck (Ed.), 15th ed. Boston: Little, Brown.

59. Maxwell, W. (1992, December 7). What he was like. *The New Yorker,* p. 122.

60. Dapkus, M. (1985). A thematic analysis of the experience of time. *Journal of Personality and Social Psychology, 49,* 408–419.

61. *Ann Arbor News,* September 18, 1989.

62. Merwin, W. S. (1973). *Writings to an unfinished accompaniment.* New York: Atheneum.

63. They are, in chronological order: Kahneman, D., & Tversky, A. (1982a). The psychology of preferences. *Scientific American, 246,* 160–173; Landman, J. (1987a). Regret and elation following action and inaction: Affective responses to positive versus negative outcomes. *Personality and Social Psychology Bulletin, 13,* 524–536; Gleicher, F., Kost, K. A., Baker, S. M., Strathman, A., Richman, S. A., & Sherman, S. J. (1990). The role of counterfactual thinking in judgments of affect. *Personality and Social Psychology Bulletin, 16,* 2284–295.

64. Kahneman & Tversky, The psychology.

65. Landman, Regret and elation.

66. Doug Hofstadter (personal communication, April 8, 1987) has convincingly argued with me that these experimental conditions do not unequivocally operationalize inaction. To decide to remain in a particular section of a course, to stay in a particular job, to return to a familiar vacation spot does not represent inaction. He has suggested to me that these experimental results would be better framed not in terms of action versus inaction, but in terms of "thwarted destiny" versus "destiny." In his reformulation, those who remain on their earlier-chosen path would be described as having submitted to destiny, and those who diverge from their

earlier-chosen path would be described as having made an active attempt to thwart destiny. The "destiny effect" can be represented graphically like this:

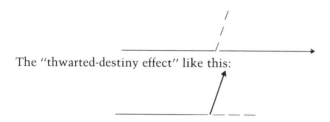

The "thwarted-destiny effect" like this:

Although his point about the arguable conceptual validity of the operationalization of inaction is well taken, I believe that in this culture the term "destiny" would raise as many questions as it is designed to quell. Ritov and Baron's way of framing this issue in terms of keeping or changing the status quo does a good job of finessing the problem (cf. Ritov, I., & Baron, J. [1990]. Reluctance to vaccinate: Omission bias and ambiguity. *Journal of Behavioral Decision Making, 3*, 263–277). But, for the time being, I have retained the currently more conventional action/inaction label.

67. Kahneman, D., & Miller, D. T. (1986). Norm theory: Comparing reality to its alternatives. *Psychological Review, 93*, 136–153.

68. None of the previous studies has directly tested Kahneman and Miller's hypothesis that differential counterfactual thinking was the operative process underlying the differential regret.

69. Fazio, R., Sherman, S. J., & Herr, P. M. (1982). The feature-positive effect in the self-perception process: Does not doing matter as much as doing? *Journal of Personality and Social Psychology, 42*, 404–411; Hearst, E. (1984a). Absence as information: Some implications for learning, performance, and representational processes. In H. L. Roitblat, T. B. Bever, & H. S. Terrace (Eds.), *Animal cognition.* Hillsdale, NJ: Lawrence Erlbaum; Hearst, E. (1984b, April 4). *Empty intervals and absent events: Something about nothing in the psychology of animals and people.* Distinguished faculty research lecture, Indiana University, Bloomington; Jenkins, H. M., & Sainsbury, R. S. (1970). Discrimination learning with the distinctive feature on positive or negative trials. In D. Mostofsky (Ed.), *Attention: Contemporary theory and analysis.* New York: Appleton-Century-Crofts; Sainsbury, R. S. (1973). Discrimination learning using positive or negative cues. *Canadian Journal of Psychology, 27*, 46–57; Nisbett, R., & Ross, L. (1980). *Human inference: Strategies and shortcomings of social judgment.* Englewood Cliffs, New Jersey: Prentice-Hall; Ross, L. (1977). The intuitive psychologist and his shortcomings: Distortions in the attribution process. In L. Berkowitz (Ed.), *Advances in experimental social psychology* (Vol. 10). New York: Academic Press; Wason, P. D., & Johnson-Laird, P. N. (1965). *Psychology of reasoning: Structure and content.* London: Batsford.

70. Ritov, I., & Baron, J. (1990). Reluctance to vaccinate: Omission bias and ambiguity. *Journal of Behavioral Decision Making, 3,* 263–277.

71. Tavris, C. (1988, August). Chasing life dreams. *Vogue,* p. 236.

72. Streshinsky, S. (1985, April). The road not taken. *Glamour,* p. 194.

73. Kuralt, C. (1990). Regrets. *A life on the road.* New York: G. P. Putnam's Sons, p. 245.

74. Kuralt, p. 247.

75. Kuralt, p. 250.

76. It appears that the hypothesis about the importance of time perspective has been borne out by empirical research not yet published. Psychologist Thomas Gilovich and his colleagues recently conducted studies that indirectly suggest that action is more regretted at the time but inaction is more regretted as time passes: Gilovich, T., Medvec, V. H., & Chen, S. (1993). Commission, omission, and dissonance reduction: Coping with regret in the three-doors problem; and Gilovich, T., Kerr, M., & Medvec, V. H. (1993). The effect of temporal perspective on subjective confidence.

77. Kinnier & Metha.

78. Ionesco, p. 131.

79. Ambiguities like these again demonstrate the limitations of experimental and survey studies as methods for delineating the nuances of regret. Face-to-face interviews might offer a better toehold for exploring exactly how it is that we experience our regrets, whether in terms of character, agency (self, other, circumstance), referent (self, other), omission, or other categories. However, the problem of the sheer inexhaustibility of description will always hamper attempts at neat categorization. What we regret can be framed in an infinite number of ways, depending on the specific angle of refraction taken.

80. I am addressing such questions through ongoing research.

5. The Logic of Regret: Its Role in Decision Making

1. I am grateful to Sidney Gendin for this distinction.

2. Luckhardt, C. G. (1975). Remorse, regret and the Socratic paradox. *Analysis, 35,* p. 159.

3. The examples of the idle rich and the unemployed poor come from a book by economist Tibor Scitovsky. (1992). *The joyless economy: The psychology of human satisfaction* (Rev. ed.). New York: Oxford University Press. I thank Hal Arkes for directing me to this book and for reminding me of the distinction between moral and pragmatic decisions, sometimes referred to as the difference between the right and the good.

4. Jungermann, H. (1986). The two camps on rationality. In H. R. Arkes, and K. R. Hammond (Eds.), *Judgment and decision making: An interdisciplinary reader* (pp. 627–641). New York: Cambridge University Press.

5. Luckhardt.

6. Luckhardt.

7. Hampshire, S. (1960). *Thought and action*. New York: Viking.

8. Luckhardt, p. 165.

9. Luckhardt, p. 165.

10. Sartre, J.-P. (1956). *Being and nothingness* (H. E. Barnes, Trans.). New York: Washington Square Books.

11. Jacobs, W. (1976). What Professor Luckhardt cannot regret. *Philosophical Research Archives, 2* (1104), 671–677.

12. Rorty, A. O. (Ed.) (1980). *Explaining emotions*. Berkeley: University of California Press.

13. Jacobs.

14. I am grateful to Joan Bossert for these examples.

15. Jacobs.

16. Luckhardt, p. 160.

17. Stocker, M. (1987). Moral conflicts: What they are and what they show. *Pacific Philosophical Quarterly, 68,* 104–123.

18. Taylor, G. (1985). *Pride, shame and guilt: Emotions of self-assessment*. New York: Clarendon Press, Oxford University Press.

19. Stocker, Moral conflicts, p. 118, emphasis added.

20. Stocker, Moral conflicts, p. 114.

21. Mill, J. S. (1859). *On liberty. Great Books of the Western World.* Vol. 43 (pp. 267–323). Chicago: Encyclopaedia Britannica, 1952, p. 295.

22. It would go beyond the scope of this volume to consider separately all the forms of standard decision theory, such as its behavioral and nonbehavioral variants, egoistic and interpersonal variants, variants that do or do not include a summative criterion across interpersonal utilities, etc. The important point for this analysis is the nonexistence of a single umbrella version capable of disabling all criticisms.

23. Machina, M. J. (1987). Decision-making in the presence of risk. *Science, 236,* p. 537.

24. Herrnstein, R. J. (1990). Rational choice theory: Necessary but not sufficient. *American Psychologist, 45,* p. 356.

25. Abelson, R. P., & Levi, A. (1985). Decision making and decision theory. In G. Lindzey & E. Aronson (Eds.), *Handbook of Social Psychology, Vol. I: Theory and Method* (pp. 231–309). New York: Random House, p. 244.

26. Coombs, C. H., Dawes, R. M., & Tversky, A. (1970). *Mathematical psychology*. Englewood Cliffs, NJ: Prentice-Hall.

27. Edwards, W., & von Winterfeldt, D. (1986). On cognitive illusions and their implications. In H. R. Arkes, & K. R. Hammond (Eds.). *Judgment and decision making: An interdisciplinary reader* (pp. 642–679). New York: Cambridge University Press, p. 663.

28. Savage, L. J. (1951). The theory of statistical decision. *Journal of the American Statistical Association, 46,* 55–67.

29. Simon, H. A. (1986). Alternative visions of rationality. In H. R. Arkes, & K. R. Hammond (Eds), *Judgment and decision making: An inter-*

disciplinary reader (pp. 97–113). New York: Cambridge University Press, p. 112.

30. Simon, Alternative visions, p. 99.

31. von Neumann, J., & Morgenstern, O. (1953). *Theory of games and economic behavior.* Princeton, NJ: Princeton University Press.

32. Arkes, H. R., & Hammond, K. R. (1986). General introduction. In H. R. Arkes, & K. R. Hammond (Eds.), *Judgment and decision making: An interdisciplinary reader* (pp.1–10). New York: Cambridge University Press.

33. One could argue that these potentials are not independent of one another. Patients who are sick enough to die in surgery may be less likely than others to experience no change without surgery, for instance. The present analysis assumes independence of probable outcomes (Dawes, personal communication, July 24, 1991).

34. Resnik, M. D. (1987). *Choices: An introduction to decision theory.* Minneapolis: University of Minnesota Press.

35. This decision is not entirely conventional, in that the options are not mutually exclusive or exhaustive, and in that the subjective probabilities sum to more than 1. But it is consistent with certain versions of SEU theory without these requirements (cf. Edwards, W. [1962]. Subjective probabilities inferred from decisions. *Psychological Review, 69,* 109–135).

36. Dawes, R. M. (1988). *Rational choice in an uncertain world.* San Diego: Harcourt Brace Jovanovich.

37. Williams, B. A. O. (1965). Ethical consistency. *Aristotelian Society, 39,* p. 110. Regret is irrational if it is based on the hindsight bias—the overestimation of one's ability, once an outcome is known, to have predicted it ahead of time. But hindsight bias does not apply whenever one's regret is based on accurate recall of the probabilities of the relevant outcomes.

38. Stocker, Moral conflicts.

39. Stocker, M. (1979). Desiring the bad: An essay in moral psychology. *The Journal of Philosophy, 76,* p. 746, n.12.

40. See Smart's side of the argument, in Smart, J. J. C., & Williams, B. (1973). *Utilitarianism for and against.* London: Cambridge University Press.

41. Stocker, Desiring the bad.

42. March, J. G. (1978). Bounded rationality, ambiguity, and the engineering of choice. *The Bell Journal of Economics, 9,* 587–608.

43. Festinger, L. (1957). *A theory of cognitive dissonance.* Evanston, Ill.: Row, Peterson; Festinger, L. (1964). *Conflict, decision, and dissonance.* Stanford, Calif.: Stanford University Press; Aronson, E. (1969). The theory of cognitive dissonance: A current perspective. In L. Berkowitz (Ed.), *Advances in experimental Social Psychology,* Vol. 4 (pp. 1–34). New York: Academic Press.

44. F. Scott Fitzgerald. In Correct Quotes. (1990–1991). WordStar software. Novato, Cal.: WordStar International, Inc.

45. Stocker, Desiring the bad, pp. 753 and 750, respectively.

46. Stocker, Desiring the bad, p. 752.

47. For a broad review, see, for example: Aronson, E. (1969). The theory of cognitive dissonance: A current perspective. In L. Berkowitz (Ed.), *Advances in experimental social psychology*, Vol. 4 (pp. 1–34). New York: Academic Press.

48. Festinger, L., & Walster, E. (1964). Post-decision regret and decision reversal. In L. Festinger (Ed.), *Conflict, decision, and dissonance* (pp. 112–127). Stanford, Cal.: Stanford University Press.

49. Thaler, R. (1980). Toward a positive theory of consumer choice. *Journal of Economic Behavior and Organization, 1*, p. 58.

50. Simon, Alternative visions, p. 112.

51. Hampshire.

52. Tversky, A., & Kahneman, D. (1981). The framing of decisions and the psychology of choice. *Science, 211*, 453–458; Tversky, A., & Kahneman, D. (1986). Rational choice and the framing of decisions. *Journal of Business, 59*, S251–S278.

53. Hampshire.

54. Simon, Alternative visions, p. 109.

55. Dawes, *Rational choice*; Kahneman, D., & Tversky, A. (1982a). The psychology of preferences. *Scientific American, 246*, 160–173; Kahneman, D., & Tversky, A. (1982b). The simulation heuristic. In D. Kahneman, P. Slovic, & A. Tversky (Eds.), *Judgment under uncertainty: Heuristics and biases*. New York: Cambridge University Press; Nisbett, R., & Ross, L. (1980). *Human inference: Strategies and shortcomings of social judgment*. Englewood Cliffs, New Jersey: Prentice-Hall.

56. Tversky & Kahneman, The framing of decisions; Tversky & Kahneman, Rational choice.

57. Tversky, A., Sattath, S., & Slovic, P. (1988). Contingent weighting in judgment and choice. *Psychological Review, 95*, 371–384.

58. Bruner, J. (1992). Another look at New Look 1. *American Psychologist, 47*, 780–783; Erdelyi, M. H. (1992). Psychodynamics and the unconscious. *American Psychologist, 47*, 784–787; Greenwald, A. G. (1992). New Look 3: Unconscious cognition reclaimed. *American Psychologist, 47*, 766–779; Jacoby, L. L., Lindsay, D. S., & Toth, J. P. (1992). Unconscious influences revealed: Attention, awareness, and control. *American Psychologist, 47*, 802–809; Kihlstrom, J. F., Barnhyardt, T. M., & Tataryn, D. J. (1992). The psychological unconscious: Found, lost, and regained. *American Psychologist, 47*, 788–791; Lewicki, P., Hill, T., & Czyzewska, M. (1992). Nonconscious acquisition of information. *American Psychologist, 47*, 796–801; Loftus, E. F., & Klinger, M. R. (1992). Is the unconscious smart or dumb? *American Psychologist, 47*, 761–765; Merikle, P. M. (1992). Perception without awareness: Critical issues. *American Psychologist, 47*, 792–795; Nisbett, R. E., & Wilson, T. D. (1977). Telling more than we can know: Verbal reports on mental processes. *Psychological Review, 84*, 231–259.

59. Cited in Gleick, J. (1987). *Chaos: Making a new science.* New York: Penguin, p. 273.

60. Simon, H. A. (1979). *Models of thought.* New Haven, Conn.: Yale University Press; and Simon, Alternative visions.

61. Simon, Alternative visions, p. 112.

62. Simon, Alternative visions, p. 101.

63. von Winterfeldt, D., & Edwards, W. (1986). *Decision analysis and behavioral research.* New York: Cambridge University Press.

64. Hal Arkes, personal communication, January 26, 1993.

65. Anderson, E. (1988, September 27). Rational choice and social behavior: A philosophical perspective. Presentation to Group Dynamics Seminar, University of Michigan, Ann Arbor.

66. Sen, A. K. (1977). Rational fools: A critique of the behavioral foundations of economic theory. *Philosophy and Public Affairs, 6,* 317–344.

67. Some decision theorists disagree that the revealed-preferences approach lacks proper constraints. For example, Dawes (personal communication, August 24, 1990) argues that a behavioral definition of preferences "prohibits certain choices: For example, a willingness to pay more for A than for B while simultaneously preferring B to A as an anonymous gift, reversing the choice A and B when they are framed in different ways that do not affect potential consequences, etc."

68. Fischhoff, Goitein, & Shapira, (1982), cited by Jungermann, H. (1986). The two camps on rationality. In H. R. Arkes, & K. R. Hammond (Eds.), *Judgment and decision making: An interdisciplinary reader* (pp. 627–641). New York: Cambridge University Press, p. 639.

69. Dawes, *Rational choice,* p. 63.

70. Robyn Dawes, personal communication, July 24, 1991.

71. See Smart's side of the argument, in Smart, J. J. C., & Williams, B. (1973). *Utilitarianism for and against.* London: Cambridge University Press.

72. See Williams's side of the argument, in Smart & Williams.

73. Walster, G. W., & Walster, E. (1970). Choice between negative alternatives: Dissonance reduction or regret? *Psychological Reports, 26,* 995–1005.

74. I am referring here to the research on the Prisoner's Dilemma. See, for instance, Hacking, I. (1984, June 28). Winner take less. [Review of *The evolution of cooperation*]. *New York Review of Books;* Hollis, M. (1979). Rational man and social science. In H. Ross (Ed.), *Rational action* (pp. 1–16). Cambridge: Cambridge University Press; Rapoport, A. (1960). *Fights, games, and debates.* Ann Arbor: University of Michigan Press; Rapoport, A., & Chammah, A. M. (1965). *Prisoner's dilemma.* Ann Arbor: University of Michigan Press. Some may argue that the results of Prisoner's Dilemma research do not reveal a weakness of economic decision theory but a tragedy inherent in the world (Hal Arkes, personal communication, January 26, 1993). The theory is not undercut insofar as it is capable of handling

whatever values are put into it—*either* those of a particular individual, *or* those of a society—but not necessarily both. But as I understand it, the claims of economic decision theory have historically been grander than this.

75. I thank Joan Bossert for this idea.

76. Anderson, Rational choice.

77. Smart & Williams.

78. Nussbaum, M. C. (1990). *Love's knowledge.* New York: Oxford University Press, p. 56.

79. Nussbaum's definition of metricity illuminates what was for me for some time inexplicable—the classic assertion of the logical absurdity (and thus nonexistence) of akrasia, weakness of will: "It is like saying, 'A, offered the choice between $50 and $200, chose the $50, because she was overcome by the quantity of the $50.' And that does seem absurd. In short, notions of *amount* and of quantitative homogeneity seem to be doing some work here in producing the absurd result." (See Nussbaum, p. 109, emphasis in original.)

80. Anderson, E. (1990). Some problems in the normative theory of rational choice with consequences for empirical research. Unpublished manuscript, p. 7.

81. Anderson, Some problems.

82. Anderson, Some problems, p. 8.

83. Sen, p. 325.

84. Edwards and von Winterfeldt, for example, define the transitivity axiom (and other axioms) as "rules of behavior that no one would wish to violate *if the stakes are high.*" (See Edwards & von Winterfeldt, p. 662, emphasis added.)

85. Another example of rational intransitivity is the Allais paradox. The Allais paradox is based on the following sort of choice outlined by Rapoport. (See Rapoport, A. [1989]. Comments on a behavioral decision teory paradox. *Behavioral Science, 34,* p. 289):

Alternative	Outcome	Probability
Choice 1 or — A₁	$10,000	1.00
— B₁ or	$20,000	.50
	$0	.50
Choice 2 or — A₂ or	$10,000	.02
	$0	.98
— B₂ or	$20,000	.01
	$0	.99

The paradox is that some people when given Choice 1 prefer A_1, the "bird-in-the-hand" choice (Resnik, p. 103) of winning $10,000 for sure, over B_1, a 50–50 chance of winning either $20,000 or nothing. Then when these same people are faced with Choice 2, they prefer B_2. This is inconsistent, or intransitive, because "to prefer A_1 to B_1 means to decline the chance of winning twice as much with a probability half as large" (Rapoport, p. 290) . . . but "to prefer B_2 to A_2 means to prefer a chance of winning twice as much with probability half as large" (ibid). It seems to me that the Allais paradox may be partially explainable in terms of context effects. Even though it is true that 1% is half as large a probability as 2% and that 50% is half as large a probability as 100%, as probability-pairs these may function as significantly different psychological contexts, leading to nontransitive choices. The Allais paradox has also been explained in terms of regret, as will be discussed later in this chapter.

86. Tversky, A. (1969). Intransitivity of preferences. *Psychological Review, 76,* 31–48.

87. Anderson, Some problems, p. 9.

88. Raz, J. (1986). *The morality of freedom.* New York: Oxford University Press, p. 324.

89. Greenspan, P. S. (1980). A case of mixed feelings: Ambivalence and the logic of emotion. In A. O. Rorty (Ed.), *Explaining Emotion* (pp. 223–250). Berkeley: University of California Press, p. 223.

90. March, p. 597.

91. Greenspan, p. 228.

92. Rorty, A., p. 494.

93. Greenspan, p. 232.

94. Greenspan, p. 232.

95. Greenspan, p. 243, emphasis in original.

96. Greenspan.

97. Greenspan, p. 237, emphasis in original.

98. Greenspan, p. 240.

99. Of course, social and interpersonal relations are also enhanced by our ability to rationally control our *behavior.* So, we might decide not to vent the unhappiness side of our ambivalence during the congratulatory party for our friend, but only in the privacy of our diary. In other words, we are in greater rational control of our behavior than of our emotions per se. But that is another issue.

100. Raz, p. 322.

101. Raz, pp. 348–349.

102. Behavioral (or act-centered) decision theorists would argue that loved ones and money are not incommensurable values, and that they can prove it by looking at people's choices. Because people do sometimes choose to be parted from a spouse, for example, to leave home for days, weeks, or even longer as part of a job or career (See Raz), they claim, people are demonstrating that it is possible to compare the two values. Raz answers: "saying

that two options are incommensurate does not preclude choice. Rational action is action for (what the agent takes to be) an undefeated reason. It is not necessarily action for a reason which defeats all others" (p. 339).

103. Raz, p. 325.

104. Although silent on incommensurability, decision theory agrees with Raz with respect to indifference: "a careful check of the axioms indicates that indifference need not be transitive. (The technical interpretation can be awkwardly phrased as 'is not unpreferred to.' " (Robyn Dawes, personal communication, August 24, 1990).

105. Williams, Ethical consistency.

106. Whitehead, J. W. (1991). The forgotten limits: Reason and regulation in economic theory. In K. R. Monroe (Ed.), *The economic approach to politics: A critical reassessment of the theory of rational action* (pp. 53–73). New York: HarperCollins.

107. Raz.

108. Sen, p. 336, emphasis in original.

109. Whitman, W. (1978). Song of myself. In N. Sullivan (Ed.), *The treasury of American poetry*. Garden City, NY: Doubleday, p. 256.

110. Emerson. *Correct quotes* (1990–1991). WordStar software. Novato, Calif.: WordStar International, Inc.

111. Smart, in Smart & Williams, p. 40.

112. Williams, in Smart & Williams, p. 113.

113. Sen.

114. Cited in *The New Yorker*, January 29, 1990, p. 95.

115. Anderson, Some problems, p. 17.

116. Banville, J. (1992, May 14). Playing house. [Review of M. Frayn's *A landing on the sun.*] *New York Review of Books*, p. 42.

117. Stocker, Moral conflicts, p. 121.

118. Tversky & Kahneman, Rational choice, p. S272.

119. Tversky & Kahneman, Rational choice, p. S252.

120. Harding, S. (1991). *Whose science? Whose knowledge?: Thinking from women's lives*. Ithaca, NY: Cornell University Press.

121. Nussbaum, p. 74.

122. Nussbaum, p. 75.

123. Nussbaum, p. 74.

124. March.

125. Simon, H.A. (1979). *Models of thought*. New Haven, Conn.: Yale University Press.

126. March, p. 592.

127. March, p. 599.

128. Elstein, A. S., Holzman, G. B., Ravitch, M. M., Metheny, W. A., Holmes, M. M., Hoppe, R. B., Rothert, M. L., & Rovner, D. R. (1986). Comparison of physicians' decisions regarding estrogen replacement therapy for menopausal women and decisions derived from a decision analytic model. *The American Journal of Medicine, 80*, 246–258.

129. Elstein, et al., p. 254.

130. Elstein, et al., p. 254.

131. Elstein, et al., p. 253.

132. Elstein, et al., p. 255.

133. See: Luce, R. D., & Raiffa, H. (1957). *Games and decisions: Introduction and critical survey.* New York: Wiley; and Savage.

134. Savage.

135. Savage.

136. Resnik.

137. Savage, p. 63.

138. McCauley, C., & Graham, N. (1971). Influence of values in risky decision making: A formalization. *Representative Research in Social Psychology, 2* (2), 3–11.

139. Myers, J. L., & Atkinson, R. C. (1964). Choice behavior and reward structure. *Journal of Mathematical Psychology, 1,* 170–203; Myers, J. L., Suydam, M. M., & Heuckeroth, O. (1966). Choice behavior and reward structure: Differential payoff. *Journal of Mathematical Psychology, 3,* 458–469; Reitsch, A. G. (1976). Selecting alpha by minimizing expected regret: An example. *Educational and Psychological Measurement, 36,* 675–678; Schoeffler, M. S. (1962). Prediction of some stochastic events: A regret equalization model. *Journal of Experimental Psychology, 64,* 615–622; Suydam, M. M. (1965). Effects of cost and gain ratios, and probability of outcome on ratings of alternative choices. *Journal of Mathematical Psychology, 2,* 171–179.

140. Grout, P. (1978). On minimax regret and welfare economics. *Journal of Public Economics, 9,* 405–410.

141. Rapoport, A. (1968). Choice behavior in a Markovian decision task. *Journal of Mathematical Psychology, 5,* 163–181.

142. McCauley & Graham.

143. Blackwell, D., & Girshick, M. A. (1954). *Theory of games and statistical decisions.* New York: Wiley.

144. Savage, p. 64.

145. Resnik, p. 30.

146. Savage, p. 63.

147. McCauley & Graham, p. 8.

148. Barron, F. H., & Mackenzie, K. D. (1973). A constrained optimization model of risky decisions. *Journal of Mathematical Psychology, 10,* 60–72.

149. But for a critical look at the action/inaction distinction, see the discussion in Chapter 4, Note 66.

150. Bell, D. E. (1980). Explaining utility theory paradoxes by decision regret. *Proceedings of the fourth international conference on multiple criteria decision making.* University of Delaware, Newark. August 10–15, 1980. New York: Springer-Verlag, 1981; Bell, D.E. (1982). Regret in decision making under uncertainty. *Operations Research, 30,* 961–981.

151. Loomes, G., & Sugden, R. (1982). Regret theory: An alternative

theory of rational choice under uncertainty. *The Economic Journal, 92,* 805–824; Sugden, R. (1985). Regret, recrimination and rationality. *Theory and Decision, 19,* 77–99.

152. Bell, Regret in decision, p. 963.

153. Lee, W. (1971a). Preference strength, expected value difference, and expected regret ratio. *Psychological Bulletin, 75,* 186–191; Lee, W. (1971b). The effects of expected value difference and expected regret ratio on preference strength. *American Journal of Psychology, 84,* 194–204.

154. There is some evidence that both factors affect choice independently (Lee, The effects).

155. Sage, A. P., & White, E. B. (1983). Decision and information structures in regret models of judgment and choice, *IEEE, SMC-13,* p. 144.

156. Loomes, G., & Sugden, R. (1987). Testing for regret and disappointment in choice under uncertainty. *The Economic Journal, 97,* p. 119.

157. Bell, Regret in decision.

158. Bell, Explaining utility theory; Sage & White, p. 144; Loomes & Sugden.

159. Sugden, Regret, recrimination.

160. One of these is the Allais paradox, discussed in Note 85. For years the pattern of choice shown in the Allais paradox puzzled orthodox decision theorists. It turns out, however, that regret reveals the reason in this paradox. "In Choice 1, if B_1 is chosen and nothing is won, regret is very strong, because in retrospect a chance of getting \$10,000 with certainty has been thrown away . . . In Choice 2, on the other hand, if B_2 is chosen and nothing is won, regret is not strong, since the chance of winning \$10,000 was very small to begin with. Thus, A_2 does not have the extra attraction that A_1 has" (Rapoport, 1989, p. 290). For other examples of decisions formerly considered irrational but now seen as explicable in regret terms see: Bell, Explaining utility theory; Loomes & Sugden, Regret theory; Machina, p. 537; Sage & White, p. 144.

161. Loomes, G. (1988). Further evidence of the impact of regret and disappointment in choice under uncertainty. *Economica, 55,* 47–62; Loomes, G., Starmer, C., & Sugden, R. (1989). Preference reversal: Information-processing effect or rational non-transitive choice? *The Economic Journal, 99,* 140–151.

162. The overall predictions of modern regret theory have been supported by the results of some experiments (Loomes, Further evidence; Loomes, Starmer, & Sugden) and not supported by others (DiCagno, D., & Hey, J. D. [1988]. A direct test of the original version of regret theory. *Journal of Behavioral Decision Making, 1,* 43–56.; Kelsey, D., & Schepanski, A. [1991]. Regret and disappointment in taxpayer reporting decision: An experimental study. *Journal of Behavioral Decision Making, 4,* 33–53).

163. Hershey, J. C., & Baron, J. (1987). Clinical reasoning and cognitive processes. *Medical Decision Making, 7,* p. 207.

164. Stocker, Moral conflicts, p. 119.

6. Personal Roots of Regret

1. Heider, F. (1958). *The psychology of interpersonal relations.* New York: Wiley.

2. Sennett, R., & Cobb, J. (1973). *The hidden injuries of class.* New York: Vintage.

3. Smith, C. A., & Lazarus, R. S. (1990). Emotion and adaptation. In L. Pervin (Ed.) *Handbook of personality theory and research* (pp. 609–637). NY: Guilford, p. 632.

4. They include everything from authoritarianism to explanatory style to state-versus action-orientation, to name just a few. See: Adorno, T. W., Frenkel-Brunswik, E., Levinson, D. J., & Sanford, R.N. (1950). *The authoritarian personality.* New York: Norton, 1969; Peterson, C., & Seligman, M. E. P. (1984). Causal explanations as a risk factor for depression: Theory and evidence. *Psychological Review, 91,* 347–374; Kuhl, J. (1981). Motivational and functional helplessness: The moderating effect of state-vs. action-orientation. *Journal of Personality and Social Psychology, 40,* 155–170.

5. Butler, R. (1968). The life review: An interpretation of reminiscence in the aged. In B. L. Neugarten (Ed.), *Middle age and aging* (pp. 486–496). Chicago: University of Chicago Press, p. 488.

6. Erikson, E. (1955). *Childhood and society.* New York: Norton.

7. Cited in Levinson, D. (with C. N. Darrow, E. B. Klein, M. H. Levinson, B. McKee). (1978). *The seasons of a man's life.* New York: Knopf, p. 250.

8. Ephron, N. (1986, November 2). Revision and life: Take it from the top—again. *New York Times Book Review,* p. 7.

9. Kincaid, J. (1989, June 26). Mariah. *The New Yorker,* p. 33.

10. Cheever, J. (1990, August 13). Journals: From the late forties and the fifties—II. *The New Yorker,* p. 39.

11. Anderson, S. (1919). *Winesburg, Ohio.* New York: Viking, 1958.

12. Piaget, J. (1952). *The origins of intelligence in children.* New York: International Universities Press.

13. Tyler, A. (1988). *Breathing lessons.* New York: Knopf, p. 327.

14. Woolf, V. (1925). *Mrs. Dalloway.* New York: Harcourt, Brace, & World, p. 14, emphasis added.

15. Levinson, p. 61.

16. Gutmann, D. L. (1975). Parenthood: A key to the comparative study of the life cycle. In N. Datan & L. Ginzberg (Eds.), *Life span developmental psychology: Normative life crises.* New York: Academic.

17. Minton, L. (1990, April 22). Fresh voices. *Parade Magazine,* p. 13.

18. Landman, J., Pais, D., & Nykiel, C. (in preparation, 1993). Regret in young adults.

19. See, for example: Boyd, J. H., & Weissman, M. M. (1981). Epide-

miology of affective disorders: A re-examination and future directions. *Archives of General Psychiatry, 38,* 1039–1046; Clayton, P. J. (1981). The epidemiology of bipolar affective disorder. *Comprehensive Psychiatry, 22,* 31–43; Nolen-Hoeksema, S. (1987). Sex differences in unipolar depression: Evidence and theory. *Psychological Bulletin, 101,* 259–282; Weissman, M. M., & Klerman, G. L. (1977). Sex differences in the epidemiology of depression. *Archives of General Psychiatry, 39,* 1397–1403.

20. Cited in *Women Pro & Con.* (1958). Mount Vernon, NY: The Peter Pauper Press, p. 56.

21. Beauvoir, Simone de. (1952). *The second sex.* New York: Bantam Books, 1961, p. 771.

22. Freud, S. (1925). Negation. *General psychological theory: Papers on metapsychology.* New York: Collier Books, 1963, p. 216.

23. Shimanoff, S. B. (1985). Rules governing the verbal expression of emotions between married couples. *The Western Journal of Speech Communication, 49,* 147–165.

24. Shimanoff, p. 161.

25. Fabes, R. A., & Martin, C. L. (1991). Gender and age stereotypes of emotion. *Personality and Social Psychology Bulletin, 17,* 532–540.

26. Erskine, H. (1973). The polls: Hopes, fears, and regrets. *Public Opinion Quarterly, 37,* 132–145.

27. Kinnier, R. T., & Metha, A. T. (1989). Regrets and priorities at three stages of life. *Counseling and Values, 33,* 182–193.

28. See Erskine.

29. See Kinnier & Metha.

30. Chin, C. (1993). The relationship between regret and rumination. Honors Thesis in Psychology, The University of Michigan, Ann Arbor, Michigan.

31. Landman, J. T. (1984). Regret and undoing: Retrospective assessment of hypothetical and real-life events. Doctoral dissertation, University of Michigan, 1984.

32. See Landman, Pais, & Nykiel.

33. See Gutmann.

34. See Kinnier & Metha.

35. See Sennett & Cobb.

36. Merton, R. K., & Kitt, A. S. (1950). Contributions to the theory of reference group behavior. In R. K. Merton & P. F. Lazarsfeld (Eds.), *Continuities in social research: Studies in the scope and method of the American soldier.* Glencoe, Ill.: Free Press; Stouffer, S. A., Suchman, E. A., DeVinney, L. C., Star, S. A., & Williams, R. M., Jr. (1949). *The American soldier: Adjustment during Army life* (Vol 1). Princeton, NJ: Princeton University Press.

37. Abramson, L. Y., Metalsky, G. I, & Alloy, L. B. (1989). Hopelessness depression: A theory-based subtype. *Psychological Review, 96,* 358–

372; Peterson, C., & Seligman, M. E. P. (1984). Causal explanations as a risk factor for depression: Theory and evidence. *Psychological Review, 91,* 347–374.

38. Jung, C. G. (1924). *Psychological types.* New York: Random House.

39. Watson, D., & Clark, L. A. (1984). Negative affectivity: The disposition to experience aversive emotional states. *Psychological Bulletin, 96,* 465–490.

40. See Nolen-Hoeksema.

41. See Chin.

42. Atthowe, J. M. (1960). Types of conflict and their resolution: A reinterpretation. *Journal of Experimental Psychology, 59,* 1–9; Kogan, N., & Wallach, M. A. (1967). Risk taking as a function of the situation, the person, and the group. In *New directions in psychology III.* New York: Holt, Rinehart, & Winston; Landman, J. (1987a). Regret and elation following action and inaction: Affective responses to positive versus negative outcomes. *Personality and Social Psychology Bulletin, 13,* 524–536; Slovic, P., & Lichtenstein, S. (1968). Importance of variance preferences in gambling decisions. *Journal of Experimental Psychology, 78,* 646–654.

43. Quammen, D. (1982, November 21). Plain folks and puzzling changes [Review of *Shiloh and other stories*]. *New York Times Book Review,* p. 7.

44. Janis, I. L., & Mann, L. (1977). Anticipatory regret. In *Decision making: A psychological analysis of conflict, choice, and commitment* (pp. 219–242). New York: Free Press, p. 231.

45. Freud, S. (1909). *Three case histories.* New York: Collier, 1963.

46. See Butler.

47. Taylor, G. (1985). *Pride, shame and guilt: Emotions of self-assessment.* New York: Clarendon Press, Oxford University Press.

48. Burks, A.W. (1946). Laws of nature and reasonableness of regret. *Mind, 55,* 1770–1772.

49. James, W. (1923). The dilemma of determinism. *The will to believe and other essays in popular philosophy.* New York: Dover, 1956.

50. Sartre's ethic takes exception to this idea, asserting that in the face of the individual's inescapable responsibility for choice, regret is simply a matter of self-indulgent bad faith. See Sartre, J.-P. (1956). *Being and nothingness* (H. E. Barnes, Trans.). NY: Washington Square Books.

51. Josephs, R. A., Larrick, R. P., Steele, C. M., & Nisbett, R. E. (1992). Protecting the self from the negative consequences of risky decisions. *Journal of Personality and Social Psychology, 62,* 26–37.

52. Steele, C. M. (1988). The psychology of self affirmation: Sustaining the integrity of the self. In L. Berkowitz (Ed.), *Advances in Experimental Social Psychology,* (Vol. 21)., 261–302.

53. Josephs, Larrick, Steele, & Nisbett.

54. Kohn, I. (1986). Counseling women who request sterilization: Psy-

chodynamic issues and interventions. *Social Work in Health Care, 11,* 35–60.

55. Isen, A. M., Shalker, T., Clark, M., & Karp, L. (1978). Affect, accessibility of material in memory and behavior: A cognitive loop? *Journal of Personality and Social Psychology, 55,* 710–717; Mischel, W., Ebbesen, E., & Zeiss, A. (1976). Determinants of selective memory about the self. *Journal of Consulting and Clinical Psychology, 44,* 92–103.

56. Alloy, L. B., & Abramson, L. Y. (1979). Judgment of contingency in depressed and nondepressed students: Sadder but wiser? *Journal of Experimental Psychology: General, 108,* 441–485; Alloy, L. B., & Abramson, L. Y. (1982). Learned helplessness, depression, and the illusion of control. *Journal of Personality and Social Psychology, 42,* 1114–1126; Lewinsohn, P. M., Mischel, W., Chaplin, W., & Barton, R. (1980). Social competence and depression: The role of illusory self-perceptions. *Journal of Abnormal Psychology, 89,* 203–212; and Watson & Clark.

57. Costa, P. T., & McCrae, R. R. (1980). Influence of extraversion and neuroticism on subjective well-being: Happy and unhappy people. *Journal of Personality and Social Psychology, 38,* 668–678; Larsen, R. J., & Ketellaar, T. (1989). Extraversion, neuroticism, and susceptibility to positive and negative mood induction procedures. *Personality and Individual Differences, 10,* 1221–1228; Larsen, R. J., & Ketellaar, T. (1991). Personality and susceptibility to positive and negative emotional states. *Journal of Personality and Social Psychology, 61,* 132–140.

58. Diener, E., & Emmons, R. A. (1985). The independence of positive and negative affect. *Journal of Personality and Social Psychology, 47,* 1105–1117.

59. Lewis, H. (1986). The role of shame in depression. In M. Rutter, C. E. Izard, & P. B. Read (Eds.), *Depression in young people* (pp. 325–339). New York: Guilford; Polivy, J. (1981). On the induction of emotion in the laboratory: Discrete moods or multiple affect states? *Journal of Personality and Social Psychology, 41,* 803–817.

60. See Kohn.

61. Ballou, J., & Bryson, J. (1983). The doing and undoing of surgical sterilization: A psychosocial profile of the tubal reimplantation patient. *Psychiatry, 46,* 161–171; Romans-Clarkson, S. E., & Gillett, W. R. (1987). Women who regret their sterilization: Developmental considerations. *Journal of Psychosomatic Obstetrics and Gynaecology, 7,* 9–17.

62. Kohn.

63. Cooper, J. E., Bledin, K. D., Brice, B., & Mackenzie, S. (1985). Effects of female sterilization: One year follow-up in a prospective controlled study of psychological and psychiatric outcome. *Journal of Psychosomatic Research, 29,* 13–22.

64. Gudjonsson, G. H. (1984). Attribution of blame for criminal acts and its relationship with personality. *Personality and Individual Differences, 5* (1), p. 53.

65. Weisman, A. D., & Worden, J. W. (1976–77). The existential plight in cancer: Significance of the first 100 days. *International Journal of Psychiatry in Medicine, 7,* 1–15.

66. Landman, J., Vandewater, E., Stewart, A., & Malley, J. (Under review, 1993). Missed opportunities: Ramifications of counterfactual thought.

67. See the discussion of the preliminary results of the Stewart, Vandewater, Landman, & Malley research described in Chapter 1.

68. Cheever, J. (1991, January 28). Journals. *The New Yorker,* p. 52.

69. Cheever (1991), p. 50.

70. See Rorty, A.

71. Nisbett, R. E., & Wilson, T. D. (1977). Telling more than we can know: Verbal reports on mental processes. *Psychological Review, 84,* 231–259.

72. Kohn; and Kopit, S., & Barnes, A. B. (1976). Patients' response to tubal division. *Journal of American Medical Association, 236* (24), 2761–2763.

73. Although it may seem presumptuous to claim that someone else has regret of which he or she remains unaware, there are ways to check the validity of such a suspicion. X's close friend or therapist might be able to tell that X is regretful, though X is not consciously aware of it. One criterion of the validity of the friend's or therapist's interpretation is if, when confronted with the other's interpretation, X figuratively slaps his or her forehead and agrees: "Yes, you're right. How could I have missed it?" (The absence of agreement does not *necessarily* guarantee that the other's interpretation was invalid. The psychoanalytic perspective tells us that the interpretation might have failed because it was premature, for example. Nor does agreement *necessarily* guarantee the validity of the interpretation. It may have "succeeded" because of its unthreatening or stabilizing nature, for example.)

74. See Watson & Clark.

75. Although Freud and Sartre agree on the fact of self-deception, they disagree on whether the concept of the unconscious validly captures the reality of self-deception.

76. Sartre, p. 82.

77. Nietzsche, F. (1887/1974). *The gay science* (W. Kaufmann, Trans.). New York: Vintage Books.

78. Erikson, E. H. (1976). Reflections on Dr. Borg's life cycle (pp. 1–31). In E. H. Erikson (Ed.), *Adulthood.* New York: Norton.

79. Barrie, J. M. (1922). *Dear Brutus: A comedy in three acts.* New York: Scribner's.

7. Occasions of Regret

1. Denzin, N. K. (1990). On understanding emotion: The interpretive-cultural agenda. In T. D. Kemper (Ed.), *Research agendas in the sociology*

of emotions (pp. 85–116). Albany: State University of New York Press; Gordon, S. L. (1990). Social structural effects on emotions. In Kemper (pp. 145–179); Hochschild, A. R. (1983). *The managed heart: Commercialization of human feeling.* Berkeley: University of California Press; Hochschild, A. R. (1990). Ideology and emotion management: A perspective and path for future research. In Kemper (pp. 117–142); Lutz, C. A., & White, G. M. (1986). The anthropology of emotions. *Annual Review of Anthropology, 15,* 405–436.

2. Briggs, J. L. (1970). *Never in anger.* Cambridge, Mass.: Harvard University Press; Levy, R. (1973). *The Tahitians.* Chicago: University of Chicago Press.

3. Lutz, C. A. (1988). *Unnatural emotions: Everyday sentiments on a Micronesian atoll and their challenge to Western theory.* Chicago: University of Chicago Press, p. 44.

4. Hochschild, Ideology and emotion management.

5. Rorty, A. O. (Ed.) (1980). *Explaining emotions.* Berkeley: University of California Press, p. 492.

6. de Rivera, cited in Adler, T. (1989, August). Culture colors experience of emotions. *APA Monitor,* p. 6.

7. Adler, p. 6.

8. Shapiro, W. (1988, July 18). When bad things are caused by good nations. *Time,* p. 20.

9. Caudill and Weinstein, cited in T. P. Rohlen (1978). The promise of adulthood in Japanese spiritualism (pp.121–147). In E. H. Erikson (Ed.), *Adulthood.* New York: Norton, p. 130.

10. Cushman, P. (1991). Ideology obscured: Political uses of the self in Daniel Stern's infant. *American Psychologist, 46,* 206–219.

11. Markus, H. R., & Kitayama, S. (1991). Culture and the self: Implications for cognition, emotion, and motivation. *Psychological Review, 98,* 224–253.

12. John Miyamoto, personal communication, April 27, 1989.

13. Gonzales, A., & Zimbardo, P. G. (1985, March). Time in perspective. *Psychology Today,* 21–26.

14. Issues concerning the formulation of probabilities and preferences are discussed in detail in Chapter 5 as well.

15. Dawes, R. M. (1988). *Rational choice in an uncertain world.* San Diego: Harcourt Brace Jovanovich, p. 275.

16. Dawes, p. 291.

17. Kahneman, D., Slovic, P., & Tversky, A. (Eds.). (1982). *Judgment under uncertainty: Heuristics and biases.* New York: Cambridge University Press.

18. Kahneman, Slovic, & Tversky.

19. Kahneman, Slovic, & Tversky.

20. Christensen-Szalanski, J. J., & Bushyhead, J. B. (1981). Physicians' use of probabilistic information in a real clinical setting. *Journal*

of Experimental Psychology: Human Perception and Performance, 7,
928–936.

21. Sugden, R. (1985). Regret, recrimination and rationality. *Theory
and Decision, 19,* 77 -99.

22. Sugden.

23. Shefrin, H. M., & Statman, M. (1986). How not to make money in
the stock market. *Psychology Today, 20,* 52–57.

24. Shefrin & Statman, p. 57.

25. March, J. G. (1978). Bounded rationality, ambiguity, and the engineering of choice. *The Bell Journal of Economics, 9,* 587–608.

26. Merton, R. K., & Kitt, A. S. (1950). Contributions to the theory of
reference group behavior. In R. K. Merton & P. F. Lazarsfeld (Eds.), *Continuities in social research: Studies in the scope and method of the American
soldier.* Glencoe, Ill.: Free Press; Stouffer, S. A., Suchman, E. A., De-
Vinney, L. C., Star, S. A., & Williams, R.M., Jr. (1949). *The American soldier: Adjustment during Army life* (Vol 1). Princeton, NJ: Princeton University Press.

27. Kopit, S., & Barnes, A. B. (1976). Patients' response to tubal division. *Journal of American Medical Association, 236* (24), 2761–2763.

28. Walsh, V.C. (1961). *Scarcity and evil.* Englewood Cliffs, NJ:
Prentice-Hall.

29. Janis, I. L., & Mann, L. (1977). Anticipatory regret. In *Decision
making: A psychological analysis of conflict, choice, and commitment*
(pp. 219–242). New York: Free Press.

30. Janis & Mann.

31. Bell, D. E. (1982). Regret in decision making under uncertainty.
Operations Research, 30, p. 969.

32. Walster, G. W., & Walster, E. (1970). Choice between negative
alternatives: Dissonance reduction or regret? *Psychological Reports, 26,*
995–1005.

33. Wicklund, R. A. (1970). Prechoice preference reversal as a result
of threat to decision freedom. *Journal of Personality and Social Psychology, 14,* 8–17.

34. Frankfurt, H. G. (1988). *The importance of what we care about:
Philosophical essays.* New York: Cambridge University Press, p. 84.

35. Abelson, R. P., & Levi, A. (1985). Decision making and decision
theory. In G. Lindzey & E. Aronson (Eds.), *Handbook of Social Psychology,
Vol. I: Theory and Method* (pp. 231–309). New York: Random House, p.
235.

36. Sen, A. K. (1977). Rational fools: A critique of the behavioral foundations of economic theory. *Philosophy and Public Affairs, 6,* p. 325.

37. Anderson, E. (1990). Some problems in the normative theory of
rational choice with consequences for empirical research; Dostoevsky, F.
(1864/1981). *Notes from underground.* New York: Bantam.

38. Edwards, W., & von Winterfeldt, D. (1986). On cognitive illusions

and their implications. In H. R. Arkes, and K. R. Hammond, Eds. *Judgment and decision making: An interdisciplinary reader* (pp. 642–679). New York: Cambridge University Press.

39. Smart, J. J. C., & Williams, B. (1973). *Utilitarianism for and against.* London: Cambridge University Press, p. 36.

40. Abelson & Levi, p. 287.

41. Abelson & Levi, p. 267.

42. Raz, J. (1986). *The morality of freedom.* New York: Oxford University Press.

43. Raz, p. 324.

44. March; Hampshire, S. (1983). *Morality and conflict.* Cambridge, Mass.: Harvard University Press; Stocker, M. (1979). Desiring the bad: An essay in moral psychology. *The Journal of Philosophy, 76,* 738–753; Stocker, M. (1987). Moral conflicts: What they are and what they show. *Pacific Philosophical Quarterly, 68,* 104–123; Williams, B. A. O. (1965). Ethical consistency. *Aristotelian Society, 39,* 103–124.

45. Shapiro, B. (1991, February 18). Hell for those who won't go. *The Nation,* pp. 194 -198.

46. Tversky, A., Sattath, S., & Slovic, P. (1988). Contingent weighting in judgment and choice. *Psychological Review, 95,* p. 384.

47. Janis & Mann.

48. Ballou, J., and Bryson, J. (1983). The doing and undoing of surgical sterilization: A psychosocial profile of the tubal reimplantation patient. *Psychiatry, 46,* 161–171.

49. Ballou & Bryson, p. 170.

50. Shain, R. N., Miller, W. P., & Holden, A. E. C. (1984). The decision to terminate childbearing: Differences in preoperative ambivalence between tubal ligation women and vasectomy wives. *Social Biology, 31* (1–2), 40–58.

51. Miller, W. B., & Shain, R. N. (1985). Married women and contraceptive sterilization: Factors that contribute to pre-surgical ambivalence. *Journal of Biosocial Sciences, 17,* 471–479.

52. Kohn, I. (1986). Counseling women who request sterilization: Psychodynamic issues and interventions. *Social Work in Health Care, 11* (20, 35–60.

53. Miller & Shain, p. 477.

54. Janis & Mann.

55. Ozick, C. (1983). *Art and ardor.* New York: Knopf, p. 200.

56. Ozick, p. 201.

57. Ozick, p. 201.

58. Kahneman, D., & Miller, D. T. (1986). Norm theory: Comparing reality to its alternatives. *Psychological Review, 93,* 136–153.

59. Kahneman, D., & Tversky, A. (1982b). The simulation heuristic. In D. Kahneman, P. Slovic, & A. Tversky (Eds.), *Judgment under uncertainty: Heuristics and biases.* New York: Cambridge University Press.

60. Kahneman & Tversky, The simulation heuristic; and Landman, J. T. (1984). Regret and undoing: Retrospective assessment of hypothetical and real-life events. Doctoral dissertation, University of Michigan, 1984.

61. Kahneman & Miller; Kahneman & Tversky. The simulation heuristic; Macrae, C. N. (1992). A tale of two curries: Counterfactual thinking and accident-related judgments. *Personality and Social Psychology Bulletin, 13,* 84–87.

62. Hearst, E. (1984a). Absence as information: Some implications for learning, performance, and representational processes. In H. L. Roitblat, T. B. Bever, & H. S. Terrace (Eds.), *Animal cognition.* Hillsdale, NJ: Lawrence Erlbaum; Hearst, E. (1984b, April 4). *Empty intervals and absent events: Something about nothing in the psychology of animals and people.* Distinguished faculty research lecture, Indiana University, Bloomington; Jenkins, H. M., & Sainsbury, R. S. (1970). Discrimination learning with the distinctive feature on positive or negative trials. In D. Mostofsky (Ed.), *Attention: Contemporary theory and analysis.* New York: Appleton-Century-Crofts; Sainsbury, R. S. (1973). Discrimination learning using positive or negative cues. *Canadian Journal of Psychology, 27,* 46–57; Wason, P. D., & Johnson-Laird, P. N. (1965). *Psychology of reasoning: Structure and content.* London: Batsford.

63. Fazio, R., Sherman, S. J., & Herr, P. M. (1982). The feature-positive effect in the self-perception process: Does not doing matter as much as doing? *Journal of Personality and Social Psychology, 42,* 404–411.

64. Nisbett, R., & Ross, L. (1980). *Human inference: Strategies and shortcomings of social judgment.* Englewood Cliffs, New Jersey: Prentice-Hall; Ross, L. (1977). The intuitive psychologist and his shortcomings: Distortions in the attribution process. In L. Berkowitz (Ed.), *Advances in experimental social psychology* (Vol. 10). New York: Academic Press.

65. Janis & Mann.

66. Landman, J. (1987a). Regret and elation following action and inaction: Affective responses to positive versus negative outcomes. *Personality and Social Psychology Bulletin, 13,* 524–536.

67. Gleicher, F., Kost, K. A., Baker, S. M., Strathman, A., Richman, S. A., & Sherman, S. J. (1990). The role of counterfactual thinking in judgments of affect. *Personality and Social Psychology Bulletin, 16,* 2284–295.

68. Otten, A. (1987, September 14). Price of progress: Efforts to predict genetic ills pose medical dilemmas. *The Wall Street Journal,* p. 21.

69. Cited by Thaler, R. (1980). Toward a positive theory of consumer choice. *Journal of Economic Behavior and Organization, 1,* p. 52, who attributes it to Ronald Howard.

70. Josephs, R. A., Larrick, R. P., Steele, C. M., & Nisbett, R. E. (1992). Protecting the self from the negative consequences of risky decisions. *Journal of Personality and Social Psychology, 62,* 26–37.

71. Johnson, J. T. (1986). The knowledge of what might have been: Affective and attributional consequences of near outcomes. *Personality and Social Psychology Bulletin, 12,* 51–62; Miller, D. T., & McFarland, C. (1986).

unterfactual thinking and victim compensation: A test of norm theory. *Personality and Social Psychology Bulletin, 12,* 513–519.

72. Kahneman, D., & Tversky, A. (1982a). The psychology of preferences. *Scientific American, 246,* 160–173.

73. Landman, J., Pais, D., & Nykiel, C. (in preparation, 1993). Regret in young adults.

74. James, H. (1903/1963). *The ambassadors.* New York: Heritage Press, pp. 310–311, emphasis mine.

75. Ishiguro, K. (1989). *The remains of the day.* New York: Knopf, p. 114.

76. Ishiguro, p. 4.

77. Ishiguro, p. 126.

78. Ishiguro, p. 201.

79. Ishiguro, p. 179.

80. Ishiguro, p. 239.

81. Ishiguro, p. 239.

82. Ishiguro, p. 242.

83. Ishiguro, p. 243.

84. Joyce, J. (1914/1946). *Ulysses.* New York: Random House, p. 414.

85. Isen, A.M., Shalker, T., Clark, M., & Karp, L. (1978). Affect, accessibility of material in memory and behavior: A cognitive loop? *Journal of Personality and Social Psychology, 55,* 710–717; Mischel, W., Ebbesen, E., & Zeiss, A. (1976). Determinants of selective memory about the self. *Journal of Consulting and Clinical Psychology, 44,* 92–103.

86. Landman, Pais, & Nykiel.

87. Butler, R. (1968). The life review: An interpretation of reminiscence in the aged. In B. L. Neugarten (Ed.), *Middle age and aging* (pp. 486–496). Chicago: University of Chicago Press.

88. Krell, D.F. (1977). *Martin Heidegger: Basic Writings.* New York: Harper & Row, p. 23.

89. Tolstoy, L. N. (1923). *The death of Ivan Ilyitch and other stories.* New York: Scribner's, pp. 62–63.

90. Tolstoy, p. 70.

91. Tolstoy, p. 71.

92. Hemingway, E. (1963). *The snows of Kilimanjaro and other stories.* Middlesex, England: Penguin Books, p. 9.

93. Atwater, L. with Brewster, T. (1991, February). Lee Atwater's last campaign. *Life,* p. 64.

94. Atwater.

95. Atwater, p. 67.

8. Transformation of Regret

1. Guilt, rather than regret, is the primary subject of Augustine's *Confessions,* another autobiography occasionally recommended to me.

2. Lazarus, R. S., & Folkman, S. (1984). *Stress, appraisal, and coping.* New York: Springer, p. 138.

3. Sartre, J.-P. (1948). *The emotions: Outline of a theory.* New York: Philosophical Library; Schafer, R. (1976). *A new language for psychoanalysis.* New Haven: Yale University Press; Solomon, R. C. (1976). *The passions: The myth and nature of human emotion.* Notre Dame, Ind.: The University of Notre Dame Press.

4. Clark, M. S., & Isen, A. M. (1982). Toward understanding the relationship between feeling states and social behavior. In A. Hastorf & A. M. Isen (Eds.), *Cognitive social psychology* (pp. 73–108). New York: Elsevier; Isen, A. M., & Levin, P. F. (1972). The effect of feeling good on helping: Cookies and kindness. *Journal of Personality and Social Psychology, 21,* 384–388; Isen, A. M., & Simmonds, S. F. (1978). The effect of feeling good on a helping task that is incompatible with good mood. *Social Psychology, 41,* 346–349; Mischel, W., Ebbesen, E., & Zeiss, A. (1976). Determinants of selective memory about the self. *Journal of Consulting and Clinical Psychology, 44,* 92–103.

5. Carlson, M., Charlin, V., & Miller, N. (1988). Positive mood and helping behavior: A test of six hypotheses. *Journal of Personality and Social Psychology, 55,* 211–229.

6. Kubler-Ross, E. (1969). *On death and dying.* New York: Macmillan; Kubler-Ross, E. (1975). *Death: The final stage of growth.* Englewood Cliffs, NJ: Prentice-Hall.

7. Brans, J., & Taylor Smith, M. (1987). *Mother, I have something to tell you.* New York: Doubleday.

8. Byrne, D. (1961). The Repression-Sensitization Scale: Rationale, reliability, and validity. *Journal of Personality, 29,* 344–349.

9. Shapiro, D. (1965). *Neurotic styles.* New York: Basic.

10. Friedman, M., & Rosenman, R.H. (1959). Association of specific overt behavior patterns with blood and cardiovascular findings: Blood cholesterol level, blood clotting time, incidence of arcus senilis, and clinical coronary artery disease. *Journal of the American Medical Association, 169,* 1286–1296.

11. See Lazarus, R. S., & Folkman, S. (1984). *Stress, appraisal, and coping.* New York: Springer.

12. See, for example, Abramson, L. Y., Seligman, M. E. P., & Teasdale, J. (1978). Learned helplessness in humans: Critique and reformulation. *Journal of Abnormal Psychology, 87,* 49–74; Brehm, J. W. (1972). *Responses to loss of freedom: A theory of psychological reactance.* Morristown, NJ: General Learning Press; Inglehart, M. R. (1991). *Reactions to critical life events: A social psychological analysis.* New York: Praeger; Klinger, E. (1975). The consequences of commitment to and disengagement from incentives. *Psychological Review, 82,* 1–25; Klinger, E. (1977). *Meaning and void: Inner experience and the incentives in people's lives.* Minneapolis: University of Minnesota Press; Lazarus, R. S. (1966). *Psychological stress and the coping process.* New York: McGraw-Hill; Lazarus, R. S. (1991). *Emotion and adaptation.* New York: Oxford University Press;

Lazarus, R. S., & Folkman, S. (1984). *Stress, appraisal, and coping.* New York: Springer; Peterson, C., & Seligman, M. E. P. (1984). Causal explanations as a risk factor for depression: Theory and evidence. *Psychological Review, 91,* 347–374; Taylor, S. E. (1983). Adjustment to threatening events: A theory of cognitive adaptation. *American Psychologist, 38,* 1161–1173; Taylor, S. E., & Brown, J. D. (1988). Illusions and well-being: Some social psychological contributions to a theory of mental health. *Psychological Bulletin, 103,* 193–210; Vaillant, G. E. (1977). *Adaptation to life.* Boston: Little, Brown.

13. Folkman, S., & Lazarus, R. S. (1985). If it changes it must be a process: Study of emotion and coping during three stages of a college examination. *Journal of Personality and Social Psychology, 48,* 150–170; Lazarus, *Emotion and adaptation;* Lazarus & Folkman, *Stress, appraisal, coping.*

14. Morris, W. N., & Reilly, N. P. (1987). Toward the self-regulation of mood: Theory and research. *Motivation and Emotion, 11,* 215–249.

15. Lazarus, *Psychological stress;* and Meichenbaum, D. (1977). *Cognitive behavior modification: An integrative approach.* New York: Plenum.

16. Morris & Reilly.

17. Lazarus & Folkman.

18. Tesser, A., Leone, C., & Clary, E. G. (1978). Affect control: Process constraints versus catharsis. *Cognitive Therapy and Research, 2,* 265–274.

19. Tesser, Leone, & Clary, p. 273.

20. Ellis, A. (1970). *Reason and emotion in psychotherapy.* New York: Lyle Stuart.

21. Beck, A. (1976). *Cognitive therapy and emotional disorders.* New York: International Universities Press; Meichenbaum, *Cognitive behavior;* Meichenbaum, D. (1985). *Stress-inoculation training.* New York: Pergamon.

22. Morris & Reilly.

23. Borkovec, T. D., & Inz, J. (1990). The nature of worry in generalized anxiety disorder: A predominance of thought activity. *Behaviour Research & Therapy, 28,* 153–158.

24. Adler, T. (1990, October). Worrywarts suppress healthy reaction to fear. *APA Monitor,* p. 12.

25. My recent computerized search of Psychological Abstracts, using the keywords of *catharsis* and *aggression* turned up 79 citations. There are many many dissertations on the topic. There is a mix of findings pro (catharsis reduces aggression) and con (catharsis does not reduce and in fact increases aggression). On the side critical of the catharsis principle, you might do well to start with these: Berkowitz, L. (1970). Experimental investigations of hostility catharsis. *Journal of Consulting and Clinical Psychology, 35,* 1–7; and Geen, R. G., Stonner, D., & Shope, G. L. (1975). The

facilitation of aggression by aggression: Evidence against the catharsis hypothesis. *Journal of Personality and Social Psychology, 31,* 721–726. On the other side, you might read these: Konecni, V. J., & Ebbesen, E.B. (1976). Disinhibition versus the cathartic effect: Artifact and substance. *Journal of Personality and Social Psychology, 34,* 352–365; Murray, J., & Feshbach, S. (1978). Let's not throw the baby out with the bathwater: The catharsis hypothesis revisited. *Journal of Personality, 46,* 462–473; and Feshbach, S. (1984). The catharsis hypothesis, aggressive drive, and the reduction of aggression. *Aggressive Behavior, 10,* 91–101.

26. Besides what was already discussed, see, for example, Tavris,C. (1982). *Anger, the misunderstood emotion.* New York: Simon and Schuster.

27. Kumin, M. (1974). *Our ground time here will be brief.* New York: Viking Penguin.

28. Freud, S. (1917). Mourning and melancholia. In *General psychological theory: Papers on metapsychology.* New York: Collier.

29. Alexander, F. (1963). *Fundamentals of psychoanalysis.* New York: Norton, p. 288.

30. Fried, E. (1982). On "working through" as a form of self-innovation. In S. Slipp (Ed.), *Curative factors in dynamic psychotherapy* (pp. 243–258). New York: McGraw-Hill, p. 244, emphasis in original.

31. Frijda, N.H. (1986). *The emotions.* Cambridge: Cambridge University Press, p. 344.

32. Freud, S. (1917). Mourning and melancholia. In *General psychological theory: Papers on metapsychology.* New York: Collier, p. 164.

33. Freud, Mourning and melancholia, p. 166.

34. Freud, Mourning and melancholia, p. 165.

35. Freud, Mourning and melancholia, p. 169.

36. Freud, Mourning and melancholia, p. 172.

37. Freud, Mourning and melancholia, p. 169.

38. Freud, Mourning and melancholia, p. 170.

39. Freud, Mourning and melancholia, p. 178.

40. Freud, Mourning and melancholia, p. 178.

41. Freud, Mourning and melancholia.

42. Klein, M. (1955a). On identification. In M. Klein, P. Heimann, & R. E. Money-Kyrle (Eds.), *New directions in psychoanalysis.* New York: Basic Books; Klein, M. (1955b). The psycho-analytic play technique: Its history and significance. In M. Klein, P. Heimann, & R. E. Money-Kyrle (Eds.), *New directions in psychoanalysis.* New York: Basic Books.

43. Klein, The psycho-analytic play technique.

44. Segal, H. (1955). A psycho-analytical approach to aesthetics. In Klein, Heimann, & Money-Kyrle; and Segal, H. (1964). *Introduction to the work of Melanie Klein.* New York: Basic Books.

45. Segal, A psycho-analytical approach, p. 403.

46. Segal, p. 388.

47. Segal, p. 388.

48. Segal, p. 389.

49. Segal, p. 389.

50. Donoghue, D. (1991, August 15). Critics at the top [Review of *Versions of Pygmalion.*] *New York Review of Books*, pp. 53–56.

51. Hirshfield, J. (1990, July 30/August 6). History as the painter Bonnard. *The Nation*, p. 143.

52. Erikson, E. (1955). *Childhood and society*. New York: Norton.

53. Carlson, C. M. (1984). Reminiscing: Toward achieving ego integrity in old age. *Social Casework, 65*, p. 85.

54. Ryff, C. D., & Heincke, S. G. (1983). Subjective organization of personality in adulthood and aging. *Journal of Personality and Social Psychology, 44*, 807–816.

55. Orwoll, L. (1989). *Wisdom in later adulthood: Personality and life history correlates*. Doctoral Dissertation, Boston University.

56. Freud, A. (1936). *The ego and the mechanisms of defense* (revised edition). New York: International Universities Press.

57. Breznitz, S. (1983). The seven kinds of denial. In S. Breznitz (Ed.), *The denial of stress*. New York: International Universities Press.

58. Joyce, J. (1914/1946). *Ulysses*. New York: Random House.

59. Hemingway, E. (1963). *The snows of Kilimanjaro and other stories*. Middlesex, England: Penguin Books.

60. Breznitz.

61. Hemingway, p. 28.

62. Tolstoy, L. N. (1923). *The death of Ivan Ilyitch and other stories*. New York: Scribner's, pp. 63, 64.

63. Tolstoy, pp. 62–63.

64. Stafford, W. (1970). *Allegiances*. New York: Harper & Row.

65. Barrie, J. M. (1922). *Dear Brutus: A comedy in three acts*. New York: Scribner's, p. 109.

66. Barrie, p. 108.

67. Barrie, p. 138.

68. Frijda, *The emotions*, p. 343.

69. Camus, A. (1956). *The fall* (J. O'Brien, Trans.). New York: Vintage, p. 147.

70. Fenichel, O. (1945). *The psychoanalytic theory of neurosis*. New York: Norton, p. 153.

71. Dostoevsky, F. (1864/1981). *Notes from underground*. New York: Bantam, p. 126.

72. Dostoevsky, p. 151.

73. Dostoevsky, p. 13.

74. Shabad, P. (1987). Fixation and the road not taken. *Psychoanalytic Psychology, 4*, p. 196.

75. Dostoevsky, p. 14.

76. Dostoevsky, p. 151.

77. Frank, J. (1986). *Dostoevsky: The stir of liberation, 1860–1865*. Princeton, NJ: Princeton University Press.

78. Dostoevsky, p. 153.

79. Dostoevsky, p. 65.

80. Shabad, p. 187.

81. For another view of the social dimension of *Notes from Underground*, see J. Frank.

82. Woolf, V. (1925). *Mrs. Dalloway.* New York: Harcourt, Brace, & World, p. 69.

83. Woolf, pp. 73–74, emphasis added.

84. Woolf, p. 115, emphasis added.

85. Woolf, p. 10, emphasis added.

86. Janis, I. L., & Mann, L. (1977). Anticipatory regret. In *Decision making: A psychological analysis of conflict, choice, and commitment* (pp. 219–242). New York: Free Press.

87. Woolf, p. 10.

88. Svenson, O., & Benthorn, L. J. (1990). Postdecision changes in attractiveness of choice alternatives. *Psychological Research Bulletin, 30,* 1–16.

89. Woolf, p. 68.

90. Woolf, p. 8.

91. Woolf, p. 116.

92. Woolf, pp. 119–120, emphasis added.

93. Woolf, p. 12.

94. Woolf, p. 55.

95. Woolf, p. 172.

96. Woolf, p. 17.

97. Greenspan, P.S. (1980). A case of mixed feelings: Ambivalence and the logic of emotion. In A. O. Rorty (Ed.), *Explaining emotion* (pp. 223–250). Berkeley: University of California Press.

98. Woolf, p. 17.

99. Sennett, R., & Cobb, J. (1973). *The hidden injuries of class.* New York: Vintage.

100. James, H. (1903/1963). *The ambassadors.* New York: Heritage Press, pp. 213–213, emphasis added.

101. Erikson.

102. James, H., p. 333.

103. James, H., p. 334.

104. I thank Sydney Warshausky for this insight.

105. I am grateful to Elizabeth Knoll for this insight.

106. Dickens, C. (1861/1978). *Great expectations.* New York: Oxford University Press, p. 308, emphasis added.

107. Dickens, p. 423.

108. Klein, The psycho-analytic play technique.

109. Kurosawa, A. (1992). *Ikiru. Seven Samurai and other screenplays* (D. Richie, Trans.). London: Faber and Faber.

110. Tyler, A. (1988). *Breathing lessons.* New York: Knopf, p. 175, emphasis added.

111. Tyler, p. 130.

112. Tyler, p. 280.

113. Tyler, pp. 280–281.

114. Tyler, p. 327.

115. Tyler, p. 323.

116. Eliot, T. S. (1975). The metaphysical poets. *Selected prose of T. S. Eliot* (F. Kermode, Ed.). New York: Harcourt Brace Jovanovich; Farrar, Straus and Giroux, p. 65.

9. The Contrary Wisdom of Regret

1. The idea of the dialectic is also present in latent form in Erik Erikson's theory of psychosocial development and certain psychoanalytic models.

2. Cornford, F. M. (1941). *The Republic of Plato.* London: Oxford University Press/Clarendon, p. 246.

3. Fish, S. E. (1972). *Self-consuming artifacts: The experience of seventeenth-century literature.* Berkeley: University of California Press, p. 8.

4. Fish, p. 3.

5. Fish; Wittgenstein is cited on the page of epigraphs.

6. Cornford/Plato, p. 221.

7. Cornford/Plato, p. 221, emphasis added.

8. Fish, p. 13.

9. Fish, p. 12.

10. Hegel, G. W. F. (1979). *Phenomenology of spirit* (A.V. Miller, Trans.). New York: Oxford University Press. (Original work published in 1807).

11. Hegel, Findlay's commentary, p. 507.

12. Hegel, Findlay's commentary, p. 512.

13. In its first century of life, the discipline of psychology has shown this progression as well, originally positing a clear-cut sensation/perception dichotomy but now more readily acknowledging the difficulty of drawing a clear line between sensation and perception. See Brown, H. I. (1977). *Perception, theory and commitment: The new philosophy of science.* Chicago: Precedent.; Gear, J. (1989). *Perception and the evolution of style: A new theory of mind.* London: Routledge.; von Fieandt, K., & Moustgaard, I. K. (1977). *The perceptual world.* London: Academic Press.

14. Hegel, p. 206.

15. Cornford/Plato, p. 228.

16. See Chapter 1; and Rosenwald, G. C., & Wiersma, J. (1983). Women, career changes, and the new self. *Psychiatry, 46,* 213–229.

17. See M. Nussbaum's (1990) *Love's Knowledge* (NY: Oxford), especially Chapter 15, for a similar analysis regarding love.

18. See Smart in Smart, J. J. C., & Williams, B. (1973). *Utilitarianism for and against.* London: Cambridge University Press.

19. Freeman, A., & DeWolf, R. (1989). *Woulda, coulda, shoulda:*

Overcoming regrets, mistakes, and missed opportunities. New York: HarperPerennial, p. 67.

20. Hampshire, S. (1983). *Morality and conflict.* Cambridge, Mass.: Harvard University Press, p. 145.

21. Lutz, C. A. (1988). *Unnatural emotions: Everyday sentiments on a Micronesian atoll and their challenge to Western theory.* Chicago: University of Chicago Press.

22. Lutz, p. 4.

23. Walsh, A. (1988, September 17). Critics singing praises of '81 Hopwood winner. *Ann Arbor News,* pp. B2–3.

24. Fabes, R. A., & Martin, C. L. (1991). Gender and age stereotypes of emotion. *Personality and Social Psychology Bulletin, 17,* 532–540; Hochschild, A. R. (1983). *The managed heart: Commercialization of human feeling.* Berkeley: University of California Press; Lutz, C. A. (1990). Engendered emotion: Gender, power, and the rhetoric of emotional control in American discourse. In C. A. Lutz, and L. Abu-Lughod (Eds.), *Language and the politics of emotion* (pp. 69–91). Cambridge: Cambridge University Press; Maccoby, E. E., & Jacklin, C. N. (1974). *The psychology of sex differences.* Stanford, CA: Stanford University Press; Shimanoff, S. B. (1985). Rules governing the verbal expression of emotions between married couples. *The Western Journal of Speech Communication, 49,* 147–165.

25. See Chapter 6 for that discussion.

26. See Lutz.

27. Lutz, p. 58.

28. Lutz, p. 56.

29. Duffy, B. (1987). *The world as I found it: A novel.* New York: Ticknor & Fields, p. 122, emphasis in original.

30. Tolstoy, L. N. (1923). *The death of Ivan Ilyitch and other stories.* New York: Scribner's, p. 238.

31. Whether Eliot's blessing of the wedding of reason and emotion is to be taken at face value is evidently a matter of controversy. George Bornstein has argued, for example, that "Eliot was in important ways afraid of imagination and emotion, and sought to contain both in various frameworks of reason, order, etc." (personal communication, January 18, 1993). See Bornstein, G. (1976). *Transformations of romanticism in Yeats, Eliot, and Stevens.* Chicago: University of Chicago Press.

32. I thank George Bornstein for referring me to Eliot's essay on Andrew Marvell, where this passage by Coleridge is cited. See Eliot, T. S. (1975). *Selected prose of T. S. Eliot* (F. Kermode, Ed.). New York: Harcourt Brace Jovanovich; Farrar, Straus and Giroux, p. 166.

33. Hogarth, R. (1986). *Judgment and choice* (2nd edition). New York: Wiley; Janis, I. L., & Mann, L. (1977). Anticipatory regret. In *Decision making: A psychological analysis of conflict, choice, and commitment* (pp. 219–242). New York: Free Press.

34. Freeman & DeWolf, p. 154, emphasis added.

35. Landman, J., Vandewater, E., Stewart, A., & Malley, J. (Under review, 1993). Missed opportunities: Ramifications of counterfactual thought; and Stewart, A., Vandewater, E., Landman, J., & Malley, J. (In preparation, 1993). Recognizing the limitations of one's own past: Motivations for change in women's lives.

36. Mack, J. E. (1976). *A prince of our disorder: The life of T. E. Lawrence.* Boston: Little, Brown.

37. Stocker, M. (1987). Moral conflicts: What they are and what they show. *Pacific Philosophical Quarterly, 68,* p. 112.

38. Mill, J. S. (1859). *On liberty* (pp. 267–323). *Great Books of the Western World.* Vol. 43. Chicago: Encyclopaedia Britannica, 1952, p. 295.

39. Cushman, P. (1991). Ideology obscured: Political uses of the self in Daniel Stern's infant. *American Psychologist, 46,* p. 208.

40. Freeman & DeWolf, p. 154, emphasis added.

41. I am referring here primarily to intellectual fashion in the sciences, rather than literary or social trends like the romantic strains of the nineteenth century, the 1960s, or the New Age 1990s.

42. Freeman & DeWolf, p. 155.

43. Shweder, R. A. (1984). Anthropology's romantic rebellion against the enlightenment, or there's more to thinking than reason and evidence. In R. A. Shweder, & R. A. LeVine (Eds.), *Culture theory: Essays on mind, self, and emotion* (pp. 27–66). New York: Cambridge University Press, p. 27.

44. Cited in Hochschild, A. R. (1983). *The managed heart: Commercialization of human feeling.* Berkeley: University of California Press, p. 185.

45. Nussbaum, p. 74.

46. Simon, H. A. (1986). Alternative visions of rationality. In H. R. Arkes, & K. R. Hammond (Eds.), *Judgment and decision making: An interdisciplinary reader* (pp. 97–113). New York: Cambridge University Press, p. 112.

47. Wittgenstein, L. (1953). *Philosophical investigations* (G. E. M. Anscomb, Trans). Oxford: Basil Blackwell & Mott, p. 17.

48. Wittgenstein, p. 34.

49. Lakoff, G. (1973). Hedges: A study in the meaning of criteria and the logic of fuzzy concepts. *Journal of Philosophical Logic, 2,* 458–508.

50. Lakoff, p. 458.

51. Johnson, J. T. (1990, July). Fuzzy logic. *Popular Science,* p. 88.

52. Johnson, p. 89, emphasis added.

53. Johnson.

54. Rosch, E., & Lloyd, B. B. (1978). *Cognition and categorization.* Hillsdale, New Jersey: Erlbaum; Rosch, E., & Mervis, C. B. (1975). Family resemblances in the internal structure of categories. *Cognitive Psychology, 7,* 573–605; Rosch, E., & Lloyd, B. B. (1978). *Cognition and categorization.* Hillsdale, New Jersey: Erlbaum; Rosch, E., & Mervis, C. B. (1975). Family

resemblances in the internal structure of categories. *Cognitive Psychology, 7*, 573–605.

55. Cantor, N., & Mischel, W. (1977). Traits as prototypes: Effects on recognition memory. *Journal of Personality and Social Psychology, 35*, 38–48; Cantor, N., Smith, E. E., French, R. D., & Mezzich. J. (1980). Psychiatric diagnosis as prototype categorization. *Journal of Abnormal Psychology, 89*, 181–193.

56. Fehr, B., & Russell, J. A. (1985). The concept of emotion viewed from a prototype perspective. *Journal of Experimental Psychology: General, 113*, 464–486.

57. Gleick, J. (1987). *Chaos: Making a new science.* New York: Penguin, p. 5.

58. Taubes, G. (1990). The body chaotic. *Discover*, pp. 49–53.

59. Gleick, p. 8.

60. Gleick, p. 299.

61. Penrose, R. (1991, March 28). The biggest enigma [Review of *Quantum Profiles*]. *New York Review of Books*, p. 37.

62. Penrose, The biggest enigma, p. 37.

63. Penrose, R. (1989). *The emperor's new mind: Concerning computers, minds, and the laws of physics.* New York: Oxford University Press, p. 149.

64. Penrose, The biggest enigma, pp. 37–38.

65. Miller was cited in Lears, J. (1989, January 9/16). Deride and conquer [Review of *The culture of TV*]. *The Nation*, p. 60.

66. Lears, p. 59.

67. Kis was cited in Newman, C. (1990, October 7). How it feels to cease to be [Review of *Hourglass*]. *New York Times Book Review*, p. 15.

68. Lears, p. 59.

69. Kiefer, C. W. (1988). *The mantle of maturity: A history of ideas about character development.* Albany: SUNY Press.

70. Kiefer, p. 210.

71. See Vaihinger, H. (1924). *The philosophy of "as if": A system of the theoretical, practical and religious fictions of mankind* (C. K. Ogden, Trans.). New York: Harcourt, Brace.

72. Vaihinger.

73. Vaihinger.

74. Messer, S. B. (1986). Behavioral and psychoanalytic perspectives at therapeutic choice points. *American Psychologist, 41*, 1261–1272.

75. Mairs, cited in Graham, L. (1990, September 2). Joy amid the pain [Review of *Carnal acts: Essays*]. *New York Times Book Review*, 7.

76. Frankfurt, H. G. (1988). *The importance of what we care about: Philosophical essays.* New York: Cambridge University Press, p. 91, n.3.

77. Mairs, p. 7.

78. Frost, R. (1977). "West-Running Brook." *North to Boston.* New York: Dodd, Mead. Emphasis added.

References

Abelson, R. P., & Levi, A. (1985). Decision making and decision theory. In G. Lindzey & E. Aronson (Eds.), *Handbook of Social Psychology, Vol. I: Theory and Method* (pp. 231–309). New York: Random House.

Abramson, L. Y., Metalsky, G. I, & Alloy, L. B. (1989). Hopelessness depression: A theory-based subtype. *Psychological Review, 96,* 358–372.

Abramson, L. Y., Seligman, M. E. P., & Teasdale, J. (1978). Learned helplessness in humans: Critique and reformulation. *Journal of Abnormal Psychology, 87,* 49–74.

Ackerman, D. (1990). *A natural history of the senses.* New York: Random House.

Adelson, J. (1983, Fall). The self and memory in *1984. American Educator,* pp. 13–15, 40–42.

Adler, T. (1989, August). Culture colors experience of emotions. *APA Monitor,* p. 6.

Adler, T. (1990, October). Worrywarts suppress healthy reaction to fear. *APA Monitor,* p. 12.

Adorno, T. W., Frenkel-Brunswik, E., Levinson, D. J., & Sanford, R. N. (1950). *The authoritarian personality.* New York: Norton, 1969.

Alexander, F. (1963). *Fundamentals of psychoanalysis.* New York: Norton.

Alloy, L. B., & Abramson, L. Y. (1979). Judgment of contingency in depressed and nondepressed students: Sadder but wiser? *Journal of Experimental Psychology: General, 108,* 441–485.

Alloy, L. B., & Abramson, L. Y. (1982). Learned helplessness, depression, and the illusion of control. *Journal of Personality and Social Psychology, 42*, 1114–1126.

Ann Arbor News, September 18, 1989.

Anderson, E. (1988, September 27). Rational choice and social behavior: A philosophical perspective. Presentation to Group Dynamics Seminar, University of Michigan, Ann Arbor.

Anderson, E. (1990). Some problems in the normative theory of rational choice with consequences for empirical research. Unpublished manuscript.

Anderson, S. (1919). *Winesburg, Ohio.* New York: Viking, 1958.

Arendt, H. (1964/1985). *Eichmann in Jerusalem: A report on the banality of evil.* New York: Penguin.

Aristotle. (1935). *Nicomachean ethics* (P. Wheelwright, Ed. and Trans.). New York: Odyssey Press.

Arkes, H. R., & Hammond, K. R. (1986). General introduction. In H. R. Arkes, & K. R. Hammond (Eds.), *Judgment and decision making: An interdisciplinary reader* (pp. 1–10). New York: Cambridge University Press.

Arnold, M. B. (1960). *Emotion and personality.* New York: Columbia University Press.

Aronson, E. (1969). The theory of cognitive dissonance: A current perspective. In L. Berkowitz (Ed.), *Advances in experimental Social Psychology,* Vol. 4 (pp. 1–34). New York: Academic Press.

Aronson, E. (1988). *The social animal* (5th ed.). San Francisco: Freeman.

Ashbery, J. (1970). *The double dream of spring.* New York: E. P. Dutton.

Atthowe, J. M. (1960). Types of conflict and their resolution: A reinterpretation. *Journal of Experimental Psychology, 59*, 1–9.

Atwater, L. with Brewster, T. (1991, February). Lee Atwater's last campaign. *Life,* pp. 58–67.

Atwood, M. (1991, Fall). Northrop Frye remembered. *Michigan Quarterly Review,* pp. 647–649.

Austen, J. (1818). *Persuasion.* New York: Bantam, 1989.

Ballou, J., & Bryson, J. (1983). The doing and undoing of surgical sterilization: A psychosocial profile of the tubal reimplantation patient. *Psychiatry, 46*, 161–171.

Banville, J. (1992, May 14). Playing house [Review of M. Frayn's *A landing on the sun.*] *New York Review of Books,* p. 42.

Barrie, J. M. (1922). *Dear Brutus: A comedy in three acts.* New York: Scribner's.

Barron, F. H., & Mackenzie, K. D. (1973). A constrained optimization model of risky decisions. *Journal of Mathematical Psychology, 10*, 60–72.

Bartlett, J. (1980). *Familiar quotations* (E. M. Beck, Ed.), 15th ed. Boston: Little, Brown.

Baumbach, J. (1989, February 5). Amorality on the rampage [Review of *The Hungry Girls*]. *New York Times Book Review*, 36.

Beauvoir, Simone de. (1952). *The second sex*. New York: Bantam Books, 1961.

Beck, A. (1976). *Cognitive therapy and emotional disorders*. New York: International Universities Press.

Beckett, S. (1958/1984). *Krapp's last tape*. In *Collected shorter plays: Samuel Beckett*. New York: Grove Press.

Bedford, E. (1956–1957). Emotions. *Proceedings of the Aristotelian Society*. London: Harrison & Sons.

Bell, D. E. (1980). Explaining utility theory paradoxes by decision regret. *Proceedings of the fourth international conference on multiple criteria decision making*. University of Delaware, Newark. August 10–15, 1980. New York: Springer-Verlag, 1981.

Bell, D. E. (1982). Regret in decision making under uncertainty. *Operations Research, 30*, 961–981.

Berkowitz, L. (1970). Experimental investigations of hostility catharsis. *Journal of Consulting and Clinical Psychology, 35*, 1–7.

Berkun, C. S. (1986). In behalf of women over 40: Understanding the importance of the menopause. *Social Work, 31* (5), 378–384.

Bevan, W. (1991). Contemporary psychology: A tour inside the onion. *American Psychologist, 46*, 475–483.

Bishop, E. (1980). *The complete poems 1927–1979*. New York: Farrar, Straus and Giroux, Inc.

Blackwell, D., & Girshick, M. A. (1954). *Theory of games and statistical decisions*. New York: Wiley.

Bleich, D. (1978). *Subjective criticism*. Baltimore, MD: Johns Hopkins University Press.

Bleich, D. (1988). *The double perspective: Language, literacy, and social relations*. New York: Oxford University Press.

Booth, W. (1988). *The company we keep: An ethics of fiction*. Berkeley: University of California Press.

Borkovec, T. D., & Inz, J. (1990). The nature of worry in generalized anxiety disorder: A predominance of thought activity. *Behaviour Research & Therapy, 28*, 153–158.

Boyd, J. H., & Weissman, M. M. (1981). Epidemiology of affective disorders: A re-examination and future directions. *Archives of General Psychiatry, 38*, 1039–1046.

Brans, J., & Taylor Smith, M. (1987). *Mother, I have something to tell you*. New York: Doubleday.

Brehm, J. W. (1972). *Responses to loss of freedom: A theory of psychological reactance*. Morristown, NJ: General Learning Press.

Brehm, J. W., & Wicklund, R. A. (1970). Regret and dissonance reduction as a function of postdecision salience of dissonant information. *Journal of Personality and Social Psychology, 14*, 1–7.

Breznitz, S. (1983). The seven kinds of denial. In S. Breznitz (Ed.), *The-denial of stress.* New York: International Universities Press.

Briggs, J. L. (1970). *Never in anger.* Cambridge, Mass.: Harvard University Press.

Brinkley, A. (1990, October 14). A savage and demeaning ritual [Review of *Pledging allegiance*]. *New York Times Book Review,* pp. 1, 28–29.

Bronowski, J. (1956). *Science and human values.* New York: Julian Messner.

Brown, H. I. (1977). *Perception, theory and commitment: The new philosophy of science.* Chicago: Precedent.

Broyard, A. (1988, May 15). All the comforts of Dickens. *New York Times Book Review,* 13.

Bruner, J. (1986). *Actual minds, possible worlds.* Cambridge, Mass.: Harvard University Press.

Bruner, J. (1992). Another look at New Look 1. *American Psychologist, 47,* 780–783.

Burks, A. W. (1946). Laws of nature and reasonableness of regret. *Mind, 55,* 1770–172.

Butler, R. (1968). The life review: An interpretation of reminiscence in the aged. In B. L. Neugarten (Ed.), *Middle age and aging* (pp. 486–496). Chicago: University of Chicago Press.

Butler, S. (1927). *Erewhon: or Over the range.* New York: The Modern Library.

Byrne, D. (1961). The Repression-Sensitization Scale: Rationale, reliability, and validity. *Journal of Personality, 29,* 344–349.

Calvino, I. (1988). *Six memos for the next millennium.* Cambridge, Mass.: Harvard University Press.

Camus, A. (1956). *The fall* (J. O'Brien, Trans.). New York: Vintage.

Cantor, N., & Mischel, W. (1977). Traits as prototypes: Effects on recognition memory. *Journal of Personality and Social Psychology, 35,* 38–48.

Cantor, N., Smith, E. E., French, R. D., & Mezzich, J. (1980). Psychiatric diagnosis as prototype categorization. *Journal of Abnormal Psychology, 89,* 181–193.

Carlson, C. M. (1984). Reminiscing: Toward achieving ego integrity in old age. *Social Casework, 65,* 81–89.

Carlson, M., Charlin, V., & Miller, N. (1988). Positive mood and helping behavior: A test of six hypotheses. *Journal of Personality and Social Psychology, 55,* 211–229.

Cassill, R. V. (1970). Symposium: The writer's situation. In T. Solotaroff (Ed.), *New American Review,* Number 9.

Chapman, R. L. (1992, February 23). Letters. *New York Times Book Review,* p. 34.

Cheever, J. (1990, August 13). Journals: From the late forties and the fifties—II. *The New Yorker,* 29–61.

Cheever, J. (1991, January 28). Journals: From the Sixties—II. *The New Yorker*, 28–59.

Chin, C. R. (1993). "Any regrets?" "Let me think about it for a minute or two, or three, or four. . . .": The relationship between regret and rumination. Psychology Honors Thesis, University of Michigan.

Christensen-Szalanski, J. J., & Bushyhead, J. B. (1981). Physicians' use of probabilistic information in a real clinical setting. *Journal of Experimental Psychology: Human Perception and Performance*, 7, 928–936.

Clark, M. S., & Isen, A. M. (1982). Toward understanding the relationship between feeling states and social behavior. In A. Hastorf & A. M. Isen (Eds.), *Cognitive social psychology* (pp. 73–108). New York: Elsevier.

Clayton, P. J. (1981). The epidemiology of bipolar affective disorder. *Comprehensive Psychiatry*, 22, 31–43.

Conrad, J. (1910/1950). *Heart of darkness.* New York: Signet.

Coombs, C. H., Dawes, R. M., & Tversky, A. (1970). *Mathematical psychology.* Englewood Cliffs, NJ: Prentice-Hall.

Cooper, J. E., Bledin, K. D., Brice, B., & Mackenzie, S. (1985). Effects of female sterilization: One year follow-up in a prospective controlled-study of psychological and psychiatric outcome. *Journal of Psychosomatic Research*, 29 (10), 13–22.

Cornford, F. M. (1941). *The republic of Plato.* London: Oxford University Press/Clarendon.

Costa, P. T., & McCrae, R. R. (1980). Influence of extraversion and neuroticism on subjective well-being: Happy and unhappy people. *Journal of Personality and Social Psychology*, 38, 668–678.

Crosby, F. (1982). *Relative deprivation and working women.* New York: Oxford University Press.

Crossman, R. (1949). *The god that failed: Why six great writers rejected communism.* New York: Harper.

Croyle, R. T., & Cooper, J. (1983). Dissonance arousal: Physiological evidence. *Journal of Personality and Social Psychology*, 45, 782–791.

Cushman, P. (1990). Why the self is empty: Toward a historically situated psychology. *American Psychologist*, 45, 599–611.

Cushman, P. (1991). Ideology obscured: Political uses of the self in Daniel Stern's infant. *American Psychologist*, 46, 206–219.

Dapkus, M. (1985). A thematic analysis of the experience of time. *Journal of Personality and Social Psychology*, 49, 408–419.

Davis, F. (1979). *Yearning for yesterday: A sociology of nostalgia.* New York: The Free Press.

Dawes, R. M. (1981). Plato vs. Russell: Hoess and the relevance of cognitive psychology. Tech. Report No. 43. Institute for Social Science Research, Eugene, OR: The University of Oregon.

Dawes, R. M. (1988). *Rational choice in an uncertain world.* San Diego: Harcourt Brace Jovanovich.

DeLillo, D. (1986). *White noise.* New York: Penguin.

DeMott, B. (1982, March 14). Funny, wise and true [Review of *Dinner at the Homesick Restaurant*]. *New York Times Book Review*, 1, 14.

Denzin, N. K. (1990). On understanding emotion: The interpretive-cultural agenda. In T. D. Kemper (Ed.), *Research agendas in the sociology of emotions* (pp. 85–116). Albany: State University of New York Press.

deSousa, R. (1987). *The rationality of emotions*. Cambridge, Mass.: MIT Press.

Descartes, R. (1641). Meditations. *Great Books of the Western World*. Chicago: Engyclopaedia Brittanica, 1952.

Dewey, J. (1960). Time and individuality. *On experience, nature, and freedom* (R. Bernstein, Ed.) (pp. 224–243). Indianapolis, Ind.: Bobbs-Merrill.

DiCagno, D., & Hey, J. D. (1988). A direct test of the original version of regret theory. *Journal of Behavioral Decision Making*, 1, 43–56.

Dickens, C. (1861/1978). *Great expectations*. New York: Oxford University Press.

Dickinson, E. (1983). *The poems of Emily Dickinson* (T. H. Johnson, Ed.). Cambridge, Mass.: The Belknap Press of Harvard University Press.

Diener, E., & Emmons, R. A. (1985). The independence of positive and negative affect. *Journal of Personality and Social Psychology*, 47, 1105–1117.

Dinesen, I. (1937). *Out of Africa*. New York: Vintage, 1985.

Donoghue, D. (1981). *Ferocious alphabets*. Boston: Little, Brown.

Donoghue, D. (1991, August 15). Critics at the top [Review of *Versions of Pygmalion.*] *New York Review of Books*, pp. 53–56.

Dostoevsky, F. (1864/1981). *Notes from underground* (M. Ginsburg, Trans.). New York: Bantam.

Duffy, B. (1987). *The world as I found it: A novel*. New York: Ticknor & Fields.

Edwards, W. (1962). Subjective probabilities inferred from decisions. *Psychological Review*, 69, 109–135.

Edwards, W., & von Winterfeldt, D. (1986). On cognitive illusions and their implications. In H. R. Arkes, & K. R. Hammond, (Eds.) *Judgment and decision making: An interdisciplinary reader* (pp. 642–679). New York: Cambridge University Press.

Eliot, T. S. (1950). *Selected essays*. New York: Harcourt, Brace and Co.

Eliot, T. S. (1975). *Selected prose of T.S. Eliot* (F. Kermode, Ed.). New York: Harcourt Brace Jovanovich; Farrar, Straus and Giroux.

Eliot, T. S. (1952). *The complete poems and plays: 1909–1950*. New York: Brace & World, 1971.

Ellis, A. (1970). *Reason and emotion in psychotherapy*. New York: Lyle Stuart.

Ellsworth, P. C., & Smith, C. A. (1988). From appraisal to emotion: Differences among unpleasant feelings. *Motivation and Emotion*, 12, 271–302.

Elstein, A. S., Holzman, G. B., Ravitch, M. M., Metheny, W. A., Holmes,

M. M., Hoppe, R. B., Rothert, M. L., & Rovner, D. R. (1986). Comparison of physicians' decisions regarding estrogen replacement therapy for menopausal women and decisions derived from a decision analytic model. *The American Journal of Medicine, 80,* 246–258.

Emerson. *Correct quotes* (1990–1991). WordStar software. Novato, Calif.: WordStar International, Inc.

Ephron, N. (1986, November 2). Revision and life: Take it from the top—again. *New York Times Book Review,* p. 7.

Erdelyi, M. H. (1992). Psychodynamics and the unconscious. *American Psychologist, 47,* 784–787.

Erikson, E. (1955). *Childhood and society.* New York: Norton.

Erikson, E. H. (1976). Reflections on Dr. Borg's life cycle. In E. H. Erikson (Ed.), *Adulthood* (pp. 1–31). New York: Norton.

Erskine, H. (1973). The polls: Hopes, fears, and regrets. *Public Opinion Quarterly, 37,* 132–145.

Fabes, R. A., & Martin, C. L. (1991). Gender and age stereotypes of emotion. *Personality and Social Psychology Bulletin, 17,* 532–540.

Faulkner, W. (1929/1987). *The sound and the fury.* New York: Vintage.

Fazio, R., Sherman, S. J., & Herr, P. M. (1982). The feature-positive effect in the self-perception process: Does not doing matter as much as doing? *Journal of Personality and Social Psychology, 42,* 404–411.

Fehr, B., & Russell, J. A. (1985). The concept of emotion viewed from a prototype perspective. *Journal of Experimental Psychology: General, 113,* 464–486.

Fenichel, O. (1945). *The psychoanalytic theory of neurosis.* New York: Norton.

Feshbach, S. (1984). The catharsis hypothesis, aggressive drive, and the reduction of aggression. *Aggressive Behavior, 10,* 91–101.

Festinger, L. (1957). *A theory of cognitive dissonance.* Evanston, Ill.: Row, Peterson.

Festinger, L. (1964). *Conflict, decision, and dissonance.* Stanford, Calif.: Stanford University Press.

Festinger, L., & Walster, E. (1964). Post-decision regret and decision reversal. In L. Festinger (Ed.), *Conflict, decision, and dissonance* (pp. 112–127). Stanford, Calif.: Stanford University Press.

Fiedler, K. (1988). Emotional mood, cognitive style, and behavior regulation. In K. Fiedler & J. Forgas (Eds.), *Affect, cognition, and social behavior* (pp. 100–119). Toronto: Hogrefe International.

Fingarette, H. (1967). Real guilt and neurotic guilt. In H. Morris (Ed.), *Guilt and shame.* Belmont, Calif.: Wadsworth, 1971.

Fischhoff, B., Goitein, B., & Shapira, Z. (1982). The experienced utility of expected utility approaches. In N. T. Feather (Ed.), *Expectations and actions* (pp. 315–339). Hillsdale, NJ: Erlbaum.

Fish, S. E. (1972). *Self-consuming artifacts: The experience of seventeenth-century literature.* Berkeley: University of California Press.

Fitzgerald, F. S. In *Correct quotes* (1990–1991). WordStar software. Novato, Calif.: WordStar International, Inc.

Folkman, S., & Lazarus, R. S. (1985). If it changes it must be a process: Study of emotion and coping during three stages of a college examination. *Journal of Personality and Social Psychology, 48,* 150–170.

Foren, J. (1989, October 5). Governor raps Flint movie without seeing it. *Ann Arbor News.*

Forster, E. M. (1924). *A passage to India.* New York: Harvest.

Frank, J. (1986). *Dostoevsky: The stir of liberation, 1860–1865.* Princeton, NJ: Princeton University Press.

Frank, R. H. (1988). *Passions within reason: The strategic role of the emotions.* New York: Norton.

Frankfurt, H. G. (1988). *The importance of what we care about: Philosophical essays.* New York: Cambridge University Press.

Freeman, A., & DeWolf, R. (1989). *Woulda, coulda, shoulda: Overcoming regrets, mistakes, and missed opportunities.* New York: Harper-Perennial.

Freud, A. (1936). *The ego and the mechanisms of defense* (revised edition). New York: International Universities Press.

Freud, S. (1907). The manifest content of dreams and the latent dream-thoughts. *Introductory lectures on psychoanalysis* (J. Strachey, Ed. & Trans.). New York: Norton, 1966.

Freud, S. (1909). *Three case histories.* New York: Collier, 1963.

Freud, S. (1915). Repression. In *General psychological theory: Papers on metapsychology.* New York: Collier.

Freud, S. (1917). Mourning and melancholia. In *General psychological theory: Papers on metapsychology.* New York: Collier.

Freud, S. (1925). Negation. *General psychological theory: Papers on metapsychology.* New York: Collier Books, 1963.

Freud, S. (1926). Beyond the pleasure principle. *Standard Edition, 18,* 7–64.

Freud, S. (1930). *Civilization and its discontents* (J. Strachey, Trans). New York: Norton, 1961.

Fried, E. (1982). On "working through" as a form of self-innovation. In S. Slipp (Ed.), *Curative factors in dynamic psychotherapy* (pp. 243–258). New York: McGraw-Hill.

Friedman, M., & Rosenman, R. H. (1959). Association of specific overt behavior patterns with blood and cardiovascular findings: Blood cholesterol level, blood clotting time, incidence of arcus senilis, and clinical coronary artery disease. *Journal of the American Medical Association, 169,* 1286–1296.

Frijda, N. H. (1986). *The emotions.* Cambridge: Cambridge University Press.

Frijda, N. H. (1987). Emotion, cognitive structure, and action tendency. *Cognition and Emotion, 1,* 115–143.

Frijda, N. H. (1988). The laws of emotion. *American Psychologist, 43,* 349–358.

Frost, R. (1977). *North to Boston.* New York: Dodd, Mead.

Frye, N. (1957). *Anatomy of criticism: Four essays.* Princeton, NJ: Princeton University Press.

Fussell, P. (1983, September). The critic as human being [Review of *Characters and their landscapes*]. *Atlantic,* p. 122.

Galassi, J. (1984, October). Still life. *Atlantic,* p. 90.

Gaylin, W. (1979, January). On feeling guilty. *Atlantic,* pp. 78–82.

Gear, J. (1989). *Perception and the evolution of style: A new theory of mind.* London: Routledge.

Geen, R. G., Stonner, D., & Shope, G. L. (1975). The facilitation of aggression by aggression: A study in response inhibition and disinhibition. *Journal of Personality and Social Psychology, 31,*721–726.

Geertz, C. (1973). *The interpretation of cultures.* New York: Basic Books.

Gleicher, F., Kost, K. A., Baker, S. M., Strathman, A., Richman, S. A., & Sherman, S. J. (1990). The role of counterfactual thinking in judgments of affect. *Personality and Social Psychology Bulletin, 16,* 2284–295.

Gleick, J. (1987). *Chaos: Making a new science.* New York: Penguin.

Gonzales, A., & Zimbardo, P. G. (1985, March). Time in perspective. *Psychology Today,* pp. 21–26.

Goodman, N. (1973). *Fact, fiction, and forecast* (3rd ed.). Indianapolis: Bobbs-Merrill.

Gordon, S. L. (1990). Social structural effects on emotions. In T. D. Kemper (Ed.), *Research agendas in the sociology of emotions* (pp. 145–179). Albany: State University of New York Press.

Graham, L. (1990, September 2). Joy amid the pain [Review of *Carnal acts: Essays*]. *New York Times Book Review,* p. 7.

Gray, J. A. (1971). *The psychology of fear and stress.* London: Weidenfeld & Nicholson.

Gray, J. A. (1982). *The neuropsychology of anxiety: An enquiry into the functions of the septohippocampal system.* Oxford: Oxford University Press.

Greenspan, P. S. (1980). A case of mixed feelings: Ambivalence and the logic of emotion. In A. O. Rorty (Ed.), *Explaining emotion* (pp. 223–250). Berkeley: University of California Press.

Greenwald, A. G. (1992). New Look 3: Unconscious cognition reclaimed. *American Psychologist, 47,* 766–779.

Grout, P. (1978). On minimax regret and welfare economics. *Journal of Public Economics, 9,* 405–410.

Gudjonsson, G. H. (1984). Attribution of blame for criminal acts and its relationship with personality. *Personality and Individual Differences, 5*(1), 53–58.

Guimond, S., & Dube-Simard, L. (1983). Relative deprivation theory and the Quebec nationalist movement: The cognition-emotion distinction and the personal-group deprivation issue. *Journal of Personality and Social Psychology, 44,* 526–535.

Gurin, P. (1987). The political implications of women's statuses. In F. Crosby (Ed.), *Spouse, parent, worker: On gender and multiple roles* (pp. 165–196). New Haven: Yale University Press.

Gutmann, D. L. (1975). Parenthood: A key to the comparative study of the life cycle. In N. Datan & L. Ginzberg (Eds.), *Life span developmental psychology: Normative life crises.* New York: Academic.

Hacking, I. (1984, June 28). Winner take less [Review of *The evolution of cooperation*]. *New York Review of Books,* 17–21.

Hampshire, S. (1960). *Thought and action.* New York: Viking.

Hampshire, S. (1983). *Morality and conflict.* Cambridge, Mass.: Harvard University Press.

Harding, S. (1991). *Whose science? Whose knowledge?: Thinking from women's lives.* Ithaca, NY: Cornell University Press.

Harré, R. (Ed.) (1986). *The social construction of emotions.* Oxford: Basil Blackwell.

Hart, H. L. A., & Honore, A. M. (1959). *Causation in the law.* London: Oxford/Clarendon Press.

Harvey, J. W. (1947). The problem of guilt. *Explanation in history and philosophy. Aristotelian Society Proceedings.* Supplementary Volume 21. London: Harrison & Sons.

Hearst, E. (1984a). Absence as information: Some implications for learning, performance, and representational processes. In H. L. Roitblat, T. B. Bever, & H. S. Terrace (Eds.), *Animal cognition.* Hillsdale, NJ: Lawrence Erlbaum.

Hearst, E. (1984b, April 4). *Empty intervals and absent events: Something about nothing in the psychology of animals and people.* Distinguished faculty research lecture, Indiana University, Bloomington.

Heat-Moon, W. L. (1991, September). PrairyErth: Portraits from Chase County, Kansas. *Atlantic,* pp. 45–74.

Hegel, G. W. F. (1979). *Phenomenology of spirit* (A. V. Miller, Trans.). New York: Oxford University Press. (Original work published in 1807).

Heider, F. (1958). *The psychology of interpersonal relations.* New York: Wiley.

Hellman, L. (1976). *Scoundrel time.* Boston: Little, Brown.

Hemingway, E. (1963). *The snows of Kilimanjaro and other stories.* Middlesex, England: Penguin Books.

Henderson, G. P. (1973). Censure under control. *Ratio, 15,* 44–56.

Herrnstein, R. J. (1990). Rational choice theory: Necessary but not sufficient. *American Psychologist, 45,* 356–367.

Hershey, J. C., & Baron, J. (1987). Clinical reasoning and cognitive processes. *Medical Decision Making, 7,* 203–211.

Hirshfield, J. (1990, July 30/August 6). History as the painter Bonnard. *The Nation,* p. 143.

Hochschild, A. R. (1983). *The managed heart: Commercialization of human feeling.* Berkeley: University of California Press.

Hochschild, A. R. (1990). Ideology and emotion management: A perspective and path for future research. In T. D. Kemper (Ed.), *Research agendas in the sociology of emotions* (pp. 117–142). Albany: State University of New York Press.

Hogarth, R. (1986). *Judgment and choice* (2nd edition). New York: Wiley.

Holland, N. N. (1975). *5 readers reading.* New Haven, Conn.: Yale University Press.

Hollis, M. (1979). Rational man and social science. In H. Ross (Ed.), *Rational action* (pp. 1–16). Cambridge: Cambridge University Press.

Huxley, A. (1963). *Literature and science.* New Haven, Conn.: Leete's Island Books.

Ibsen, H. (1884/1954). *The wild duck.* In *Three plays* (U. Ellis-Fermor, Trans.). Baltimore: Penguin.

Inglehart, M. R. (1991). *Reactions to critical life events: A social psychological analysis.* New York: Praeger.

Ionesco, E. (1940–41/1971). *Present past, past present: A personal memoir* (H. R. Lane, Trans.). New York: Grove.

Isen, A. M., & Levin, P. F. (1972). The effect of feeling good on helping: Cookies and kindness. *Journal of Personality and Social Psychology, 21,* 384–388.

Isen, A. M., Shalker, T., Clark, M., & Karp, L. (1978). Affect, accessiblity of material in memory and behavior: A cognitive loop? *Journal of Personality and Social Psychology, 55,* 710–717.

Isen, A. M., & Simmonds, S. F. (1978). The effect of feeling good on a helping task that is incompatible with good mood. *Social Psychology, 41,* 346–349.

Ishiguro, K. (1989). *The remains of the day.* New York: Knopf.

Izard, C. E. (1972). *Patterns of emotions.* New York: Academic Press.

Izard, C. E. (1977). *Human emotions.* New York: Plenum.

Jacobs, W. (1976). What Professor Luckhardt cannot regret. *Philosophical Research Archives, 2* (1104), 671–677.

Jacoby, L. L., Lindsay, D. S., & Toth, J. P. (1992). Unconscious influences revealed: Attention, awareness, and control. *American Psychologist, 47,* 802–809.

James, H. (1903/1963). *The ambassadors.* New York: Heritage Press.

James, W. (1890). *The principles of psychology* (Vol. I). New York: Henry Holt.

James, W. (1923). The dilemma of determinism. *The will to believe and other essays in popular philosophy.* New York: Dover, 1956.

Janis, I. L., & Mann, L. (1977). Anticipatory regret. In *Decision making: A psychological analysis of conflict, choice, and commitment* (pp. 219–242). New York: Free Press.

Jaspers, K. (1947). Differentiation of German guilt. In H. Morris (Ed.), *Guilt and shame.* Basic Problems in Philosophy Series. Belmont, Calif.: Wadsworth, 1971.

Jenkins, H. M., & Sainsbury, R. S. (1970). Discrimination learning with the distinctive feature on positive or negative trials. In D. Mostofsky (Ed.), *Attention: Contemporary theory and analysis.* New York: Appleton-Century-Crofts.

Johnson, J. T. (1986). The knowledge of what might have been: Affective and attributional consequences of near outcomes. *Personality and Social Psychology Bulletin, 12,* 51–62.

Johnson, J. T. (1990, July). Fuzzy logic. *Popular Science,* pp. 87–89.

Johnson, M. K., & Sherman, S. J. (1990). Constructing and reconstructing the past and the future in the present. In E. T. Higgins, & R. M. Sorrentino (Eds.), *Handbook of motivation and cognition: Foundations of social behavior* (Vol. 2) (pp. 482–526). New York: Guilford.

Jones, D. H. (1966). Freud's theory of moral conscience. *Philosophy, 41,* 34–57.

Josephs, R. A., Larrick, R. P., Steele, C. M., & Nisbett, R. E. (1992). Protecting the self from the negative consequences of risky decisions. *Journal of Personality and Social Psychology, 62,* 26–37.

Joyce, J. (1914/1946). *Ulysses.* New York: Random House.

Jung, C. G. (1924). *Psychological types.* New York: Random House.

Jungermann, H. (1986). The two camps on rationality. In H. R. Arkes, & K. R. Hammond (Eds), *Judgment and decision making: An interdisciplinary reader* (pp. 627–641). New York: Cambridge University Press.

Kahneman, D., & Miller, D. T. (1986). Norm theory: Comparing reality to its alternatives. *Psychological Review, 93,* 136–153.

Kahneman, D., Slovic, P., & Tversky, A. (Eds.). (1982). *Judgment under uncertainty: Heuristics and biases.* New York: Cambridge University Press.

Kahneman, D., & Tversky, A. (1982a). The psychology of preferences. *Scientific American, 246,* 160–173.

Kahneman, D., & Tversky, A. (1982b). The simulation heuristic. In D. Kahneman, P. Slovic, & A. Tversky (Eds.), *Judgment under uncertainty: Heuristics and biases.* New York: Cambridge University Press.

Keillor, G. (1983, July 11). The current crisis in remorse. *The New Yorker,* pp. 36–37.

Kelsey, D., & Schepanski, A. (1991). Regret and disappointment in taxpayer reporting decision: An experimental study. *Journal of Behavioral Decision Making, 4,* 33–53.

Kemper, T. D. (Ed.) (1990). *Research agendas in the sociology of emotions.* Albany: State University of New York Press.

Kempton, M. (1992, April 23). Brother, can you spare a dime? *New York Review of Books*, p. 55.

Kenny, D. (1979). *Correlation and cauality.* New York: Wiley.

Kernberg, O. (1975). *Borderline conditions and pathological narcissism.* New York: Jason Aronson.

Kiefer, C. W. (1988). *The mantle of maturity: A history of ideas about character development.* Albany: SUNY Press.

Kierkegaard, S. (1967). *The journals of Soren Kierkegaard: A selection* (A. Dru, Ed. & Trans.). Bloomington, Ind.: Indiana University Press.

Kihlstrom, J. F., Barnhyardt, T. M., & Tataryn, D. J. (1992). The psychological unconscious: Found, lost, and regained. *American Psychologist, 47,* 788–791.

Kincaid, J. (1989, June 26). Mariah. *The New Yorker.*

Kinnier, R. T., & Metha, A. T. (1989). Regrets and priorities at three stages of life. *Counseling and Values, 33,* 182–193.

Klein, M. (1955a). On identification. In M. Klein, P. Heimann, & R. E. Money-Kyrle (Eds.), *New directions in psychoanalysis.* New York: Basic Books.

Klein, M. (1955b). The psycho-analytic play technique: Its history and significance. In M. Klein, P. Heimann, & R. E. Money-Kyrle (Eds.), *New directions in psychoanalysis.* New York: Basic Books.

Kleinginna, P. R., & Kleinginna, A. M. (1981). A categorized list of emotion definitions, with suggestions for a consensual definition. *Motivation and Emotion, 5,* 345–379.

Klinger, E. (1975). The consequences of commitment to and disengagement from incentives. *Psychological Review, 82,* 1–25.

Klinger, E. (1977). *Meaning and void: Inner experience and the incentives in people's lives.* Minneapolis: University of Minnesota Press.

Kogan, N., & Wallach, M. A. (1967). Risk taking as a function of the situation, the person, and the group. In *New directions in psychology III.* New York: Holt, Rinehart, & Winston.

Kohn, I. (1986). Counseling women who request sterilization: Psychodynamic issues and interventions. *Social Work in Health Care, 11* (20), 35–60.

Konecni, V. J., & Ebbesen, E. B. (1976). Disinhibition versus the cathartic effect: Artifact and substance. *Journal of Personality and Social Psychology, 34,* 352–365.

Kopit, S., & Barnes, A. B. (1976). Patients' response to tubal division. *Journal of American Medical Association, 236* (24), 2761–2763.

Krell, D. F. (1977). *Martin Heidegger: Basic writings.* New York: Harper & Row.

Kripke, S. A. (1980). *Naming and necessity.* Cambridge, Mass.: Harvard University Press.

Kubler-Ross, E. (1969). *On death and dying.* New York: Macmillan.

Kubler-Ross, E. (1975). *Death: The final stage of growth.* Englewood Cliffs, NJ: Prentice-Hall.

Kuhl, J. (1981). Motivational and functional helplessness: The moderating effect of state- vs. action-orientation. *Journal of Personality and Social Psychology, 40,* 155–170.

Kumin, M. (1974). *Our ground time here will be brief.* New York: Viking Penguin.

Kundera, M. (1981). *The book of laughter and forgetting.* New York: Penguin.

Kuralt, C. (1990). Regrets. *A life on the road.* New York: G. P. Putnam's Sons.

Kurosawa, A. (1992). *Ikiru. Seven Samurai and other screenplays* (D. Richie, Trans.). London: Faber and Faber.

Lakoff, G. (1973). Hedges: A study in the meaning of criteria and the logic of fuzzy concepts. *Journal of Philosophical Logic, 2,* 458–508.

Lakoff, G., & Johnson, M. (1980). *Metaphors we live by.* Chicago: The University of Chicago Press.

Lampedusa, G. di. (1960). *The leopard* (A. Colquhoun, Trans.). New York: Pantheon.

Landau, M. (1984). Human evolution as narrative. *American Scientist, 72,* 262–268.

Landman, J. T. (1984). Regret and undoing: Retrospective assessment of hypothetical and real-life events. Doctoral dissertation, University of Michigan, 1984.

Landman, J. (1987a). Regret and elation following action and inaction: Affective responses to positive versus negative outcomes. *Personality and Social Psychology Bulletin, 13,* 524–536.

Landman, J. (1987b). Regret: A theoretical and conceptual analysis. *Journal for the Theory of Social Behaviour, 17,* 135–160.

Landman, J., & Manis, J. (1992). What might have been: Counterfactual thought concerning personal decisions. *British Journal of Psychology, 83,* 473–477.

Landman, J., Pais, D., & Nykiel, C. (in preparation, 1993). Regret in young adults.

Landman, J., Vandewater, E., Stewart, A., & Malley, J. (Under review). Missed opportunities: Ramifications of counterfactual thought.

Laplanche, J. and Pontalis, J.-B. (1973). *The language of psycho-analysis* (D. Nicholson-Smith, Trans.). New York: Norton.

Larsen, R. J., & Ketelaar, T. (1989). Extraversion, neuroticism, and susceptibility to positive and negative mood induction procedures. *Personality and Individual Differences, 10,* 1221–1228.

Larsen, R. J., & Ketelaar, T. (1991). Personality and susceptibility to positive and negative emotional states. *Journal of Personality and Social Psychology, 61,* 132–140.

Lasch, C. (1979). *The culture of narcissism.* New York: Warner.

Lawrence, T. E. (1927). *Seven pillars of wisdom.* Garden City, NY: Doubleday, 1935.

Lazarus, R. S. (1966). *Psychological stress and the coping process.* New York: McGraw-Hill.

Lazarus, R. S. (1982). Thoughts on the relations between emotion and cognition. *American Psychologist, 37,* 1019–1024.

Lazarus, R. S. (1991). *Emotion and adaptation.* New York: Oxford University Press.

Lazarus, R. S., & Folkman, S. (1984). *Stress, appraisal, and coping.* New York: Springer.

Lears, J. (1989, January 9/16). Deride and conquer [Review of *The culture of TV*]. *The Nation,* 59–61.

Lee, W. (1971a). Preference strength, expected value difference, and expected regret ratio. *Psychological Bulletin, 75,* 186–191.

Lee, W. (1971b). The effects of expected value difference and expected regret ratio on preference strength. *American Journal of Psychology, 84,* 194–204.

Leventhal, H. (1980). Toward a comprehensive theory of emotion. In L. Berkowitz (Ed.), *Advances in experimental social psychology.* (Vol. 13). New York: Academic Press.

Levinson, D. (with C. N. Darrow, E. B. Klein, M. H. Levinson, B. McKee). (1978). *The seasons of a man's life.* New York: Knopf.

Levy, R. (1973). *The Tahitians.* Chicago: University of Chicago Press.

Lewicki, P., Hill, T., & Czyzewska, M. (1992). Nonconscious acquisition of information. *American Psychologist, 47,* 796–801.

Lewinsohn, P. M., Mischel, W., Chaplin, W., & Barton, R. (1980). Social competence and depression: The role of illusory self-perceptions. *Journal of Abnormal Psychology, 89,* 203–212.

Lewis, D. K. (1973). *Counterfactuals.* Cambridge, Mass.: Harvard University Press.

Lewis, H. B. (1971). *Shame and guilt in neurosis.* New York International Universities Press.

Lewis, H. D. (1947). The problem of guilt. *Explanation in history and philosophy. Aristotelian Society Proceedings* (Vol. 21). London: Harrison & Sons.

Lewis, H. (1986). The role of shame in depression. In M. Rutter, C. E. Izard, & P. B. Read (Eds.), *Depression in young people* (pp. 325–339). New York: Guilford.

Loewenstein, S. F., Bloch, N. E., Campion, J., Epstein, J. S., & Salvatore, M. (1981). A study of satisfactions and stresses of single women in midlife. *Sex Roles, 7* (11), 1127–1141.

Loftus, E. F., & Klinger, M. R. (1992). Is the unconscious smart or dumb? *American Psychologist, 47,* 761–765.

Loomes, G. (1988). Further evidence of the impact of regret and disappointment in choice under uncertainty. *Economica, 55,* 47–62.

Loomes, G., Starmer, C., & Sugden, R. (1989). Preference reversal: Information-processing effect or rational non-transitive choice? *The Economic Journal, 99,* 140–151.

Loomes, G., & Sugden, R. (1982). Regret theory: An alternative theory of rational choice under uncertainty. *The Economic Journal, 92,* 805–824.

Loomes, G., & Sugden, R. (1987). Testing for regret and disappointment in choice under uncertainty. *The Economic Journal, 97,* 118–129.

Lowry, M. (1947/1971). *Under the volcano.* New York: New American Library.

Luce, R. D., & Raiffa, H. (1957). *Games and decisions: Introduction and critical survey.* New York: Wiley.

Luckhardt, C. G. (1975). Remorse, regret and the Socratic paradox. *Analysis, 35,* 159–166.

Lukacs, J. (1968/1985). *Historical consciousness or The remembered past.* New York: Schocken.

Lutz, C. A. (1988). *Unnatural emotions: Everyday sentiments on a Micronesian atoll and their challenge to Western theory.* Chicago: University of Chicago Press.

Lutz, C. A. (1990). Engendered emotion: Gender, power, and the rhetoric of emotional control in American discourse. In C. A. Lutz, & L. Abu-Lughod (Eds.), *Language and the politics of emotion* (pp. 69–91). Cambridge: Cambridge University Press.

Lutz, C. A., & White, G. M. (1986). The anthropology of emotions. *Annual Review of Anthropology, 15,* 405–436.

Maccoby, E. E., & Jacklin, C. N. (1974). *The psychology of sex differences.* Stanford, Calif.: Stanford University Press.

Machina, M. J. (1987). Decision-making in the presence of risk. *Science, 236,* 537–543.

Mack, J. E. (1976). *A prince of our disorder: The life of T. E. Lawrence.* Boston: Little, Brown.

Macrae, C. N. (1992). A tale of two curries: Counterfactual thinking and accident-related judgments. *Personality and Social Psychology Bulletin, 13,* 84–87.

Mansfield, K. In *Correct quotes* (1990–1991). WordStar software. Novato, Calif.: WordStar International, Inc.

March, J. G. (1978). Bounded rationality, ambiguity, and the engineering of choice. *The Bell Journal of Economics, 9,* 587–608.

Markman, K. D., Gavanski, I., Sherman, S. J., & McMullen, M. N. (1993). The mental simulation of better and worse possible worlds. *Journal of Experimental Social Psychology 29,* 87–109.

Markus, H. R., & Kitayama, S. (1991). Culture and the self: Implications for cognition, emotion, and motivation. *Psychological Review, 98,* 224–253.

Markus, H., & Nurius, P. (1986). Possible selves. *American Psychologist,* *41,* 954–969.

Maxwell, W. (1992, December 7). What he was like. *The New Yorker,* pp. 122–123.

McAdams, D. P. (1985). *Power, intimacy, and the life story: Personological inquiries into identity.* Homewood, Ill.: Dorsey Press.

McCauley, C., & Graham, N. (1971). Influence of values in risky decision making: A formalization. *Representative Research in Social Psychology, 2* (2), 3–11.

Meehl, P. E. (1979). A funny thing happened to us on the way to the latent entities. *Journal of Personality Assessment, 43,* 564–581.

Meichenbaum, D. (1977). *Cognitive behavior modification: An integrative approach.* New York: Plenum.

Meichenbaum, D. (1985). *Stress-inoculation training.* New York: Pergamon.

Mendelsohn, G., Weiss, D., & Feimer, N. (1982). Conceptual and empirical analysis of the typological implications of patterns of socialization and femininity. *Journal of Personality and Social Psychology, 42,* 1157–1170.

Merikle, P. M. (1992). Perception without awareness: Critical issues. *American Psychologist, 47,* 792–795.

Merton, R. K., & Kitt, A. S. (1950). Contributions to the theory of reference group behavior. In R. K. Merton & P. F. Lazarsfeld (Eds.), *Continuities in social research: Studies in the scope and method of the American soldier.* Glencoe, IL: Free Press.

Mervis, C. B., & Rosch, E. (1981). Categorization of natural objects. *Annual Review of Psychology, 32,* 89–115.

Merwin, W. S. (1973). *Writings to an unfinished accompaniment.* New York: Atheneum.

Messer, S. B. (1986). Behavioral and psychoanalytic perspectives at therapeutic choice points. *American Psychologist, 41,* 1261–1272.

Mill, J. S. (1859). *On liberty.* In *Great Books of the Western World* (Vol. 43) (pp. 267–323). Chicago: Encyclopaedia Britannica, 1952.

Miller, D. T., & McFarland, C. (1986). Counterfactual thinking and victim compensation: A test of norm theory. *Personality and Social Psychology Bulletin, 12,* 513–519.

Miller, W. B., & Shain, R. N. (1985). Married women and contraceptive sterilization: Factors that contribute to pre-surgical ambivalence. *Journal of Biosocial Sciences, 17,* 471–479.

Minton, L. (1990, April 22). Fresh voices. *Parade Magazine,* p. 13.

Mischel, W., Ebbesen, E., & Zeiss, A. (1973). Selective attention to the self: Situational and dispositional determinants. *Journal of Personality and Social Psychology, 27,* 129–142.

Mischel, W., Ebbesen, E., & Zeiss, A. (1976). Determinants of selective memory about the self. *Journal of Consulting and Clinical Psychology, 44*, 92–103.

Montaigne, M. de. (1580/1936). Of repentance. *The essays of Michel de Montaigne* (J. Zeitlin, Trans.). Vol III. New York: Knopf.

Moracco, J. C., D'Arienzo, R. V., & Danford, D. (1983). Comparison of perceived occupational stress between teachers who are contented and discontented in their career choices. *The Vocational Guidance Quarterly, 32* (1), 44–51.

Morris, J. N. (1966). *Versions of the self.* New York: Basic Books.

Morris, W. N., & Reilly, N. P. (1987). Toward the self-regulation of mood: Theory and research. *Motivation and Emotion, 11*, 215–249.

Morrow, L. (1983, May 23). The morals of remembering. *Time,* p. 88.

Mowrer, O. H. (1960). *Learning theory and behavior.* New York: Wiley.

Murray, J., & Feshbach, S. (1978). Let's not throw the baby out with the bathwater: The catharsis hypothesis revisited. *Journal of Personality, 46*, 462–473.

Myers, J. L., & Atkinson, R. C. (1964). Choice behavior and reward structure. *Journal of Mathematical Psychology, 1*, 170–203.

Myers, J. L., Suydam, M. M., & Heuckeroth, O. (1966). Choice behavior and reward structure: Differential payoff. *Journal of Mathematical Psychology, 3*, 458–469.

Nagel, T. (1993, March 4). The mind wins! [Review of *The rediscovery of the mind*]. *New York Review of Books,* 37–41.

Newman, C. (1990, October 7). How it feels to cease to be [Review of *Hourglass*]. *New York Times Book Review,* 14–15.

Nietzsche, F. (1887/1974). *The gay science* (W. Kaufmann, Trans.). New York: Vintage Books.

Nisbett, R., & Ross, L. (1980). *Human inference: Strategies and shortcomings of social judgment.* Englewood Cliffs, New Jersey: Prentice-Hall.

Nisbett, R. E., & Wilson, T. D. (1977). Telling more than we can know: Verbal reports on mental processes. *Psychological Review, 84*, 231–259.

No comment. (1991, May). *The Progressive,* p. 10.

Nolen-Hoeksema, S. (1987). Sex differences in unipolar depression: Evidence and theory. *Psychological Bulletin, 101*, 259–282.

Noted with pleasure. (1990, October 21). *New York Times Book Review,* 43.

Nussbaum, M. C. (1990). *Love's knowledge.* New York: Oxford University Press.

Oatley, K. (1992). *Best laid schemes: The psychology of emotions.* New York: Cambridge University Press.

O'Brien, C. C. (1988, Nov. 24). Keeping up with the Shaws [Review of *Bernard Shaw: The Search for Love. Vol I, 1856–1898*]. *New York Review of Books,* 3–6.

Olney, J. (1972). *Metaphors of self.* Princeton, NJ: Princeton University Press.

Ortony, A., Clore, G., & Collins, A. (1988). *The cognitive structure of emotions.* New York: Cambridge University Press.

Orwell, G. (1949). *1984.* New York: Signet, 1983.

Orwoll, L. (1989). *Wisdom in later adulthood: Personality and life history correlates.* Doctoral Dissertation, Boston University.

Otten, A. (1987, September 14). Price of progress: Efforts to predict genetic ills pose medical dilemmas. *The Wall Street Journal,* p. 21.

Ozick, C. (1983). *Art and ardor.* New York: Knopf.

Parfit, D. (1984). *Reasons and persons.* New York: Clarendon/Oxford.

Penrose, R. (1989). *The emperor's new mind: Concerning computers, minds, and the laws of physics.* New York: Oxford University Press.

Penrose, R. (1991, March 28). The biggest enigma [Review of *Quantum Profiles*]. *New York Review of Books,* pp. 37–38.

Peterson, C. (1991). *Health and optimism.* New York: Free Press.

Peterson, C., & Seligman, M. E. P. (1984). Causal explanations as a risk factor for depression: Theory and evidence. *Psychological Review, 91,* 347–374.

Piaget, J. (1952). *The origins of intelligence in children.* New York: International Universities Press.

Plato. (1952). *The republic.* Great Books of the Western World (R. M. Hutchins, Ed.). Chicago: Encyclopaedia Britannica.

Platonov, A. (1975). *The foundation pit* (M. Ginsburg, Trans.). New York: E. P. Dutton.

Plutchik, R. (1980). *Emotion: A psychoevolutionary synthesis.* New York: Harper & Row.

Polivy, J. (1981). On the induction of emotion in the laboratory: Discrete moods or multiple affect states? *Journal of Personality and Social Psychology, 41,* 803–817.

Pribram, K. H. (1971). *Languages of the brain: Experimental paradoxes and principles of neuropsychology.* Englewood Cliffs, NJ: Prentice-Hall.

Price, E. (1979). *Leave your self alone.* Grand Rapids, Mich.: Zondervan.

Price, M. H. (1992, February 9). Author reflects on screen adaptation of his novel. *Ann Arbor News,* p. E5.

Proust, M. (1948). *Pleasures and regrets* (L. Varese, Trans.). New York: Lear/Crown.

Quammen, D. (1982, November 21). Plain folks and puzzling changes [Review of *Shiloh and other stories*]. *New York Times Book Review,* 7.

Rapoport, A. (1960). *Fights, games, and debates.* Ann Arbor: University of Michigan Press.

Rapoport, A. (1968). Choice behavior in a Markovian decision task. *Journal of Mathematical Psychology, 5,* 163–181.

Rapoport, A. (1989). Comments on a behavioral decision theory paradox. *Behavioral Science, 34,* 289–290.

Rapoport, A., & Chammah, A. M. (1965). *Prisoner's dilemma.* Ann Arbor: University of Michigan Press.

Rawls, J. (1963). The sense of justice. In H. Morris (Ed.), *Guilt and shame.* Basic Problems in Philosophy Series. Belmont, Calif.: Wadsworth, 1971.

Raz, J. (1986). *The morality of freedom.* New York: Oxford University Press.

Reitsch, A. G. (1976). Selecting alpha by minimizing expected regret: An example. *Educational and Psychological Measurement, 36,* 675–678.

Resnik, M. D. (1987). *Choices: An introduction to decision theory.* Minneapolis: University of Minnesota Press.

Ritov, I., & Baron, J. (1990). Reluctance to vaccinate: Omission bias and ambiguity. *Journal of Behavioral Decision Making, 3,* 263–277.

Rohlen, T. P. (1978). The promise of adulthood in Japanese spiritualism. In E. H. Erikson (Ed.). *Adulthood* (pp.121–147). New York: Norton.

Romaker, R. S. (1991, December 2). U-M memories. *Ann Arbor News,* p. C1.

Romans-Clarkson, S. E., & Gillett, W. R. (1987). Women who regret their sterilization: Developmental considerations. *Journal of Psychosomatic Obstetrics and Gynaecology, 7,* 9–17.

Rorty, A. Oksenberg. (Ed.). (1980). *Explaining emotions.* Berkeley: University of California Press.

Rorty, R. (1982). *Consequences of pragmatism (Essays: 1972–1980).* Minneapolis: University of Minnesota Press.

Rosch, E., & Lloyd, B. B. (1978). *Cognition and categorization.* Hillsdale, New Jersey: Erlbaum.

Rosch, E., & Mervis, C. B. (1975). Family resemblances in the internal structure of categories. *Cognitive Psychology, 7,* 573–605.

Roseman, I. (1979, September). *Cognitive aspects of emotion and emotional behavior.* Paper presented at the meeting of the American Psychological Association, New York City.

Roseman, I. J., Spindel, M. S., & Jose, P. E. (1990). Appraisals of emotion-eliciting events: Testing a theory of discrete emotions. *Journal of Personality and Social Psychology, 59,* 899–915.

Roseman, I. J. (1991). Appraisal determinants of discrete emotions. *Cognition and Emotion, 5,* 161–200.

Rosenblatt, L. M. (1968). *Literature as exploration.* New York: Noble and Noble.

Rosenwald, G. C., & Wiersma, J. (1983). Women, career changes, and the new self. *Psychiatry, 46,* 213–229.

Ross, L. (1977). The intuitive psychologist and his shortcomings: Distortions in the attribution process. In L. Berkowitz (Ed.), *Advances in experimental social psychology* (Vol. 10). New York: Academic Press.

Russell, D., & McAuley, E. (1986). Causal attributions, causal dimensions, and affective reactions to success and failure. *Journal of Personality and Social Psychology, 50,* 1174–1185.

Russell, J. A. (1978). Evidence of convergent validity on the dimensions of affect. *Journal of Personality and Social Psychology, 36,* 1152–1168.

Russell, J. A., & Mehrabian, A. (1977). Evidence for a three-factor theory of emotions. *Journal of Research in Personality, 11,* 273–294.

Ruvolo, A. P., & Markus, H. R. (1992). Possible selves and performance: The power of self-relevant imagery. *Social Cognition, 10,* 95–124.

Ryff, C. D., & Heincke, S. G. (1983). Subjective organization of personality in adulthood and aging. *Journal of Personality and Social Psychology, 44,* 807–816.

Sage, A. P., & White, E. B. (1983). Decision and information structures in regret models of judgment and choice, *IEEE, SMC-13,* 136–145.

Sainsbury, R. S. (1973). Discrimination learning using positive or negative cues. *Canadian Journal of Psychology, 27,* 46–57.

Sandelands, L. E. (1988). The concept of work feeling. *Journal for the Theory of Social Behaviour, 18,* 437–457.

Sartre, J.-P. (1948). *The emotions: Outline of a theory.* New York: Philosophical Library.

Sartre, J.-P. (1956). *Being and nothingness* (H.E. Barnes, Trans.). New York: Washington Square Books.

Savage, L. J. (1951). The theory of statistical decision. *Journal of the American Statistical Association, 46,* 55–67.

Schafer, R. (1976). *A new language for psychoanalysis.* New Haven: Yale University Press.

Scherer, K. R., & Ekman, P. (Eds.) (1984). *Approaches to emotion.* Hillsdale, NJ: Erlbaum.

Schoeffler, M. S. (1962). Prediction of some stochastic events: A regret equalization model. *Journal of Experimental Psychology, 64,* 615–622.

Schwartz, G. E., & Weinberger, D. A. (1980). Patterns of emotional responses to affective situations: Relations among happiness, sadness, anger, fear, depression, and anxiety. *Motivation and Emotion, 4,* 175–191.

Schwarz, N. (1990). Feelings as information: Informational and motivational functions of affective states. In E. T. Higgins & R. M. Sorrentino (Eds.), *Handbook of motivation and cognition: Foundations of social behavior* (Vol 2) (pp. 527–561). New York: Guilford.

Schwarz, N., Bless, H., & Bohner, G. (1991). Mood and persuasion: Affective states influence the processing of persuasive communications, pp. 161–199. In M. P. Zanna (Ed.), *Advances in experimental social psychology* (Vol. 24). San Diego, CA: Academic Press.

Scitovsky, T. (1992). *The joyless economy: The psychology of human satisfaction* (Rev. ed.). New York: Oxford University Press.

Sears, P. S. (1979). The Terman genetic studies of genius, 1922–1972. In A. H. Passow (Ed.), *The gifted and the talented: Their education and development.* The 78th Yearbook of the National Society for the Study of Education, Part I. Chicago: University of Chicago Press.

Segal, H. (1955). A psycho-analytical approach to aesthetics. In M. Klein, P. Heimann, R. E. Money-Kyrle (Eds.), *New directions in psychoanalysis.* New York: Basic Books.

Segal, H. (1964). *Introduction to the work of Melanie Klein.* New York: Basic Books.

Sen, A. K. (1977). Rational fools: A critique of the behavioral foundations of economic theory. *Philosophy and Public Affairs, 6,* 317–344.

Sennett, R., & Cobb, J. (1973). *The hidden injuries of class.* New York: Vintage.

Shabad, P. (1987). Fixation and the road not taken. *Psychoanalytic Psychology, 4,* 187–205.

Shain, R. N., Miller, W. P., & Holden, A. E. C. (1984). The decision to terminate childbearing: Differences in preoperative ambivalence between tubal ligation women and vasectomy wives. *Social Biology, 31* (1–2), 40–58.

Shapiro, B. (1991, February 18). Hell for those who won't go. *The Nation,* pp. 194–198.

Shapiro, D. (1965). *Neurotic styles.* New York: Basic.

Shapiro, W. (1988, July 18). When bad things are caused by good nations. *Time,* p. 20.

Shea, J. (1989, January 13). Without a radio, Shea takes a final look at life. *Michigan Daily/Weekend,* p. 10.

Shefrin, H. M., & Statman, M. (1986). How not to make money in the stock market. *Psychology Today, 20,* 52–57.

Shimanoff, S. B. (1984). Commonly named emotions in everyday conversations. *Perceptual and Motor Skills, 58,* 514.

Shimanoff, S. B. (1985). Rules governing the verbal expression of emotions between married couples. *The Western Journal of Speech Communication, 49,* 147–165.

Shweder, R. A. (1984). Anthropology's romantic rebellion against the enlightenment, or there's more to thinking than reason and evidence. In R. A. Shweder, & R. A. LeVine (Eds.), *Culture theory: Essays on mind, self, and emotion* (pp. 27–66). New York: Cambridge University Press.

Silber, J. R. (1967). Being and doing: A study of status responsibility and voluntary responsibility. *University of Chicago Law Review, 35,* 47–91.

Siler, T. (1991, February 3). Noted with pleasure. *New York Times Book Review,* p. 35.

Simon, H. A. (1956). Rational choice and the structure of the environment. *Psychological Review, 63,* 129–138.

Simon, H. A. (1979). *Models of thought.* New Haven, Conn.: Yale University Press.

Simon, H. A. (1986). Alternative visions of rationality. In H. R. Arkes, & K. R. Hammond (Eds), *Judgment and decision making: An interdisciplinary reader* (pp. 97–113). New York: Cambridge University Press.

Sinclair, R. C. (1988). Mood, categorization breadth, and performance appraisal: The effects of order of information acquisition and affective state on halo, accuracy, information retrieval, and evaluations. *Organizational Behavior and Human Decision Processes, 42,* 22–46.

Slavitt, D. (1990, January 29). Quoted in Briefly Noted [Review of *Lives of the saints*]. *The New Yorker,* p. 95.

Slovic, P., & Lichtenstein, S. (1968). Importance of variance preferences in gambling decisions. *Journal of Experimental Psychology, 78,* 646–654.

Smart, J. J. C., & Williams, B. (1973). *Utilitarianism for and against.* London: Cambridge University Press.

Smith, A. (1759/1793). *The theory of moral sentiments* (Vol I). Basil:J. J. Tourneisen.

Smith, C. A., & Ellsworth, P. C. (1985). Patterns of cognitive appraisal in emotion. *Journal of Personality and Social Psychology, 48,* 813–838.

Smith, C. A., & Ellsworth, P. C. (1987). Patterns of appraisal and emotion related to taking an exam. *Journal of Personality and Social Psychology, 52,* 475–488.

Smith, C. A., & Lazarus, R. S. Emotion and adaptation. In L. Pervin (Ed.), *Handbook of personality theory and research* (pp. 609–637). NY: Guilford.

Snow, C. P. (1956/1963). The two cultures. In S. Weintraub (Ed.), *C. P. Snow: A spectrum* (pp. 30–33). New York: Scribner.

Smith, T. R. (Ed.) (1919). *Baudelaire: His prose and poetry* (F. P. Sturm, Trans.). New York: Modern Poetry.

Solomon, R. C. (1976). *The passions: The myth and nature of human emotion.* Notre Dame, Ind.: The University of Notre Dame Press.

Spinoza, B. (1952). Ethics. In R. M Hutchins, (Ed.), *Great books of the western world* (Vol. 31). Chicago: Encyclopaedia Britannica.

Stafford, W. (1970). *Allegiances.* New York: Harper & Row.

Staw, B. M. (1976). Knee-deep in the big muddy: A study of escalating commitment to a chosen course of action. *Organizational Behavior and Human Performance, 16,* 27–44.

Steele, C. M. (1988). The psychology of self affirmation: Sustaining the integrity of the self. In L. Berkowitz (Ed.), *Advances in Experimental Social Psychology* (Vol. 21), (261–302). New York: Academic Press.

Steiner, G. (1961). *The death of tragedy.* New York: Hill and Wang.

Stevens, W. (1972). *The palm at the end of the mind: Selected poems and a play by Wallace Stevens* (H. Stevens, Ed). New York: Vintage Books.

Stewart, A. J., Vandewater, E. A., Landman, J., & Malley, J. E. (Under review). Recognizing the limitations of one's own past: Motivations for change in women's lives.

Stipek, D., Weiner, B., & Li, K. (1989). Testing some attribution-emotion relations in the People's Republic of China. *Journal of Personality and Social Psychology, 56,* 109–116.

Stocker, M. (1979). Desiring the bad: An essay in moral psychology. *The Journal of Philosophy, 76*, 738–753.

Stocker, M. (1987). Moral conflicts: What they are and what they show. *Pacific Philosophical Quarterly, 68*, 104–123.

Storm, C., & Storm, T. (1987). A taxonomic study of the vocabulary of emotions. *Journal of Personality and Social Psychology, 53*, 805–816.

Stouffer, S. A., Suchman, E. A., DeVinney, L. C., Star, S. A., & Williams, R. M., Jr. (1949). *The American soldier: Adjustment during Army life* (Vol 1). Princeton, NJ: Princeton University Press.

Streshinsky, S. (1985, April). The road not taken. *Glamour*, pp. 192–197.

Sugden, R. (1985). Regret, recrimination and rationality. *Theory and Decision, 19*, 77–99.

Suydam, M. M. (1965). Effects of cost and gain ratios, and probability of outcome on ratings of alternative choices. *Journal of Mathematical Psychology, 2*, 171–179.

Svenson, O., Benthorn, L. J. (1990). Postdecision changes in attractiveness of choice alternatives. *Psychological Research Bulletin, 30*, 1–16.

Tangney, J. P. (1992). Situational determinants of shame and guilt in young adulthood. *Personality and Social Psychology Bulletin, 18*, 199–206.

Taubes, G. (1990). The body chaotic. *Discover*, pp. 49–53.

Tavris, C. (1982). *Anger, the misunderstood emotion.* New York: Simon and Schuster.

Tavris, C. (1988, August). Chasing life dreams. *Vogue*, p. 236.

Taylor, G. (1985). *Pride, shame and guilt: Emotions of self-assessment.* New York: Clarendon Press, Oxford University Press.

Taylor, S. E. (1983). Adjustment to threatening events: A theory of cognitive adaptation. *American Psychologist, 38*, 1161–1173.

Taylor, S. E., & Brown, J. D. (1988). Illusions and well-being: Some social-psychological contributions to a theory of mental health. *Psychological Bulletin, 103*, 193–210.

Tesser, A., Leone, C., & Clary, E. G. (1978). Affect control: Process constraints versus catharsis. *Cognitive Therapy and Research, 2*, 265–274.

Thalberg, I. (1963). Remorse. *Mind, 72*, 545–555.

Thaler, R. (1980). Toward a positive theory of consumer choice. *Journal of Economic Behavior and Organization, 1*, 39–60.

Tolstoy, L. N. (1923). *The death of Ivan Ilyitch and other stories.* New York: Scribner's.

Tolstoy, L. (1869/1952). *War and peace* (L. and A. Maude, Trans.). Chicago: Encyclopaedia Britannica, Inc.

Trilling, L. (1953). *The liberal imagination.* Garden City, NY: Anchor.

Tversky, A. (1969). Intransitivity of preferences. *Psychological Review, 76*, 31–48.

Tversky, A., & Kahneman, D. (1981). The framing of decisions and the psychology of choice. *Science, 211*, 453–458.

Tversky, A., & Kahneman, D. (1986). Rational choice and the framing of decisions. *Journal of Business, 59,* S251–S278.

Tversky, A., Sattath, S., & Slovic, P. (1988). Contingent weighting in judgment and choice. *Psychological Review, 95,* 371–384.

Tyler, A. (1988). *Breathing lessons.* New York: Knopf.

Vaihinger, H. (1924). *The philosophy of "as if": A system of the theoretical, practical and religious fictions of mankind* (C. K. Ogden, Trans.). New York: Harcourt, Brace.

Vaillant, G. E. (1977). *Adaptation to life.* Boston: Little, Brown.

Van Amerongen, J. (1989, March 12). The Neighborhood cartoon. *Ann Arbor News.*

von Fieandt, K., & Moustgaard, I. K. (1977). *The perceptual world.* London: Academic Press.

von Neumann, J., & Morgenstern, O. (1953). *Theory of games and economic behavior.* Princeton, NJ: Princeton University Press.

von Winterfeldt, D., & Edwards, W. (1986). *Decision analysis and behavioral research.* New York: Cambridge University Press.

Walsh, A. (1988, September 17). Critics singing praises of '81 Hopwood winner. *Ann Arbor News,* pp. B2–3.

Walsh, V. C. (1961). *Scarcity and evil.* Englewood Cliffs, NJ: Prentice-Hall.

Walster, G. W., & Walster, E. (1970). Choice between negative alternatives: Dissonance reduction or regret? *Psychological Reports, 26,* 995–1005.

Wason, P. D., & Johnson-Laird, P. N. (1965). *Psychology of reasoning: Structure and content.* London: Batsford.

Watson, D., & Clark, L. A. (1984). Negative affectivity: The disposition to experience aversive emotional states. *Psychological Bulletin, 96,* 465–490.

Weisman, A. D., & Worden, J. W. (1976–77). The existential plight in cancer: Significance of the first 100 days. *International Journal of Psychiatry in Medicine, 7*(10), 1–15.

Weiner, B. (1985). An attributional theory of achievement motivation and emotion. *Psychological Review, 92,* 548–573.

Weissman, M. M., & Klerman, G. L. (1977). Sex differences in the epidemiology of depression. *Archives of General Psychiatry, 39,* 1397–1403.

Whitehead, J. W. (1991). The forgotten limits: Reason and regulation in economic theory. In K. R. Monroe (Ed.), *The economic approach to politics: A critical reassessment of the theory of rational action* (pp. 53–73). New York: HarperCollins.

Whitman, W. (1978) Song of myself. In *The treasury of American poetry* (p. 256). (N. Sullivan, Ed.). Garden City, NY: Doubleday.

Wicker, F. W., & Payne, G. C., & Morgan, R. D. (1983). Participant descriptions of guilt and shame. *Motivation and Emotion, 7,* 25–39.

Wicklund, R. A. (1970). Prechoice preference reversal as a result of threat to decision freedom. *Journal of Personality and Social Psychology, 14,* 8–17.

Wicklund, R. A., & Brehm, J. W. (1976). *Perspectives on cognitive dissonance.* New York: Wiley.

Wideman, J. E. (1984). *Brothers and keepers.* New York: Holt, Rinehart & Winston.

Williams, B. A. O. (1965). Ethical consistency. *Aristotelian Society, 39,* 103–124.

Williams, B. A. O. (1976). Moral luck. *Aristotelian Society, 50,* 115–136.

Wills, G. (1983, February 20). An American family [Review of *Descent from glory*]. *New York Times Book Review,* p. 1.

Wittgenstein, L. (1953). *Philosophical investigations* (G.E.M. Anscomb, Trans). Oxford: Basil Blackwell & Mott.

Wolitzer, M. (1990, July 15). Review of *The body and its dangers. New York Times Book Review,* p. 17.

Women Pro & Con. (1958). Mount Vernon, NY: The Peter Pauper Press.

Woolf, V. (1925). *Mrs. Dalloway.* New York: Harcourt, Brace, & World.

Zajonc, R. B. (1980). Cognition and social cognition: A historical perspective. In L. Festinger (Ed.), *Retrospections on social psychology.* New York: Oxford University Press.

Index